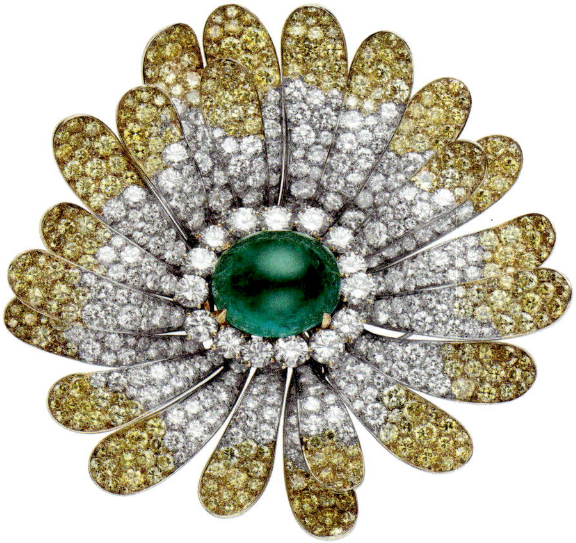

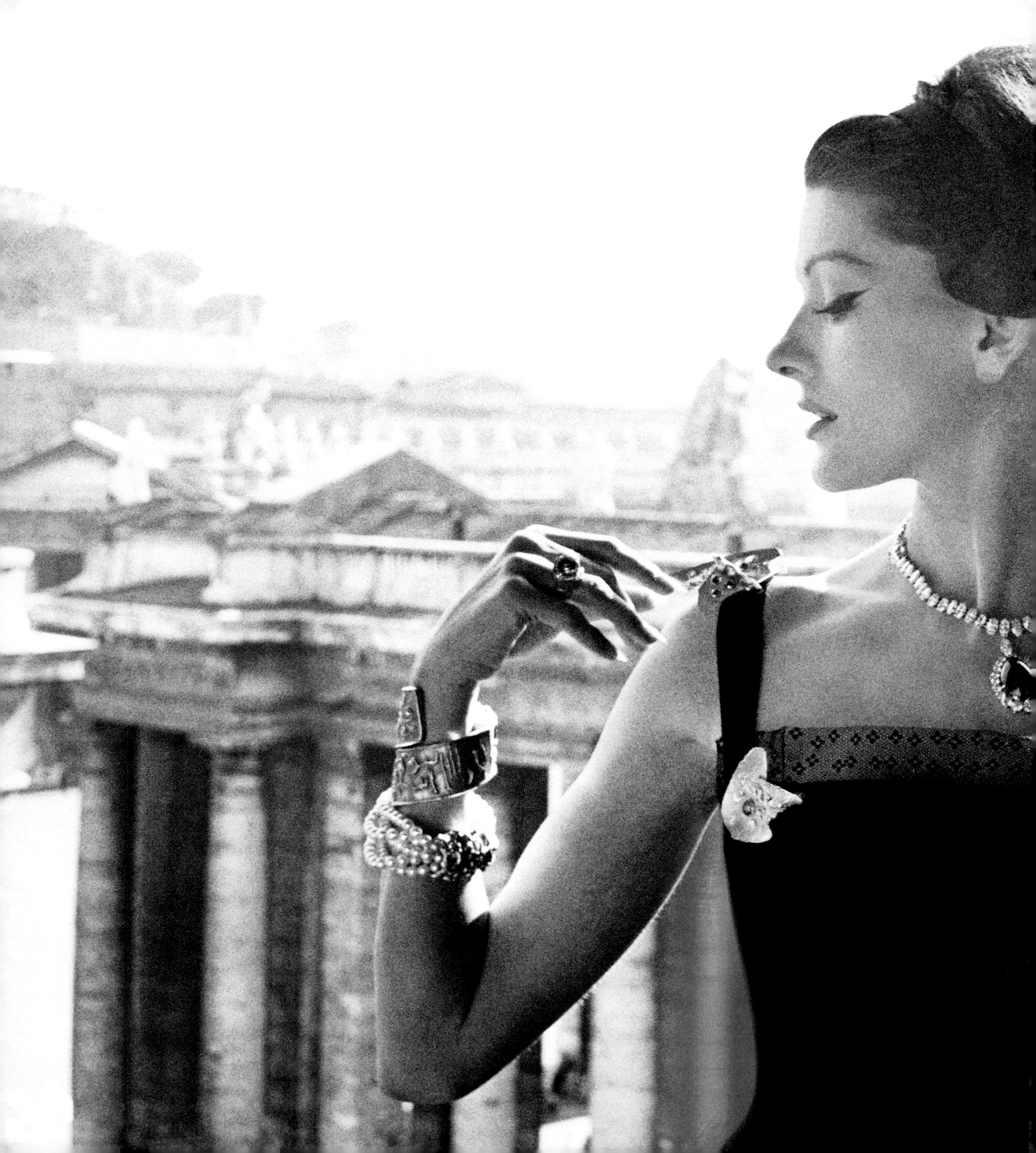

THE ART OF BVLGARI

LA DOLCE VITA AND BEYOND 1950–1990

MARTIN CHAPMAN AND AMANDA TRIOSSI

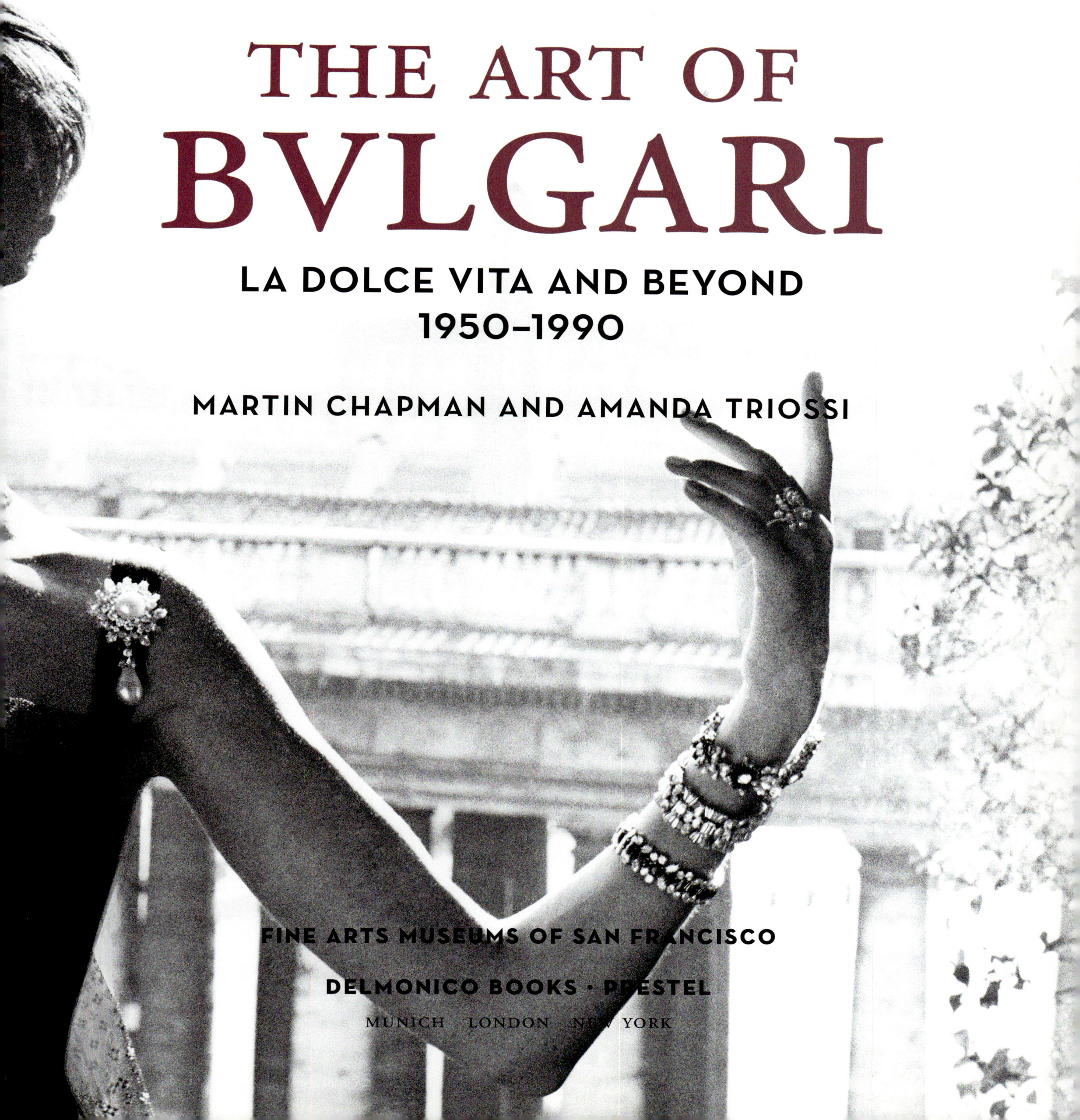

FINE ARTS MUSEUMS OF SAN FRANCISCO

DELMONICO BOOKS · PRESTEL

MUNICH LONDON NEW YORK

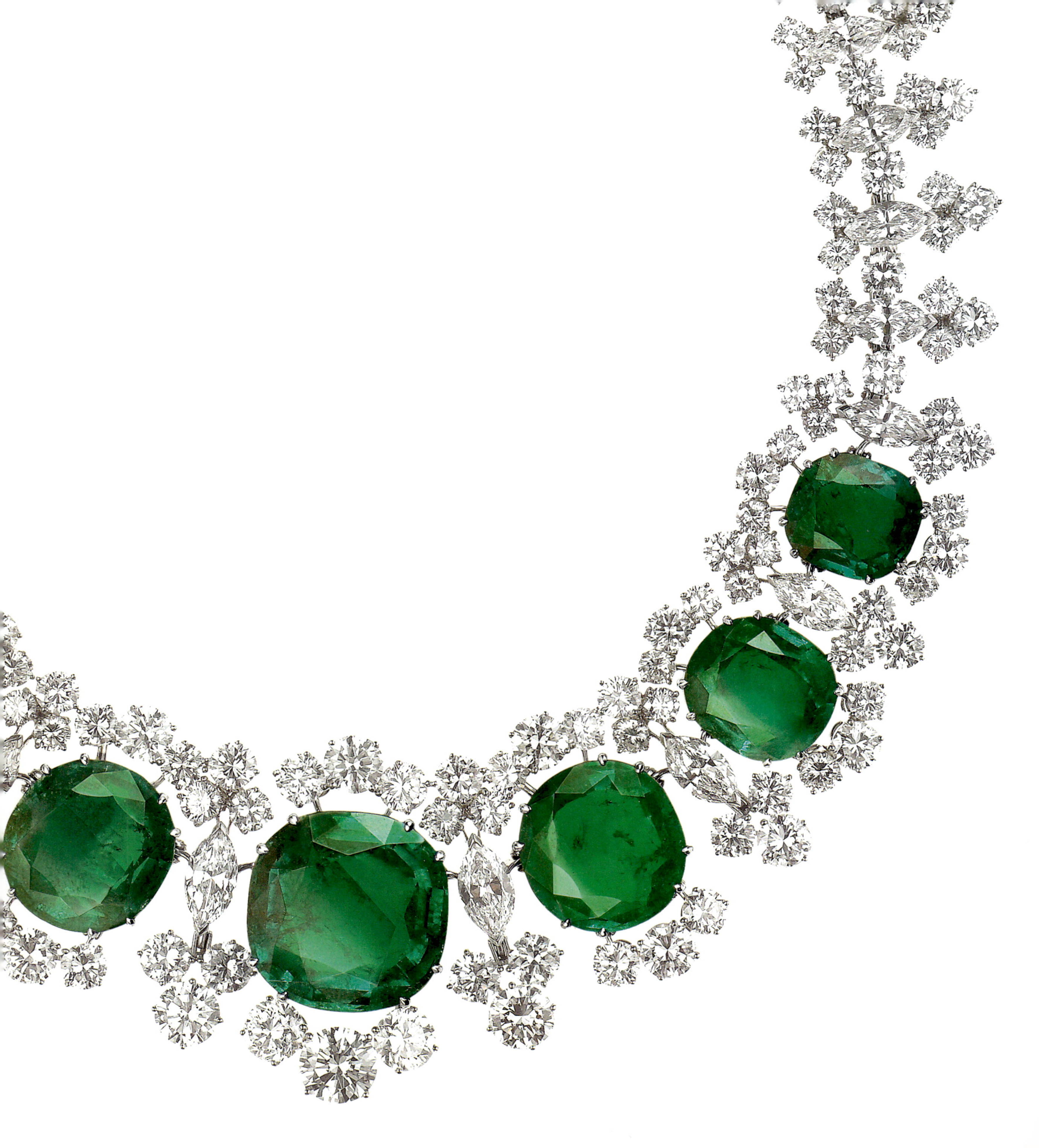

Contents

Foreword

The Fine Arts Museums of San Francisco are pleased to welcome *The Art of Bulgari: La Dolce Vita and Beyond, 1950–1990*, an exhibition of 145 pieces created by the renowned Italian jeweler over four decades. This show highlights jewelry that defined a pivotal period in Italian design, from the post–World War II era to 1990. It further includes many pieces from the collection of Elizabeth Taylor only recently reacquired by Bulgari from the auction of her jewelry in 2011.

In the 1960s Bulgari's jewelry began to move beyond the traditional designs established by Parisian jewelers toward boldly colored combinations of gemstones and the broad use of yellow gold with forms derived from Greco-Roman classicism, the Italian Renaissance, and nineteenth-century Roman goldsmiths. This new style, which came to be known as the "Italian school" of jewelry design, became a hallmark of Bulgari throughout the 1970s, the 1980s, and beyond.

Bulgari became known to a much wider American audience after it opened its first US store in New York in 1972. By then it had already been attracting international patrons and celebrities such as Sophia Loren, Ingrid Bergman, and perhaps most notably, Elizabeth Taylor. As this exhibition and catalogue reveal, Bulgari's cultural context offers a fascinating intersection of celebrity, design, and fine craftsmanship.

The Art of Bulgari: La Dolce Vita and Beyond, 1950–1990 continues the Fine Arts Museums' tradition of mounting exhibitions dedicated to the work of decisive figures and movements in the world of fashion and design, including *Cartier and America*, *Balenciaga and Spain*, *Yves Saint Laurent*, and *The Fashion World of Jean Paul Gaultier: From the Sidewalk to the Catwalk*.

We wish to thank our lenders, including Claire M. A. Beaulieu, Camilla Dietz Bergeron Ltd., Linda S. Chaiken, Jill and Allen Chozen, Denise Hale, Jennifer Tilly, Diane B. Wilsey, and others who have shared pieces from their personal collections. We also thank Carl and Yurie Pascarelli, Denise Fitch, Dr. Alan R. Malouf, and Wells Fargo for their early commitments to sponsor the exhibition.

We are grateful to Bulgari S.p.A., including Nicola Bulgari, Alberto Festa, and Jean-Christophe Babin, for working with us to bring this show to fruition. Thanks are also due to Martin Chapman, curator in charge of European decorative arts and sculpture for the Fine Arts Museums, and Amanda Triossi, author, jewelry historian, and the definitive expert on all things Bulgari, who collaborated on this illustrious exhibition and catalogue. It is my great pleasure to share this presentation with our audiences.

COLIN B. BAILEY
Director of Museums
Fine Arts Museums of San Francisco

Original design sketch for Bulgari necklace of yellow gold, emeralds, rubies, sapphires, and diamonds (cat. 28)

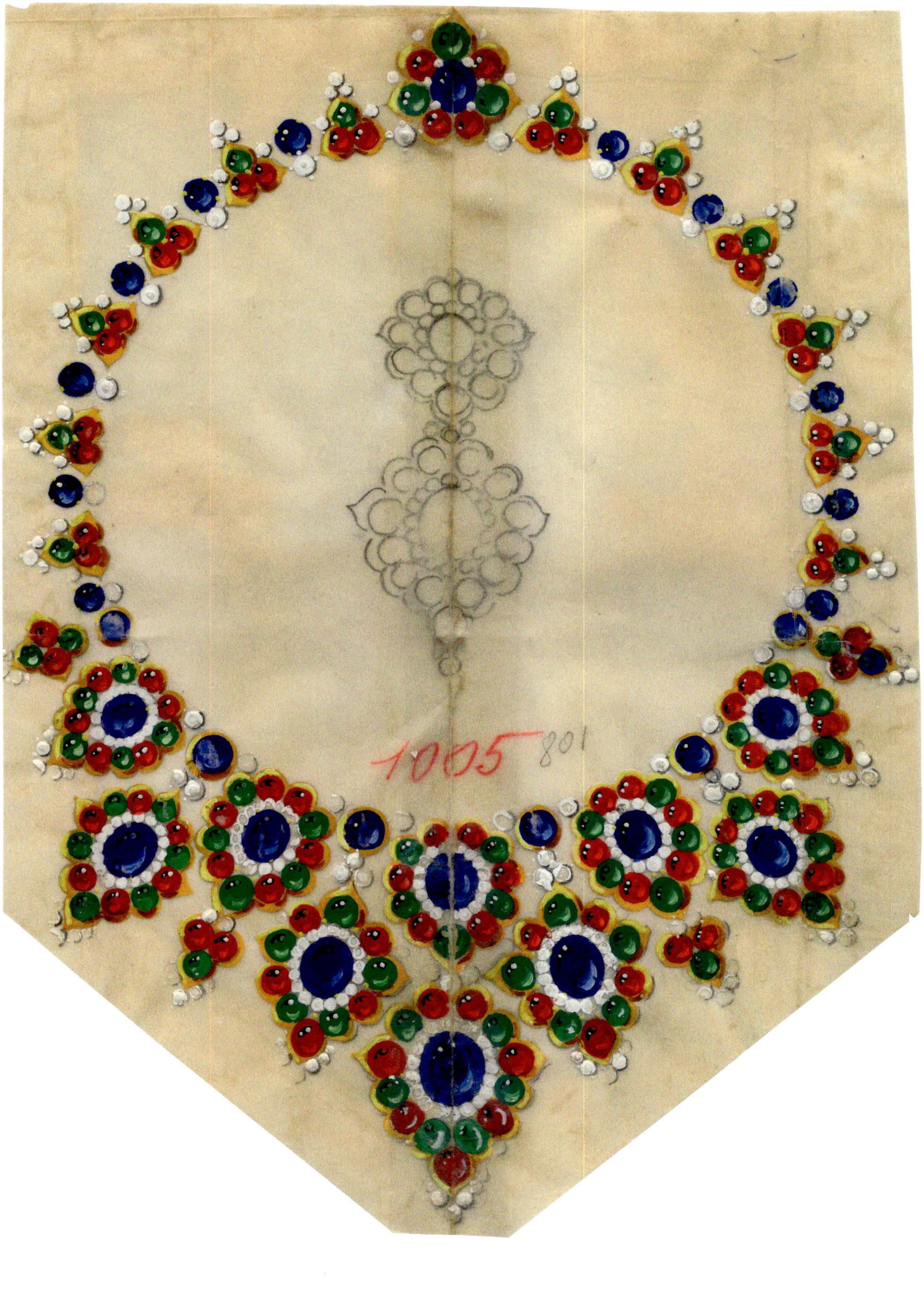
1005
801

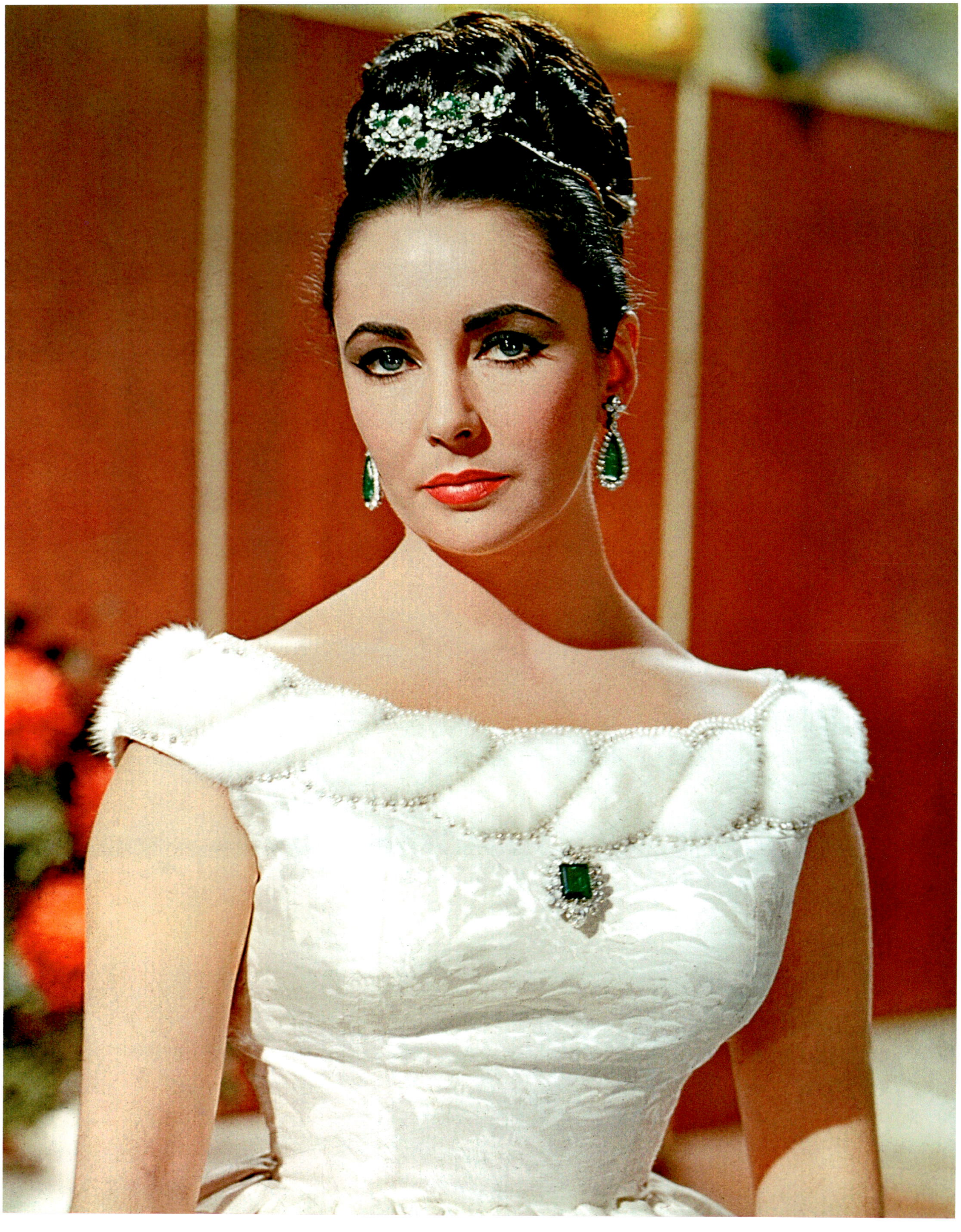

Introduction: Bulgari for Americans

MARTIN CHAPMAN

Bulgari has been an attraction for Americans visiting Rome since the 1930s. But the store on via dei Condotti began to draw more visitors from the States during the 1960s, when many film stars were in Rome making films at Cinecittà—the principal Italian movie studio. Elizabeth Taylor was a great fan of the jewelry house, frequenting it on breaks from filming *Cleopatra* in 1961–1962 and continuing her patronage long after the production finished. Such was her fervor for the jeweler that her husband Richard Burton said, "The only word that Elizabeth knows in Italian is *Bulgari*." For their engagement he gave her a substantial emerald brooch from Bulgari and followed it up on their wedding day in 1964 with an enormous matching necklace (cat. 92). Over the years Taylor was to acquire significant Bulgari pieces, seven of which are included in this exhibition to show her special love of this jeweler's work.

Bulgari, founded in 1884, blossomed during the reconstruction of Rome after the difficult times of World War II (see Triossi, "When in Rome," this volume). Before movie stars began arriving in the 1960s, Bulgari's principal American clients came from high society. Clare Boothe Luce was a glamorous society figure, writer, and politician who in 1953 was named US ambassador to Italy—the first woman to be appointed to such a major diplomatic post. In 1955 she commissioned an important emerald necklace from Bulgari (see figs. 2–4). Made of twenty-seven oval emeralds surrounded by baguette- and brilliant-cut diamonds, it is an impressive collar of vivid color that shows the elegance and restraint of the jewelry created in the traditional Parisian style that Bulgari was producing in the 1950s. As recorded in the drawing in the Bulgari archives for the piece (fig. 3), the necklace took some eight months to make; but Luce had to leave Rome abruptly after it was delivered in 1956 because she succumbed to poisoning from the flakes of arsenic-laden paint that had been falling from her ceiling onto her bed.[1] However, after her return to the United States she remained loyal to Bulgari, buying pieces from the jeweler throughout her life.

Woolworth heiress and archetypal "poor little rich girl" Barbara Hutton was one of the world's greatest jewelry collectors in the mid-twentieth century. Famously married—and divorced—many times, she had better luck in obtaining jewelry, which she bought from all the major houses. From Bulgari in the early 1950s she purchased the Pasha diamond, also known as the Pasha of Egypt.[2] A large octagonal stone of about forty carats, this historic diamond was purchased by Bulgari from King Farouk of Egypt. It was recut on the orders of Hutton and mounted into a ring (see fig. 5). Like all great jewelers Bulgari traded in high-quality gemstones, but it was unusual in also selling works of art. The silver sold in the early days of Bulgari was succeeded by more precious objets d'art. The store on via dei Condotti once had a room devoted to jades and still has an impressive Florentine pietre-dure clock from the early eighteenth century on view.[3] In the 1950s the American collector Robert Lehman bought from the jeweler

---

Fig. 1. Elizabeth Taylor, in a publicity photograph for *The V.I.P.s*, wearing her Bulgari platinum, emerald, and diamond *tremblant* brooch (cat. 91), Colombian emerald brooch (shown attached to necklace, cat. 92), and matching earrings, 1963

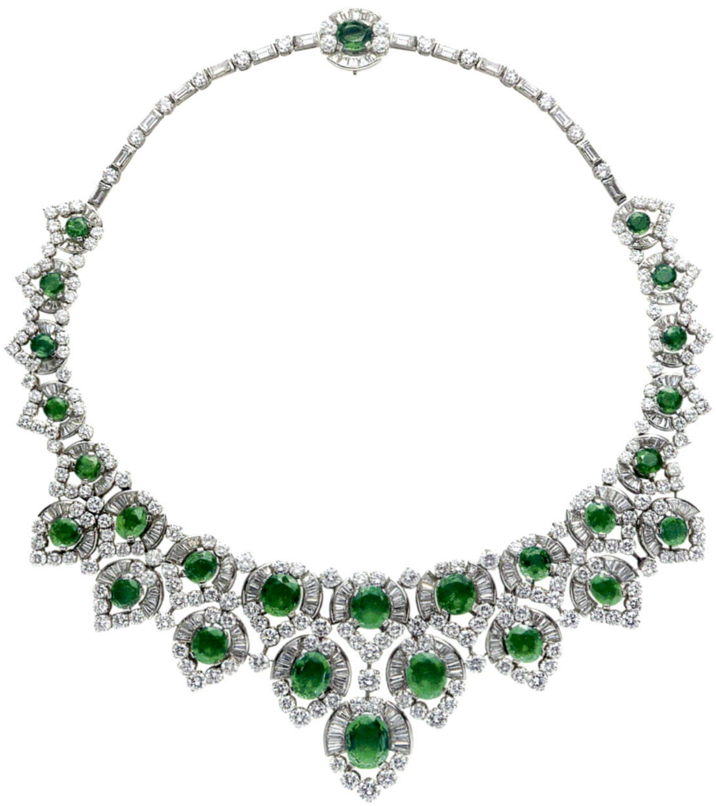

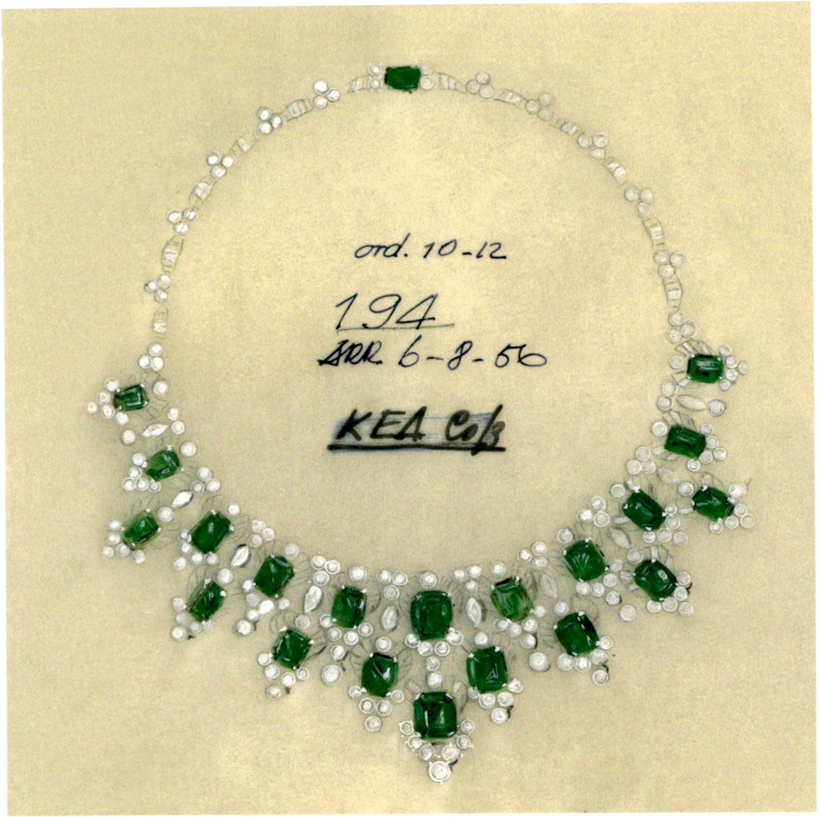

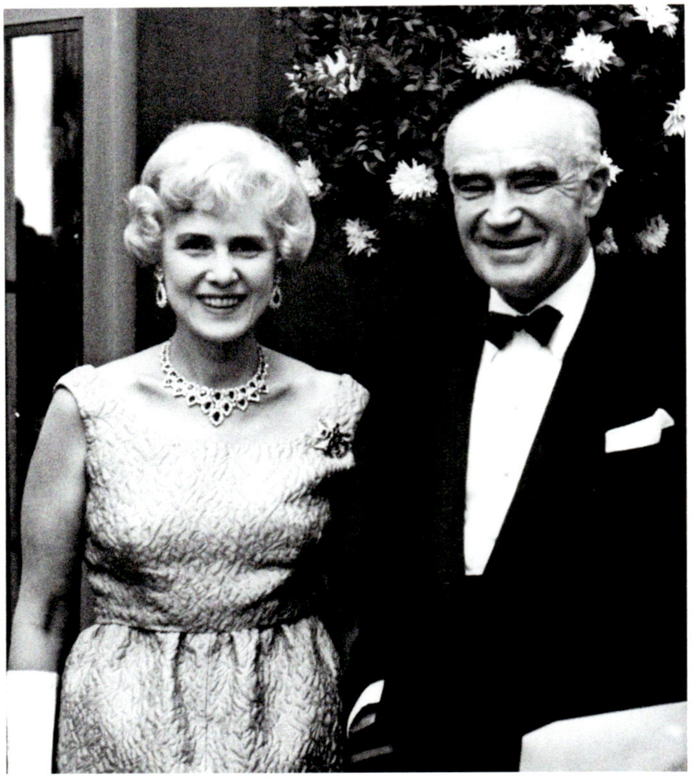

Fig. 2. Necklace of platinum, emeralds, and diamonds, 1956, owned by Clare Boothe Luce

Fig. 3. Bulgari's original design sketch for the Luce necklace, with the inscription "ord. 10-12" indicating the date of order and "ARR 6-8-56" the date of consignment

Fig. 4. Clare Boothe Luce, wearing her Bulgari necklace, and Henry R. Luce, 1963

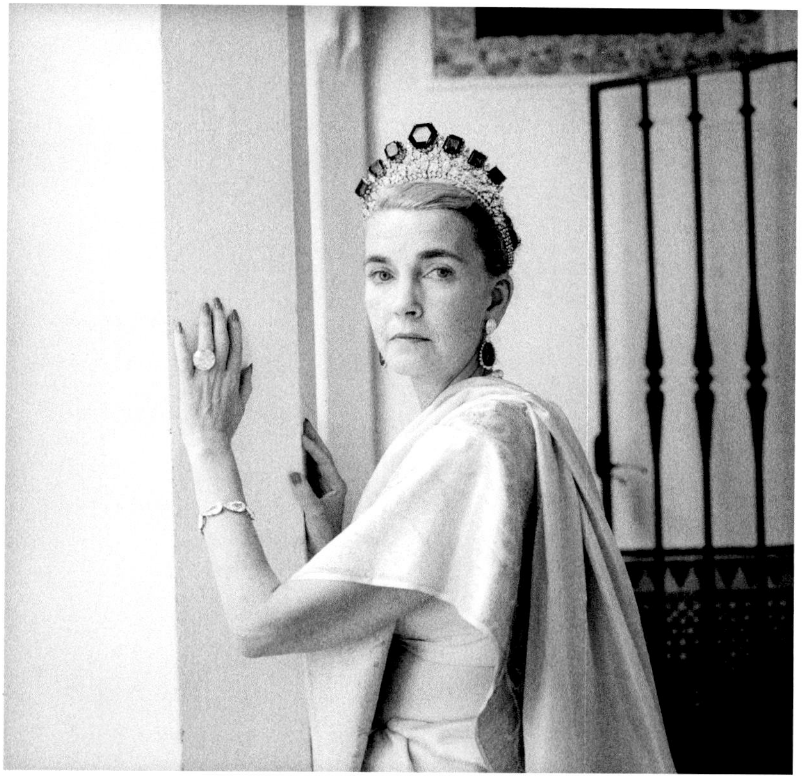

Fig. 5. Barbara Hutton, wearing the Pasha diamond as a ring and the Grand Duchess Vladimir's emeralds as a tiara, 1961

two spectacular gem-set, eighteenth-century snuff boxes that had belonged to Frederick the Great, king of Prussia, one of which is on view at the Metropolitan Museum of Art in New York today.

A leader of New York society in the latter part of the twentieth century, Brooke Astor owned an impressive emerald necklace that her husband, Vincent, commissioned from Giorgio Bulgari in 1958. Bulgari, who traveled to see the Astors in London, produced a design that was as grand as it was subdued (fig. 6). Completed after her husband's death in 1959, the necklace was ultimately bought by Mrs. Astor (see fig. 7), who wrote in her autobiography, "Vincent liked jewelry and had very good taste. It is pretty and not ostentatious but very elegant, so I bought it. Considering it was Vincent's last personal gift to me I am very sentimental about it."[4] Lyn Revson (see fig. 41), wife of Revlon owner Charles Revson, possessed one of the most iconic suites of Bulgari jewels made in the mid-1960s. It comprises a magnificent bib necklace and matching pair of earrings with the unusual color combination of emeralds, amethysts, and turquoise cut *en cabochon* and surrounded by brilliant-cut diamonds (cat. 35). The rounded forms, the sense of volume, and the unexpected palette are all features that made Bulgari stand out in the jewelry world of the 1960s.

San Franciscans were also drawn to Bulgari. Diane B. Wilsey, today the president of the Fine Arts Museums, first came across the Bulgari store in Rome as a young girl traveling with her father, Wiley T. Buchanan, an American ambassador to Luxembourg and Austria. Years later she acquired a spectacular brooch in the form of a stylized flower with a diamond of some twenty-seven carats (cat. 43).

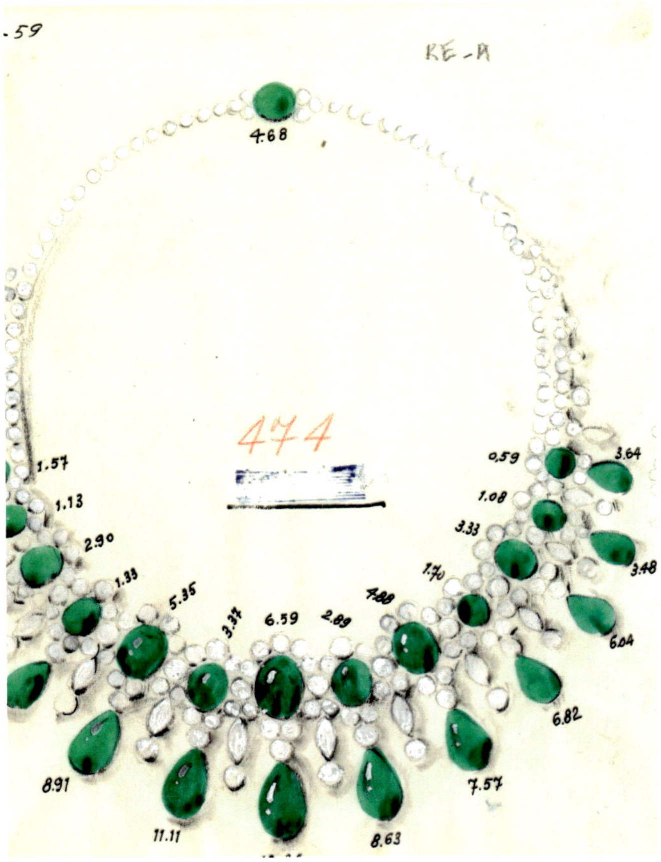

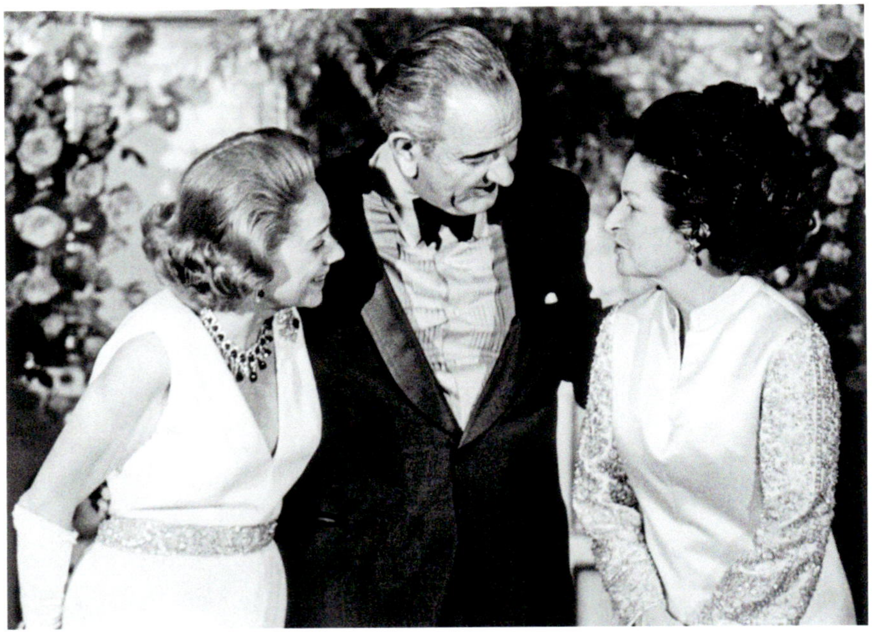

Fig. 6. Bulgari's original design sketch for Brooke Astor's 1959 necklace of gold, platinum, emeralds, and diamonds

Fig. 7. Brooke Astor, in her Bulgari necklace, with Lyndon and Lady Bird Johnson, 1969

Another San Francisco society figure, Denise Hale (see fig. 8), was a client of Bulgari in the late 1950s and early 1960s, when she lived in Rome. She admired the great lengths to which Giorgio Bulgari would go in order to please his clients. Hale recalls that he reset three times the thirty-seven-carat sapphire that she had inherited from her grandmother until they were satisfied with the resulting ring (cat. 7).[5] She also acquired an important Bulgari diamond bracelet in those years, as well as two fine brooches that are very typical of Bulgari's signature designs at this time—one densely packed with turquoise and sapphire cabochons, and the other a stylized flower of sapphires edged in diamonds (cats. 8, 9, 24). Hale said, "I've always worn beautiful jewelry. It's my second skin."[6] The writer Dominick Dunne, who was very taken with Hale after she moved to Hollywood in the 1960s and married the movie director Vincente Minnelli, said of her: "She was a glamorous Serbian with a great jewelry collection."[7]

Audrey Hepburn, Ingrid Bergman, Ava Gardner, and other movie stars patronized the Bulgari store in Rome during the so-called "dolce vita" years of the 1960s, but the most famous client of all was Elizabeth Taylor. She spent many afternoons there with Giorgio Bulgari and received gifts of Bulgari jewels, first from her husband Eddie Fisher and then, more famously, from Richard Burton. One of

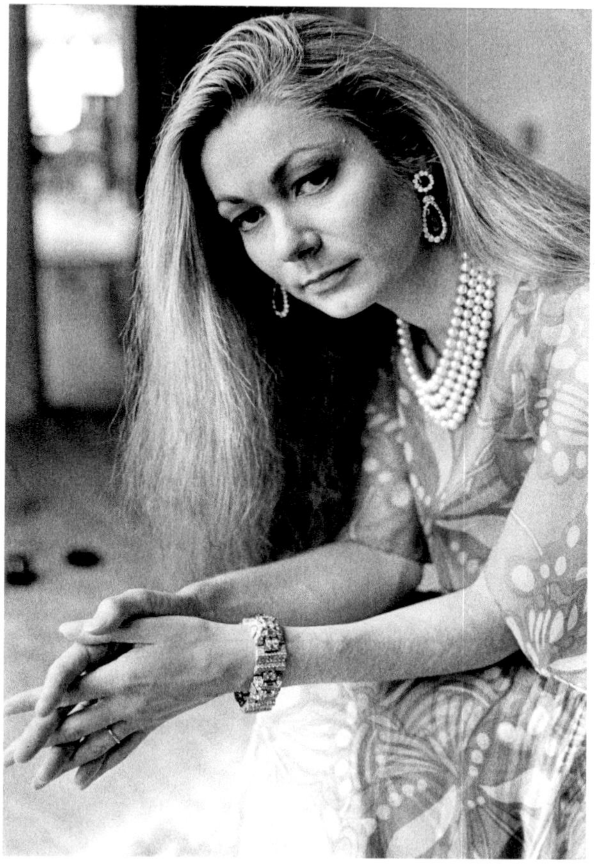

Fig. 8. Denise Hale, wearing her Bulgari platinum and diamond bracelet (cat. 9), ca. 1960s

Fisher's gifts to her, a *tremblant* brooch of yellow diamonds, is included in this exhibition (cat. 90). It represents one of Bulgari's greatest successes in jewelry design in the late fifties and early sixties. Brooches made of sprays or small bouquets of flowers became very popular in the mid-eighteenth century and have remained so on and off ever since. Bulgari reworked this traditional design by making brooches with colored diamonds and setting the heads on springs, so that they shivered when they moved; this technique, known as *en tremblant* ("trembling"), gave the diamonds extra sparkle and appeal. Fisher gave this brooch to Taylor on her thirtieth birthday, in February 1962, although she would soon be separated from him as she became more deeply involved with Burton, whom she married in 1964.

Knowing how much it meant to her, Burton continued giving Bulgari jewelry to Taylor, presenting his wife with major pieces on her birthdays, but also on other occasions, sometimes for no other reason than "it was Tuesday."[8] In 1972, for her fortieth birthday, he presented her with a Bulgari sapphire and diamond sautoir (cat. 96; see also fig. 49). This impressive piece, which started life as a brooch in 1969, is composed of a large sugarloaf Burmese sapphire of about sixty-five carats, set into a pavé of diamonds, outlined in calibré sapphires. It is suspended from a long chain with similar workmanship. Both the technique and the form are reminiscent of Art Deco jewelry. Taylor also acquired a sapphire ring made the previous year (cat. 95), in 1971, which was probably intended to complement the sautoir.

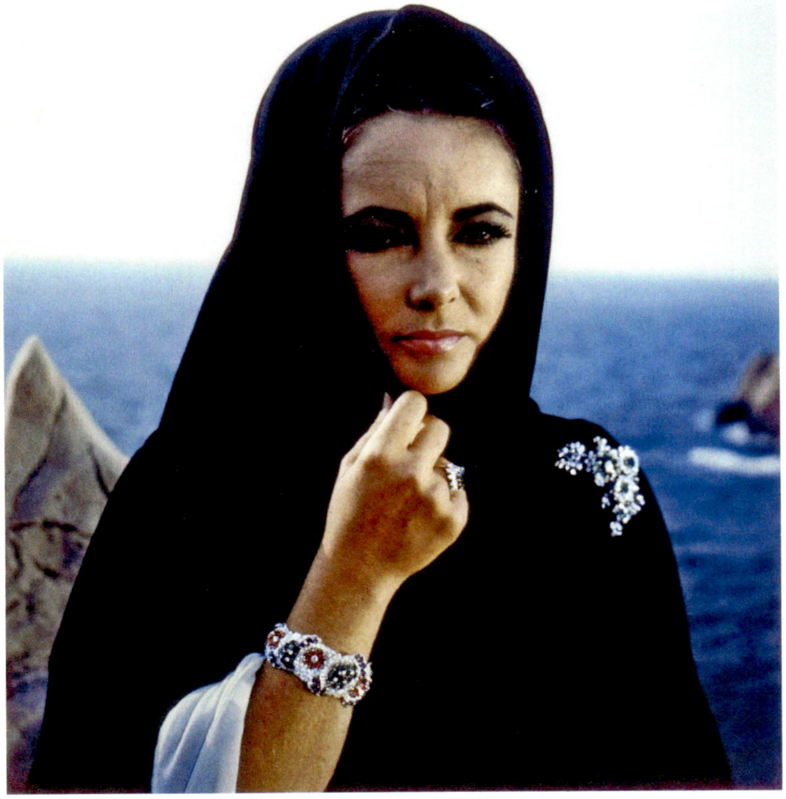

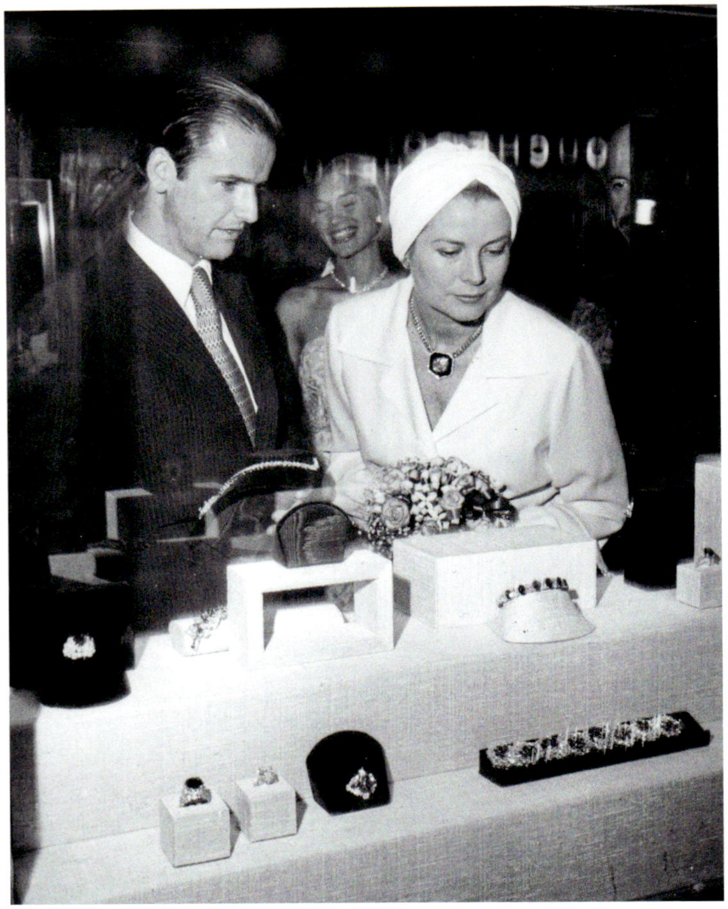

Fig. 9. Elizabeth Taylor, wearing her own Bulgari jewelry, including a *tremblant* brooch (cat. 91) and a ring (cat. 93), both of platinum, emeralds, and diamonds, in *Boom!*, 1968

Fig. 10. Princess Grace of Monaco, wearing a Bulgari gold coin-set necklace, in Monte Carlo, 1978

In the tradition of other movie stars before her, Taylor often wore her own jewels in her films. She donned several of her Bulgari pieces in *The V.I.P.s* (1963), including the diamond and emerald *tremblant* brooch (cat. 91), as well as the brooch she later received from Richard Burton on their engagement (see cat. 92; see also fig. 1). Taylor can also be seen wearing the same *tremblant* brooch, her emerald and diamond ring (cat, 93), and her floral-motif bracelet in *Boom!* (1968) (see fig. 9), and her pearl earrings in *Ash Wednesday* (1973) (see fig. 46), all from Bulgari.

Americans were especially drawn to the coin-set jewelry that was one of the firm's hallmarks in the 1960s and became so popular that it undoubtedly influenced the stereotypical image of a bronzed Hollywood producer sporting a shirt undone to the navel and a medallion on a heavy gold chain. Taking cues from ancient jewelry types that were revived in the nineteenth century, Bulgari first reintroduced ancient coins into its jewelry in the 1960s, reflecting the jeweler's Roman location and heritage. As these designs proved popular Bulgari expanded the range from necklaces and sautoirs (often mounted on chains) to rings, bracelets, and earrings. This motif was also highly adaptable, enabling the house to

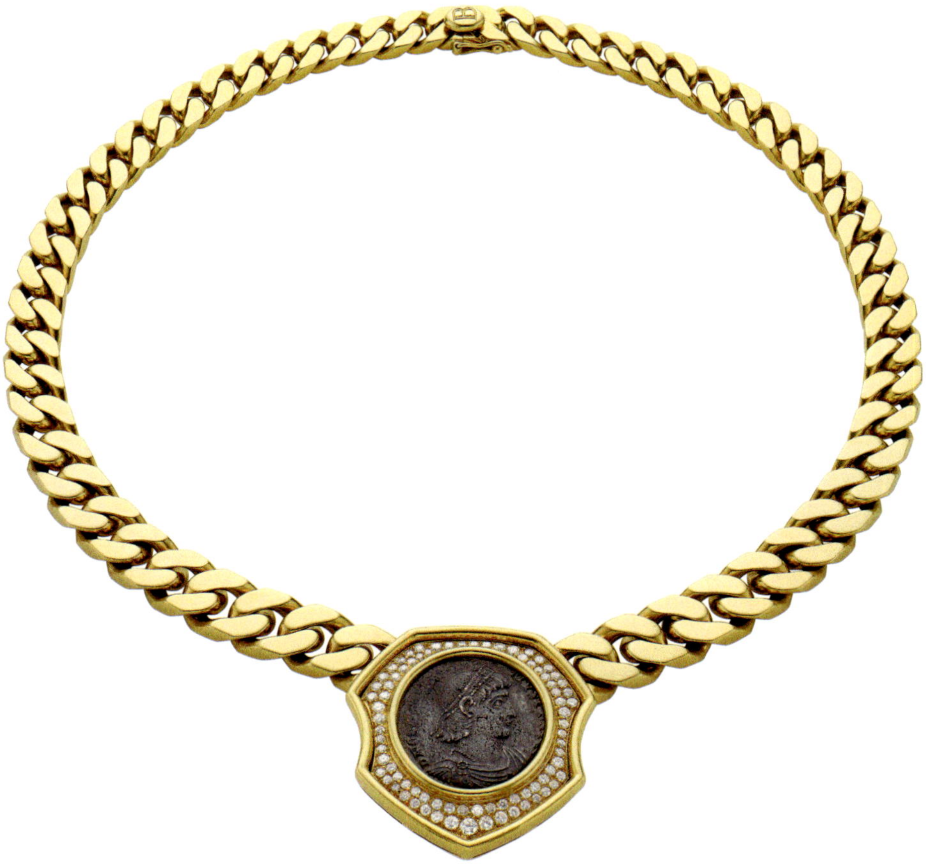

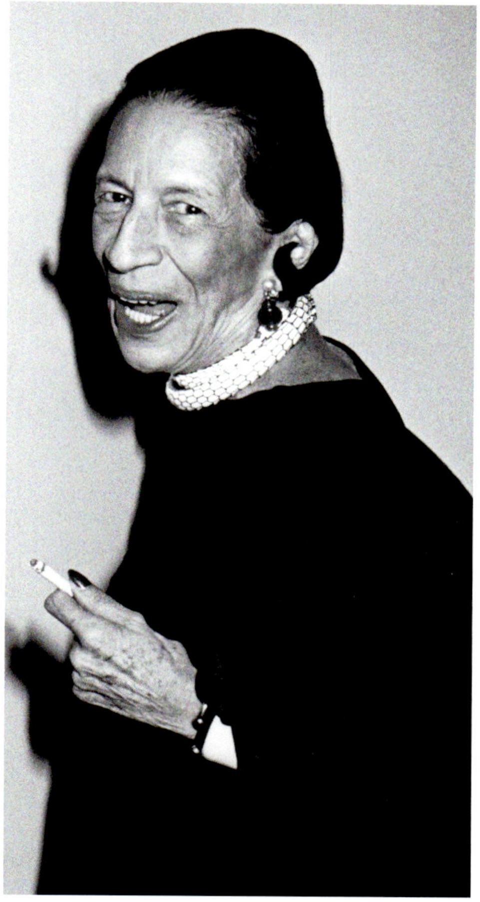

Fig. 11. Bulgari gold coin-set chain necklace from the collection of Elizabeth Taylor, ca. late 1970s–early 1980s

Fig. 12. Diana Vreeland, in her Bulgari snake belt worn as a choker, 1980

produce jewelry that was easily wearable for everyday occasions. Bulgari coin-set jewelry became de rigueur for daywear; necklaces with coins set in large gold chains were worn by both Princess Grace of Monaco (see fig. 10) and her daughter Princess Caroline in the 1970s. Taylor also had similar coin-set necklaces (see fig. 11) and a chain set with six Byzantine coins (cat. 97; see also fig. 43).

Although Elizabeth Taylor was one of the last actresses of old-school Hollywood to wear her own jewelry on the set, American celebrities would continue to turn to Bulgari to adorn themselves for the red carpet throughout the 1980s and up to the present day. They were also enlisted by Bulgari to wear its jewelry to promote the brand. In the 1970s Cher wore part of the Star-Spangled Banner collection (also known as the Stars-and-Stripes collection) for a publicity shoot in conjunction with the opening of the first Bulgari boutique in the United States, the New York shop in the Pierre Hotel, in 1972 (see fig. 13). This collection represented Bulgari's new direction, which was less about the sheer luxury of gemstone-set jewelry and more about innovative design that would make their products more accessible to a broader clientele—although they would continue to make great bejeweled pieces whenever they could.

Jewelry created for a wider market was the trend of the 1970s, and Bulgari experimented at this time with bold design, bright color, and yellow gold. Art Deco–influenced pieces with hard edges and geometric shapes were arguably the most characteristic designs of the decade (see cats. 58–60, for example); while other motifs, such as snake jewelry, remained popular throughout the 1970s and beyond. The eccentric arbiter of New York taste Diana Vreeland wore her enameled gold Bulgari snake belt doubled up as a necklace during these years (see fig. 12). "Don't forget the serpent," she said in 1968. "The serpent should be on every finger and on all wrists and everywhere. The serpent is the motif of Horus in jewelry. We cannot see enough of them."[9]

Pop artist Andy Warhol was a collector of Bulgari jewelry and in 1979 stated, "I always visit Bulgari, because it is the most important museum of contemporary art."[10] His magazine *Interview* featured actress Jessica Lange on its cover in 1979, wearing a pair of geometric Bulgari Art Deco–style earrings set with emeralds and yellow diamonds (see fig. 52). The following year, in an interview with Nicola Bulgari, Warhol stated, "Well I think your jewelry is the 1980s. Everybody's trying to copy this look."[11]

One of the new looks the house developed in the 1980s became another landmark for Bulgari. The Parentesi (parenthesis) line, featuring jewelry made of interlocking modular sections, has a strong design that is almost architectural (see cat. 99). Indeed, it is said to be based on the interlocking curbstones found all over Rome. It is bold, voluminous, and almost endlessly variable, and its strong design was probably one of the reasons Andy Warhol and other Americans were so impressed by the jewelry house during these years.

Bulgari continues its close relationship with Americans today by draping a new generation of celebrities with its jewelry on the red carpet (see fig. 35) and by establishing stores in most major US cities. However, looking back to the period of the 1950s through the 1980s, we can see how Bulgari first made its way into American hearts with its high craftsmanship and its singular designs that remain staples of Bulgari today, and which are still instantly recognizable.

1. "Foreign Relations: Arsenic for the Ambassador," *Time*, July 23, 1956, http://www.time.com/time/magazine/article/0,9171,865337,00.html

2. Stefano Papi and Alexandra Rhodes, *Famous Jewelry Collectors* (London: Thames and Hudson, 1999), 186.

3. Alvar Gonzales-Palacios, "The Name of the Bulgari," in *Between Eternity and History; Bulgari from 1884 to 2009* (Milan: Skira, 2009), 12.

4. Brooke Astor, *Footprints: An Autobiography* (Garden City, New York: Doubleday & Company, Inc., 1980), quoted in Amanda Triossi and Daniela Mascetti, *Bulgari* (Milan: Electa, 2007), 32.

5. Conversation with the author, April 2013.

6. Quoted in John Heilpern, "Out to Lunch: Society by the Bay," *Vanity Fair*, August 2009, 81.

7. Dominick Dunne, *The Way We Lived Then: Recollections of a Well-Known Name Dropper* (New York: Crown, 1999), 82.

8. Elizabeth Taylor, *My Love Affair with Jewelry* (London: Thames and Hudson, 2002), 55, 66.

9. Quoted in "Vreeland Memos," *Visionaire* 37 (2002).

10. Triossi and Mascetti, *Bulgari*, 38.

11. Quoted in Andy Warhol, "Nicola Bulgari: Wearable Wealth," *Interview*, November 1980, 62–63.

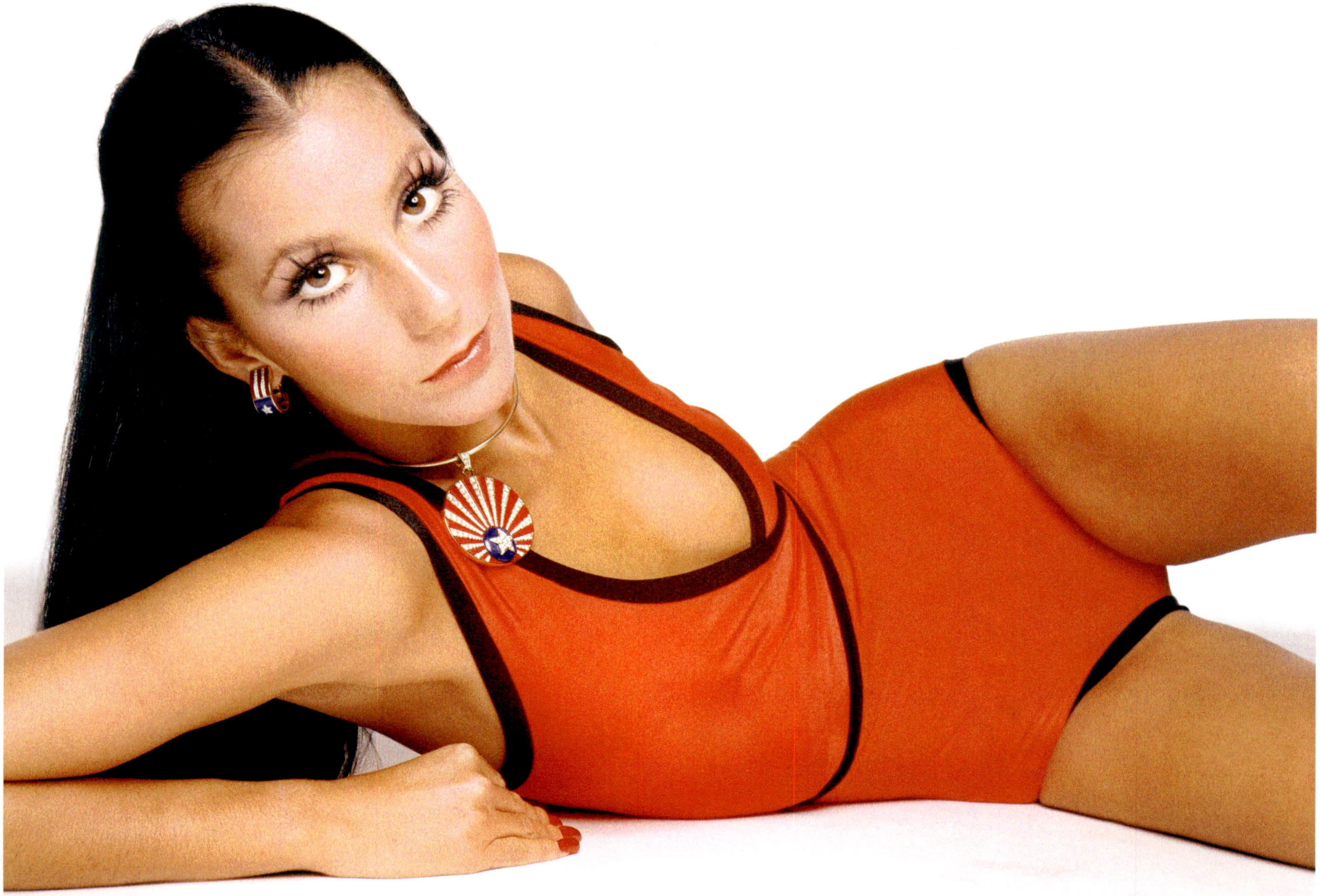

Fig. 13. Cher, wearing pieces from the Star-Spangled Banner collection, photographed by Richard Avedon for *Vogue*, April 1972

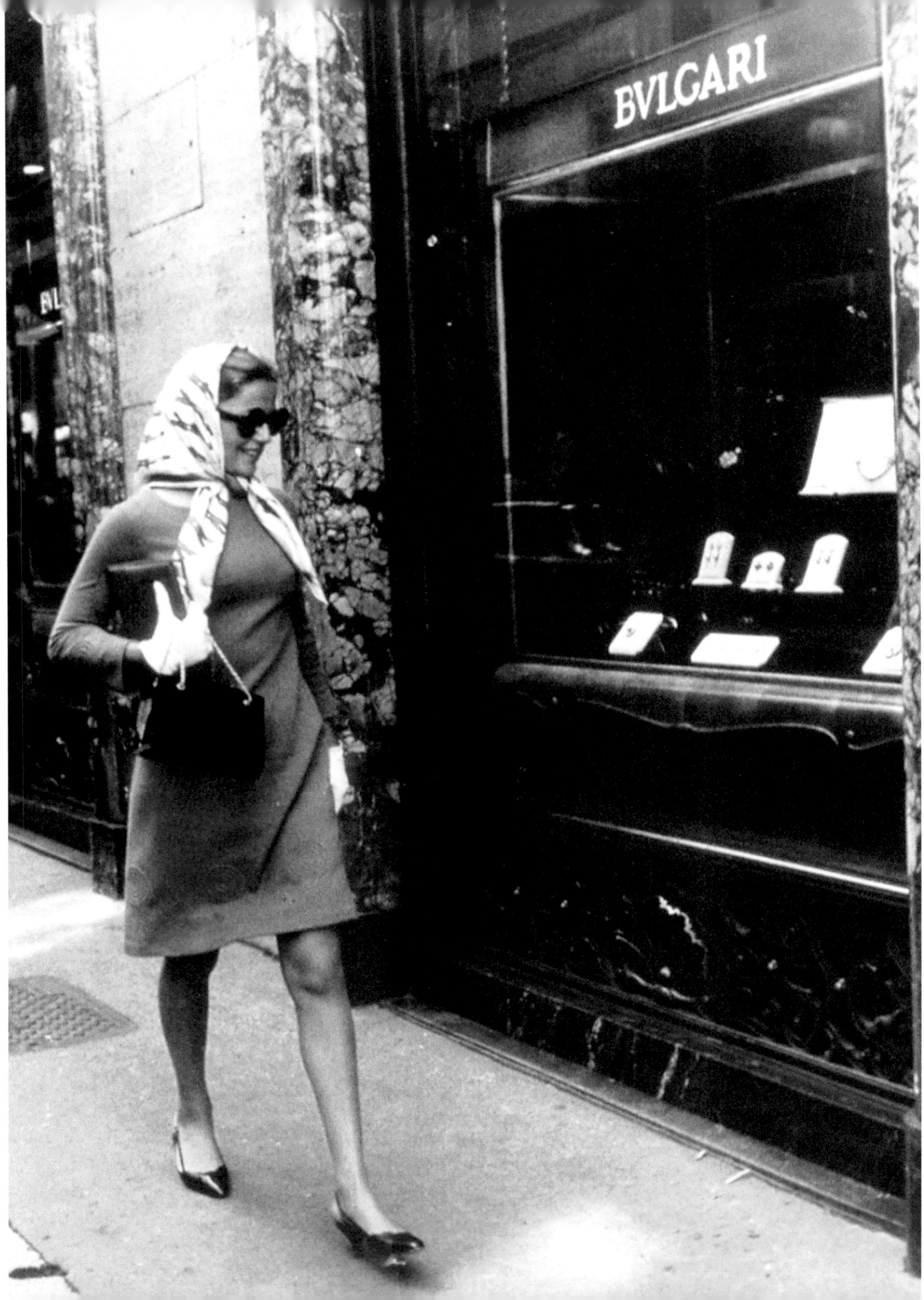
BVLGARI

“When in Rome”: The History of Bulgari

AMANDA TRIOSSI

The Bulgari brand is more than a century old, but the unique aesthetic that many associate with the company did not emerge until the middle of the twentieth century, when an explosion of creativity surrounded not just the jeweler, but all of Italian culture—from street life to art, from film to fashion, and beyond. During Italy’s postwar era, Hollywood stars and other members of the wealthy elite descended upon Rome, eagerly embracing the resurgent city’s lifestyle and luxury goods. Bulgari, along with other innovative artists and manufacturers of the time, became an active participant in creating and disseminating a uniquely Italian style, one that would distinguish the country as both a modern society and one with a deep history and rich artisan traditions. As Italy transformed itself and Rome, in particular, metamorphosed into the heart of “la dolce vita” (the sweet life), Bulgari was perfectly placed as the jeweler of choice, standing at the forefront of fashion and capturing the attention of the world.

BULGARI’S BEGINNINGS

One can trace the origins of Bulgari to a family of Greek silversmiths in the village of Kalarites (or Kallarytes) in Epirus, a region of northwestern Greece near the Albanian border that in the first half of the nineteenth century, prior to Greek independence, was part of the Ottoman Empire. Sotiris Boulgaris, who later Italianized his name to Sotirio Bulgari (see fig. 15), was born in 1857 to Giorgio and Elena Boulgaris in Paramythia, a prosperous market town. The only surviving child of eleven, Sotirio learned his trade from his father, creating silver objects for personal adornment such as belts and large buckles in the traditional local style, known as Neo-Hellenic (see fig. 16). This style, which developed gradually between the fifth and late nineteenth centuries, successfully combined elements of Byzantine and Islamic traditions; the shapes are Byzantine in origin while the floral and foliate patterns derive from Islamic art. In 1877, due to growing political unrest, the Boulgaris family decided to move from Epirus to Corfu, a Greek island off the coast of Epirus, separated from Italy by the Ionian Sea.

In 1880 Sotirio Bulgari, together with another silversmith, Demetrios Kremos, traveled to Naples to set up a retail shop; when it failed after a few months, the men moved to Rome, the capital of a newly united Italy, where they attempted to sell their wares in Piazza della Trinità dei Monti, at the top of the Spanish Steps. There they met a Greek merchant who offered them space to display their goods in his store on nearby via Sistina, a street lined with antique dealers, silversmiths, marble carvers, and numerous painters’ studios. The enterprise worked well and enabled Bulgari and Kremos to open a silversmiths’ shop on the same street. After about a year, business disagreements caused the two friends to part ways, and Sotirio independently opened the first Bulgari store at 86 via Sistina in 1884.

Along with his artistic skill, Sotirio had an acute business sense, and he quickly realized the advantages of establishing a presence in various fashionable resorts in Italy and Switzerland such as

Fig. 14. Italian actress Virna Lisi, in front of the Bulgari shop on via dei Condotti, Rome, 1971

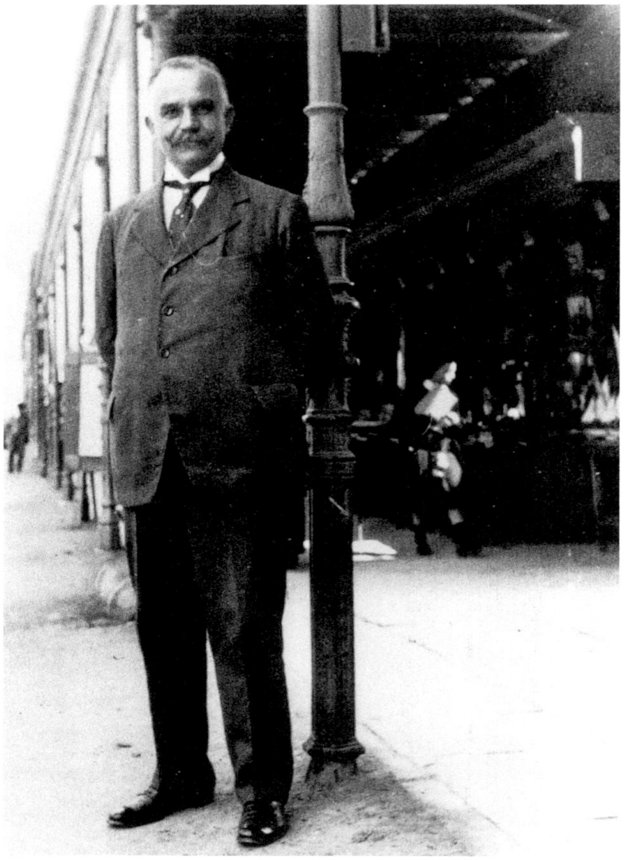

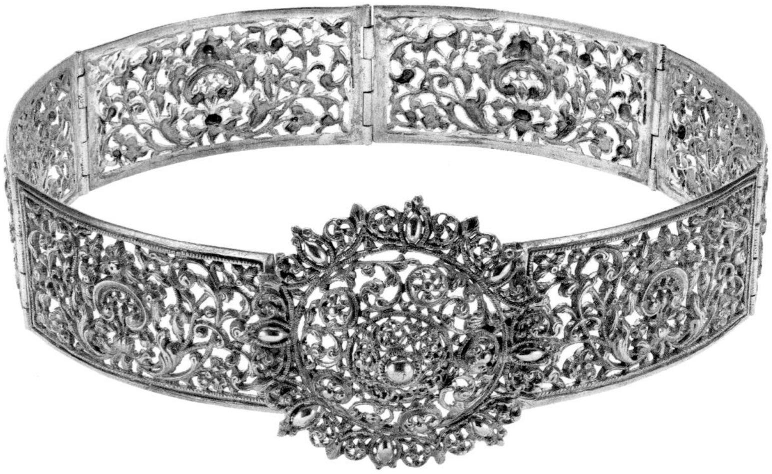

Fig. 15. Sotirio Bulgari, Saint Moritz-Bad, 1906

Fig. 16. Silver belt, created between 1895 and 1905, an example of Sotirio Bulgari's silversmithing

Fig. 17. The Bulgari store at 28 via dei Condotti, Rome, ca. 1900

Naples, Sorrento, San Remo, Bellagio, Saint Moritz, and Lucerne, while maintaining the original store in Rome. Sotirio was able to expand his business in a fairly short period of time, largely relying on the support of relatives and craftsman friends whom he summoned from Greece. For example, his brother-in-law was entrusted with the direction of the Sorrento store, while his friend Alexi Giannopulos was in charge of the one in Naples. Together they worked to satisfy a clientele that likely consisted of wealthy tourists, in particular travelers from Britain, who in the second half of the nineteenth century had cultivated a taste for traditional, ethnic, silver jewels and ornaments.

In 1886 Sotirio returned to see his parents in Corfu, where he married Elena Basios. The couple would eventually have six children, two of whom would grow up to continue the family business. In 1894 Sotirio opened a second shop in Rome at 28 via dei Condotti (see fig. 17), and then in 1905 he added a larger, third one just a few doors away, at 10 via dei Condotti.

With the success of having established fourteen shops across Italy and Switzerland, in 1907 Sotirio began to change course. By entrusting the management of most of these shops to his relatives

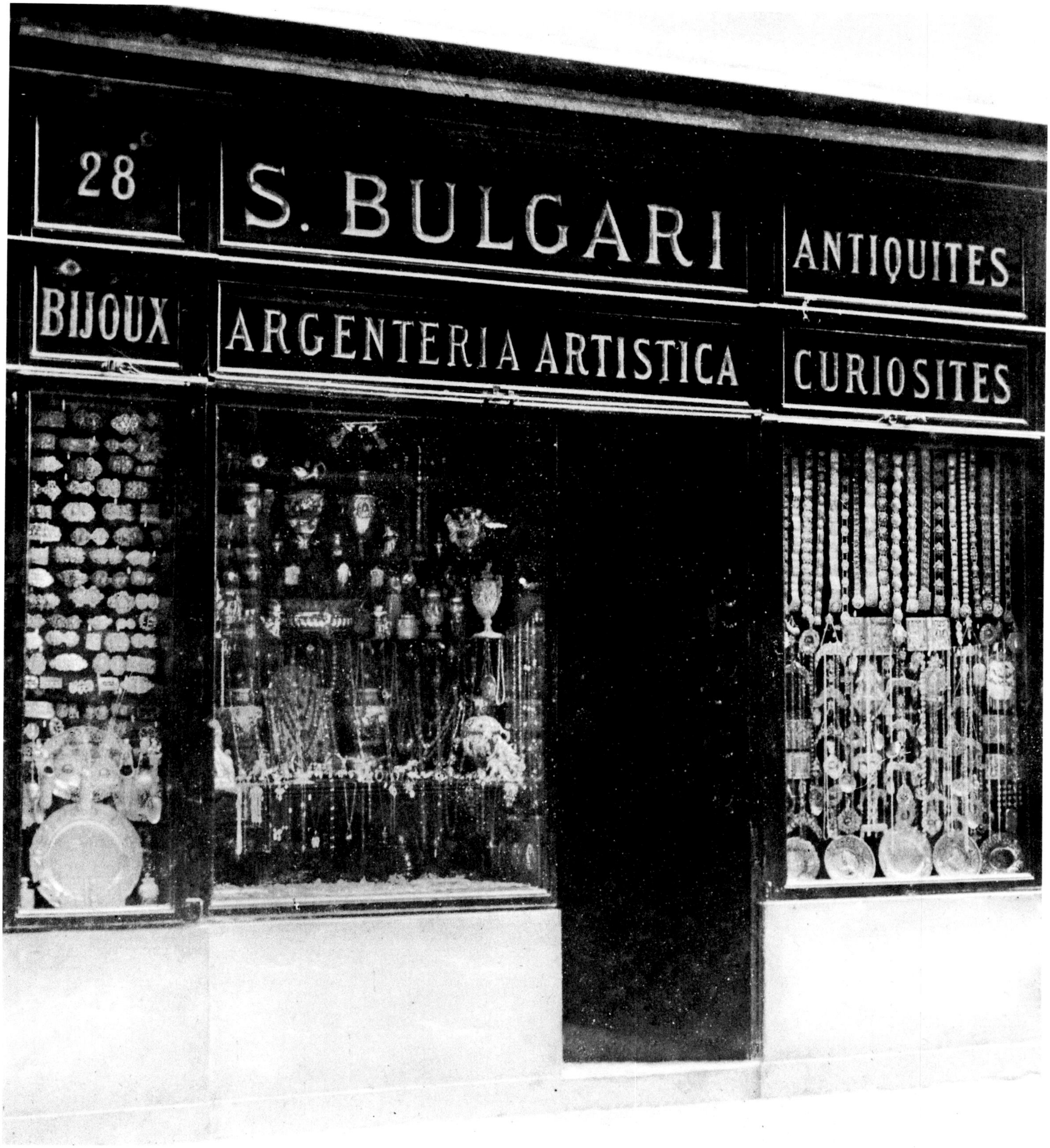
28
S. BULGARI
ANTIQUITES
BIJOUX
ARGENTERIA ARTISTICA
CURIOSITES

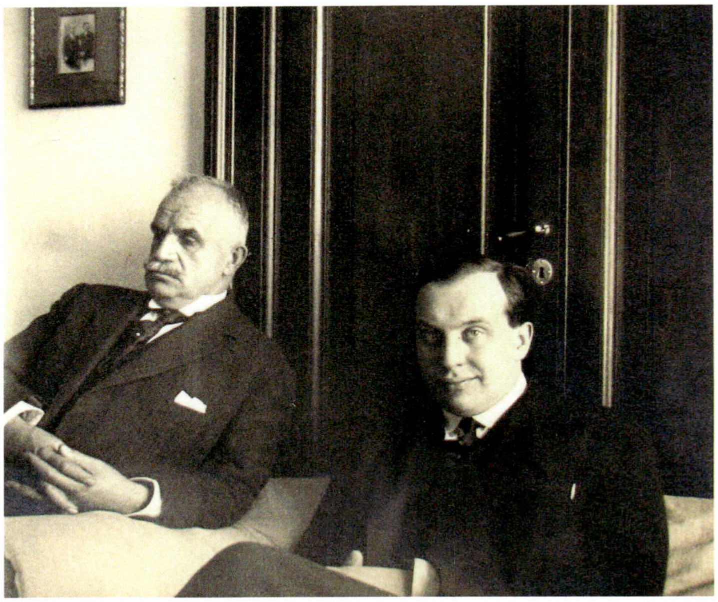

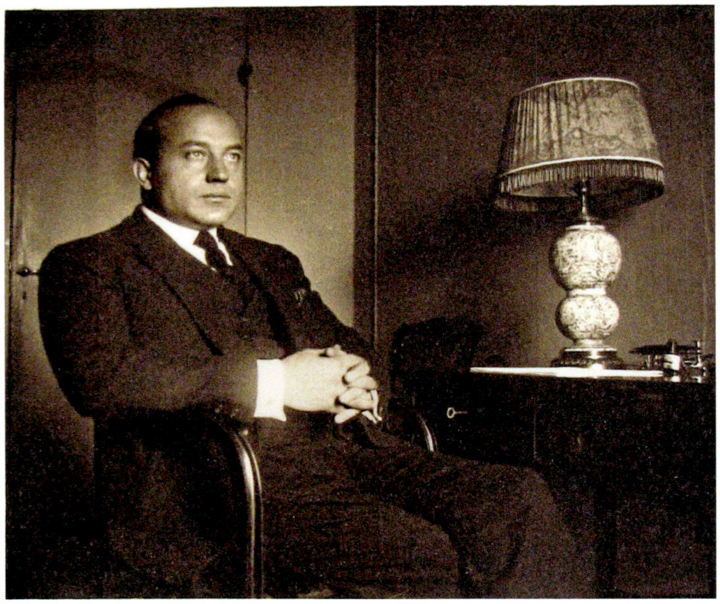

Fig. 18. Sotirio and Giorgio Bulgari, 1921

Fig. 19. Costantino Bulgari, 1921

Fig. 20. The Bulgari store at 10 via dei Condotti, Rome, 1934

and associates, he could focus primarily on the ones in the heart of Rome. There he expanded his original trade by creating his first pieces of luxury jewelry, as is testified by the entries in the Roman trade directories from 1915 on. By the end of World War I he decided to devote himself mainly to jewelry, and to conserve his resources he gradually sold off his shops, ultimately keeping only the one on via dei Condotti. For a long time this location would remain Bulgari's only retail showroom, and to this day it continues to be the brand's flagship store.

The lack of much archival material, and the fact that Bulgari jewels were not stamped at this time, has made attribution of pieces from this period very difficult. At present, no jewels dating from 1915 to 1920 have been identified (except for a design for a diamond bracelet); but from the few identifiable examples from the mid-twenties, it appears that early Bulgari works conformed to the fashionable styles then dictated by Parisian jewelers, such as geometric patterns and stylized naturalistic motifs set in platinum with brightly colored gems that were often calibré cut (shaped to enable the gemstones to fit together in clusters) to fit the mount.

In the early twentieth century two of Sotirio's sons, Giorgio (see fig. 18) and Costantino (see fig. 19), joined their father's business. The two brothers learned from their father both the secrets of jewelry-making and the aspects of running a business, gradually taking on more responsibility in the firm, so that when Sotirio died, in 1932, they were positioned to successfully take over Bulgari and lead it toward new horizons. In 1934 the shop on via dei Condotti was expanded and completely refurbished (see fig. 20). Its facade was clad in travertine with its four front windows and doorway framed in African marble

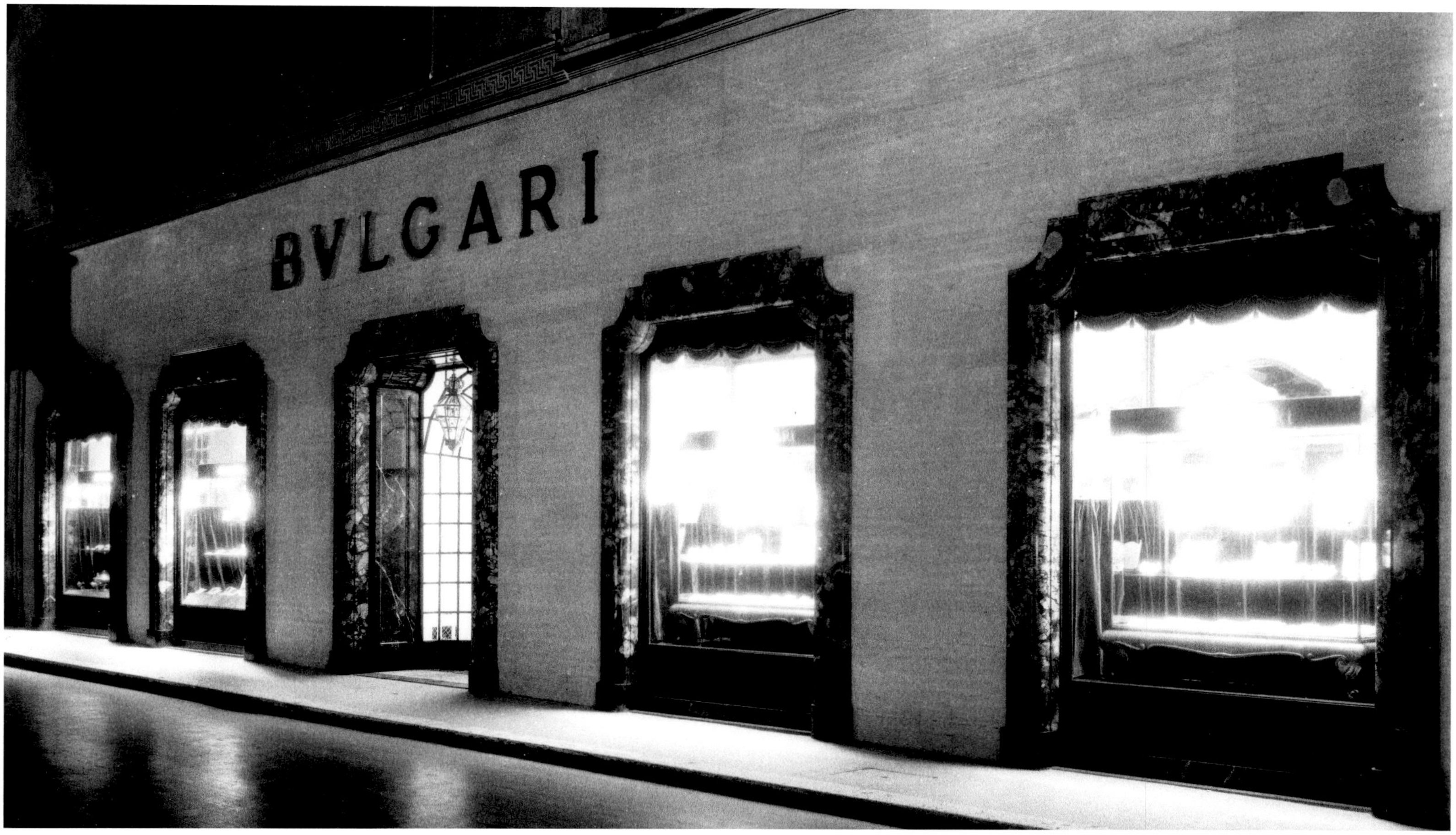

and surmounted by bronze letters spelling "BVLGARI"—a restyling considered so chic, modern, and representative that a photograph of the storefront was chosen to illustrate the entry for "shop" in the Italian *Enciclopedia Treccani* that was published that same year.

Behind the facade at Bulgari, Costantino and Giorgio took on different responsibilities. While the latter focused on the purchase of gemstones and the making of jewelry, the former concentrated on the family tradition of silversmithing, acquiring antique silver and studying the history of the metal in Italian manufacture. Costantino produced the most extensive study ever made of Italian gold jewelry and silver; his five-volume work *Argentieri, Gemmari e Orafi d'Italia* (Silversmiths, gem engravers, and goldsmiths of Italy) was published between 1958 and 1974, and today still constitutes the only existing directory of Italian silversmiths' hallmarks from every era.[1]

Meanwhile, Giorgio focused on acquiring fine gemstones and designing and producing exclusive jewelry. As a young man he had frequently traveled to Paris, where he became familiar with that city's style, design, and production techniques. As a result, the jewels that were sold at Bulgari continued to be steeped in the French tradition. Some precious pieces would be produced in Rome from designs purchased in Paris, while others would be commissioned directly from Parisian workshops (as evidenced by a number of jewels from this period inscribed "Bulgari" and bearing French assay marks and maker's marks). Starting in 1925 Bulgari entrusted the manufacture of its jewels in Rome to a single workshop owned and managed by Ubaldo Crescenzi, *maestro orafo* (master goldsmith). Crescenzi, who had long been a business partner and loyal friend of the Bulgari family, fostered the success of the firm by intimately understanding the house style and guaranteeing high standards of workmanship. This partnership continues to prosper today, with the workshop under the reins of Crescenzi's daughters and grandchildren.

Costantino and Giorgio Bulgari married two sisters—respectively, Laura (in 1926) and Leonilde (in 1932) Gulienetti—daughters of a merchant who owned a shop on via dei Condotti. The children from these two unions would, in the decades to follow, enter the firm and become important contributors, ensuring that the Bulgari legacy would maintain both family traditions and its historically high-quality standards well into the future. However, it was at a unique point in time, as World War II drew to a close and a new Italy dawned, that Bulgari's own "sweet life" truly began to blossom against a glittering backdrop of glamour, celebrity, fashion, and a rapidly changing modern world.

BULGARI AND THE WAR

Between World War I and World War II Italy came under the rule of the Italian Fascist party, whose policy was that of order, discipline, and hierarchy; the Fascists considered Italy to be the heir of the Roman Empire and sought expansion in all directions. The Bulgaris, as foreigners in Rome, were able to take advantage of the international presence in the city brought about by the government's global affairs, while other Roman shopkeepers drew a primarily local clientele.[2] However, given their Greek origin, the Bulgaris may have feared the rise of Fascism and its overt Italian nationalism. In fact, the Fascist secret police were keeping the Bulgari establishment under close observation, but as they did so, they recognized the firm's prominence. In a 1940 report a secret informant stated: "[Bulgari] is considered the first in Italy, and nearly all other Italian jewelers copy their jewels, using them as models for their own creations. The Bulgari firm has the same status in Italy as that of Cartier abroad. Politically they have always demonstrated [themselves as] excellent Italian citizens [and] they have never taken part in any political activity, as they regard themselves as completely apolitical."[3]

During the 1920s and 1930s Bulgari counted among its habitual foreign customers the great American magnates Samuel H. Kress and Robert Lehman; the millionaire Frank Jay Gould and his wife Florence; and the heiress Barbara Hutton. Italian clients included Count Giuseppe Volpi, finance minister and governor of Libya; and the Venetian Count Vittorio Cini, who purchased an exceptional lilac-pink diamond weighing 24.44 carats, along with countless other objets d'art.

At the outbreak of World War II and Italy's invasion of Greece, the Bulgari family requested Italian citizenship, thereby avoiding confiscation of their property that could result from being citizens of an "enemy nation." Although men of the Fascist regime frequented their shop, the Bulgaris were not directly involved in any such political activity and, in fact, have since been recognized for supporting the Allied troops after the armistice, and for sheltering Jewish families during the time of the racial laws.[4] By the end of World War II the Bulgari establishment had successfully maintained its business, well positioning itself for the thriving years that would follow.

POSTWAR ROME: FROM DEFEAT TO CELLULOID DREAM

On May 8, 1945, World War II came to an end following the surrender of Germany.[5] Italy had signed an armistice with the Allied powers in 1943, but a civil war was waged for another eighteen months. The country that finally emerged was deeply divided and impoverished. After the war Italy came forth with a constitution and held its first election with universal suffrage;[6] its political rehabilitation was accompanied by economic reconstruction (aided by the US government through the Marshall Plan), and by 1951 Italy was able to surpass its prewar production levels.[7]

Before the war Italy was predominantly agrarian; much of its rural population, especially in the south, was poor, illiterate, unemployed, and living in almost primitive conditions. The decade of economic growth and great social change experienced by the young republic after the war turned the old Italy on its head.[8] Financial support enabled industry to modernize and enter foreign markets, and literally millions of people left their rural homes, headed to jobs in manufacturing regions. [9] Soon homes had refrigerators, washing machines, television sets, and telephones. The growth was so exceptional that, in 1959, the *Daily Mail* spoke of the "economic miracle" in Italy.[10]

Likewise, Bulgari prospered, producing dazzling precious jewels for an increasing clientele of rich Italian industrialists, aristocrats, foreign royalty, diplomats, and celebrities. Gianni Agnelli, heir of the Italian car industry Fiat, spent an exorbitant sum at Bulgari on the engagement ring he bought for Marella Caracciolo di Castagneto, a socialite and style icon known for her inclusion in Truman Capote's famous circle of "swans." In 1953, in Rome for a two-week stay with her mother, the Iranian empress Soraya Pahlavi visited Bulgari. And later, in 1956, at the end of her own three-year stay in Rome, the ambassador Clare Boothe Luce, nicknamed "Luce Americana," bought a Bulgari emerald and diamond necklace (fig. 2) as a grand souvenir.

The film stars who began frequenting the shop on via dei Condotti during this time reflected a growing fascination with the screen as Italian culture dropped many of its traditions and welcomed new trends and technologies. Television broadcasting began in Italy in 1954 and within ten years reached an audience of eleven million viewers;[11] but even television's potent influence pales in comparison to the tremendous and lasting effects of this era's emergence of Italian cinema.

LA DOLCE VITA: FILM AND FAME IN MODERN ITALY

Protagonist of and witness to the nation's dynamic social evolution, Italian cinema of this era largely encompassed films of the neorealist genre[12] and of the *commedia all'italiana* (Italian comedy). Both reflected a desire among writers and directors to commit to Italy's political and social realities by recounting truer-to-life stories that differed from the lavishly false ones in films that were popular during the twenty-year Fascist period.[13] Cinema proved to be an effective instrument, furthermore, for the diffusion of fashion, design, and the new way of life based, at least in part, on an infatuation with America, the epitome of modernity.

At this time, the American film industry took advantage of the European economy, producing many of their expensive epics in, among other places, Rome. "The arrival of the Americans turned into a clamorous embarkation of personages. Celebrities and directors . . . became elements of the cinematographic landscape of the fifties," wrote Alberto Crespi in the book *Hollywood sul Tevere* (Hollywood on the Tiber).[14] The coming and going was so intense that magazines devoted huge spaces to that glittering world and substantial attention was dedicated to the animated nightlife of the capital. It was de rigueur to spend evenings walking along via Veneto, the chosen stage for the film stars and the entire exhibitionist circus—unknown and aspiring actors, aristocrats, playboys, writers, wannabes, curious onlookers, and the inevitable photographers (including, of course, the paparazzi)—that revolved around them. Jewels sparkled on Claudia Cardinale, Anna Magnani, Sophia Loren, Gina Lollobrigida, and Monica Vitti (see figs. 24, 25, 27, 30, 36), to name just a few of the stars who wore Bulgari.

The lifestyle that pervaded the eternal city at this time was savagely described by Federico Fellini (see fig. 21) in *La Dolce Vita* (1960). The film enjoyed an immediate and long-lasting success, perhaps because at the time of its release no other film had yet, as Crespi wrote, "touched the spirit of the times, the exposed nerve of the enormous changes that were going on."[15] The film describes that glittering parade based on the most fantastic gossip about "Hollywood on the Tiber" that was circulating from the street to the wildest cocktail parties.[16] It was not, of course, Fellini's intent to strictly report on such lifestyle, but rather to describe the existential hollowness of his characters. With the passage of time the title *La Dolce Vita* surprisingly seems to have survived and become part of a universal vocabulary—although not so much to convey the emptiness of the society portrayed in the film, but as a shorthand reference to the period straddling the fifties and early sixties viewed nostalgically as a lost era of extraordinary glamour and elegance.

THE MARKETPLACE OF THE "ROMAN DREAM"

Today, scenes from *La Dolce Vita* or *Roman Holiday* (1953) can be seen as historical documents, depicting luxury and poverty side by side in the heart of Rome. It was in this setting, which probably seemed very exotic and picturesque, that the stars lived their "Roman dreams." Hundreds of photos immortalize those now-legendary protagonists in the history of cinema—Kirk Douglas, Audrey Hepburn, Gregory Peck, Anthony Quinn, Peter Sellers, and others—in their moments of relaxation, with wives and husbands or alleged lovers, strolling, shopping, fighting, or simply sitting at Rosati in Piazza del Popolo enjoying the Roman climate.[17]

A myriad of shops catered to these wealthy American stars who were accustomed to a luxury and grandeur only previously afforded in that city by the popes. Italian fashion was able to satisfy this new clientele due to a longstanding artisan tradition that assured the quality of materials, along with a low-cost labor force that guaranteed the execution and delivery of final pieces. Bulgari, too, was able to satisfy its customers with fine gemstones set in impeccably manufactured works. Giorgio Bulgari was known to be a perfectionist; if he was not satisfied with a piece of jewelry, even after a master goldsmith had completely finished it, he would return it to the workshop for alterations and adjustments until he considered it fit to be sold.

The quality and competitive pricing of Italian goods may have helped lead Italian fashion to international fame, but other factors also contributed to its reputation. Due to exorbitant import taxes

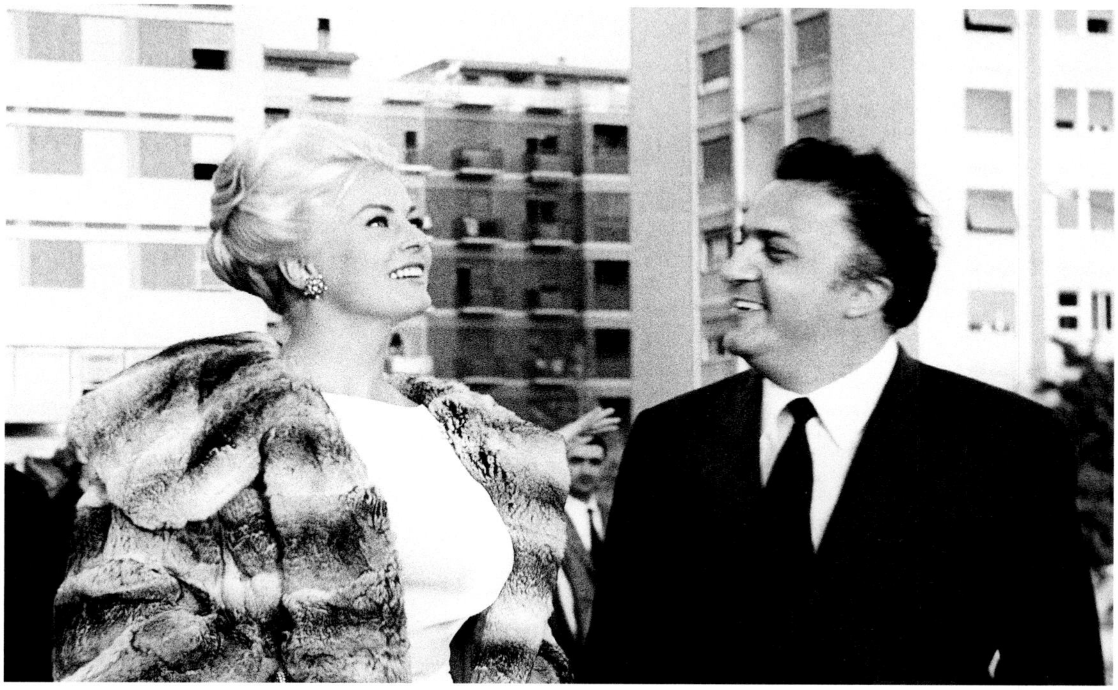

Fig. 21. Anita Ekberg, wearing Bulgari earrings with sapphires and diamonds, with Federico Fellini in Rome, 1961

placed on luxury products by both Britain and the United States after the economic crisis of 1929, as well as the difficulties that arose following World War II that made the export of Parisian works nearly impossible, the influence of French couture was in decline worldwide.

Until Italy's Fascist period the country's fashion was heavily dependent on the French; the templates were copied with slight changes, and French provenance was considered an asset. During the 1930s this custom became untenable to the Fascist regime, which attempted to "Italianize" fashion, creating, in 1935, the Ente Nazionale della Moda (National Fashion Authority), which dictated creations and materials and issued "certificates of Italian character." The authority went so far as to promote the image of the shapely, fertile Italian woman in contrast with her thin French counterpart. Cinema was used as a means of propaganda for the authorized styles, but even among the most dedicated Fascists, American films continued to inspire dressmakers and their customers. Over time a new Italian style developed, one freed from self-imposed submission to French couture.

Two events are commonly considered to mark the birth of postwar Italian fashion: first, the 1949 marriage in Rome, seen in newsreels around the world, of movie star Tyrone Power to actress Linda Christian, complete with a wedding dress by the Sorelle Fontana atelier and wedding rings by Bulgari (see fig. 22); and second, two fashion shows organized by Giovanni Battista Giorgini in Florence, in 1951, to showcase the best creations from the most important Italian stylists for the buyers for major American department stores, who were in Europe to attend the Paris shows. Press accounts recount the Italians' great success with the Americans—*La Stampa Sera* wrote, "The Roman and Milanese models have enthused the Americans [with] simple, sporty lines in a great variety of colors" (July 25, 1951),

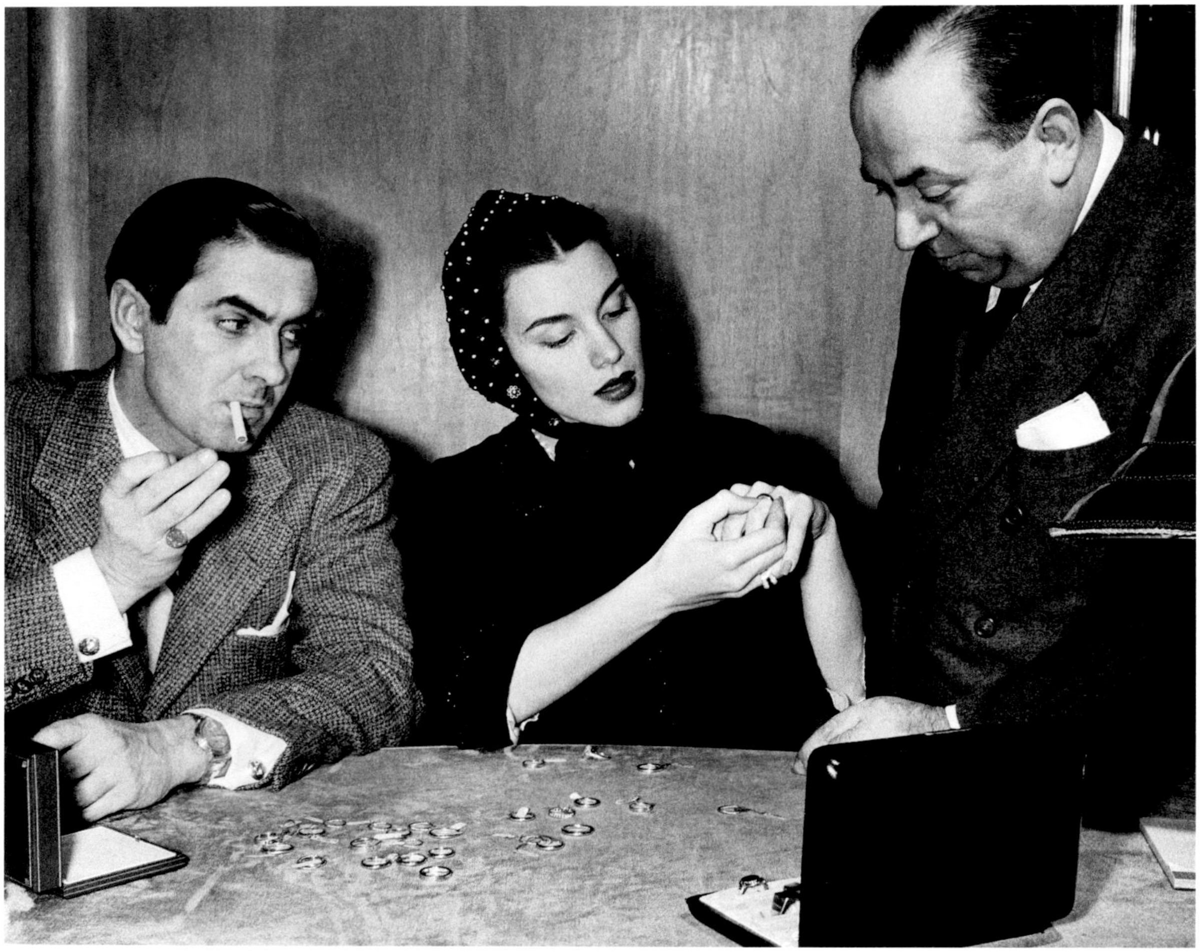

Fig. 22. Tyrone Power and Linda Christian, shopping for wedding rings at Bulgari, 1949

and the *Los Angeles Times* headlined their article "Italian Couturiers Capture Colors of Rare Beauty at Florence Show" (July 27, 1951)—suggesting that a mélange of Mediterranean exoticism and functionality compatible with the "American look" was the key to this victory.

LA DOLCE VITA AND BEYOND AT BULGARI

During all this activity, as Italian fashion emerged internationally, the Bulgari shop at 10 via dei Condotti was perfectly situated within the Roman Trident, the chic center of Rome.[18] Giorgio and Costantino Bulgari, now running the business after the death of their father, spoke several languages and were well accustomed to dealing with a wealthy foreign clientele. Alongside their fine jewelry, which was still heavily influenced by the French style, they also sold antiquities: important collections of icons, Chinese jades, and antique silver—all enhancing the interior beauty of the shop (fig. 23). In the store today one can still see fine examples of the objects that were handled at that time, including a rare clock in ebony, hardstones, and gilt bronze with bronze sculptures by Giovanni Battista Foggini, which was created in the workshops of the Grand Duchy of Tuscany and dates to the early 1700s.

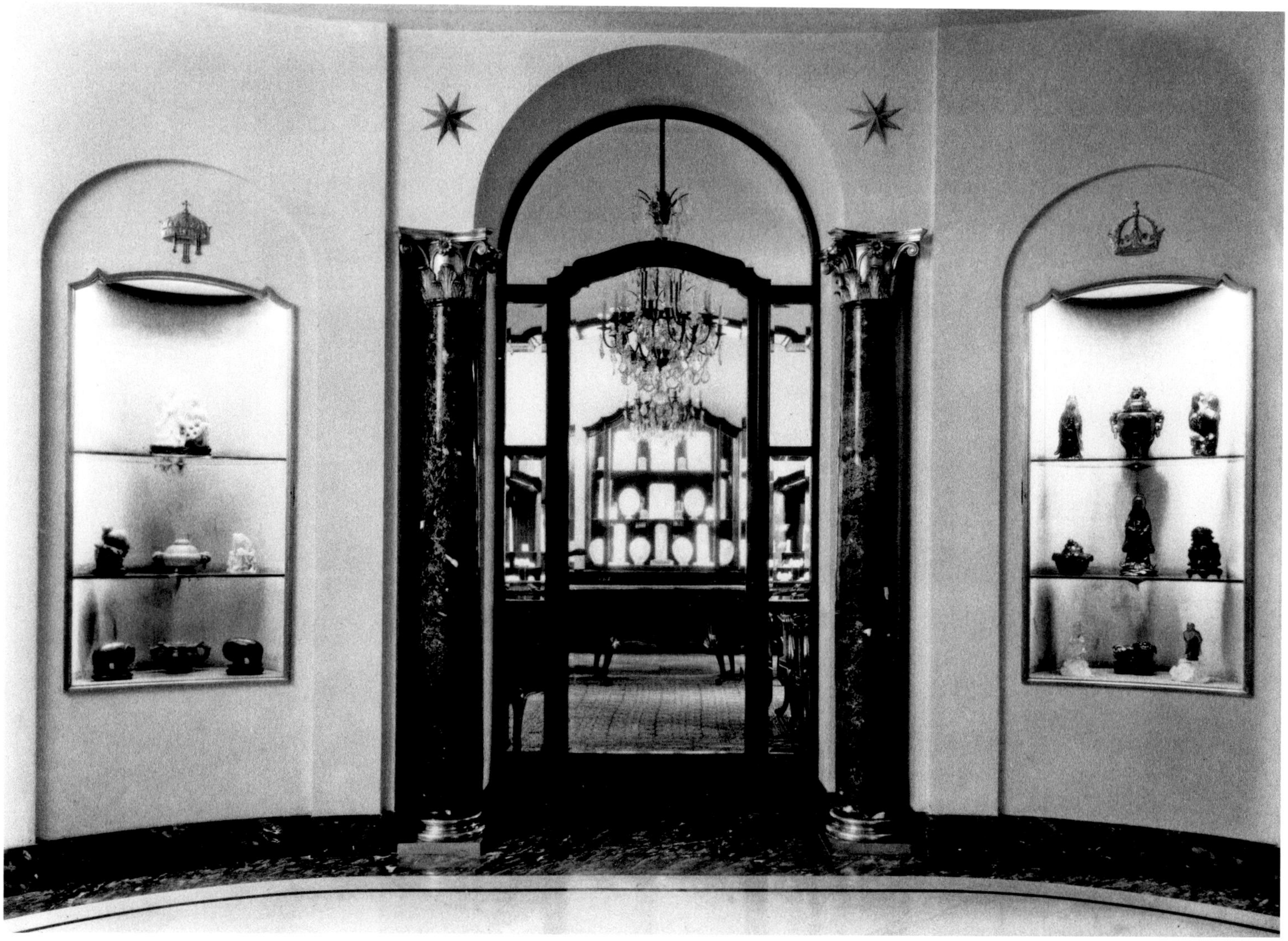

Fig. 23. The interior of the Bulgari store at 10 via dei Condotti, Rome, 1934

When Tyrone Power and Linda Christian decided to marry in Rome, it was almost inevitable that their wedding rings would come from Bulgari—by then the most stylish and prominent jeweler in Rome. The establishment was gaining cachet among international as well as Italian film stars and other celebrities. It should also be mentioned that Audrey Hepburn, at the time she was filming *Roman Holiday*, bought a gold bag there for her mother, and director Luchino Visconti stopped in to purchase gold cigarette cases with engraved dedications to thank some of his collaborators. Italian actress Gina Lollobrigida (see fig. 24) spent some of her first earnings in the shop to buy a convertible diamond necklace, while Sophia Loren opted for a necklace of cabochon sapphires, rubies, and diamonds (see figs. 25, 27). Anna Magnani (see fig. 30), who also held a great passion for Bulgari jewels, was affronted upon being greeted at the store by the young Paolo Bulgari (Giorgio's son, then just twenty), responding, "I'm an important client—who is this boy?"[19]

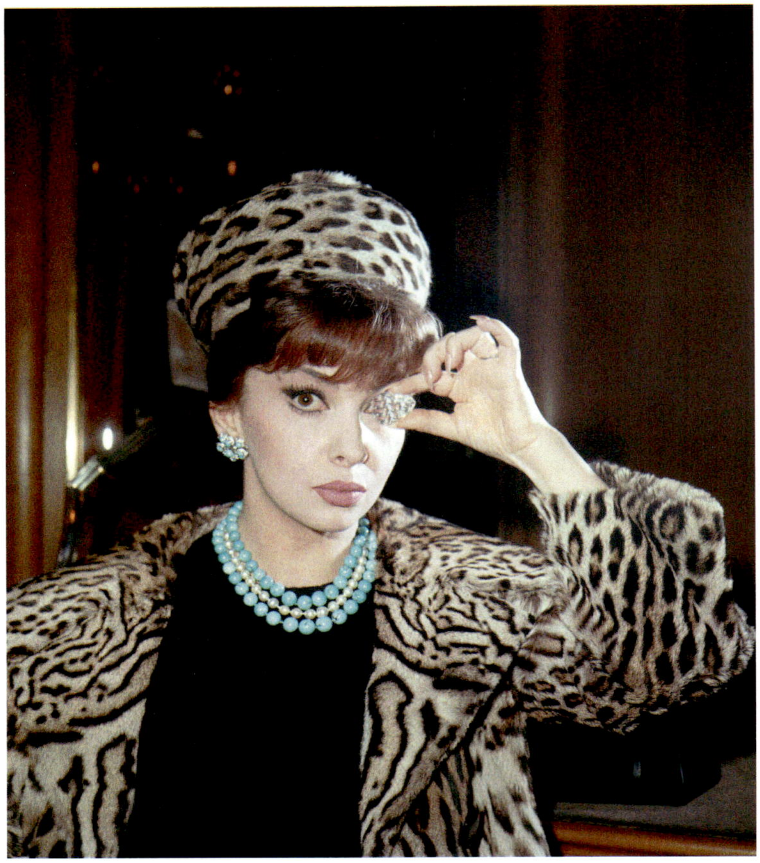

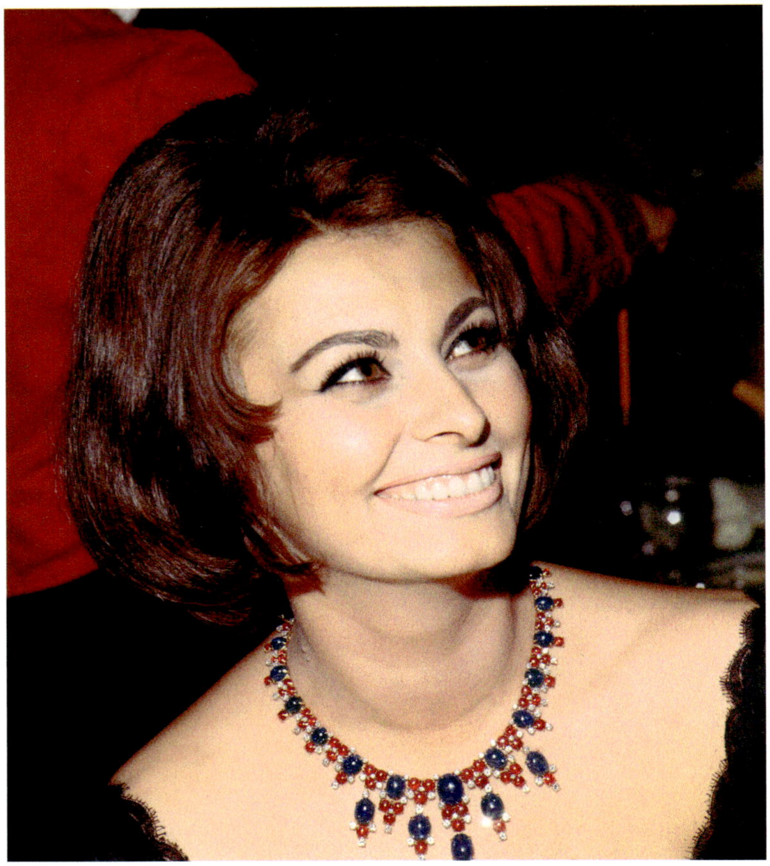

Fig. 24. Gina Lollobrigida, in a Bulgari turquoise parure, at the jeweler's shop in Rome, 1965

Fig. 25. Sophia Loren in her Bulgari necklace of cabochon sapphires and rubies with diamonds, 1962

Bulgari jewels were brought to the set of *Cleopatra* in the film studios of Cinecittà, where Richard Burton initially selected a Bulgari ring for his then-wife, Sybil. He later went to the via dei Condotti shop to bedeck Elizabeth Taylor—then married to Eddie Fisher—in emeralds (see Triossi, "The Elizabeth Taylor Collection," this volume). The store that Taylor called "a nice little shop" was the scene of furious fights and costly reconciliations between the two scandalous lovers (see fig. 26).[20] On a silver box with coins that these actors presented to the producer of *Cleopatra*, it is amusing to read the dedication that is engraved in Taylor's facsimile handwriting: *To our favorite Producer & Wife / Lest we forget the glamour of it all / All love / Elizabeth & Rich*. The gift was an exquisite and typically Bulgari object. The fame of such clientele and the attention the world devoted to the Roman dolce vita endowed the shops and ateliers frequented by those stars with wide media coverage, something that was otherwise difficult for design houses and retailers to achieve at that time.

Yet while an Italian style in fashion had been evolving since the thirties, it was not until the end of the fifties that an Italian style of jewelry can be said to have made an appearance. This is not surprising: clothing is perceived as seasonal and has rhythms that dictate rapid renewal; since fashion makes use of

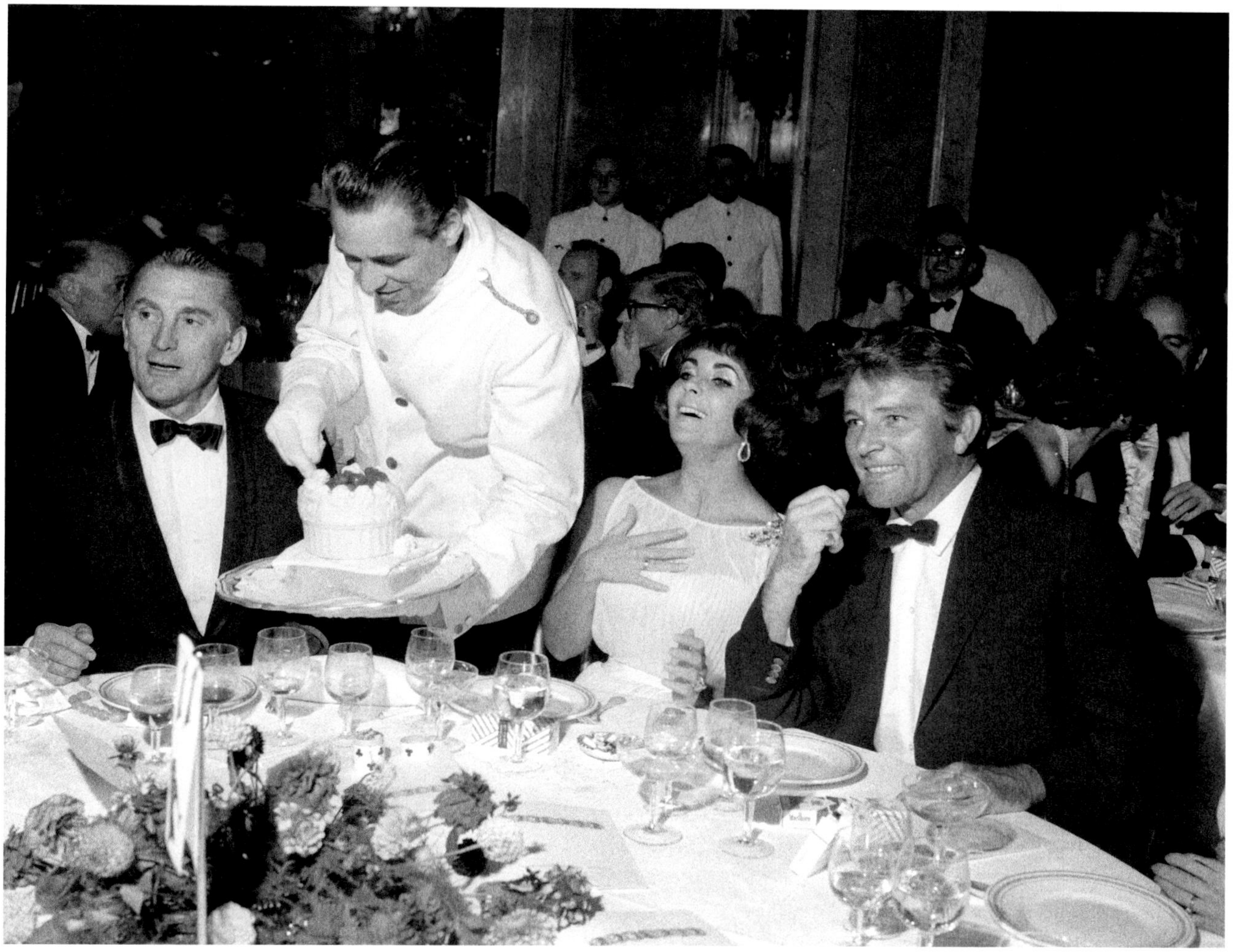

Fig. 26. Elizabeth Taylor, in her Bulgari platinum, emerald, and diamond *tremblant* brooch (cat. 91), out on the town with Richard Burton in Rome, 1961

materials of minor intrinsic value, it allows for greater experimentation and less adherence to the dictates of tradition. Meanwhile, precious jewels are considered eternal, and their high cost requires designs that will not rapidly fade out of style. This phenomenon was quite clear in the second quarter of the twentieth century when the Art Deco style—named for the 1925 Exposition Universelle des Arts Décoratifs in Paris—emerged decades after the Fauvist, Cubist, and Futurist art movements that inspired it.

Therefore, even though Italian fashion had already achieved recognition by 1951, such awareness did not extend to the world of jewelry until the subsequent decade. Bulgari was among the first jewelers to introduce products reflecting Italian taste. Their innovations in this arena were acknowledged in a 1963 article in *Connaissance des Arts*, written by well-known art historian Evelyne Schlumberger, who wrote, "A Bulgari jewel is as recognizable as a Chanel suit."[21]

What was emerging was a distinctive look that could be said to convey "casual formality." The contradiction inherent in this term describes the spirit of Italian-style jewels, which are precious, yet wearable, and frequently incorporate less expensive materials juxtaposed with those of greater value, such as steel with gold. They are colorful, bold, and rounded, with an unusual mix of gemstones, and the warm tones of yellow gold are preferred to the cool white metals such as platinum. Taken together, these characteristics make a Bulgari jewel thoroughly original and immediately recognizable.

The four decades that are the focus of the chapters that follow further investigate Bulgari's creativity in two very important watersheds in the history of the company: the first, which occurred in the late 1950s to early 1960s, when Bulgari, under the leadership of Giorgio and Costantino, began to forge a distinctive new style unique to Bulgari but at the same time "Italian" in spirit; and the second, between the late seventies and early eighties, under the leadership of the family's third and fourth generations, when Bulgari realized the necessity of modernizing jewelry to render it wearable and distinct. Following this design edict and a desire to create an international presence, Bulgari expanded with numerous shops overseas and transformed itself from a family-run business into a globally recognized brand. These two periods introduced numerous motifs, lines, and collections that have since become significant and recognizable characteristics unique to Bulgari, lasting even through the present day.

1. Costantino Bulgari, *Argentieri, Gemmari e Orafi d'Italia* (Rome: Fratelli Palombi, 1958–1974).

2. In the nearby Piazza di Spagna, for example, the Petochi firm of jewelers, also founded in 1884, was frequented by members of the Roman aristocracy when they were not buying from the great Parisian houses. Despite its illustrious clientele and long history, Petochi, like the other established Roman jewelers, never enjoyed international fame.

3. Amanda Triossi and Daniela Mascetti, *Bulgari* (Milan: Electa, 2007), 19.

4. Ibid., 24.

5. On September 2, 1943, after long and secret negotiations, an armistice was signed between the Allied forces and Italy. Announced by a brief government communiqué on September 8, but without any directives to the Italian armed forces or the nation's structures, it threw the country into a state of confusion and at the mercy of the Germans, who managed to maintain control, together with the Fascists, of northern Italy and a good part of central Italy. The royal family, the government, and other leaders of the armed forces fled Rome. There followed a war of resistance between the partisans and the Fascist/Nazi forces.

6. The diverse post–World War II governing class headed, if not actually led, Italy toward its new republican life, notwithstanding the great social conflicts of a strong pro-Soviet Communist party, an intrusive Vatican, the Cold War, and the demands of the victors. On June 2, 1946, an institutional referendum sanctioned the end of the monarchy and the birth of the Italian republic; its constitution went into effect on January 1, 1948. The first parliamentary elections, after a government of national unity, were held in May 1948. Women's suffrage was conceded in 1946.

7. According to some historians, the Marshall Plan fell short of its original goals because of the extremity of the basic needs of the recipient nations, which had been destroyed by the war, and because the economic growth, due to low labor costs, did not immediately produce great consumer growth. It is certain, however, that the plan was a great economic accelerator for the future of Europe.

8. This productive euphoria did not involve the agrarian economy, which was sacrificed to the needs of the northern European countries and, in Italy, to the interests of industrialists; employment in agriculture, in fact, dropped from forty to twenty-five percent in ten years, while the number of service workers increased.

9. It has been calculated that, between the end of the war and 1970, there was a migration of twenty-five million people, about ten million of whom moved from their places of origin to other regions of Italy, while about four million emigrated to other countries. See Guido Crainz, *Il paese mancato. Dal miracolo economico agli anni ottanta* (Rome: Donzelli editore, 2003), 14.

10. "Non si perda mai di vista il dato centrale del nostro miracolo, connesso alle arretratissime condizioni di partenza: in Italia, più che in altri paesi europei, antiche aspirazioni ed elementari esigenze iniziano a realizzarsi contemporaneamente all'irrompere di consumi e bisogni

nuovi." (Do not lose sight of the central fact of our miracle, related to the very backward starting conditions: in Italy, more than in other European countries, old aspirations and basic needs begin to be achieved at the same time as consumption and new needs burst on the scene.) Ibid., 14.

11. Ibid., 15.

12. "Neorealism was not a school, but a group of voices, peripheral in a large part, a multiple discovery of the different Italys, especially of the Italys that until then were the least known in literature." Italo Calvino, preface to *The Path to the Spiders' Nests*, rev. ed. (New York: Harper Collins, 2000).

13. The works of such directors as Luchino Visconti (*Ossessione*, *Bellissima*, *La terra trema*), Roberto Rossellini (*Germany Year Zero*, *Paisà*), Vittorio De Sica (*Sciuscià*, *The Bicycle Thief*), Giuseppe De Santis (*Riso amaro*), and Pietro Germi (*Il cammino della speranza*, *Il ferroviere*) greatly influenced international cinema. The director Martin Scorsese, in his documentary about Italian movies, *My Voyage to Italy* (1999), discusses the films mentioned here at length.

14. Alberto Crespi, "Non solo divi. I registi della Hollywood sul Tevere," in Stefano Della Casa and Dario Viganò, *Hollywood sul Tevere: Anatomia di un fenomeno* (Milan: Electa, 2010), 45.

15. Ibid., 48.

16. Orio Caldiron, "Il divismo fra mito e gossip," in Della Casa and Viganò, *Hollywood sul Tevere*, 65.

17. Rosati is a café in Rome that was famously frequented by many writers, actors, and directors from the 1950s through the 1970s.

18. The Roman Trident is positioned between the Piazza del Popolo and the three streets that merge into it: via Ripetta, via del Corso, and via del Babuino.

19. Paolo Bulgari, quoted in Ettore Livini, "Bulgari, i gioielli e le attrici 'Ho venduto la Dolce Vita,'" in *La Repubblica* (Affari & Finanza), March 9, 2011.

20. Ibid.

21. Quoted in Evelyne Schlumberger, "Un présent pour le souverain pontife et d'autres joyaux des XVI et XVII siècles vus chez un grand antiquaire de Rome," in *Connaissance des Arts* (Paris), December 1963, 145.

The Art of Bulgari

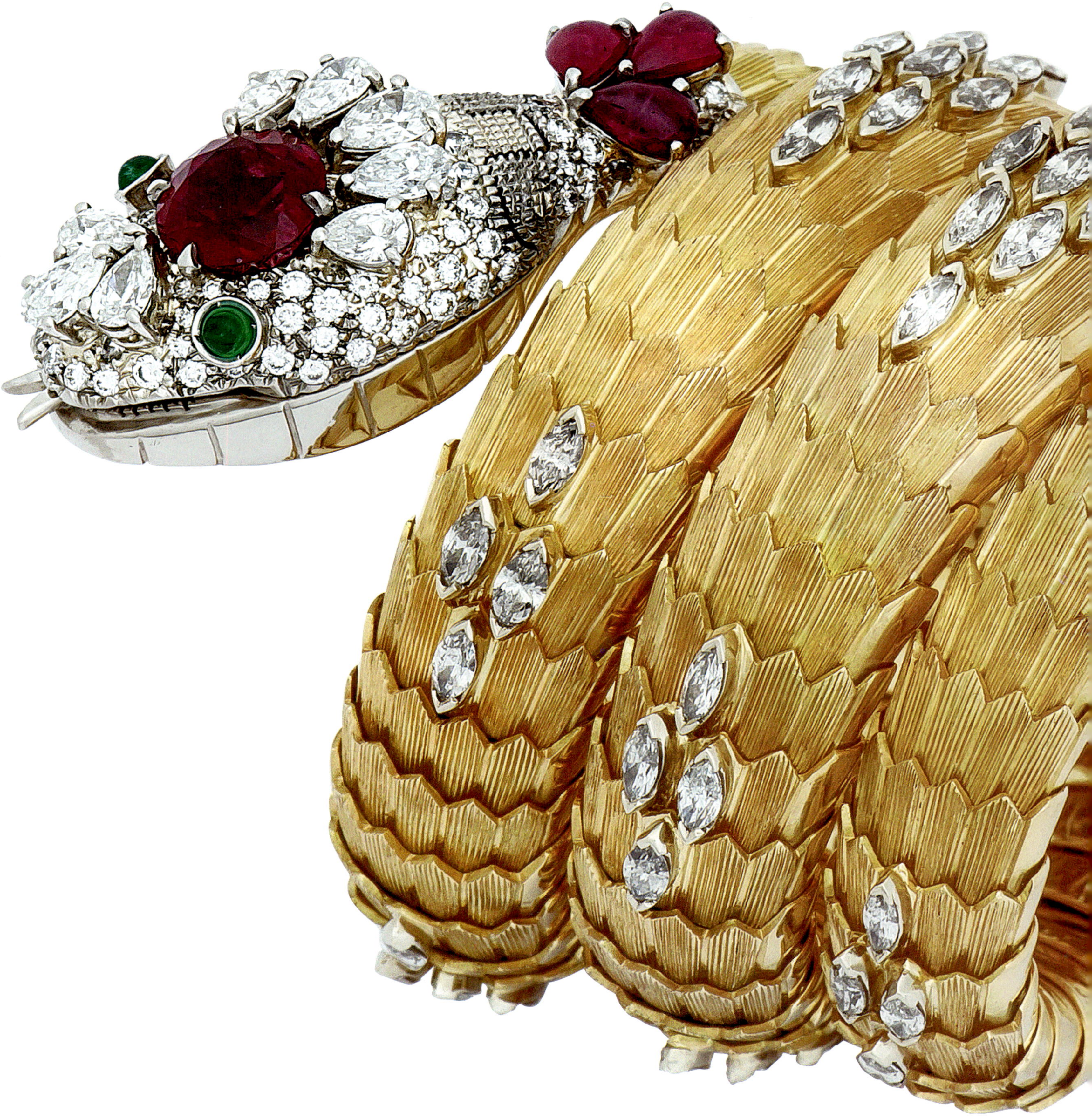

1950s

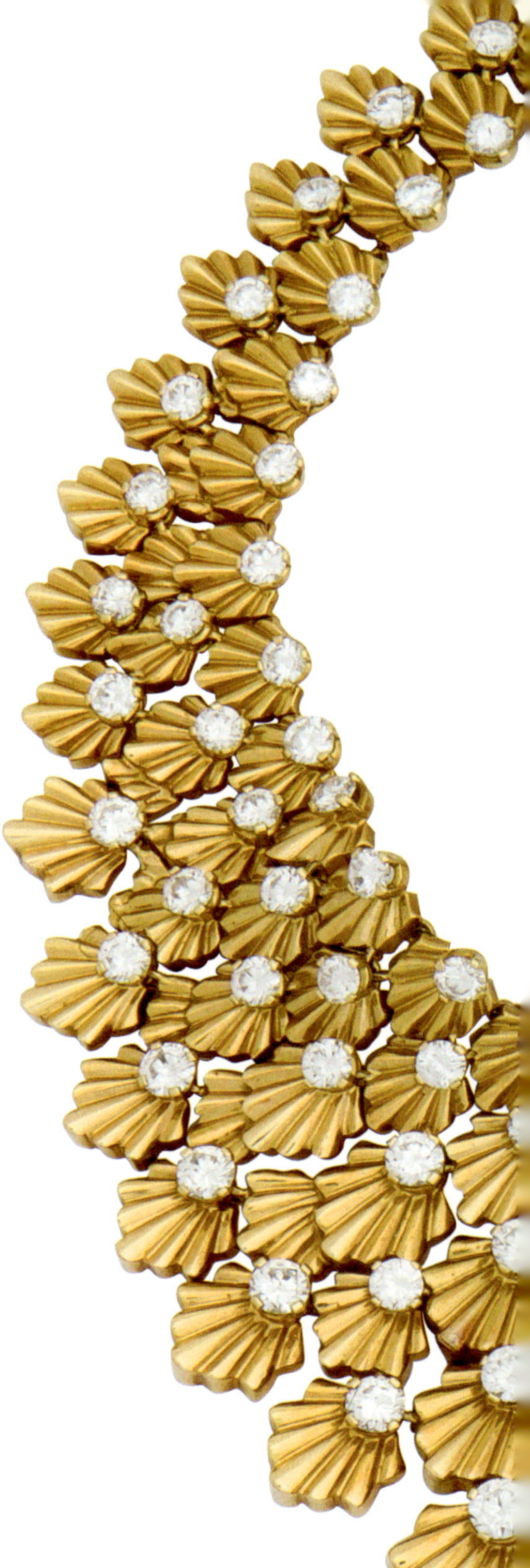

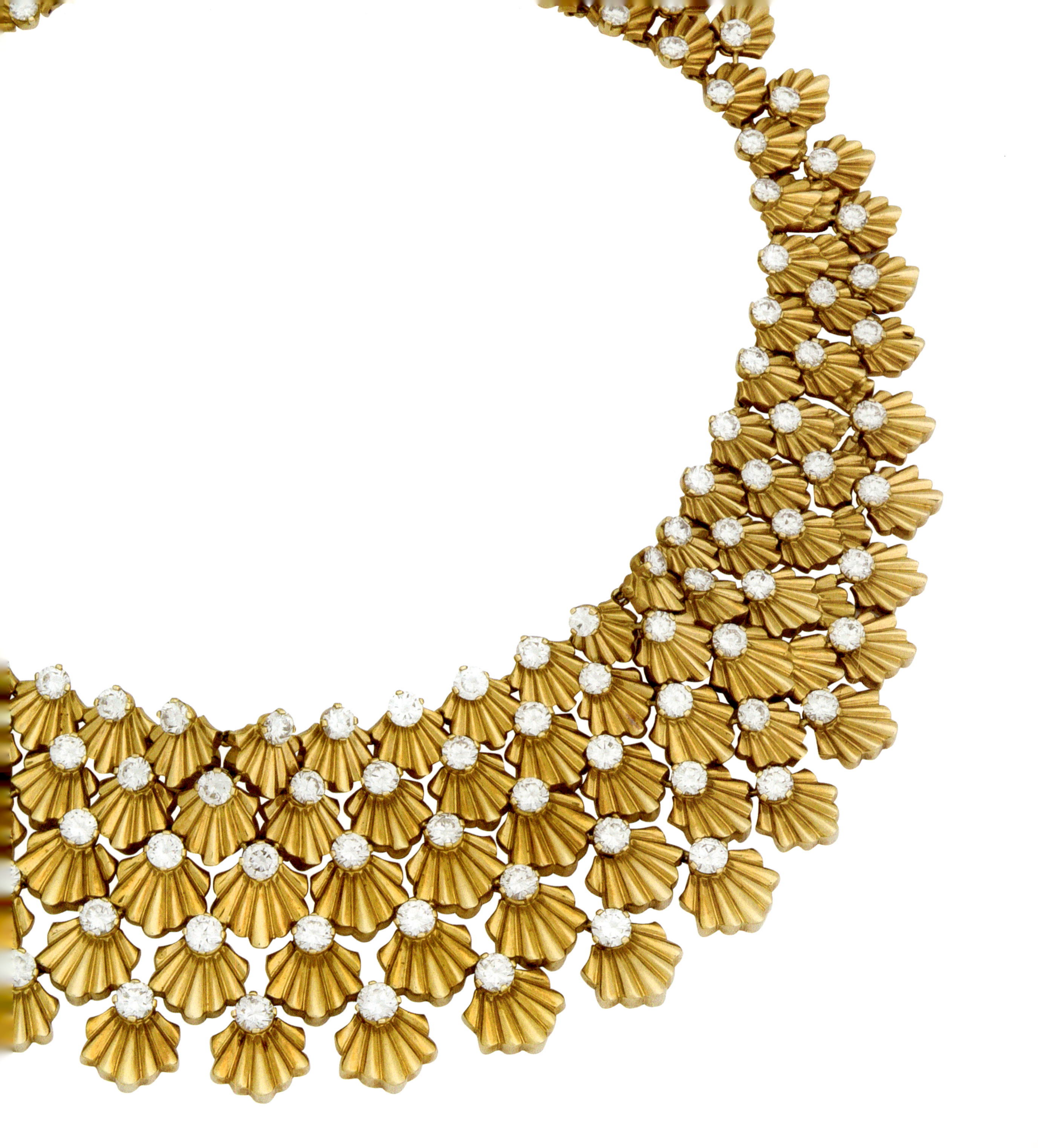

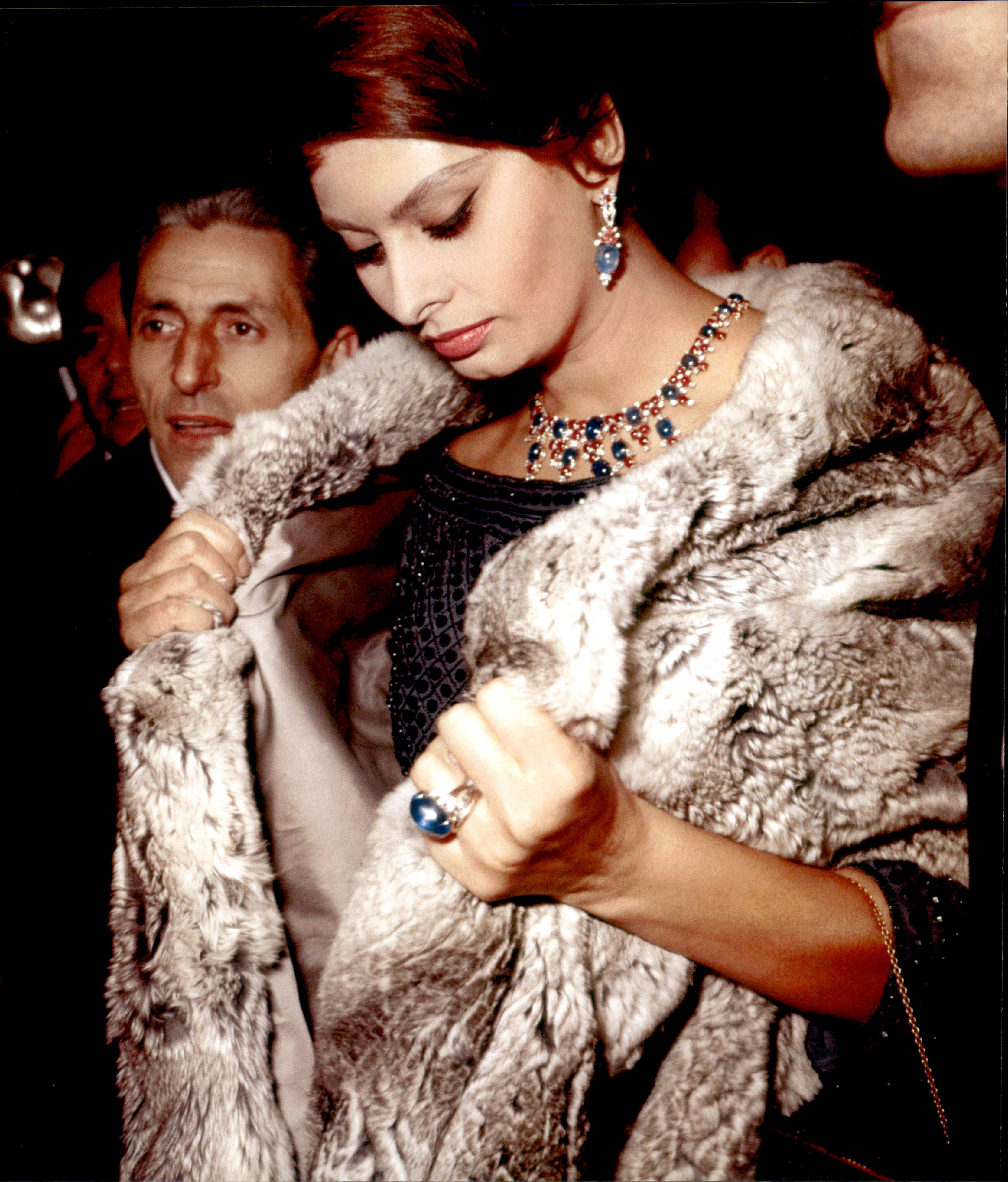

1950s: From Diamonds to Color

The postwar boom in the Western world created a demand for lavishly set gemstone jewelry as the economic and industrial development of the period led to the rapid growth of an affluent upper-middle class eager to reveal its newly acquired wealth and status. Jewelry featuring a generous display of gems undoubtedly reflected this spirit, with diamonds in particular reigning supreme.

It is no coincidence that De Beers, the consortium of companies that largely controls the diamond trade, began promoting these gems on a large scale by coining, in 1948, the very successful slogan "diamonds are forever," and by establishing, in 1954, the annual Diamonds International Awards, which were intended to promote designs that incorporated the stones in both formal and casual settings. Furthermore, in 1953, the diamond grading system based on the "4Cs" (color, cut, clarity, and carat weight), which had initially been introduced by the Gemological Institute of America (the GIA), became the universal grading standard for these gems; in 1955 the GIA began to issue the first diamond grading reports, providing expert analyses of a gem's identity and quality characteristics, which have since become the international jewelry industry's benchmark. Therefore the song "Diamonds Are a Girl's Best Friend," famously sung by Marilyn Monroe in the 1953 film *Gentlemen Prefer Blondes*, could not have been timelier.[1] Its lyrics perfectly express the appeal of diamonds at that time: "Men grow cold as girls grow old / and we all lose our charms in the end / but square cut or pear shape / these rocks don't lose their shape . . ."

The international style of "fine jewelry"of the 1950s was characterized by jewels encrusted with diamonds, which were typically mounted in precious white metal.[2] When colored gemstones, such as rubies, emeralds, and sapphires, were introduced, they were seldom mixed together, but rather each was combined with diamonds. Sinuous curving lines featuring asymmetrical openwork motifs were also popular in the jewelry of the 1950s, as were floral sprays, bows, and tassels, all of which were often set with diamond baguettes.

Bulgari generally adhered to this international style, which since the eighteenth century had been championed by the trendsetting Parisian jewelers. Similar to the fine Parisian jewelry of the day, Bulgari pieces in this decade tended to be asymmetrical in shape and often featured cascading motifs of baguette diamonds, as documented in countless designs in the Bulgari archives (see fig. 28). Among the numerous jewels created at the time, a pair of ruby and diamond tassel earrings of 1954 (fig. 29), purchased by the Italian actress Anna Magnani (see fig. 30), exemplifies the Parisian style. Bulgari also looked to France when it came to the less formal "day jewelry," which was typically mounted in yellow gold and decorated with small diamonds. Yellow gold, which is more malleable than platinum, can be knotted, woven, or trimmed; its surface can also be developed in interesting openwork patterns. One

Fig. 27. Sophia Loren in a Bulgari parure of cabochon sapphires and rubies highlighted with diamonds, 1960

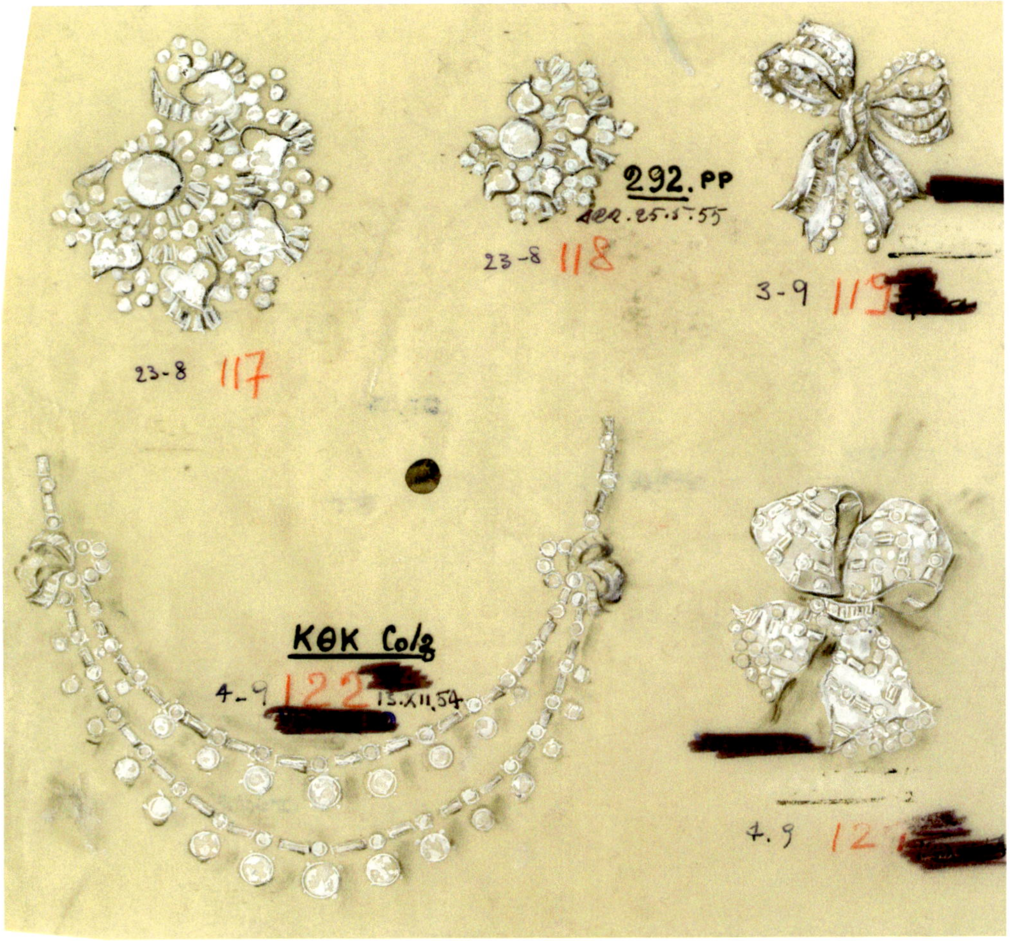

Fig. 28. Original design sketch showing bows, cascades, and other designs with diamonds, ca. 1950s

necklace from the mid-fifties is a fine example of how yellow gold can be formed, with its multiple rows of fan-shaped "palmettes," each studded with a small brilliant-cut diamond (cat. 3).

Later in the decade, however, the Bulgari style evolved as the diverse interests of the second-generation Bulgari brothers, Costantino and Giorgio, became more clearly defined, as did their roles within the firm. With Giorgio's understanding of gemstones and production techniques (acquired in part through his visits to the French capital) and Costantino's connoisseurship (he collected, along with antique silver, Renaissance objects, snuff boxes, icons, and jade), Bulgari was positioned to make its own mark on jewelry design and began to develop a more distinctive and independent style.

Bulgari's works became monumental, which set them apart from more delicate French jewels. Preferences for rounded contours, more compact shapes, and volume emerged, as did the prevalence of cabochon gemstones (rather than angular, faceted ones), as shown in the sapphire and diamond necklace of 1955 (cat. 2) and the emerald and diamond necklace commissioned by Brooke Astor (see figs. 6, 7). These styles demonstrate a growing favor for three-dimensionality in Bulgari's designs, as can be

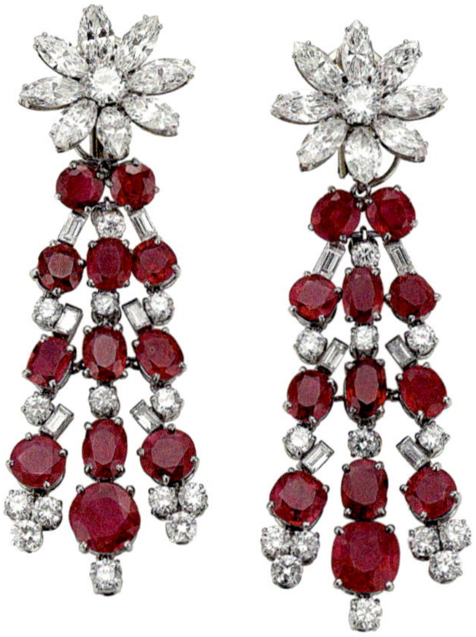

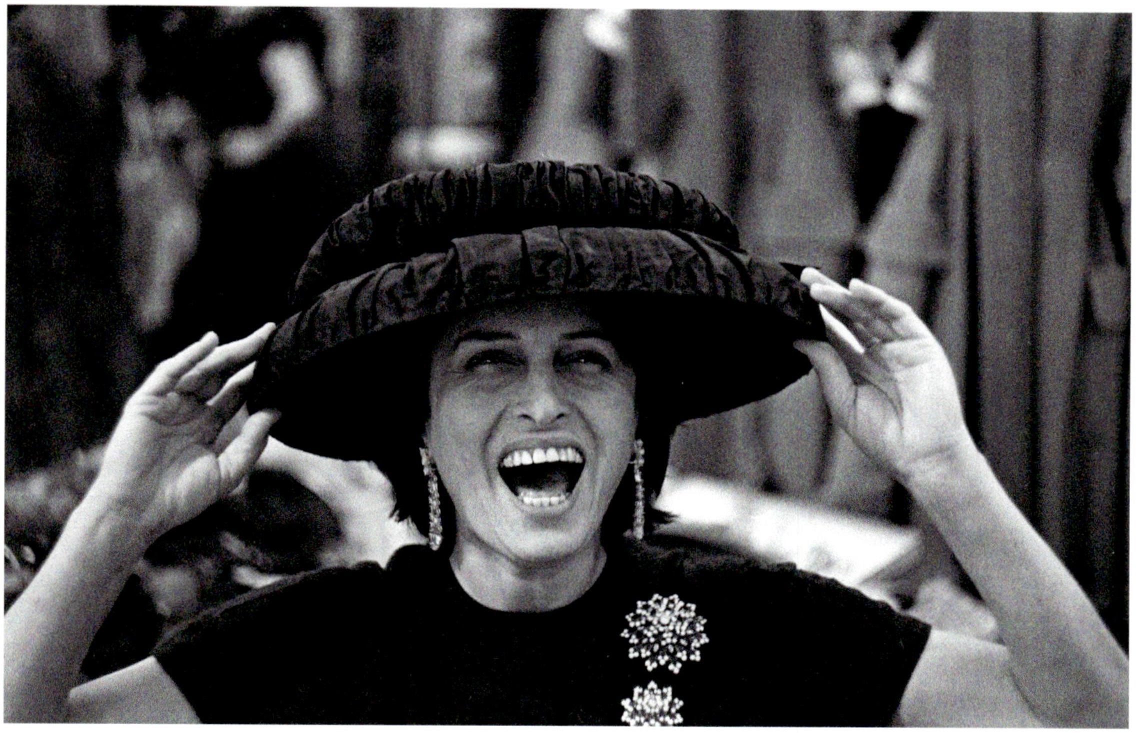

Fig. 29. Bulgari platinum, ruby, and diamond earrings, 1954

Fig. 30. Anna Magnani wearing her Bulgari platinum, ruby, and diamond earrings with matching brooches, 1959

seen in a pair of platinum bracelets from 1955 and 1959 (cat. 15), which are composed of a succession of diamond-set domed plaques.[3]

Bulgari also began to create inventive floral-spray brooches in the late fifties. French jewelers since the eighteenth century have frequently incorporated into their pieces realistically rendered floral motifs, often arranged in free-form compositions. Reaching what may be considered its apogee during the mid-nineteenth century, due to the work of the master Parisian jeweler Oscar Massin, this floral motif continued to spread thereafter, remaining fashionable well into the twentieth century and beyond (except during the Art Deco period, when flower motifs became extremely stylized). During the latter half of the eighteenth century, some floral brooches were innovatively made by attaching the flower heads to the mounts with springs, thereby allowing them to quiver at a wearer's every movement, creating shimmering visual effects. This kind of mount was referred to as *en tremblant* (trembling).

During the late fifties Giorgio Bulgari acquired from an Armenian gem dealer a sizable collection of colored diamonds that were tremendously varied in size, shape, and hue, ranging from golden-yellow to cognac, pink to lilac, and blue to green. Their diversity, rather than daunting Giorgio and his chief designer, Gianni Valli, challenged them, leading to the creation of a series of large floral-spray brooches with flowers of different shapes and colors. This motif enabled Bulgari to make the most of this heterogeneous group of diamonds that would have otherwise been difficult to mount together.

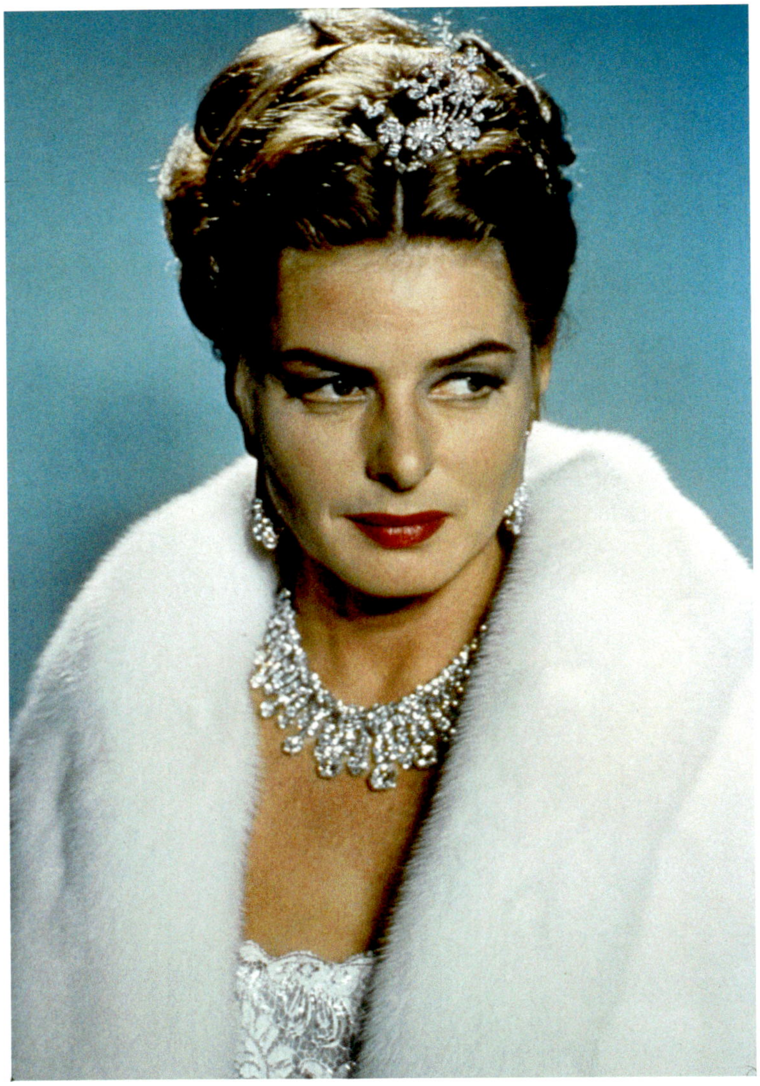

Fig. 31. Ingrid Bergman, wearing a Bulgari *tremblant* diamond brooch, in *The Visit*, 1964

As these works also utilized the special spring mount, they became known as the *tremblant* brooches (see cats. 4–6, 90–91). Though Giorgio had not invented the mechanism, he made it his own by perfecting it in his designs of the mid-twentieth century. The variety of his floral compositions is remarkable, ranging from sprays to bouquets to baskets full of bejeweled flowers. In the majority of cases, the mounts were in platinum and the springs and pins in white gold, set with colored and white diamonds or, less frequently, gemstones such as rubies, sapphires, and emeralds. They were best sellers in their day, and were also popularly worn as hair ornaments by the likes of Ingrid Bergman (see fig. 31), Princess Soraya Pahlavi of Iran, Gina Lollobrigida, and Elizabeth Taylor (see fig. 1).

As the 1950s moved into the 1960s, a series of brooches were created in the shapes of vases or baskets of flowers with leaves. These creations, known in jewelry circles from the eighteenth century by the name *giardinetto* (little garden), allowed Bulgari to experiment with vast combinations of colored

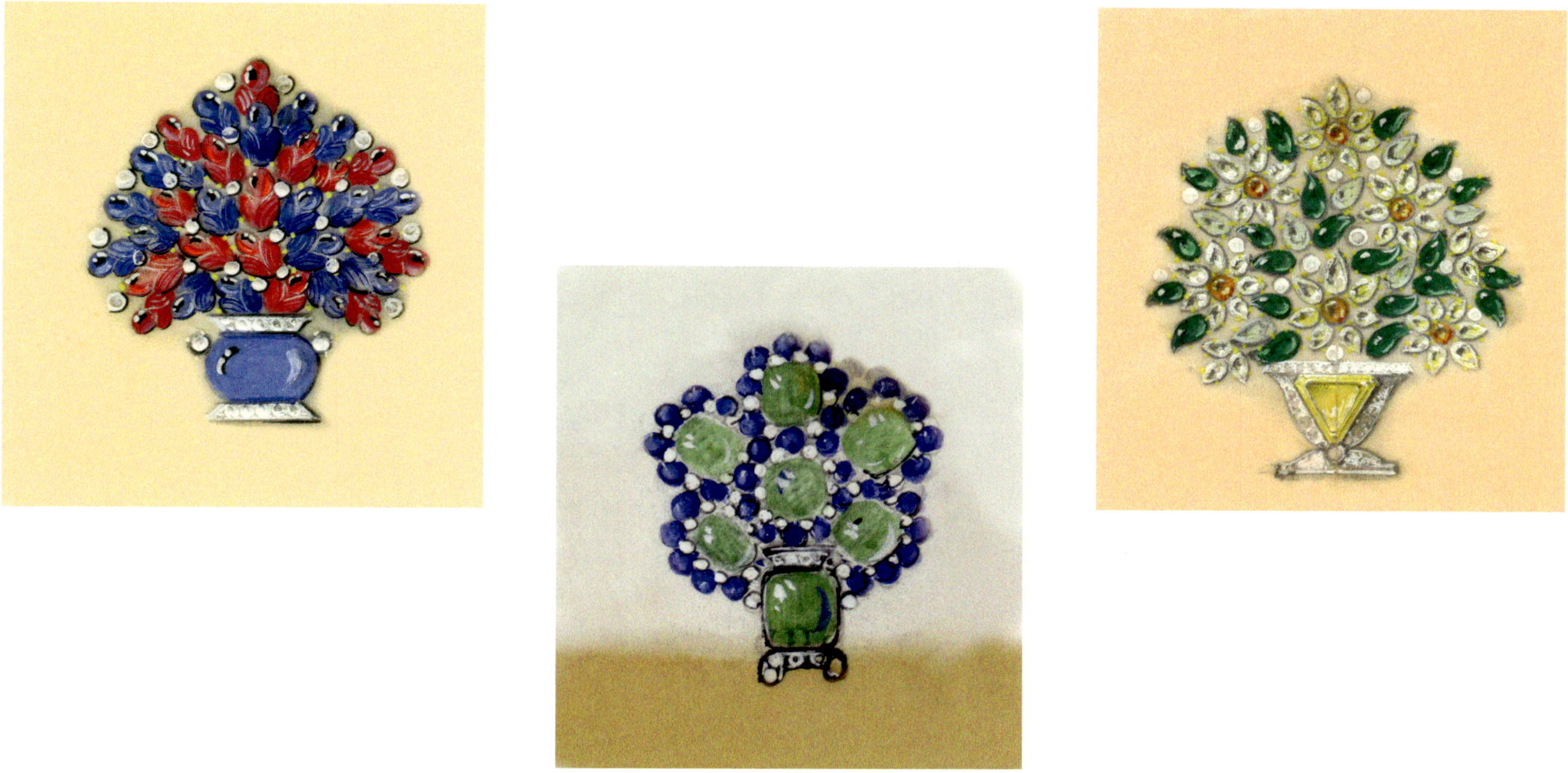

Figs. 32a–c. Original design sketches for *giardinetto* brooches, ca. 1965

gemstones. Sometimes faceted, sometimes carved, and sometimes cabochon, the primary gems representing the flowers were embellished with diamond highlights, while another larger stone served as the vase or basket (cats. 10–14; see also figs. 32a–c). Apart from the range of colors, the real innovation displayed in these pieces was in the extensive use of precious gemstones fashioned as cabochons and placed in prominent positions, which marked a departure from the prevailing twentieth-century tradition of reserving the cabochon cut mainly for stones of lesser intrinsic value.

Bulgari undoubtedly reached a high level of success in the 1950s with an ever-growing national and international clientele, but unlike Italian couture fashion, which had begun to establish its own identity by this time, the jeweler's creations were still largely indebted to French styles. Yet the charming *giardinetto* brooches first introduced by Bulgari in this decade present a striking range of hues that may be regarded as an anticipation of the colorful jewels of the decades that would follow.

1. The 1953 film was an adaptation of the earlier musical that premiered on Broadway in 1949.

2. This term indicates individually conceived jewels mounted with gemstones of great intrinsic value. This type of jewelry is also referred to as "high jewelry," a direct translation from the French *haute joaillerie*.

3. It is intriguing to note that these particular bracelets were once in the collection of American actress Ellen Barkin; one of them appeared on the wrist of Elizabeth Taylor in the film *Boom!* (1968), although there is no record of her owning it.

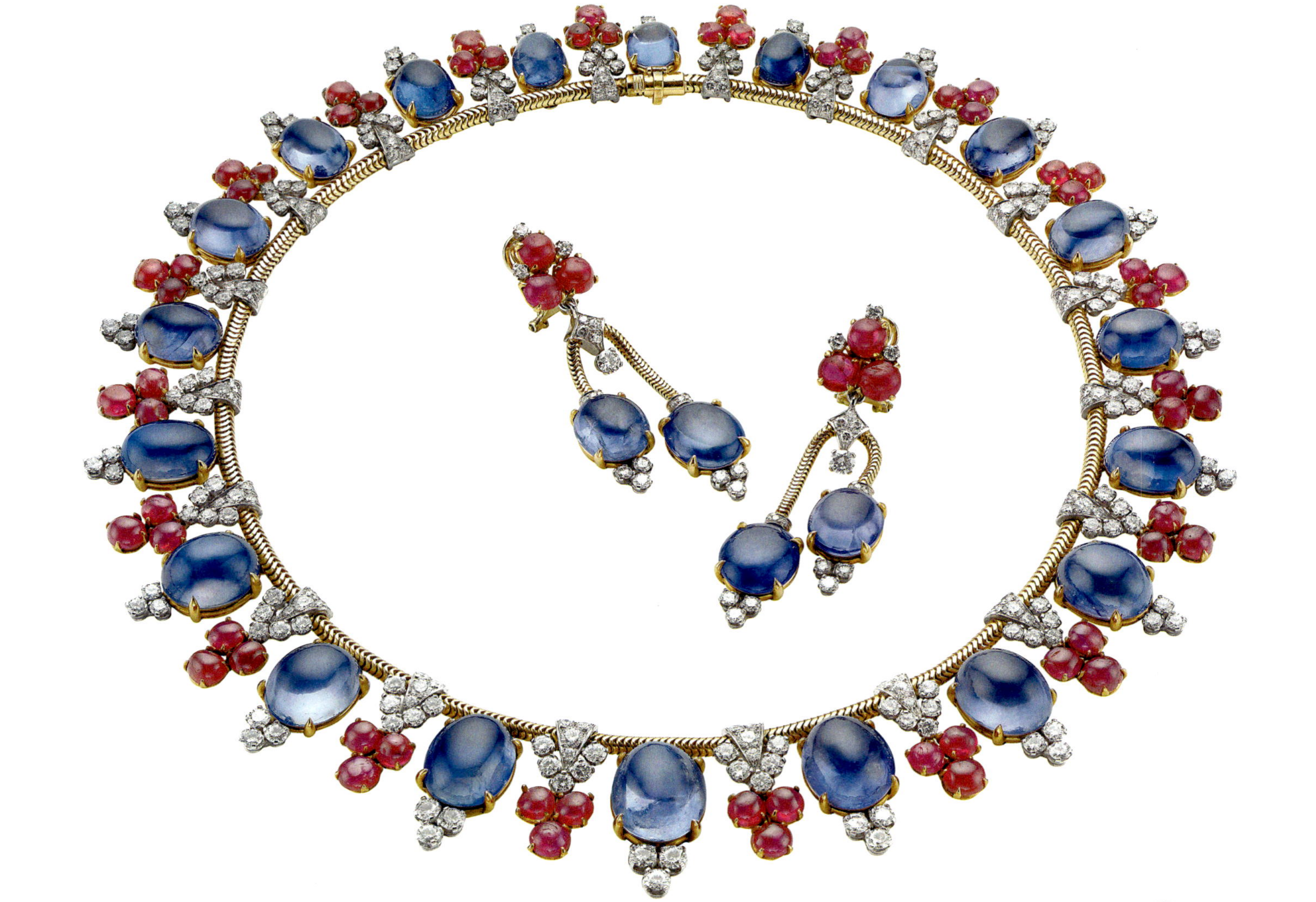

1. Parure (suite), 1955–1956
Gold and platinum with sapphires, rubies, and diamonds

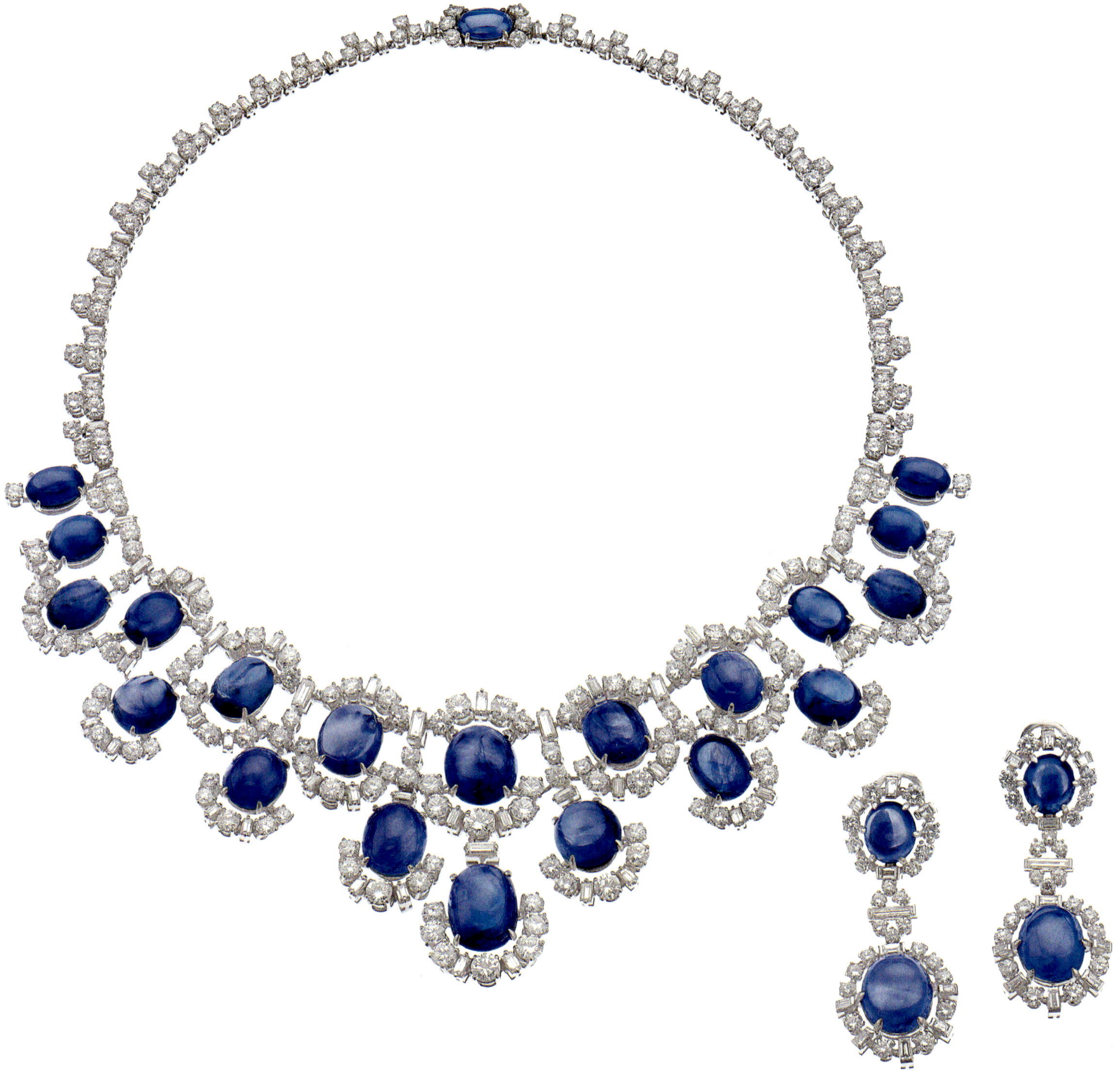

2. Necklace and pendant earrings, 1955
Platinum with sapphires and diamonds

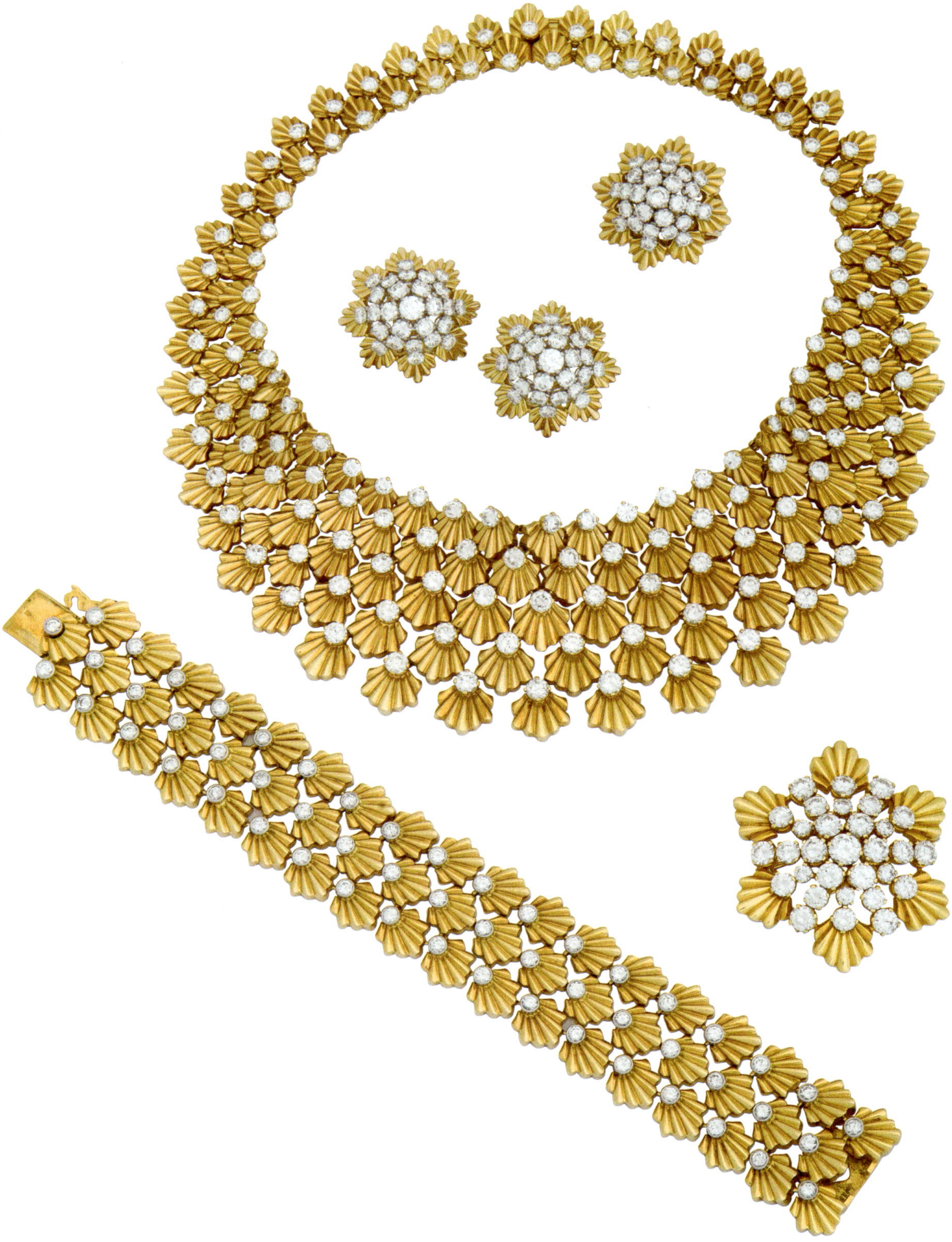

3. Parure, 1954–1958
Gold and platinum with diamonds

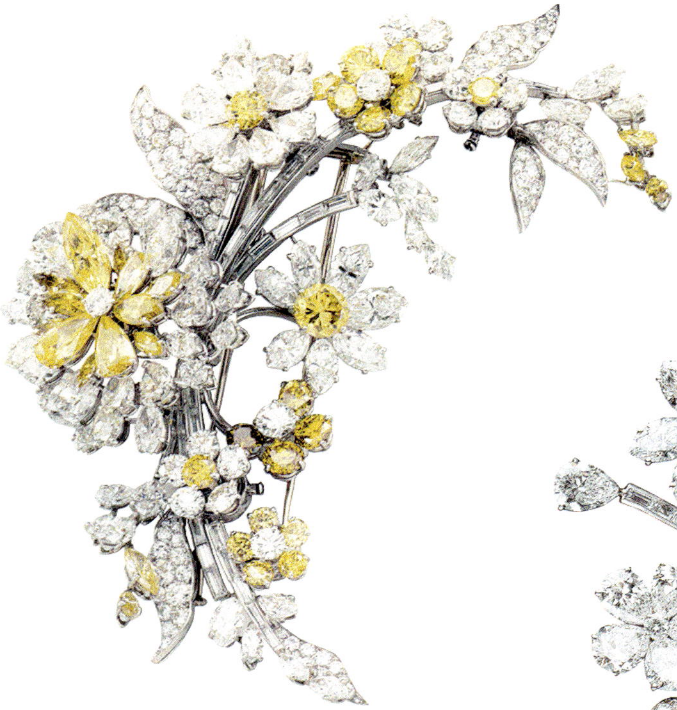

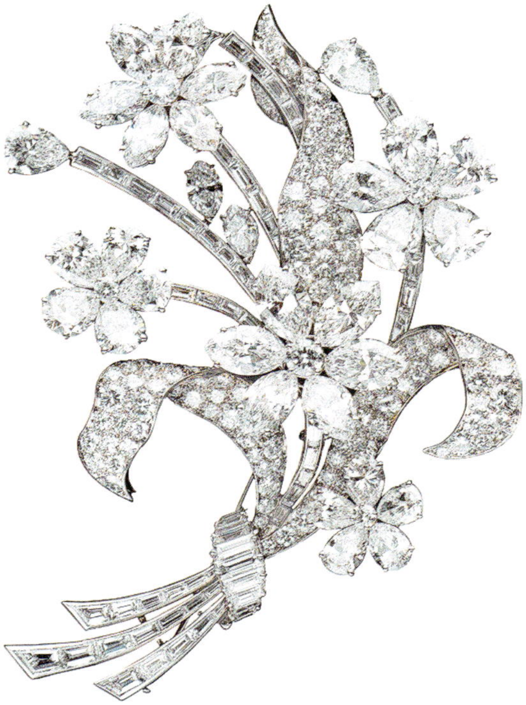

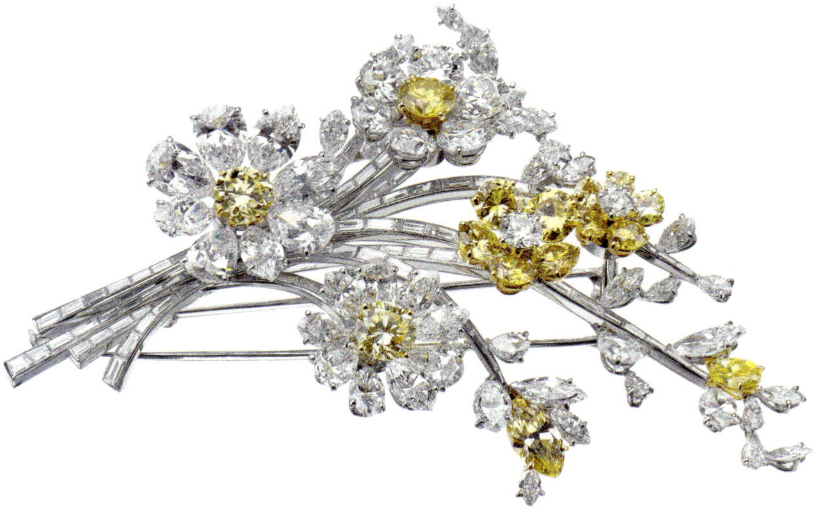

4. *Tremblant* brooch, 1960
Platinum with yellow and white diamonds

5. *Tremblant* brooch, 1962
Platinum with yellow and white diamonds

6. *Tremblant* brooch, 1958
Platinum with diamonds

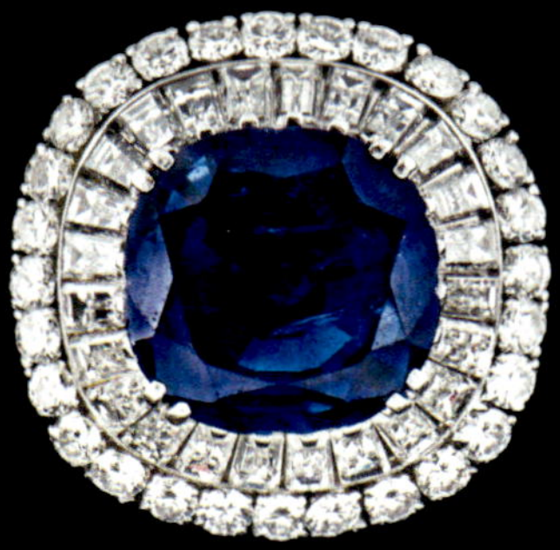

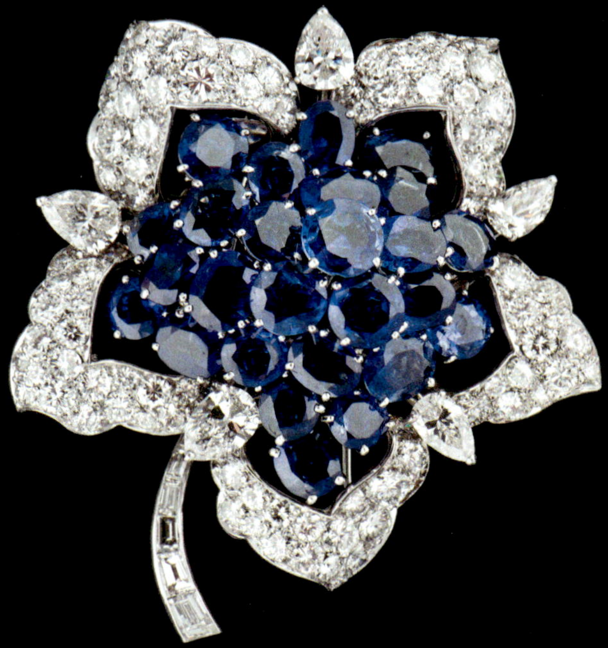

7. Ring, ca. 1960
Platinum with sapphire and diamonds

8. Brooch, 1961
Platinum with sapphires and diamonds

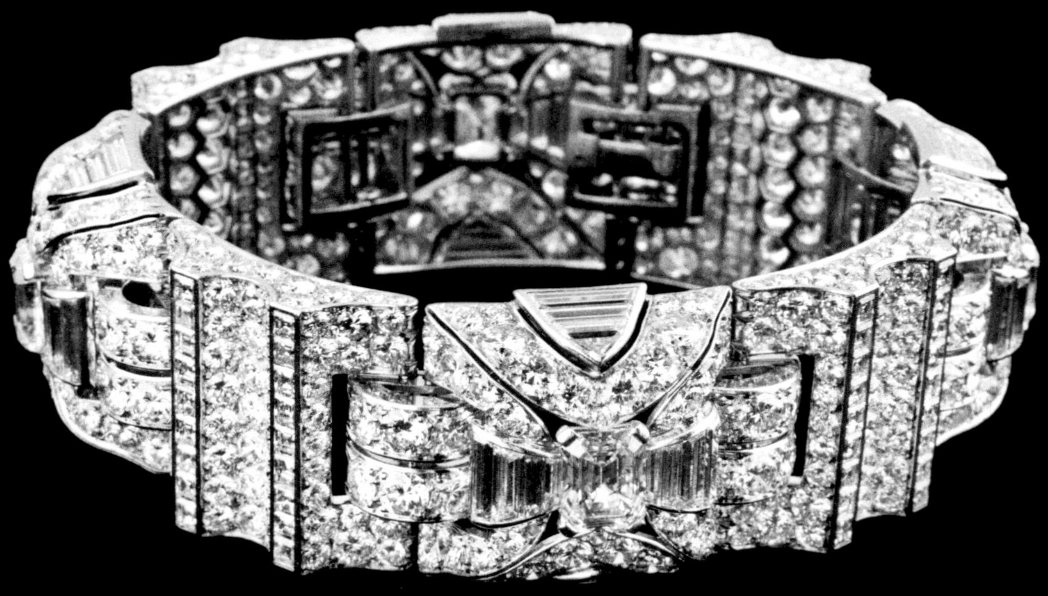

9. Bracelet, ca. 1950
Platinum with diamonds

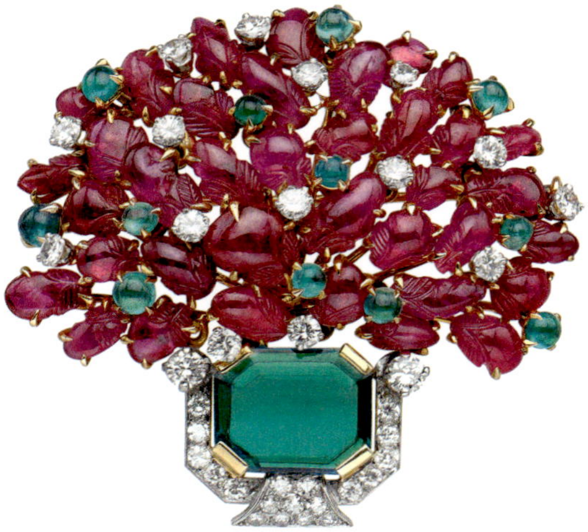

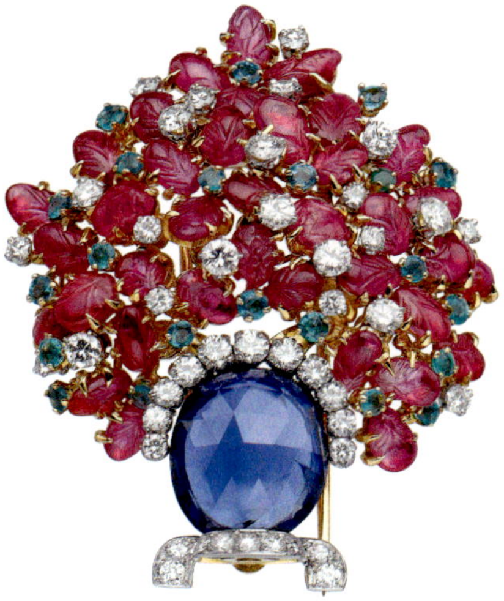

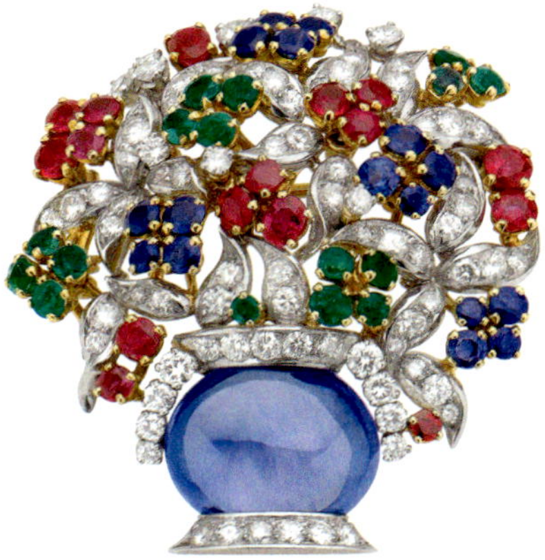

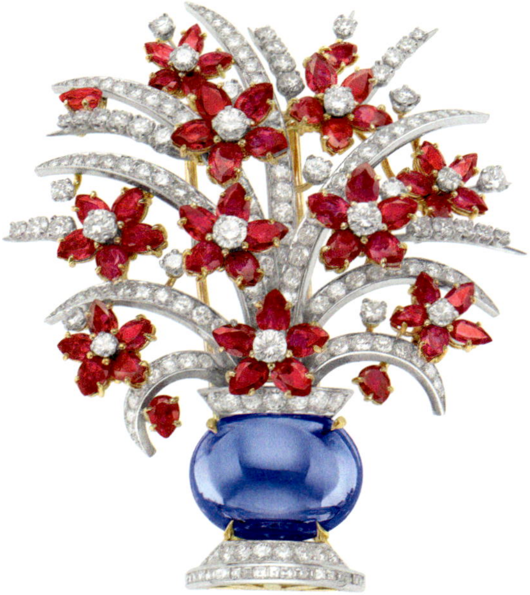

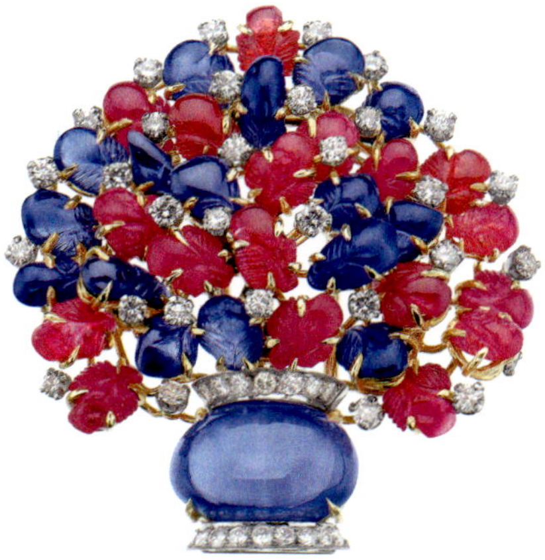

10. *Giardinetto* brooch, ca. 1959
Gold and platinum with emeralds, rubies, and diamonds

11. *Giardinetto* brooch, 1964
Gold and platinum with sapphire, rubies, emeralds, and diamonds

12. *Giardinetto* brooch, 1960
Gold and platinum with sapphires, emeralds, rubies, and diamonds

13. *Giardinetto* brooch, 1966
Gold and platinum with sapphire, rubies, and diamonds

14. *Giardinetto* brooch, 1968
Gold with sapphires, rubies, and diamonds

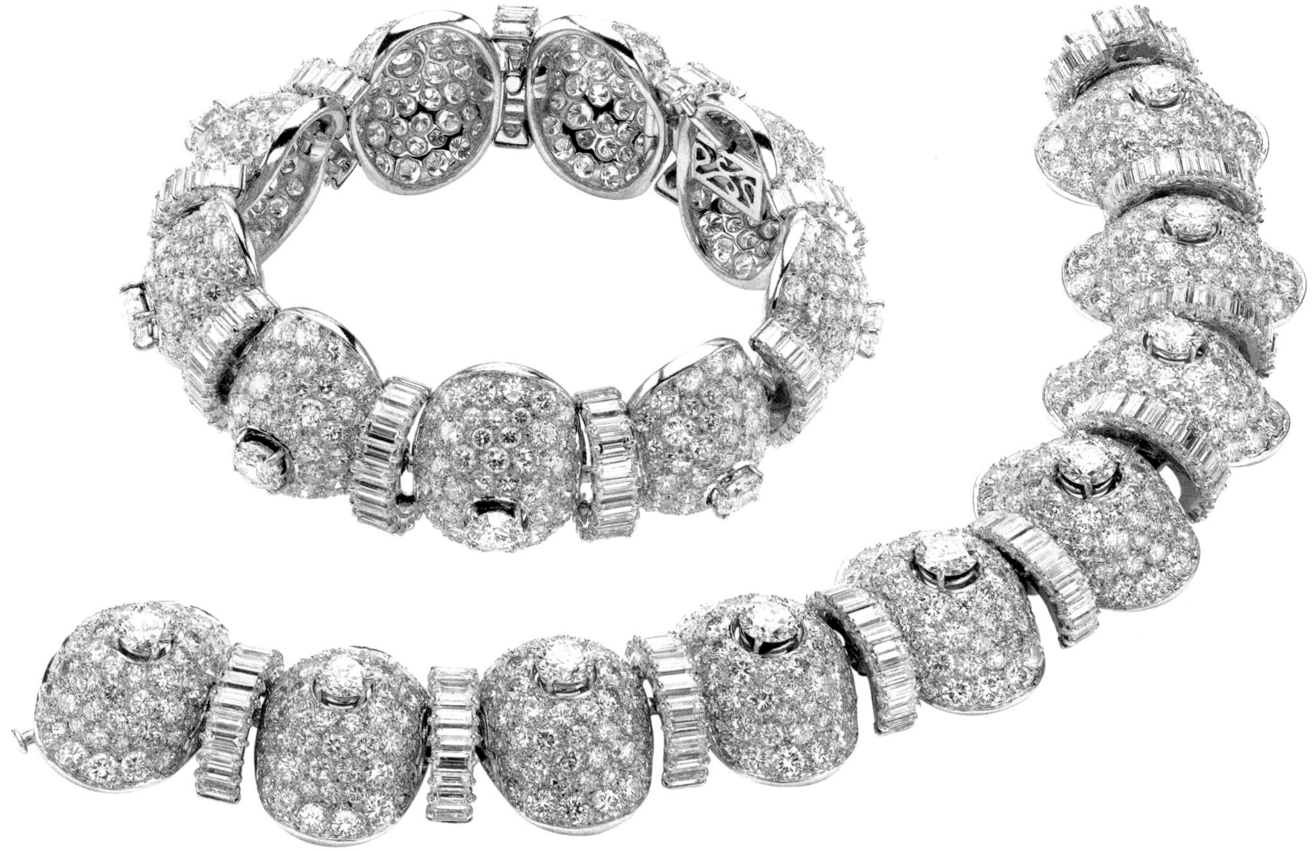

15. Bracelets, 1955 and 1959
Platinum with diamonds

1960s

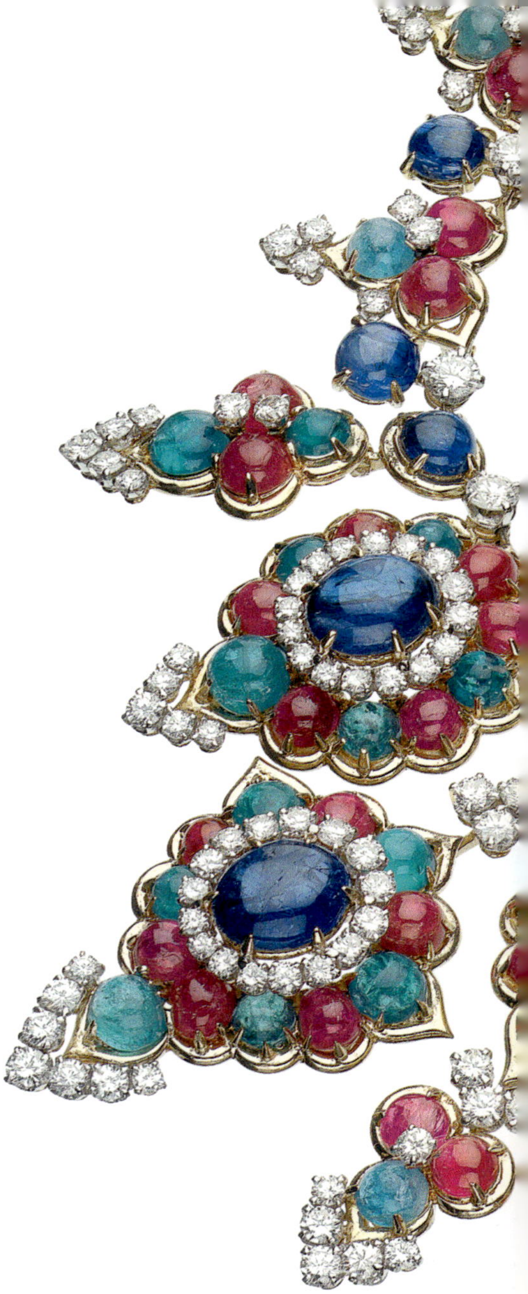

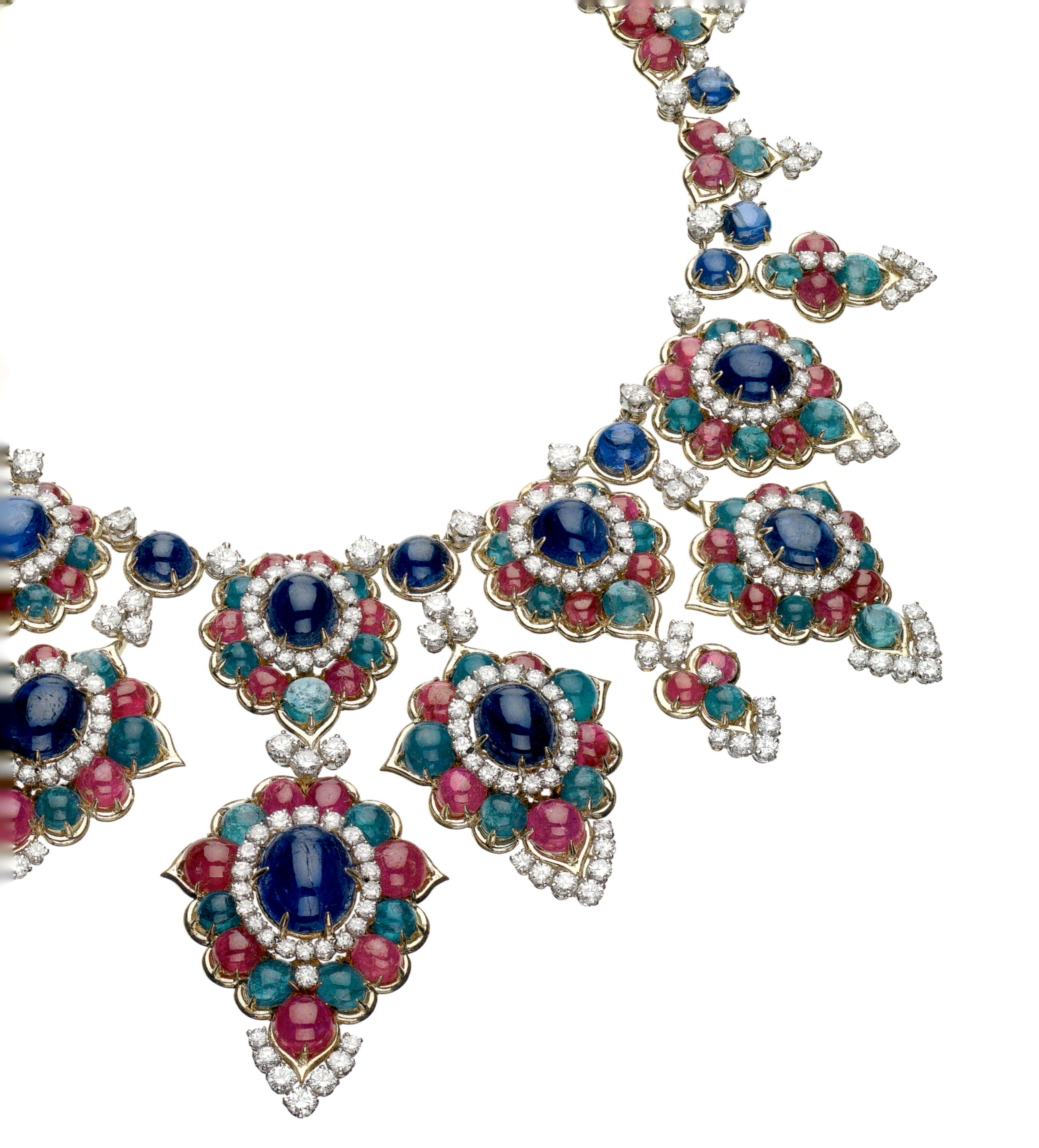

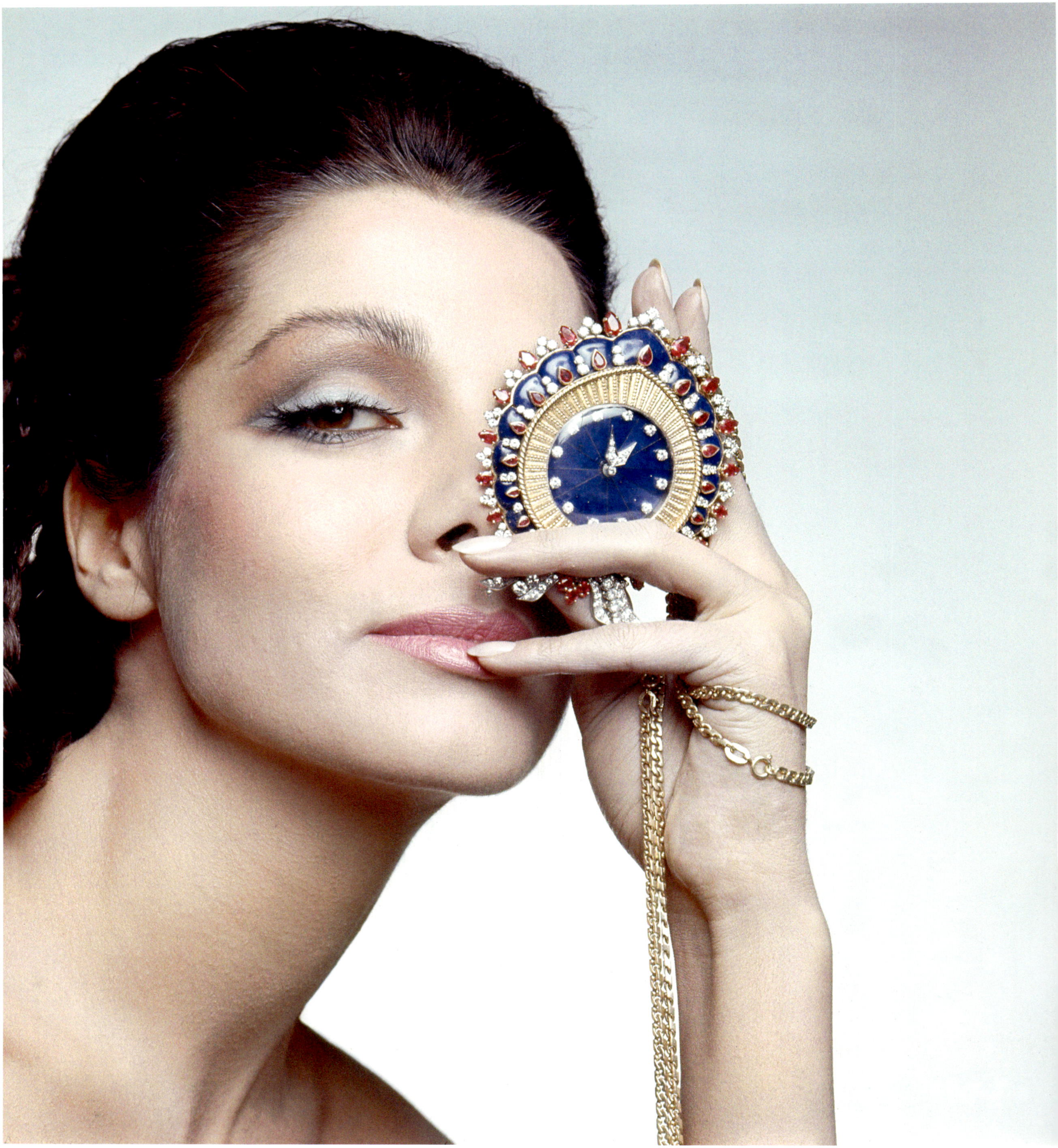

1960s: The Bulgari Style Emerges

As memories of the war faded into the past, a reconstructed Italy began to flourish during the 1950s and was booming by the 1960s. Life had become easier; the American "comfort lifestyle" had made its way to Europe. In Italy a television set could be found in every living room, and families proudly owned cars and summer homes.

As demand grew for new consumer objects, attention to production design with a uniquely Italian sensibility came to the fore, starting in the automobile and household appliance industries. By 1962 an Italian style in jewelry-making would begin to emerge. That year an exhibition sponsored by the Italian government was held at the Istituto Italiano di Cultura in Paris: *Bijoux italiens: Goût et tradition dans la joaillerie italienne* (Italian jewels: Taste and tradition in Italian jewelry). Seventy-five Italian jewelers participated in this first-of-its-kind event that showcased a shrine of fine jewelry to an international audience. Later that year the British magazine *Watchmaker, Jeweller and Silversmith* extolled Italian design with these words: "Italy has built her post-war revival upon design. She has, in the space of a few years, come to be the design center of Europe. Europe drives cars designed by Italians, buys Italian furniture or furniture copied from Italian models, and Europe walks in Italian shoes; Europe is currently also buying Italian jewellery."[1]

As Italy launched its own individual style in jewelry design, Bulgari, which had already come to prominence in the prewar years, became the unquestionable leader of innovation in this development. The process of Italy's emancipation from the legacy of Parisian jewelry design had been gradual (see Triossi, "1950s: From Diamonds to Color," this volume); it began in the second half of the 1950s but arrived at its maturity in the following decade. The 1960s saw Bulgari definitively distancing itself from Parisian edicts and abandoning the asymmetrical floral motif first popularized by the French, favoring instead more structured, symmetrical, and compact shapes.

Another characteristic of the emerging Bulgari style was its use of bold color. By breaking away from the traditional chromatic triad of emeralds, rubies, and sapphires typically combined exclusively with diamonds, Bulgari began to explore new and fresh combinations. Juxtapositions at first predictable (red and blue) turned increasingly robust and surprising (purple, turquoise, and green; see cat. 35) as gemstones began to be used not purely for their intrinsic value but for their chromatic effect as well.

The combination of red rubies and blue sapphires (usually enhanced by a few diamonds) could already be seen in the jewelry of the 1940s. It was in the 1960s, however, that these innovations began to fully take root, with the color revolution reinforced by the use of stones fashioned as cabochons rather than as faceted gems, and of more subdued sapphires of lighter sky-blue hues.

Fig. 33. Model Ivana Bastianello with Bulgari alarm clock of gold, platinum, lapis lazuli, rubies, and diamonds (cat. 27), *Vogue*, 1968

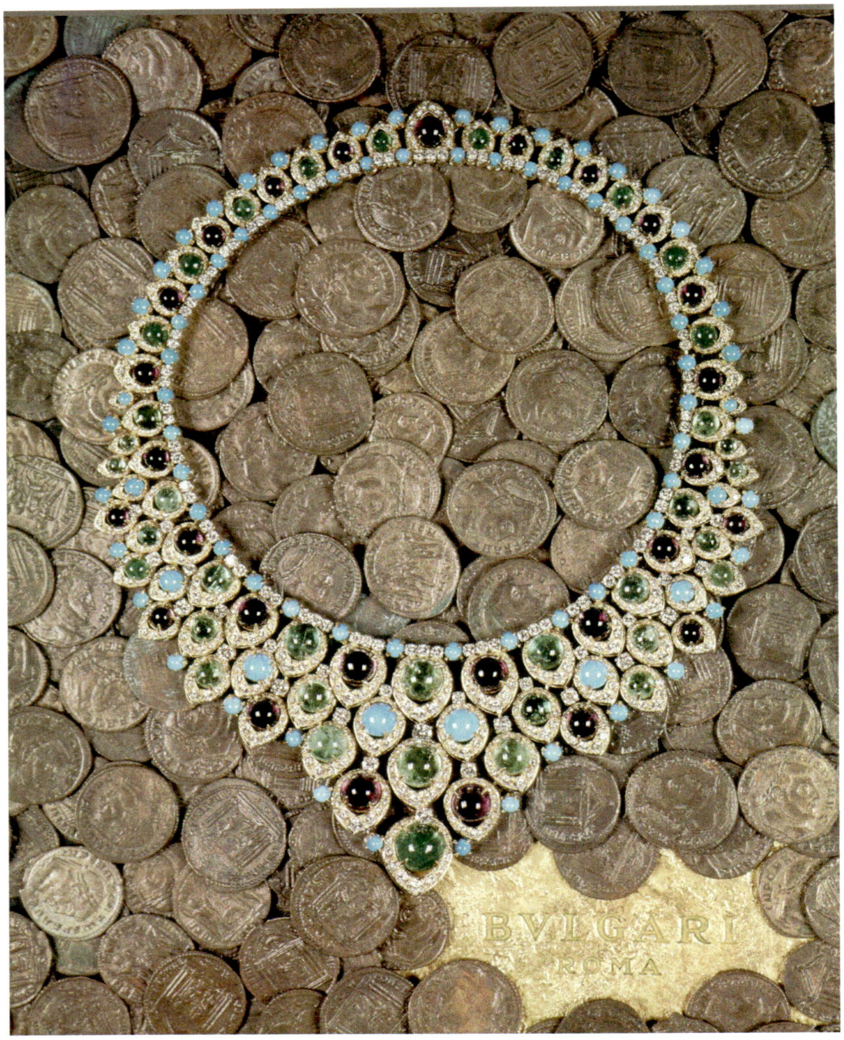

Fig. 34. Bulgari advertisement featuring the 1965 bib necklace of yellow gold, emeralds, amethysts, turquoise, and diamonds later owned by Lyn Revson (cat. 35)

It is interesting to note that blue sapphires come in various gradations and intensities of color, factors that contribute to identifying their origins: velvety blue or cornflower-colored sapphires come from Kashmir; intensely blue ones with touches of violet are from Burma; and pale, watery blue gems derive from Sri Lanka (formerly Ceylon, thus the "Ceylon sapphire"). Although it is not the color that certifies a stone's origins, but rather its inclusions (the materials that are trapped inside a mineral during its formation), the hue is often indicative.[2]

The pale, sky-blue sapphires from Sri Lanka were used so extensively by Bulgari in the second half of the 1950s that the cabochon Ceylon sapphire became something of a signature for the jeweler. One fine example is a splendid parure, or set, of matching jewelry pieces, dating to 1955–1956, which is adorned with thirty-two cabochon sapphires alternating with small cabochon rubies and brilliant-cut diamonds (cat. 1). This work was soon followed by an abundance of brooches, earrings, and bracelets

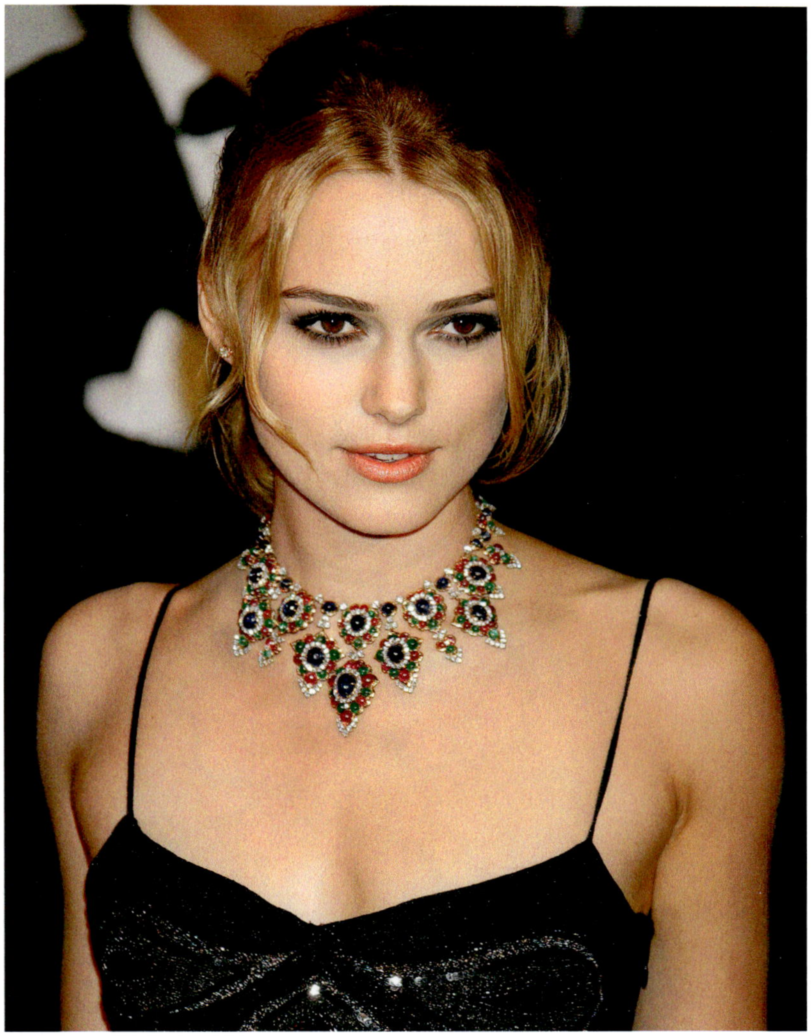

Fig. 35. Keira Knightley, in a 1967 Bulgari necklace of gold, emeralds, rubies, sapphires, and diamonds (cat. 28), worn for the 2006 Academy Awards

that were designed as stylized flowers with compact outlines, set in similar combinations (see cats. 16, 17).

As time passed, the variety of color combinations increased. Some works mixed sapphires of multiple colors, whereas others juxtaposed different gems such as rubies, sapphires, and emeralds. The arrangements became more daring over time, from green juxtaposed with blue, to red matched with green and blue, and then violet, turquoise, and green together. The magnificent necklace and earrings of 1965 owned by Lyn Revson, wife of the founder of Revlon (cat. 35; see also fig. 34), and the spectacular necklace of 1967 set with large sapphires, rubies, and emeralds (cat. 28; see also page 7), worn years later by Keira Knightley at the 2006 Academy Awards (see fig. 35), could not better illustrate the new Bulgari taste for color and cabochon gems during the 1960s.

The nascent Bulgari style of this period also displayed an increasing predilection for compact, rounded shapes that conveyed a sense of volume and three-dimensionality, nearly always mounted in yellow gold. A typical Bulgari shape in these years was the shield (sometimes called "chestnut") form. A great many jewels were created in this design, in numerous color combinations that ranged from turquoise with sapphires or rubies (see cat. 24) to sapphires with emeralds; but even when entirely set with diamonds, as illustrated by the platinum and diamond brooch of 1967 (cat. 25), the shape still pointed to Bulgari's new design directions. The popularity of the shield form is also reflected in a series of luxury clocks bearing this shape. Among the most striking of these timepieces is an alarm clock in gold and platinum decorated with fine, deep-blue lapis lazuli, rubies, and diamonds (cat. 27; see also fig. 33).

Even when gemstone combinations continued to follow the more conventional traditions of Paris, Bulgari's jewels relied on tighter arrangements, thus achieving smooth contours and bolder, more compact designs. This style is exemplified in the magnificent emerald and diamond necklace nicknamed the "Seven Wonders" (cat. 18; see also fig. 36). Instead of using the marquise-cut, pear-shaped, and brilliant-cut diamonds commonly found in Parisian jewels, Bulgari chose round, brilliant-cut trefoil motifs to trim this piece. On other occasions, continuing a preference for rounded contours, the makers employed marquise-shaped diamonds all aligned in the same direction—an arrangement so frequently used thereafter that it now unequivocally denotes Bulgari.

Another design that came to be synonymous with Bulgari at this time is the snake bracelet-watch. Since ancient times the serpent motif has symbolized wisdom, life, and eternity, and has been used in jewelry both ornamentally and apotropaically (to ward off evil). Representations of the serpent disappeared during the Middle Ages, as it was considered a symbol of evil, but reappeared in the mid-nineteenth century, especially in jewelry design, where it was perfectly suited for bracelets and necklaces that were created in flexible gold chain, often paved with turquoise. Bulgari was undoubtedly one of the twentieth-century jewelers responsible for successfully reintroducing the serpent motif, as well as, for the first time, turning it into a watch.

The initial examples of Bulgari's snake-shaped bracelet-watches date to the late 1940s, with coils made of gold mesh or using the *tubogas* technique. Literally translated as "gas pipe," *tubogas* describes a type of chain made from interlocking gold strips wrapped tightly together to form a flexible and hollow tube. Spiraling multiple times around the wrist, with a rectangular or square watchcase placed at one end to suggest a serpent's head (or sometimes positioned in the center of the band), these particular watches were later produced in many versions that exploited every possible shape of case and dial: round, square, octagonal, pear-, and cushion-shaped, with or without diamond-set bezels. Such watches were created initially either solely in, or in combinations of, yellow, white, and rose gold; and, from the 1970s onward, versions were introduced in steel, blackened steel, or a combination of gold and steel. The leading watchmakers—Audemars Piguet, Jaeger-LeCoultre, Movado, and Vacheron Constantin—customized their movements for Bulgari, with the logo of the respective movements' maker appearing alongside that of Bulgari's on the dial.

The first models to display a more literal interpretation of the serpent appeared in the 1960s (cats. 19–23; see also fig. 37), and represented a more explicit reconnection with the ancient Roman tradition of gold bracelets featuring realistically rendered snakes. The "scales" of these serpents were

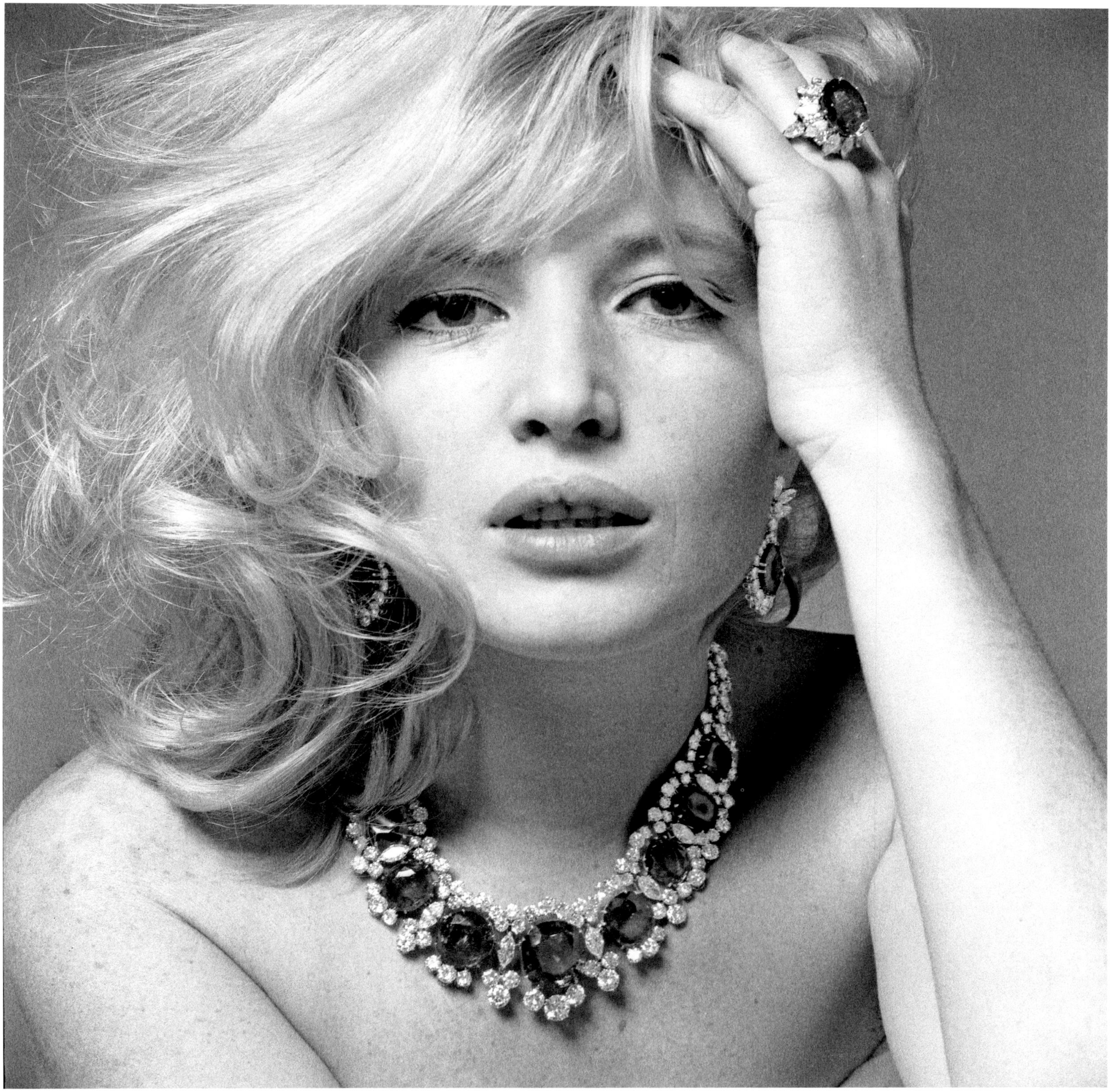

Fig. 36. Monica Vitti, wearing the Bulgari "Seven Wonders" necklace of platinum, emeralds, and diamonds (cat. 18), 1965

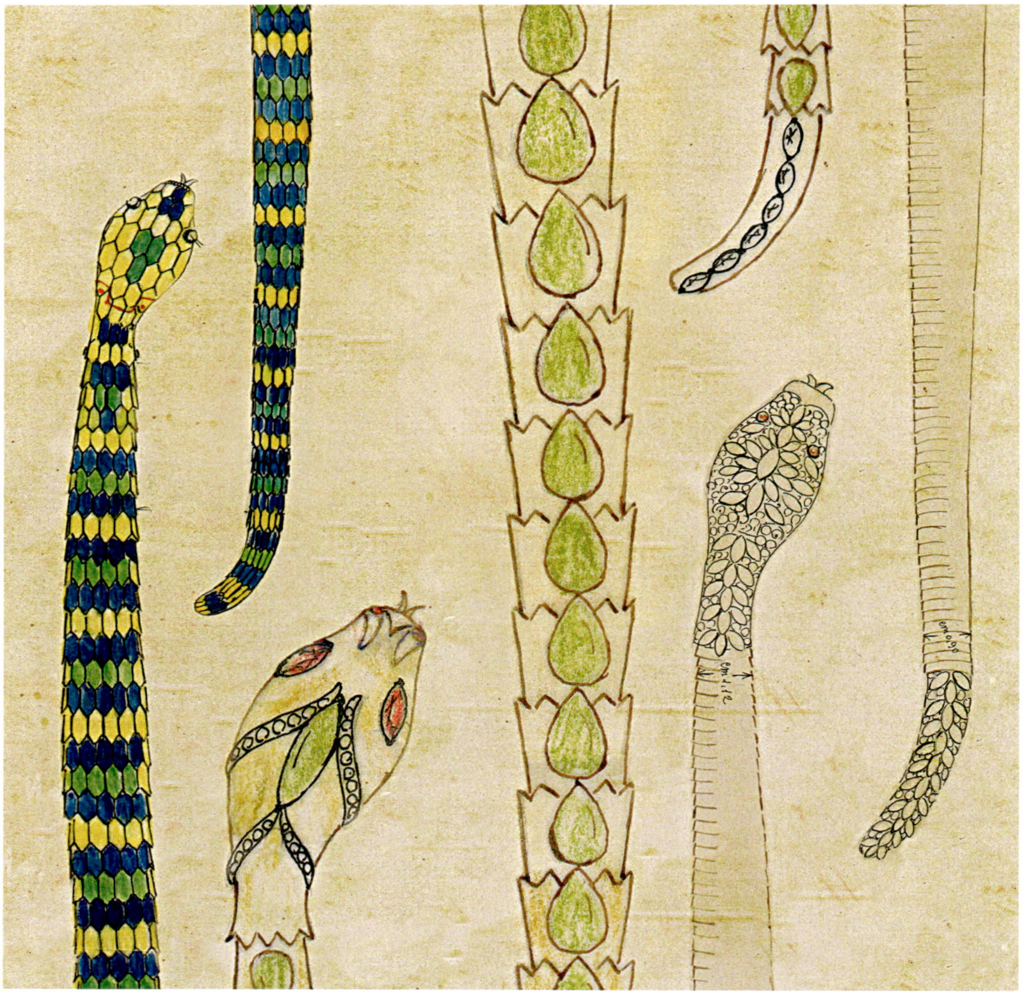

Fig. 37. Original design sketch for serpent bracelet-watches, ca. 1960

handmade out of sheet gold and attached to one another by soldered gold pivots or, in the case of the enameled versions, screwed together. A white-gold spring coiled inside the snake's body is the secret behind the watch's extraordinary flexibility and its serpentlike motion. Concealed in the reptile's head is the watchcase, while the dial can be found under a hinged cover on the upper and central part of the skull. The earliest models of the sixties were created exclusively in yellow gold, with diamond-encrusted heads and tails. Elizabeth Taylor's watch, which was immortalized on the actress's wrist in a photograph taken on the *Cleopatra* set in 1962, is a magnificent example (see fig. 44). The serpent's head is decorated with pavé-set diamonds, its eyes are made of emeralds, and it is embellished with a crest of marquise-shaped diamonds (see cat. 23 for a similar model).

The following years saw the production of many other such pieces as well as similar bracelets without the watch itself. While the serpent's body was always in gold, the small scales of the early models were later transformed into larger ones and ornamented with polygonal diamond patterns or multicolored enamel in extremely varied and flamboyant combinations that included turquoise and white;

red and yellow; and green, red, black, and pale blue. In addition to this variety of enamels, some rare and beautiful examples were made with variegated shades of coral (see cat. 22). Other stones were also employed to simulate the serpents' eyes: yellow or white diamonds, rubies, sapphires, and pear-shaped, marquise-shaped, or circular emeralds. The bracelet itself could vary in length, the most striking examples being those that spiraled several times around the wrist and up the arm.

Certainly one of the most unusual Bulgari creations is a gold serpent belt with pink, cream, and white enamel scales and with sapphire eyes. The belt belonged to (and was probably commissioned by) the then-queen of fashion, Diana Vreeland, who was famous for her large and eccentric accessories. The serpent motif held a particular fascination for Vreeland. In 1968 she recorded: "The serpent should be on every finger and on all wrists and everywhere."[3] By what can be judged from various portrait photographs, it appears that Vreeland preferred to wrap the serpent around her neck rather than her waist (see fig. 12).

The 1960s represent the decade when Bulgari's style began to emerge and develop independently from Parisian design. The jeweler created innovative and characteristic designs using colored gems arranged in daring combinations, with new shapes, and set in yellow gold. This is also the decade when Bulgari introduced the serpent bracelet-watches rendered as "real" snakes—a motif that would be successfully revisited time and again by the company well into the twenty-first century.

1. Quoted in Lia Lenti, *Gioielli e gioiellieri di Valenza: Arte e storia orafa 1825–1975* (Torino: Umberto Allemandi, 1994), 191.

2. Sapphires also come in a variety of other colors, including lilac, pink, orange, and green, although many sapphires are actually colorless. The stones are formed from the mineral corundum, which is colorless when pure but takes on various hues from impurities present during a stone's composition. The presence of titanium and iron produces the well-known blue. Rubies are sapphires given a red color through the presence of chromium.

3. Quoted in "Vreeland Memos," *Visionaire* no. 37 (2002).

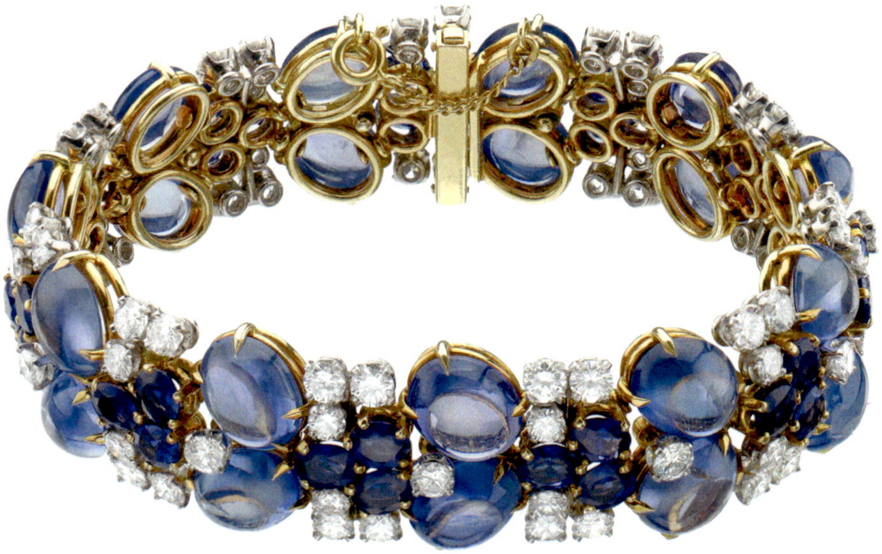

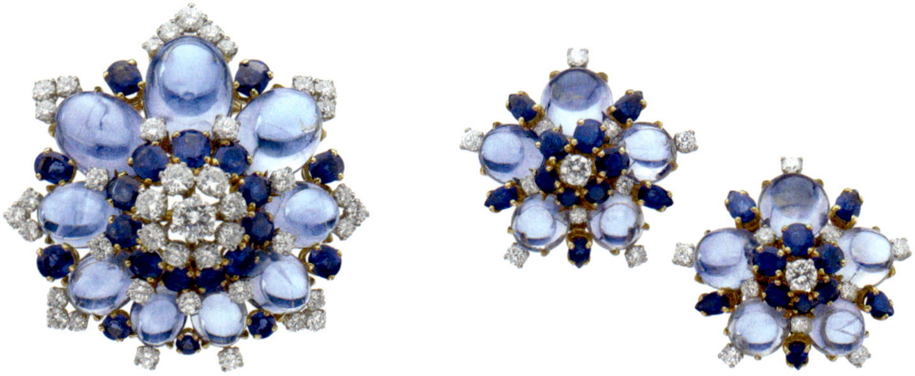

16. Bracelet, 1960
Gold with sapphires and diamonds

17. Brooch and earrings, 1960
Gold with sapphires and diamonds

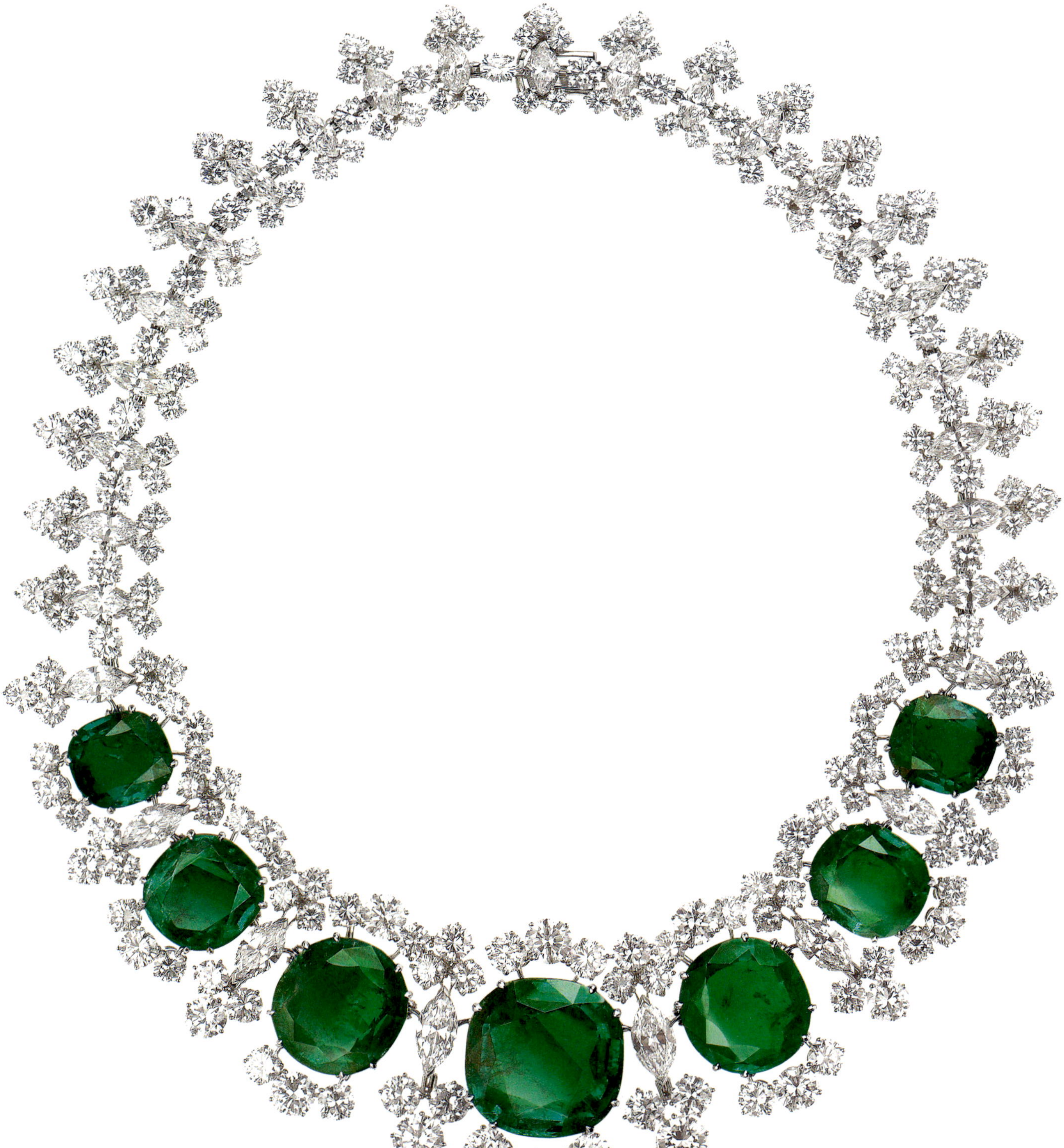

18. Necklace, 1961
Platinum with emeralds and diamonds

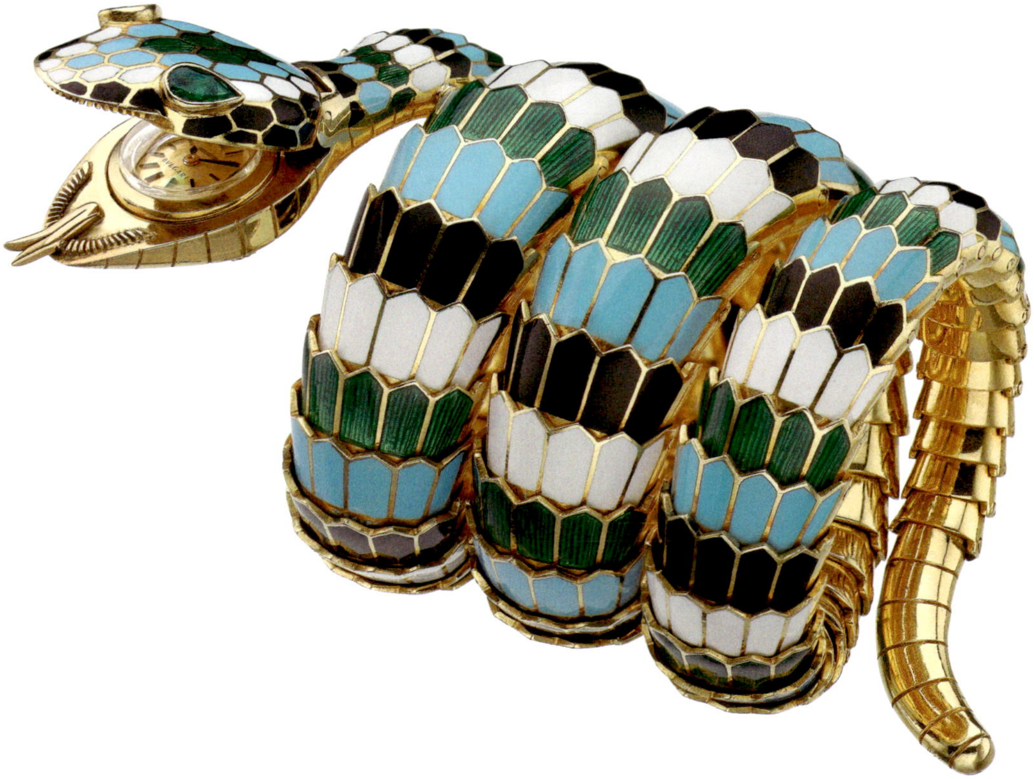

19. Snake bracelet-watch, 1967
Gold with polychrome enamel and emeralds

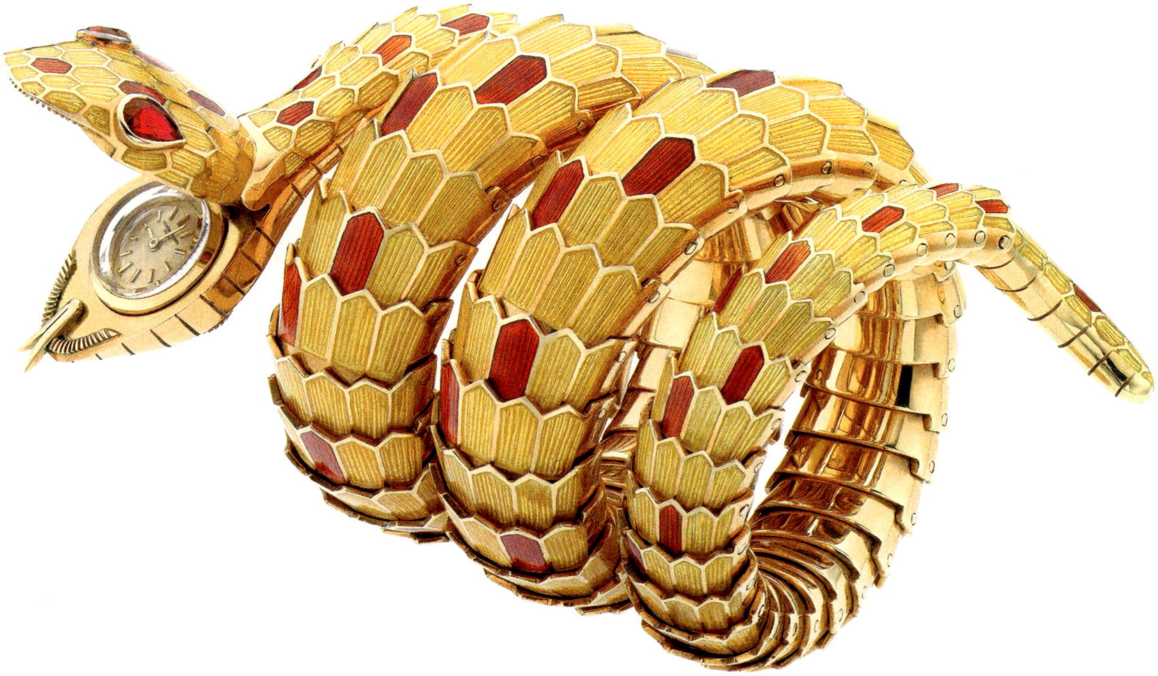

20. Snake bracelet-watch, ca. 1967
Gold with yellow and red enamel and rubies

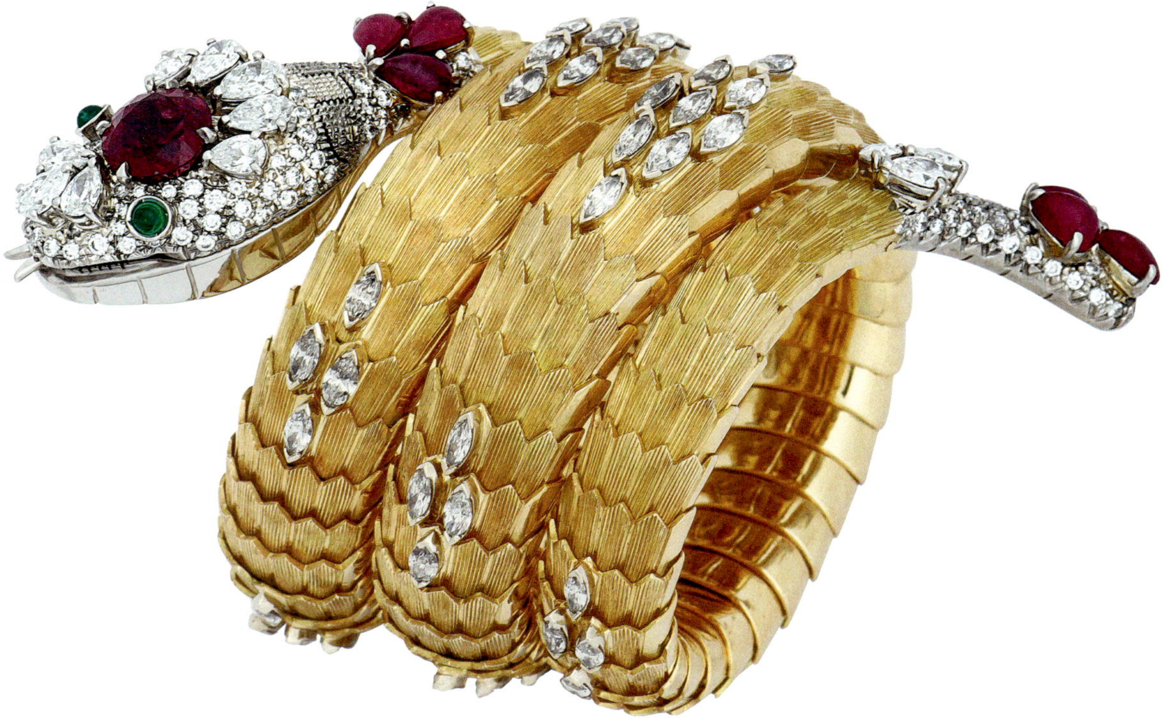

21. Snake bracelet-watch, ca. 1962
Gold with rubies, emeralds, and diamonds

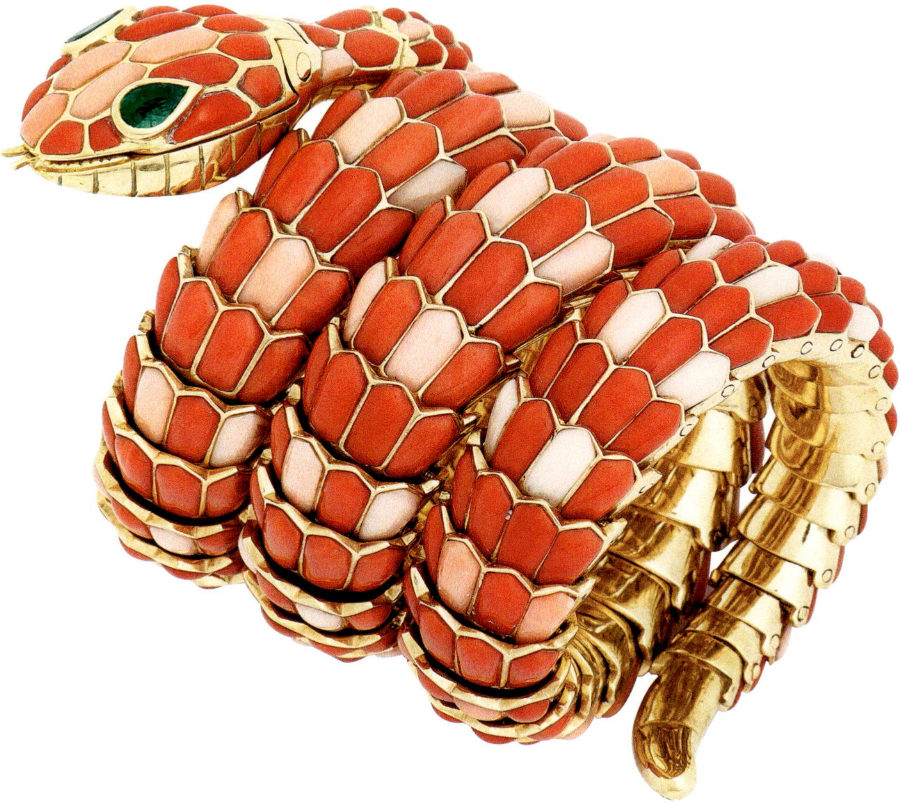

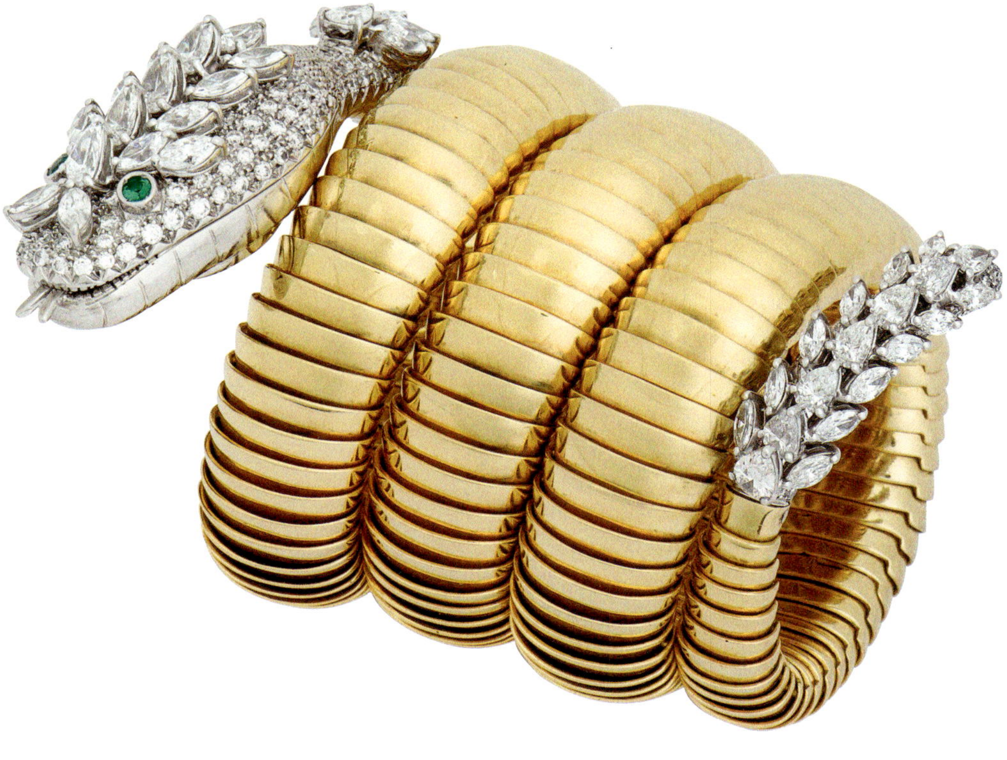

22. Snake bracelet-watch, ca. 1965
Gold with coral, emeralds, and diamonds

23. Snake bracelet-watch, ca. 1962
Gold and platinum with emeralds and diamonds

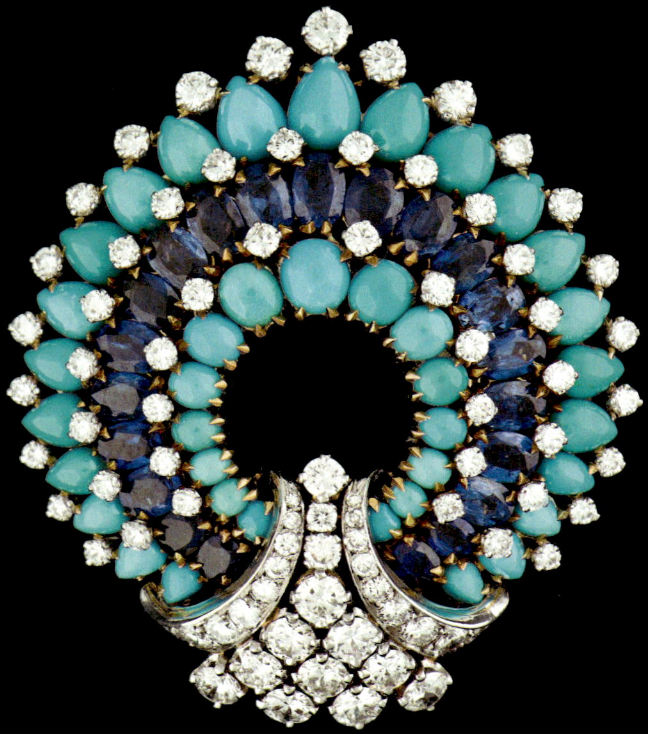

24. Brooch, 1959
Platinum with turquoise, sapphires, and diamonds

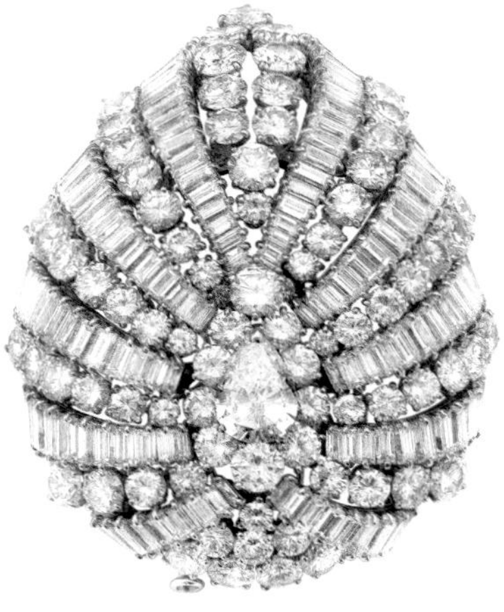

25. Shield brooch, 1967
Platinum with diamonds

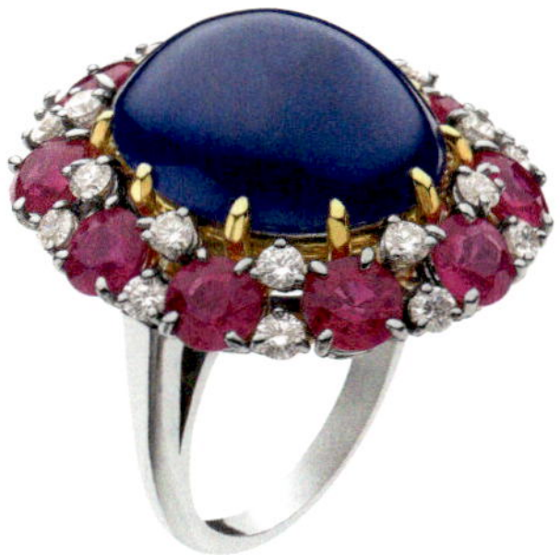

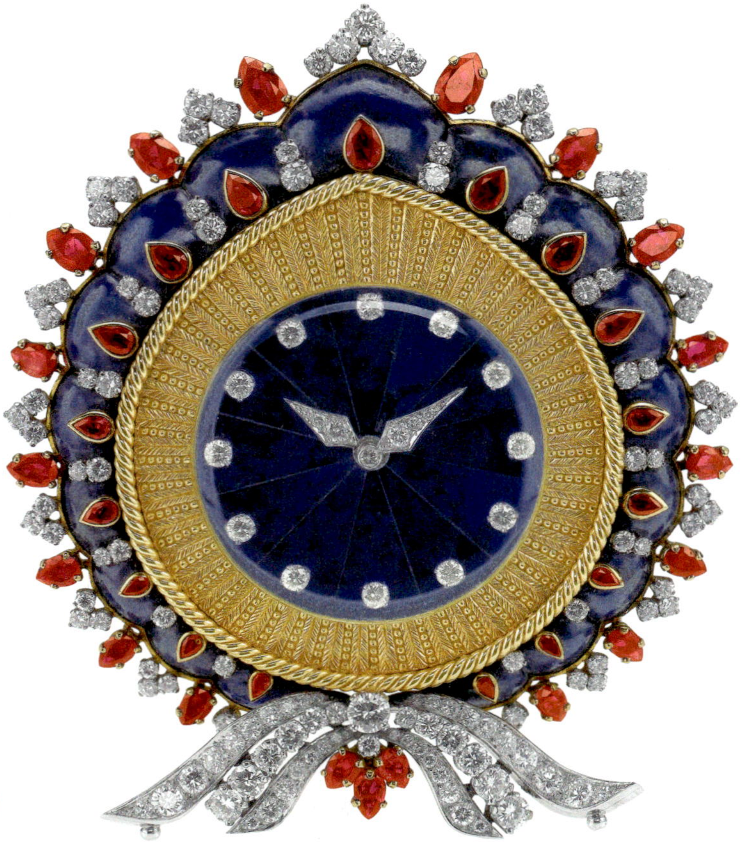

26. Ring, ca. 1960
Platinum and gold with sapphire, rubies, and diamonds

27. Table clock, 1968
Gold and platinum with lapis lazuli, rubies, and diamonds

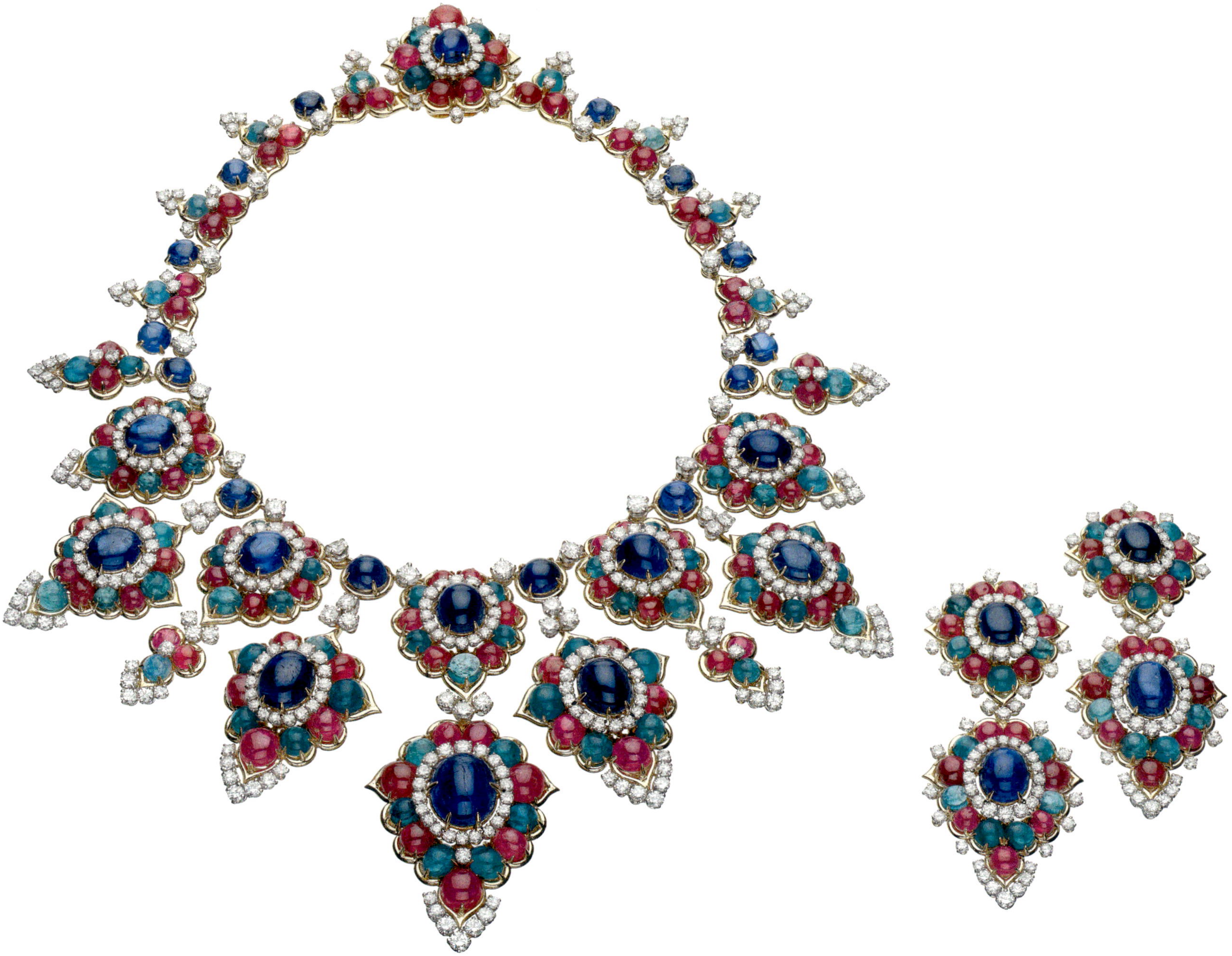

28. Necklace and pendant earrings, 1967
Gold with sapphires, emeralds, rubies, and diamonds

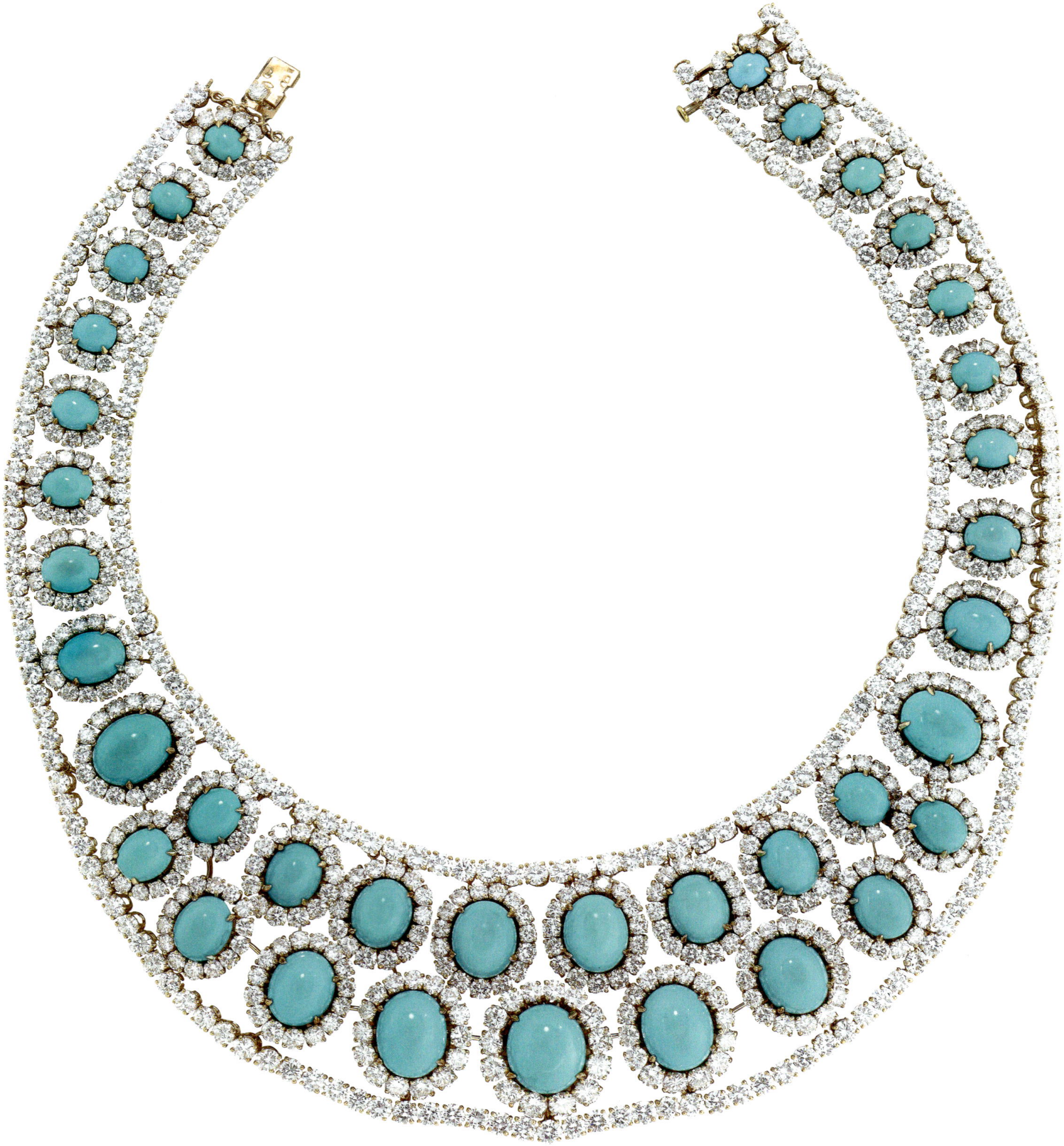

29. Necklace, 1972
Platinum with turquoise and diamonds

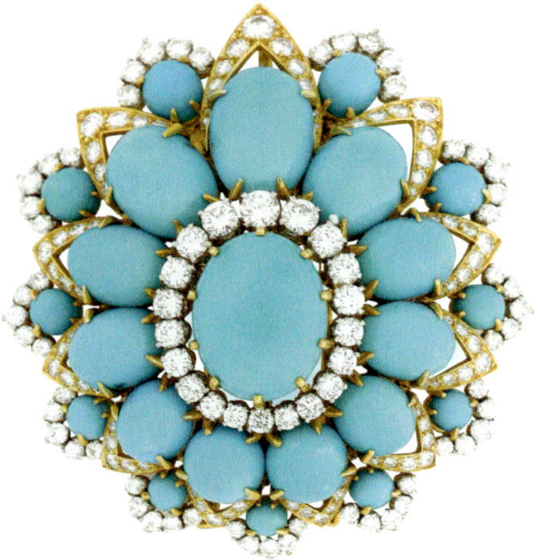

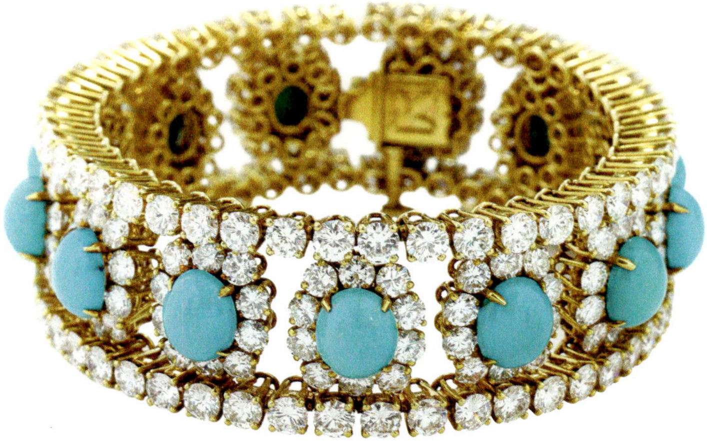

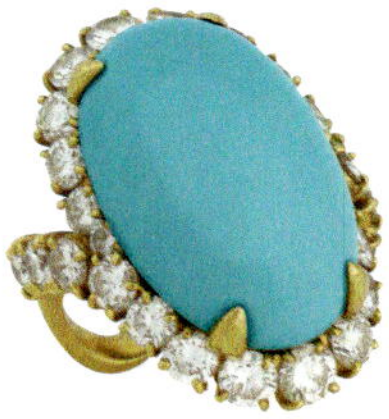

30. Bracelet, 1972
Platinum with turquoise and diamonds

31. Brooch, ca. 1969
Platinum with turquoise and diamonds

32. Ring, ca. 1969
Platinum with turquoise and diamonds

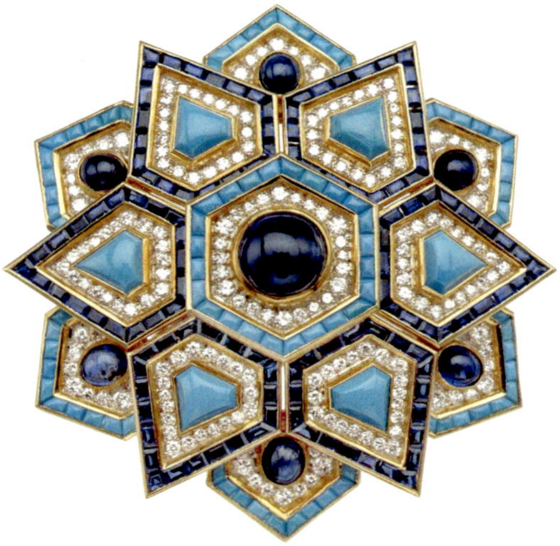

33. Brooch, 1969
Gold and platinum with turquoise, sapphires, and diamonds

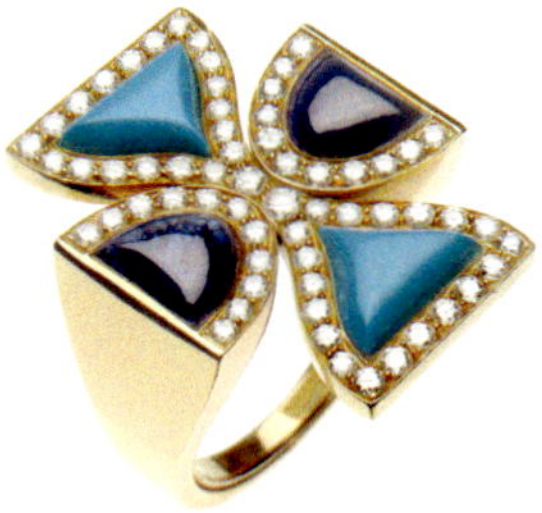

34. Ring, ca. 1975
Gold with sapphires, turquoise, and diamonds

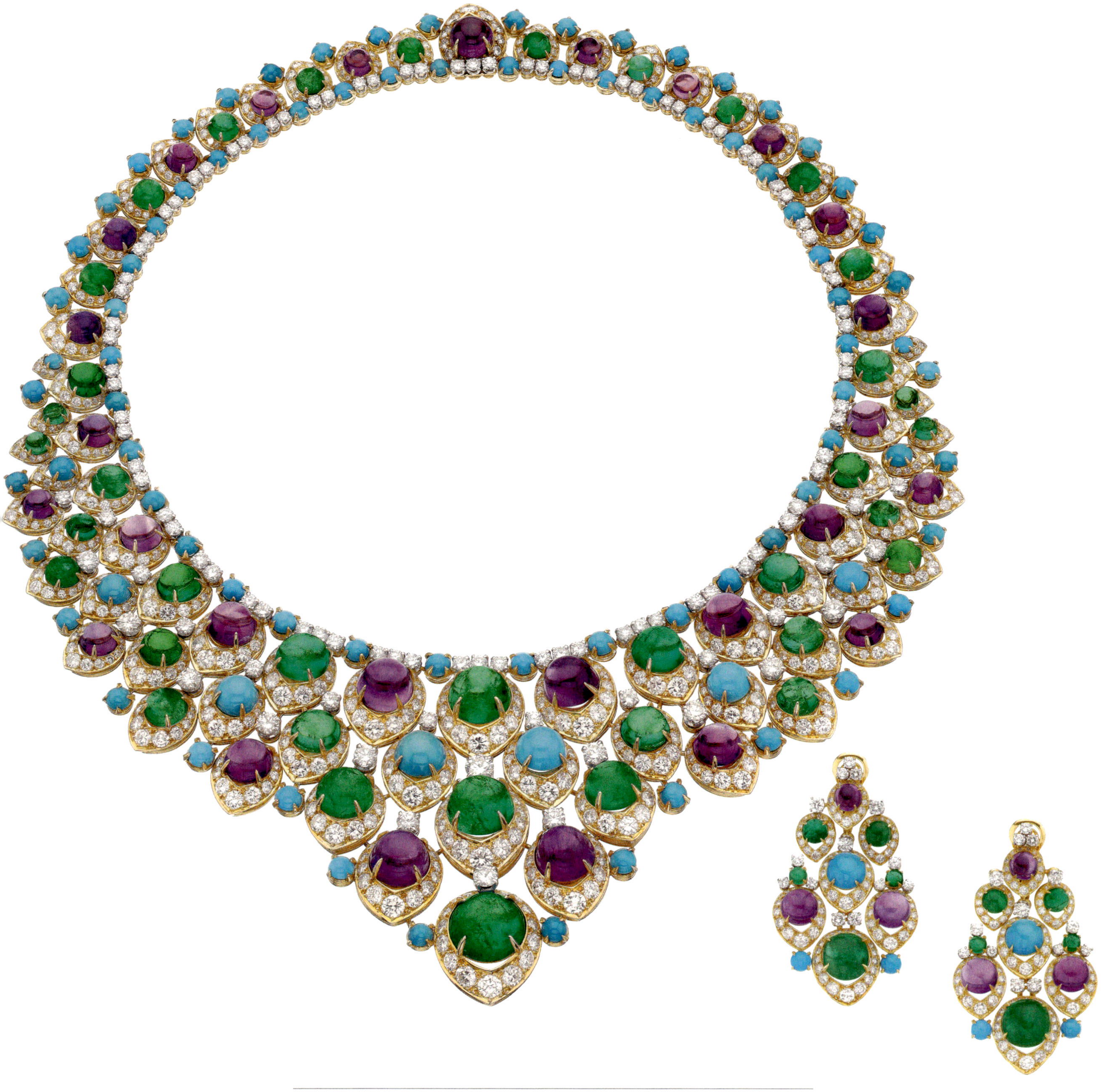

35. Bib necklace and pendant earrings, 1965
Gold with emeralds, amethysts, turquoise, and diamonds

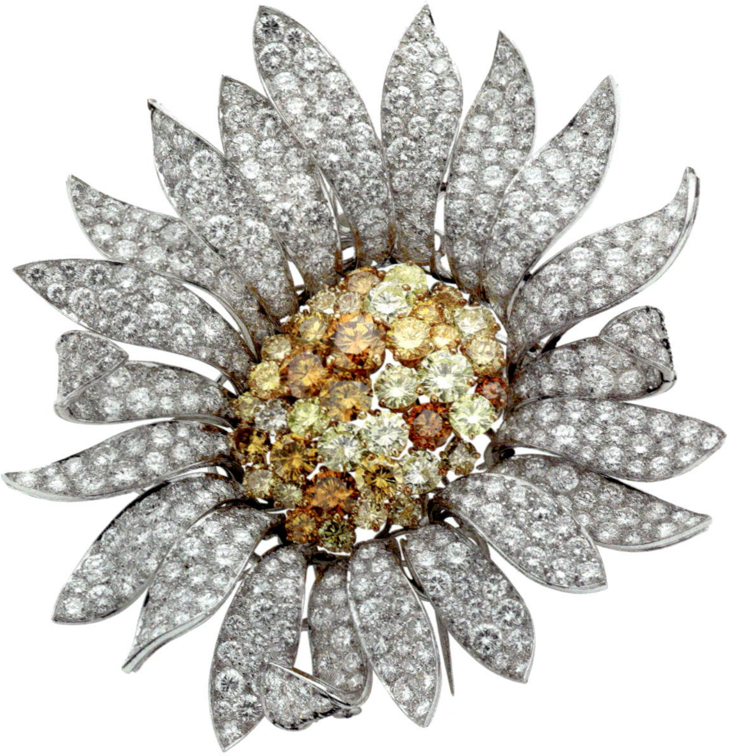

36. Flower brooch, 1968

Platinum and gold with yellow and white diamonds

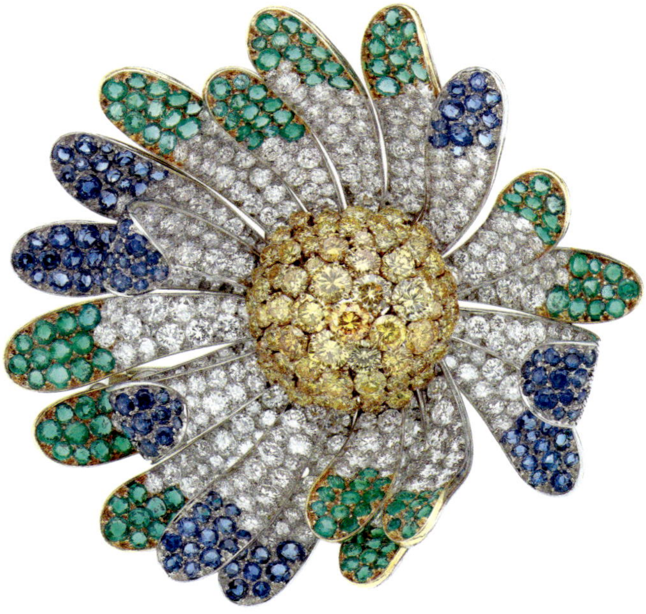

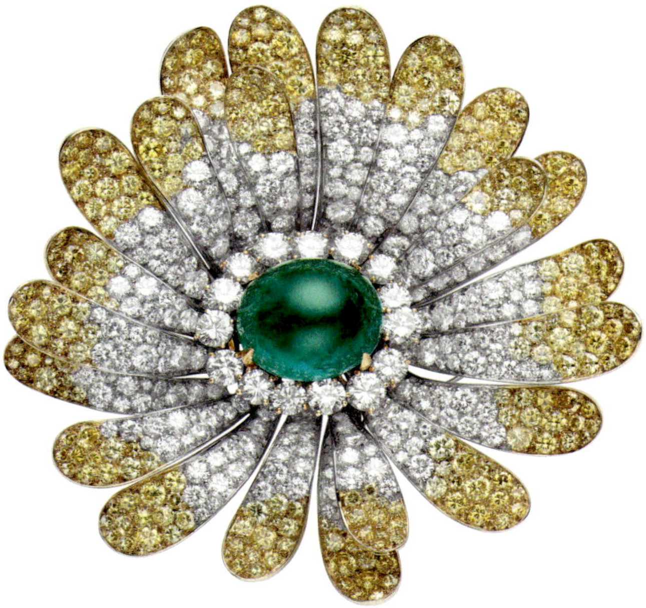

37. Flower brooch, 1969
Platinum with emeralds, sapphires, and yellow and white diamonds

38. Daisy brooch, 1969
Platinum with emerald and yellow and white diamonds

1970s

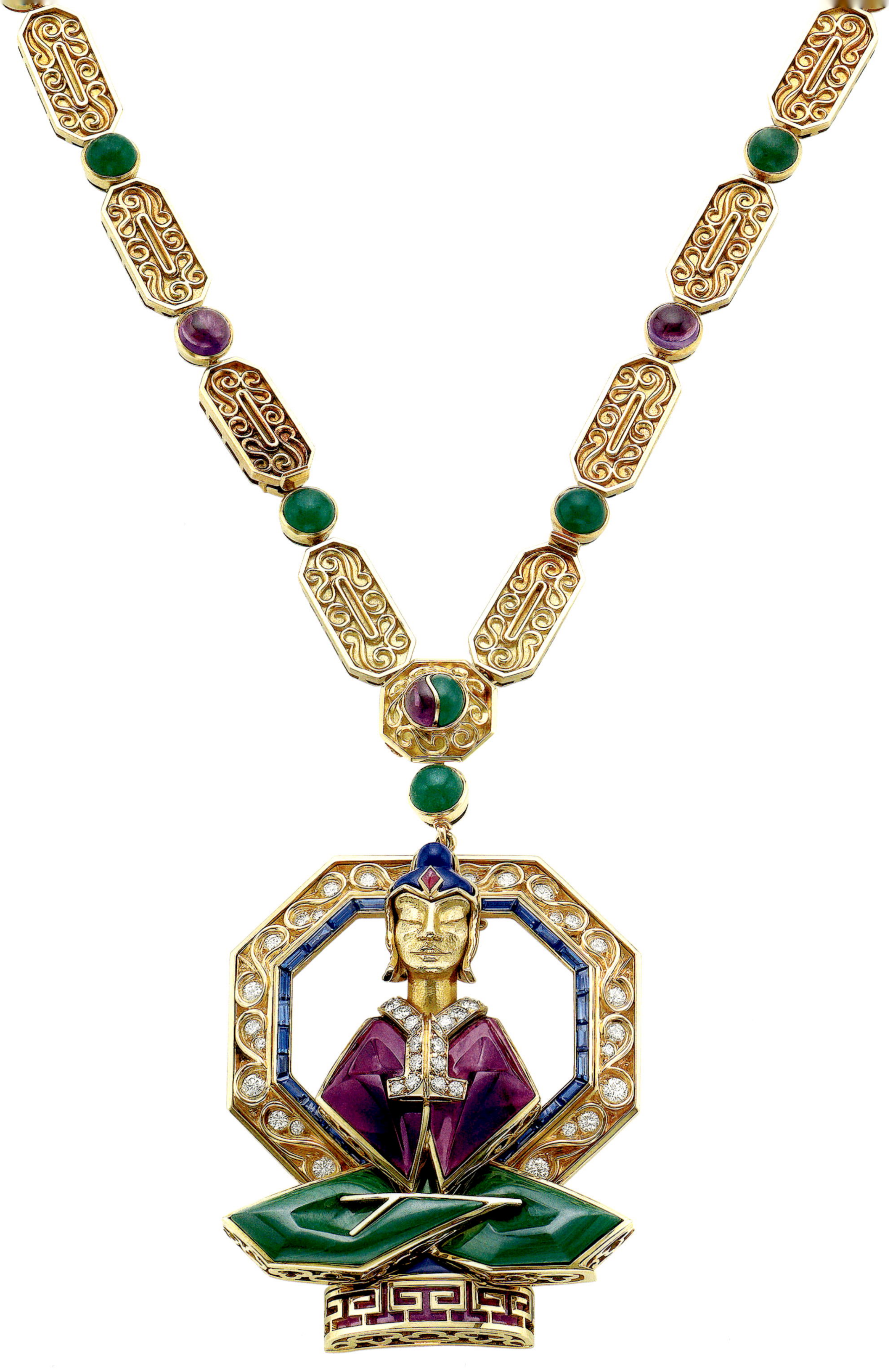

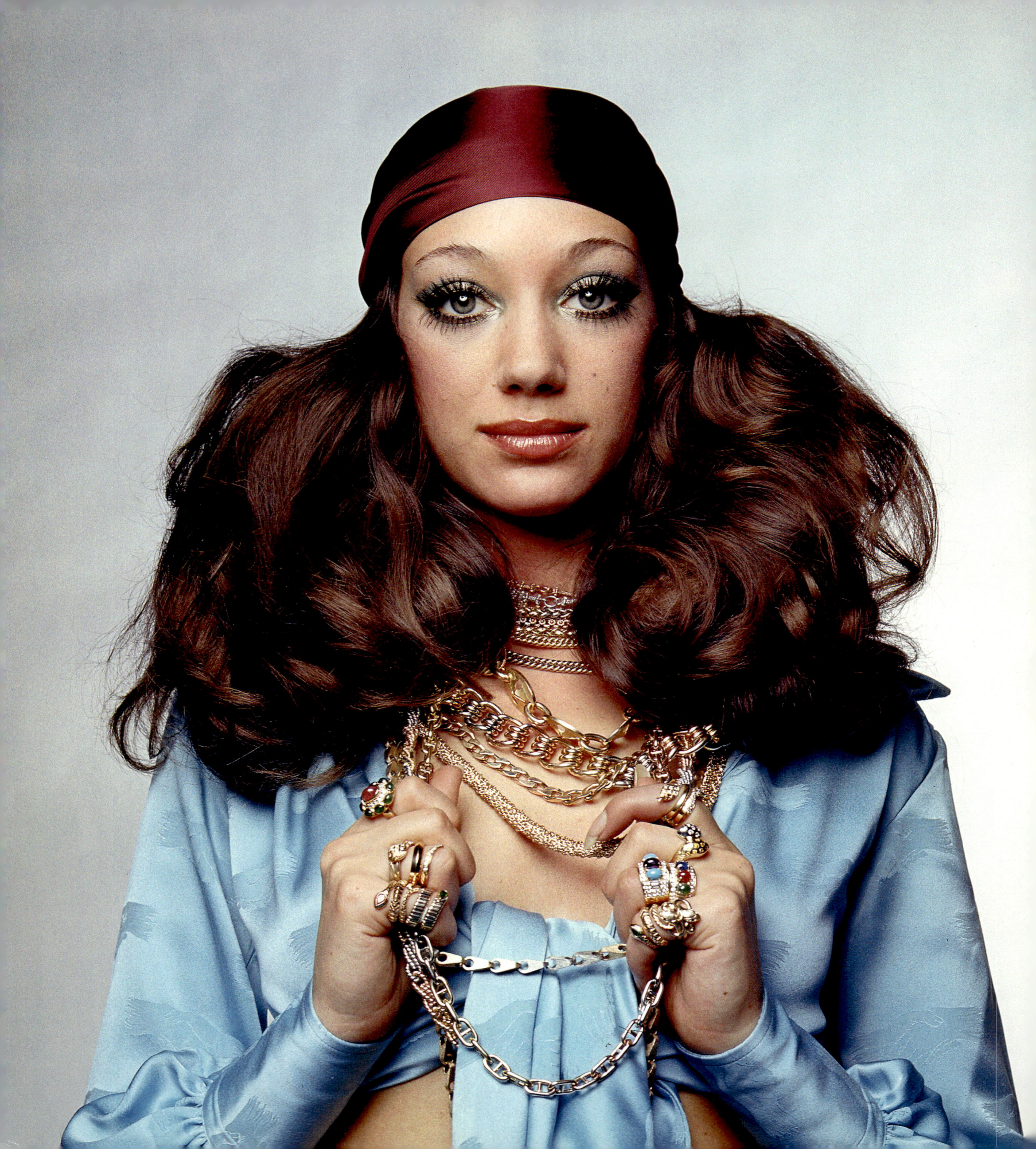

1970s: Modern Designs for Every Day

By the 1970s Rome was no longer "Hollywood on the Tiber," and Italy was plunged into a recession due to the international oil crisis, to which it responded with countrywide austerity. Following the death of their father, Giorgio, in 1966, Gianni, Paolo, and Nicola Bulgari (see fig. 39) took over the management of Bulgari, aware that the time had come to modernize it beyond its "la dolce vita" image. Catering to an affluent elite outside of Italy, the company opened a new shop at the Pierre Hotel in New York in 1972, soon following it with others in Geneva, Monte Carlo, and Paris.

The Bulgari image was not the only thing to undergo a radical transformation: the idea of jewelry was changing as well. At the time of the opening of the New York store, Gianni Bulgari stated, "[Women] no longer want something they put on or carry for great occasions, but jewelry they wear often with many things."[1] This new modern jewelry needed to be wearable for both special and everyday events while remaining valuable, sophisticated, and even amusing. Creations utilized important gems in more casual jewelry or mixed with less valuable materials. Yellow gold, which in the past was reserved mainly for daytime jewelry (while platinum and white gold were used for formal, evening dress), became popular for the most prestigious pieces of jewelry, which were now also worn informally.

The youthful exuberance of Bulgari's third generation resulted in a great variety of designs produced during this decade that reflect experimentation and audacity. A motif taking the form of what might be considered a stylized eye—an oval element with a cabochon gem often set off-center and partly framed by brilliant-cut diamonds (and, in some cases, shaped gemstones)—was introduced by Bulgari and was so extensively employed for most types of jewelry that it came to be described as the "Bulgari eye." The most striking results were achieved when this eye was applied to sautoirs, made at this time of heavy, gold-filed chains of curb linking. A sautoir's elongated shape, which well suited the "maxi" fashions of the times, provided ample scope for the display of the eye with its remarkable combinations of colored gems (see cats. 59, 60, 62, 65). The version here in gold, yellow sapphire, tiger's eye, citrine, and diamonds (cat. 59) is just one of the many magnificent examples created in this decade; it adorned the neck of the elegant Italian actress Silvana Mangano in the 1974 Luchino Visconti film *Conversation Piece*.

Bulgari also drew inspiration at this time from very diverse and wide-ranging sources, with jewelry designs clearly indebted to the cultures of ancient Egypt, the Far East, and India (see cats. 55–57; see also figs. 40, 41). It is not surprising to find Bulgari jewels from this decade with colorful lotus and papyrus motifs, views of Mount Fuji, Buddhas, and gemstones derived from seventeenth-century Indian jewels. Emeralds were the gemstones par excellence for the Mughal emperors, and it was not uncommon for Bulgari to take apart antique Indian jewels and remount the gems in contemporary settings. An example of this is the magnificent pendant suspended from a long sautoir set with a hexagonal cabochon emerald of 300.93 carats (cat. 58). Its earlier Mughal provenance is exposed by its slightly irregular outline

Fig. 38. Marisa Berenson in a variety of Bulgari rings and gold chain necklaces, 1969

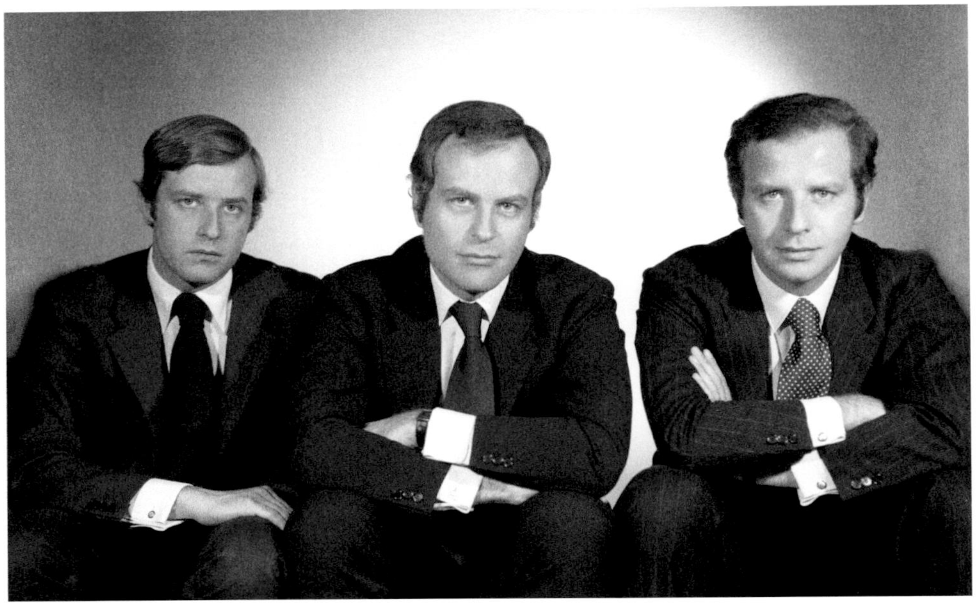

Fig. 39. Nicola, Gianni, and Paolo Bulgari, 1971

(which reflects how a gem was formerly cut to maximize the stone's weight rather than the perfection of its cut) and the presence of drill holes, common in traditional Indian jewelry, enabling important gems to be strung on silk cords.

Pop art and its transformation of everyday objects into "high art" inspired a variety of jewels in the seventies, including objects created on the theme of playing cards: for example, a pendant made of gold, mother-of-pearl, and coral; and a sautoir in onyx, mother-of-pearl, coral, and diamonds (see cats. 75–79). Pop art continued to prevail throughout the 1980s, when candies, ice pops, and ice cream cones became inspirations for precious, colored brooches (see cats. 120–124). This particular theme was extended to gold, silver, or combined gold and silver manifestations of everyday objects: a Coca-Cola bottle complete with logo, postage stamps, origami paper boats, tennis-ball canisters, and cigarette cases in the same shapes and bearing the same prints as their real-life models; such reproductions even included a folding measuring stick, a hammer, and champagne corks (see cats. 47–54).

Following the trend of Pop art and its transformation of the American flag into a pop icon, Bulgari introduced the popular Stars-and-Stripes motif. This particular design element was not entirely new. Between 1889 and 1912 Tiffany & Co. made numerous brooches with faithful reproductions of the American flag, but it was after the artist Jasper Johns painted his Stars-and-Stripes canvases in the mid-fifties that the motif would achieve its full impact. Although Bulgari never made an exact reproduction of the flag, it did evoke its image by adopting its colors and its elements (see figs. 42a–b). Necklaces, sautoirs, earrings, rings, bracelets, and cuff links using red and blue enamel or lapis lazuli and red coral with diamonds in a Stars-and-Stripes theme were publicized as the "Star-Spangled Banner" collection (see cats. 81–83). In a 1972 *Vogue* advertisement, the singer Cher appeared in a swimsuit wearing Bulgari's US flag–themed jewelry (see fig. 13). The ad copy read: "Contemporary flash: modern girl, modern

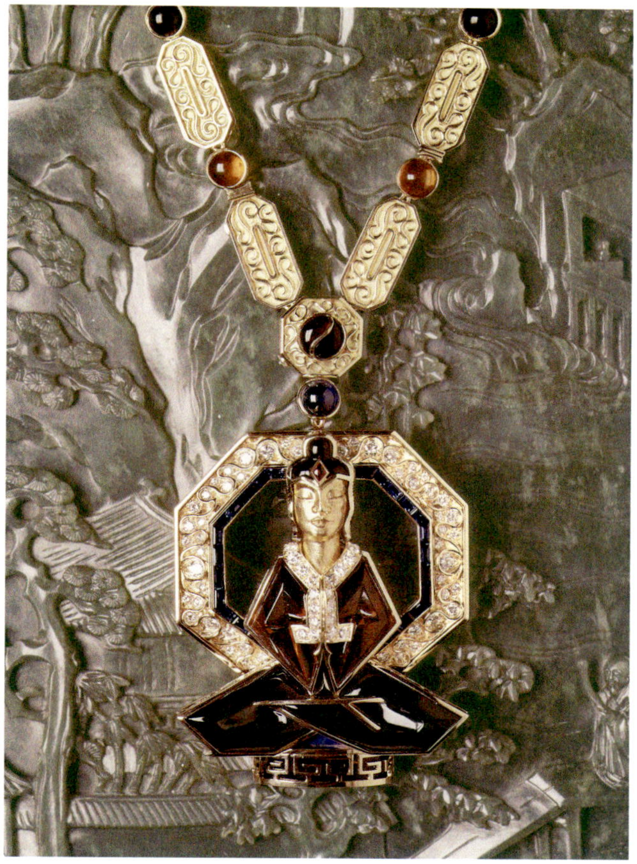

Fig. 40. Bulgari advertisement for Buddha sautoir, ca. early 1970s

jewels—Cher and Bulgari's stars and stripes of coral, diamonds, and lapis—real, but not too serious. . . . And that is the whole point about today's jewelry—it's to wear, to use, and to enjoy." Along with these jewels a limited number of small precious table clocks were also manufactured, such as the one featured here (cat. 80). This line, specially created for the opening of the New York shop, was successful, and it anticipated—with great sophistication—the 1976 bicentennial celebration of the United States' signing of the Declaration of Independence.

A luxury accessory par excellence, the Melone (melon) bag, named for its oval shape, was another great success of the 1970s (see cats. 67–70). In a perfect combination of utility and beauty, the famous and unmistakable evening bag was distinguished by its simple, rounded form and its weight from the smaller, conventional evening bags of the time. The Melone was made in a variety of finishes and embellishments, the most memorable among them being tortoiseshell, hued gold, and decorations of antique coins or blackened steel inlay. Its unique design allows it to be opened into two hinged halves by pressing a gem-set thumbpiece, and a mirror, comb, and lidded compartment are often found inside. Any of these bags can be suspended from interchangeable silk cords decorated with tassels in a range of colors to match different outfits. The demand for these evening bags was so great that Bulgari often had to draw up waiting lists for what had become one of the most fashionable of luxury accessories.

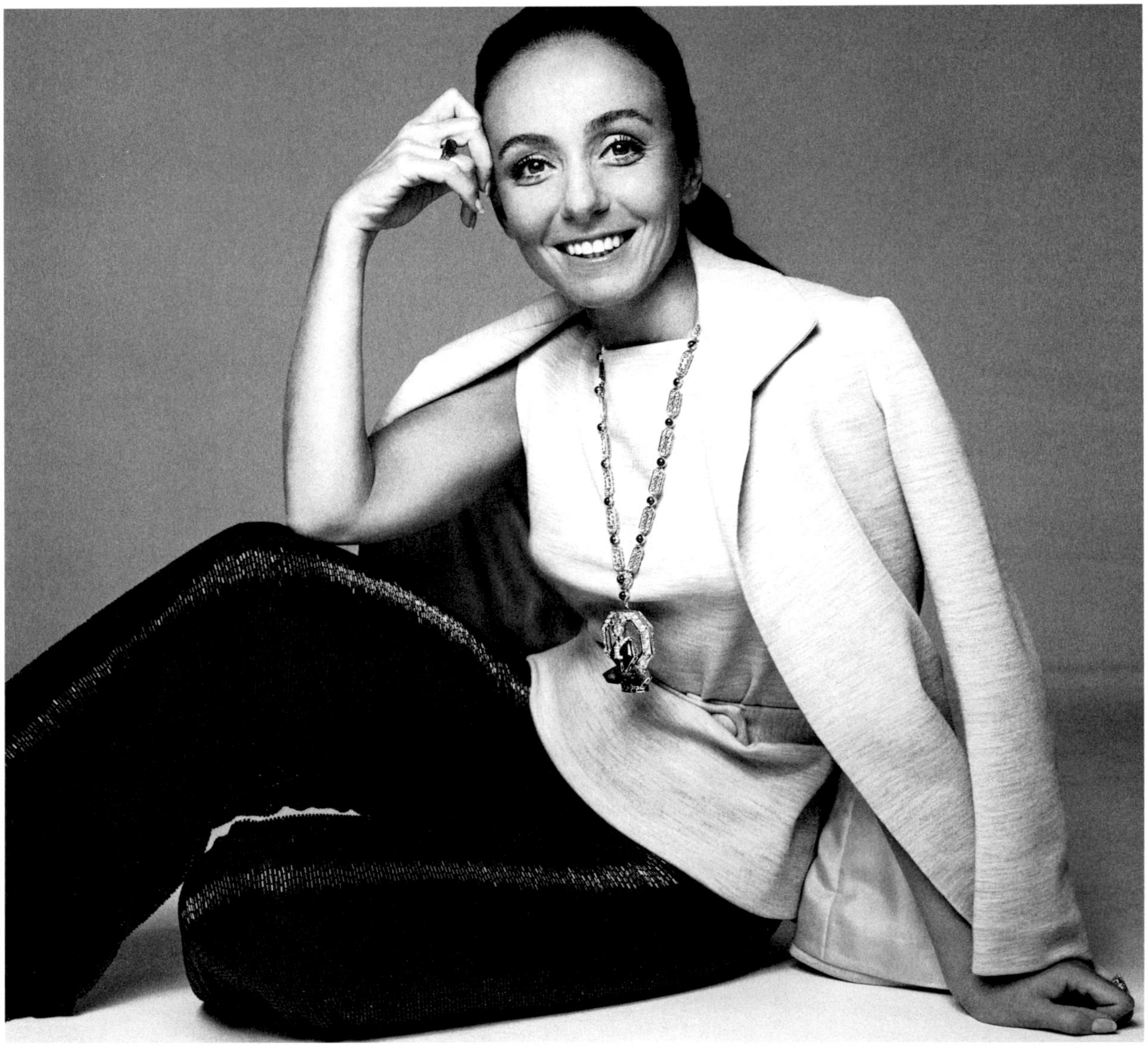

Fig. 41. Lyn Revson, wearing her Bulgari Buddha sautoir, photographed by Richard Avedon for French *Vogue*, April 1972

It was also during the seventies that Bulgari began to consistently mount coins as centerpieces in its jewels, thus laying the foundation for what would, by the twenty-first century, become the Monete (coins) collection. Though Bulgari had exploited the decorative value of ancient and antique coins as early as the 1930s to embellish cigarette cases and precious boxes, it was only in the mid-sixties that the company began mounting them on jewels. According to family tradition, the driving force behind this particular new endeavor was Nicola Bulgari, who, due in part to the coins he had received as a young boy from his godfather, the master goldsmith Ubaldo Crescenzi, had grown to appreciate their particular beauty and historic value.

By mounting coins as jewels, Bulgari revived a tradition that dates to the Hellenistic period (fourth century BC) and continued through ancient Rome, flourishing until the seventh century AD, particularly in Byzantine and Anglo-Saxon cultures. Coins can be found on rare examples of silver objects made throughout the centuries that followed, but were not popularized again in jewelry until the second half of the 1800s. The famous Castellani dynasty of Roman goldsmiths and its circle began to set ancient Greek and Roman coins in the manner of precious gemstones in what is called a "neo-archaeological" style—not only looking to the past for inspiration, but also taking authentic fragments from it and incorporating them into modern jewels.[2] Goldsmiths working in the neo-archaeological style generally used silver coins such as the Hellenistic tetradrachm or the Roman denarius, both of which were plentiful in archaeological digs of the time. The contrast between the coin's original antique silver patina and the matte nineteenth-century gold mount was exploited to great advantage. Though these settings were plain (sometimes the only decoration was a beaded frame), they offset the coin's intrinsic beauty.

Bulgari continued to adhere to many well-established traditions in coin jewelry, yet its interpretations of the motif resulted in totally modern and original creations. Bulgari in the twentieth century had access to a much broader range of coins than what was previously available on the world market, including bronze, silver, gold, and electrum specimens from the ancient Mediterranean world, and ancient and modern coins from Europe, North Africa, and America, covering a period of time from the fifth century BC to Bulgari's present day (see cats. 84–89, 97, 115–117; see also figs. 11, 43).

Intrinsic beauty was the criterion at Bulgari for selecting the appropriate "gem coins." Heads were favored overall, especially profiles of Alexander the Great, Medusa, the nymph Arethusa, the armored goddess Roma, and the Caesars, or the more recent (1795) personification of Liberty found on the American silver dollar (see cat. 87). The coins, usually framed by a single or double gold collet, were used in a broad range of Bulgari jewels that included rings, necklaces, earrings, and bracelets, as well as evening bags. They also decorated such objects as boxes, paper knives, ashtrays, and bowls. Coins in circular settings with typical Bulgari elements and decorative motifs could be found on chains of filed curb linking or on flattened or tubular sections of *tubogas* (gas pipe; see below); they were often suspended from silk cords or inserted into modular jewelry. Occasionally coins were mounted on pivots enabling their rotation to show both of their sides.

The round shapes of coins harmonized perfectly with Bulgari's jewels, which often had the same outlines. If a coin was irregular in shape or worn down, its setting was designed to prevent further damage and loss to its numismatic value. A play of contrasts was also applied to these works: the worn, matte finish of the coin against the smooth, polished shine of its setting; the color of the coin's bronze, silver, electrum, or gold metal against its gold or steel mount; and the coin's ancient heritage against Bulgari's modern sensibility. Inscribed on the reverse of each mount are the coin's name, nominal value, and year of issue.

The seventies saw the expanding use of the so-called *tubogas* technique, a method developed during the second half of the nineteenth century, which began to be used by a number of jewelers, including Bulgari, in the 1940s. However, starting in the 1970s, Bulgari made such extensive use of it—and employed it so effectively in the creation of some of its watches, bracelets, necklaces, and rings—that it soon became one of the firm's hallmarks (see cats. 39–42). The Bulgari *tubogas* is a flexible band with

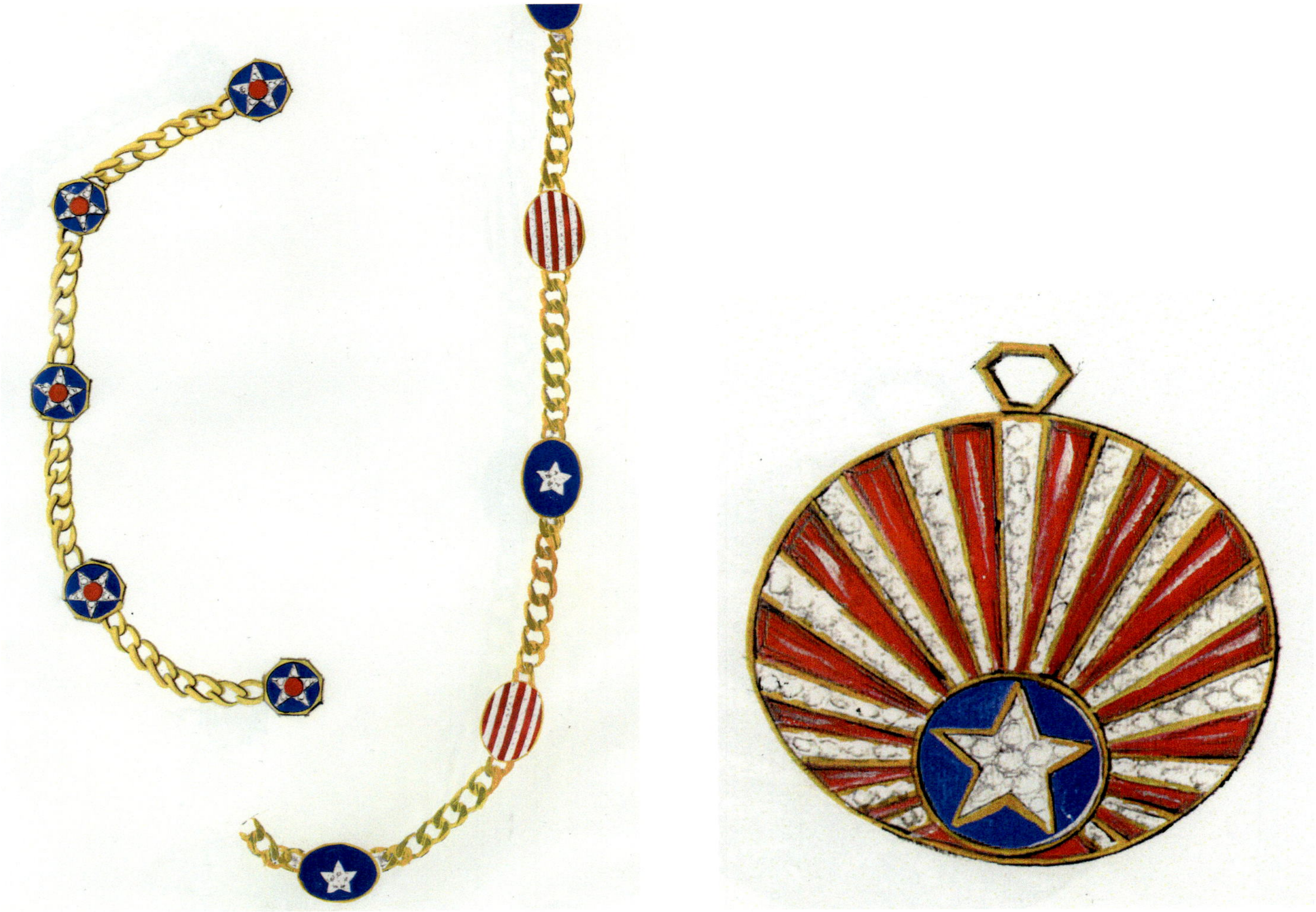

Figs. 42a–b. Original design sketches for the Star-Spangled Banner collection, ca. 1970

sleek, rounded contours that is produced without soldering. It takes hours of specialized work to make *tubogas*, as the process involves wrapping two long gold strips with raised edges around a copper or wood core so that the edges firmly interlock with each other to form a continuous unsoldered piece. The core is then removed or dissolved in acid.

The flexibility of these metallic bands is truly remarkable and has produced impressive results. Among the most successful and striking examples are those composed of multiple *tubogas* coils placed one on top of the other (see cats. 115, 117). To create heightened chromatic effects Bulgari used alternating yellow, pink, and white gold strips of *tubogas* for bracelets and necklaces that change color with every coil. The use of gray steel combined with yellow gold was also introduced in the 1970s. Lengthy and detailed technical research was undertaken to find a suitable type of stainless steel in the exact shade of gray to complement the warm-hued pink and yellow gold. Researchers identified a certain type of steel that was usually employed in the aeronautical, naval, chemical, and medical industries, but discovered that it was difficult to work with steel's high melting point (2600–2800° Fahrenheit) and its low malle-

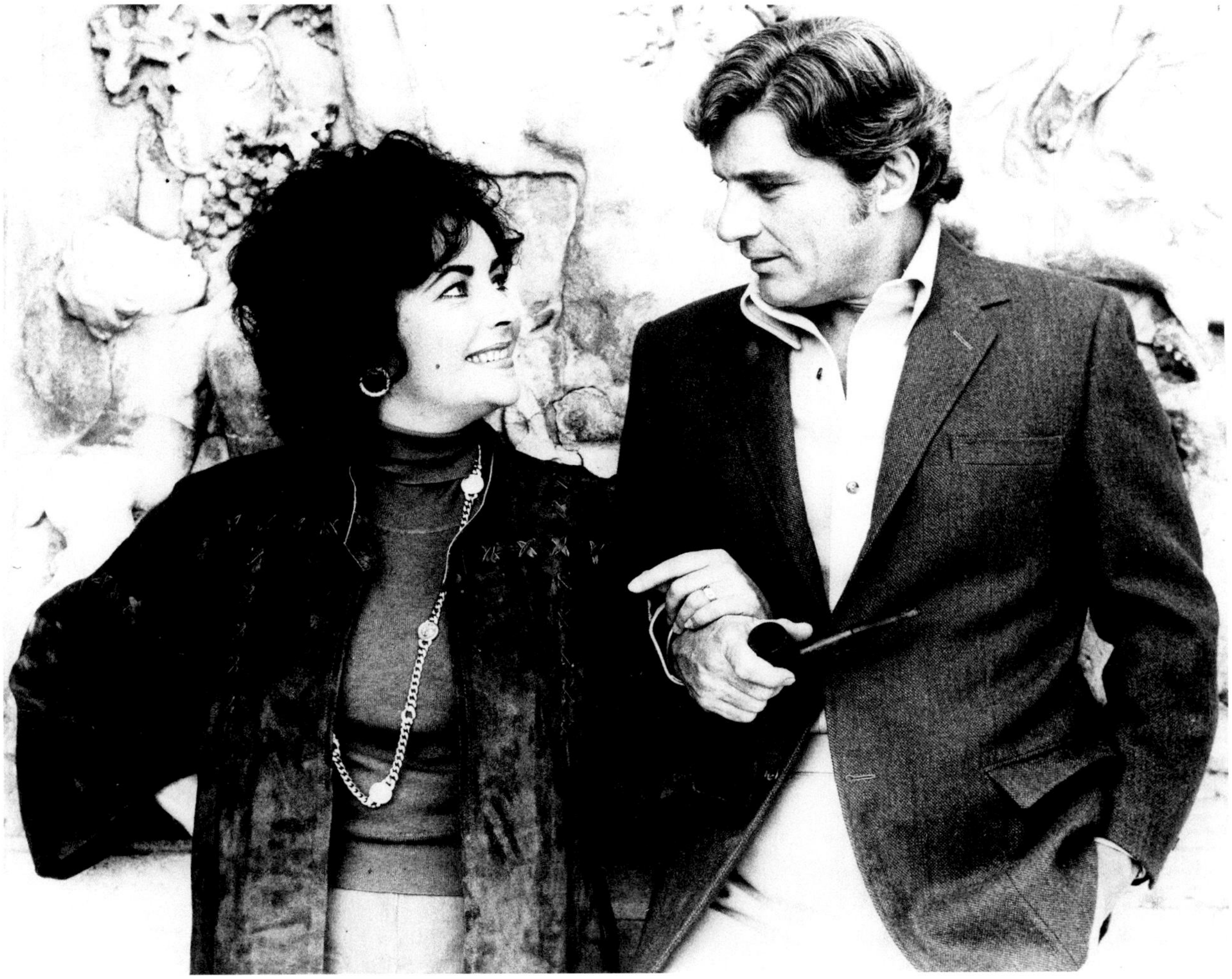

Fig. 43. Elizabeth Taylor, wearing her Bulgari gold sautoir with six Byzantine coins and diamonds (cat. 97), with John Warner, 1976

ability (particularly in comparison with eighteen-karat gold). Given the material's more labor-intensive techniques, the steel *tubogas* were, paradoxically, more expensive than those made of gold.

Bulgari's jewels of the seventies may be remembered for their extraordinary range of designs and eclectic sources of inspiration. Between the "Bulgari eye," coins mounted as jewelry centerpieces, and sleek *tubogas* ornaments in steel and gold, the decade brought to the fore a number of motifs that would become iconic for the company. In the following decade an increased concentration on global expansion and brand identity would result in these designs gaining an instantly recognizable pedigree.

1. Interview with Gianni Bulgari, *New York Post*, September 1, 1970.

2. For more detailed information on the Castellanis and their jewelry creations with coins, see "Alessandro e Augusto Castellani: collezionismo, museologia e mercato antiquario," in *I Castellani e l'oreficeria archeologica italiana*, exh. cat. (Rome: L'Erma di Bretschneider, 2005).

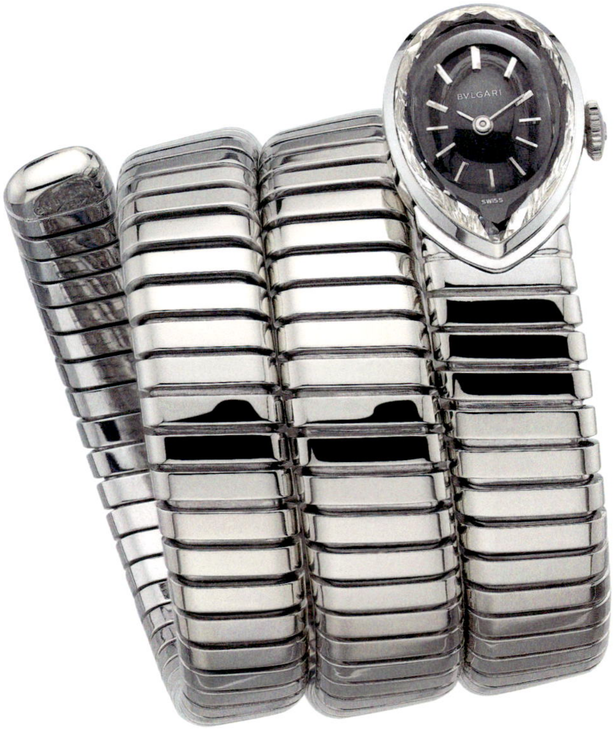

39. *Tubogas* bracelet-watch, ca. 1960
White gold

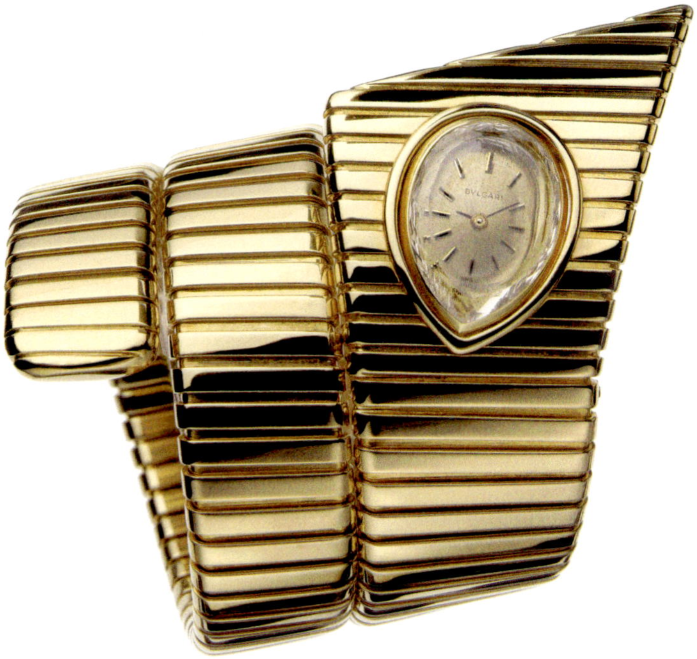

40. *Tubogas* bracelet-watch, ca. 1972
Gold

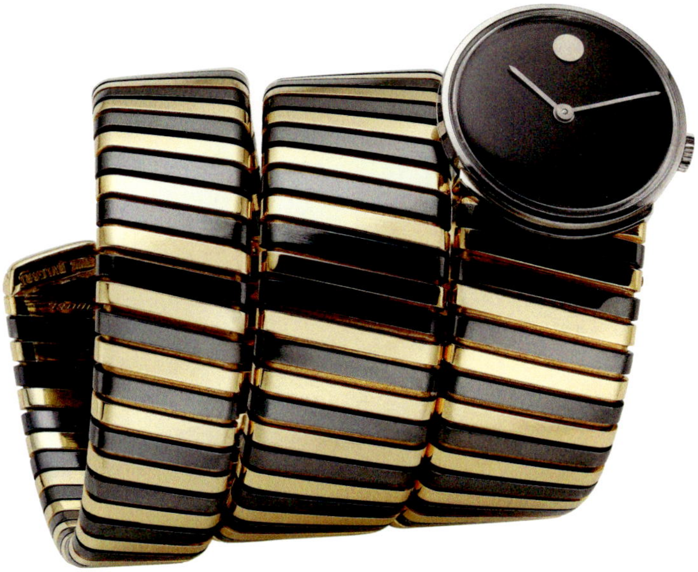

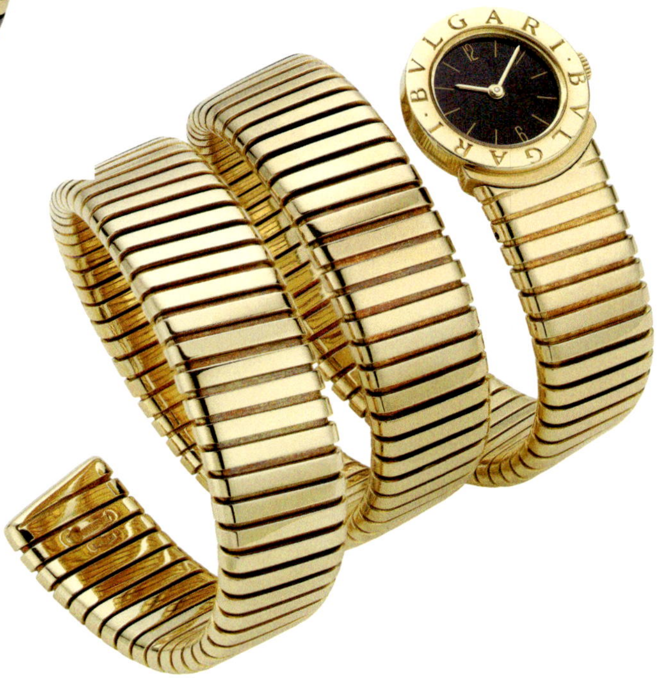

41. ***Tubogas*** **bracelet-watch, ca. 1972**
Gold and burnished steel

42. ***Tubogas*** **"BVLGARI-BVLGARI" bracelet-watch, 1980**
Gold

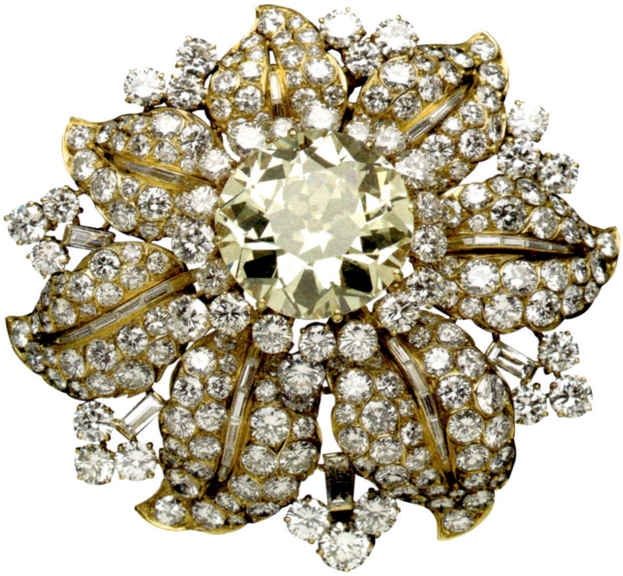

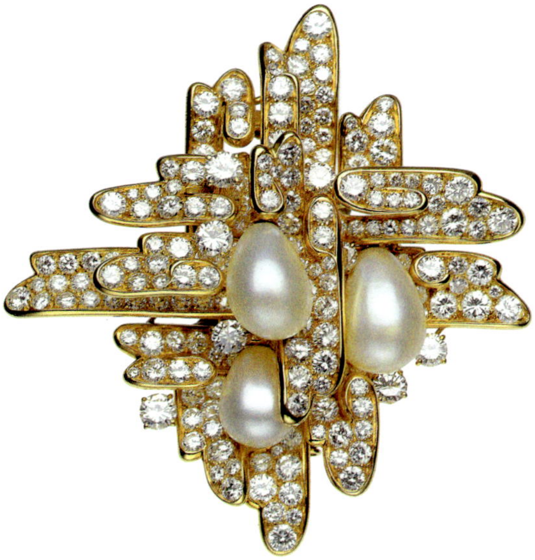

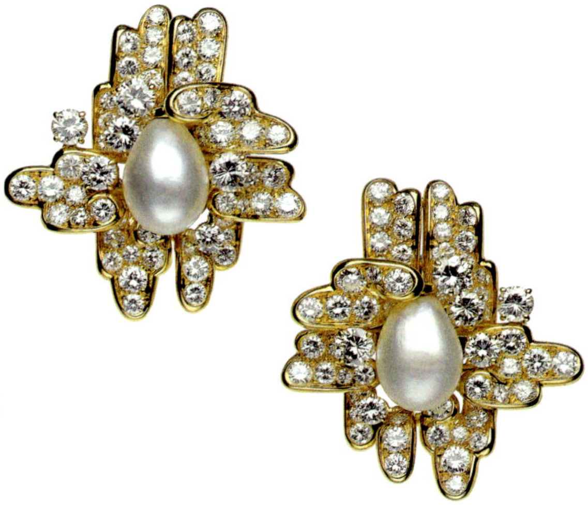

43. Brooch, ca. 1968
Gold with diamonds

44. Brooch, 1970
Gold with natural pearls and diamonds

45. Earrings, 1970
Gold with natural pearls and diamonds

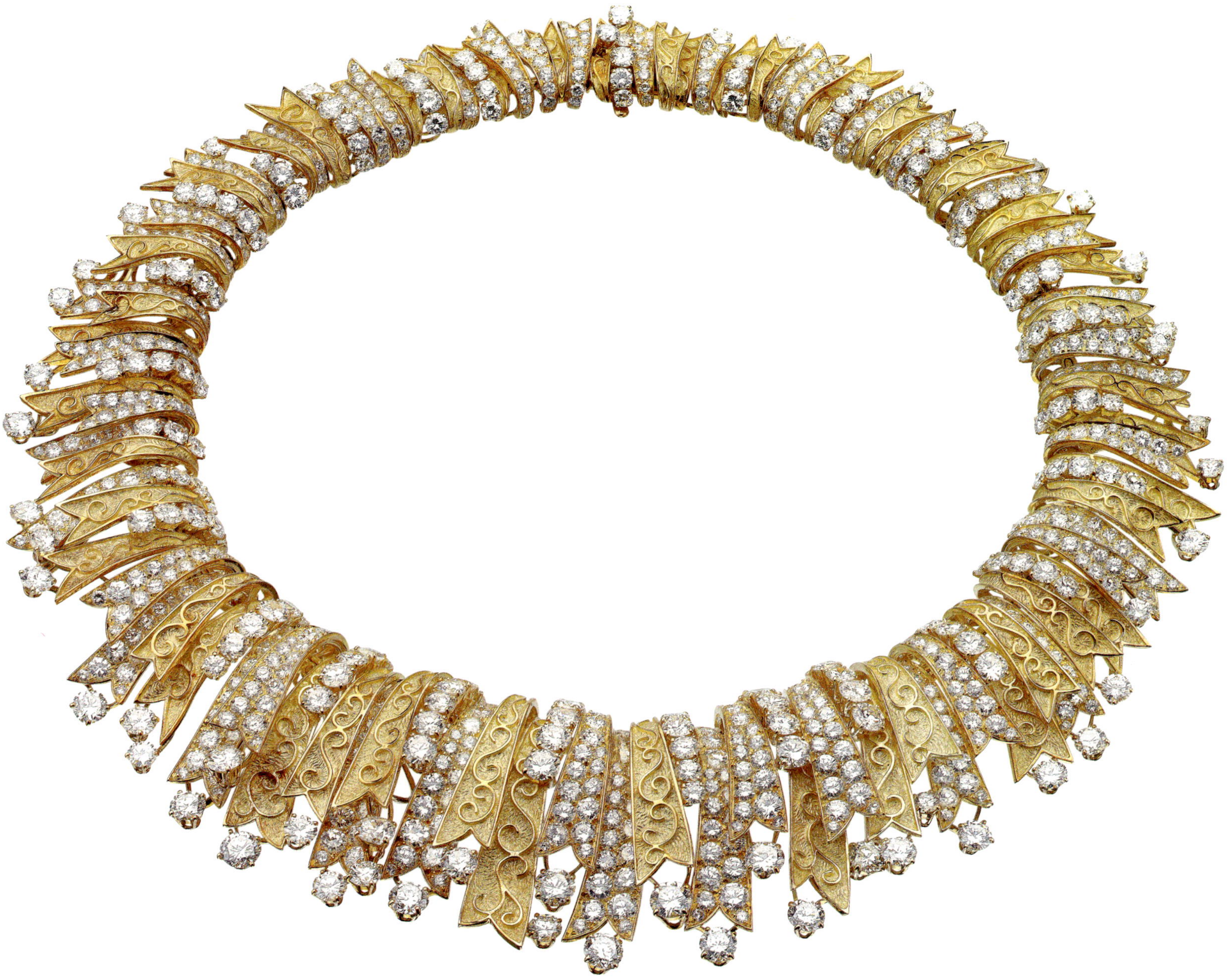

46. Fireworks necklace, 1969
Gold with diamonds

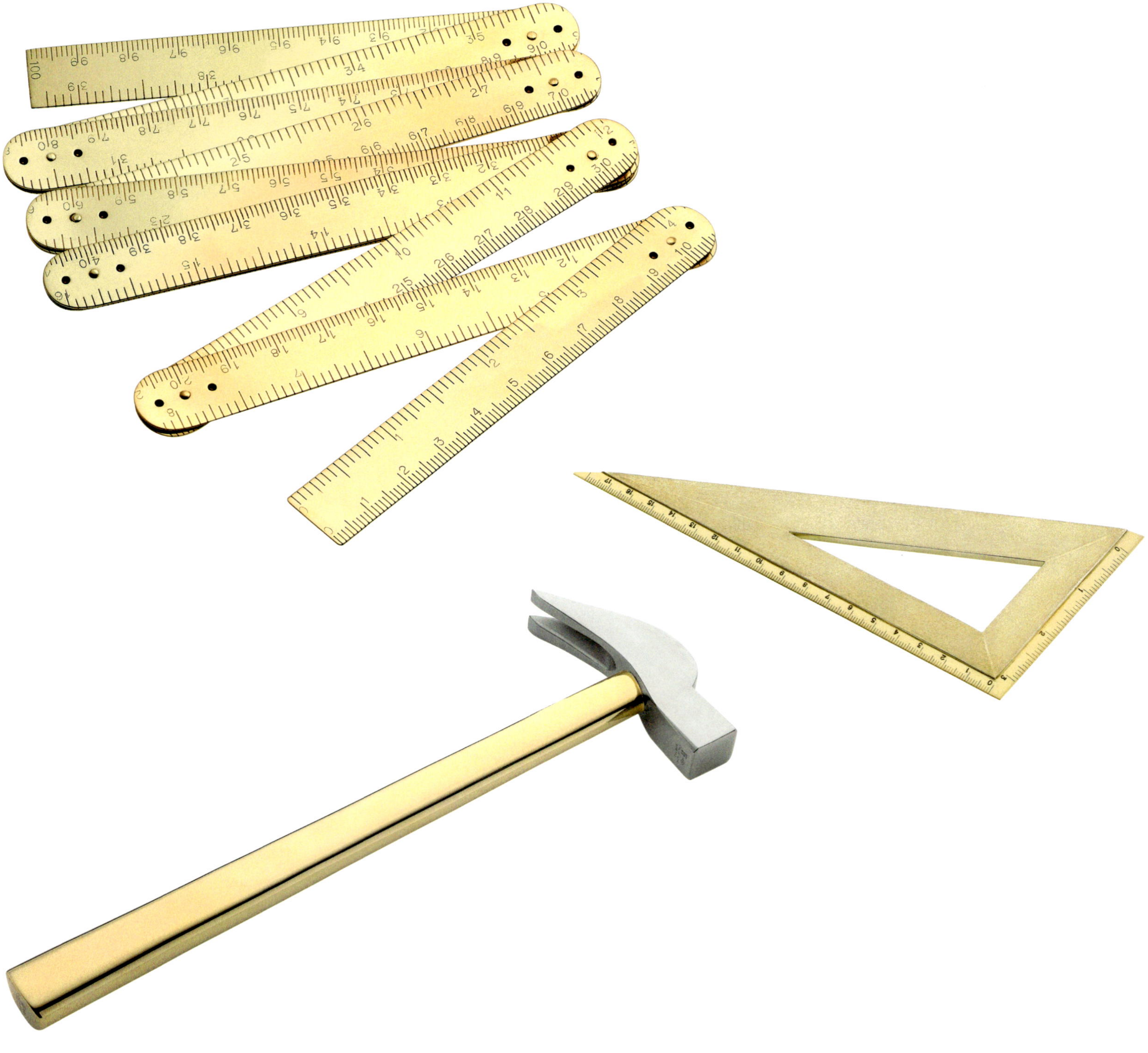

47. Measuring stick, ca. 1970
Gold

48. Hammer, 1972
Two-color gold

49. Square, ca. 1970
Gilded silver and gold

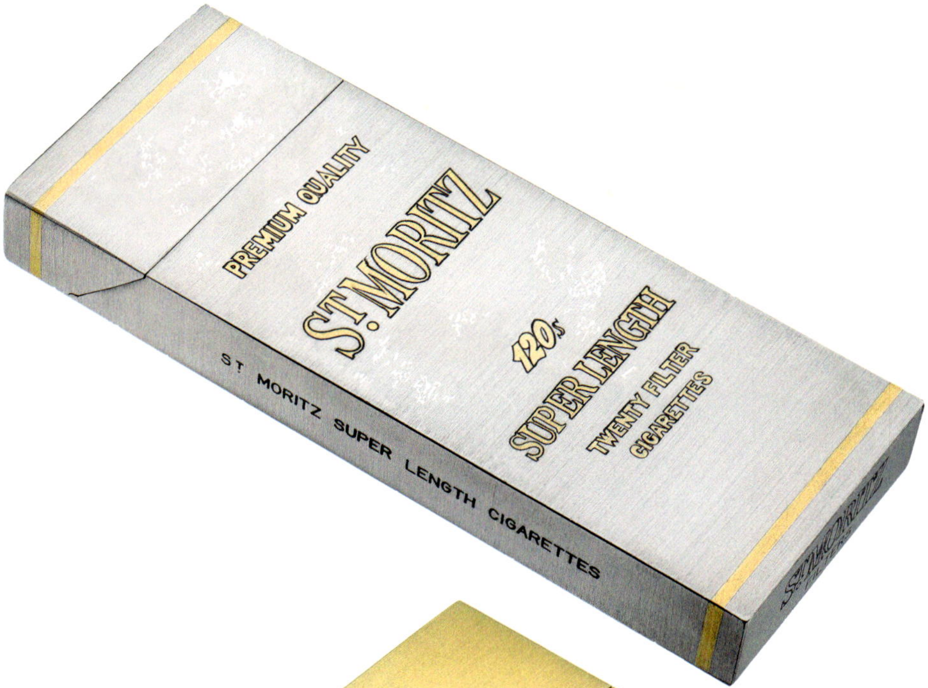

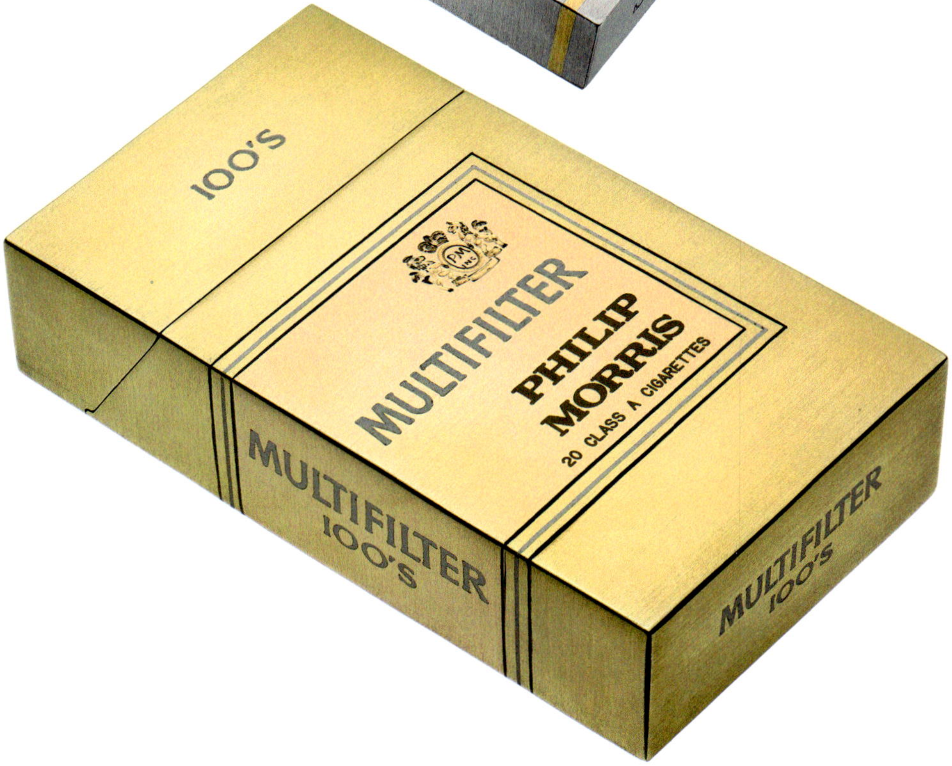

50. "St. Moritz" cigarette case, 1977
Silver and gold

51. "Multifilter Philip Morris" cigarette case, 1977
Two-color gold with white and black enamel

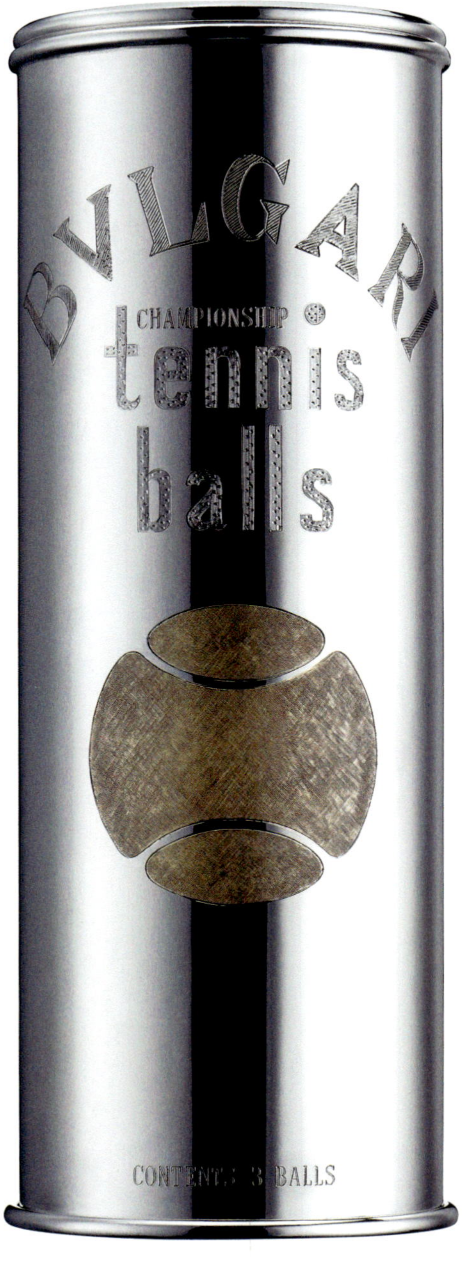

52. Tennis-ball canister, 1980
Silver and gold

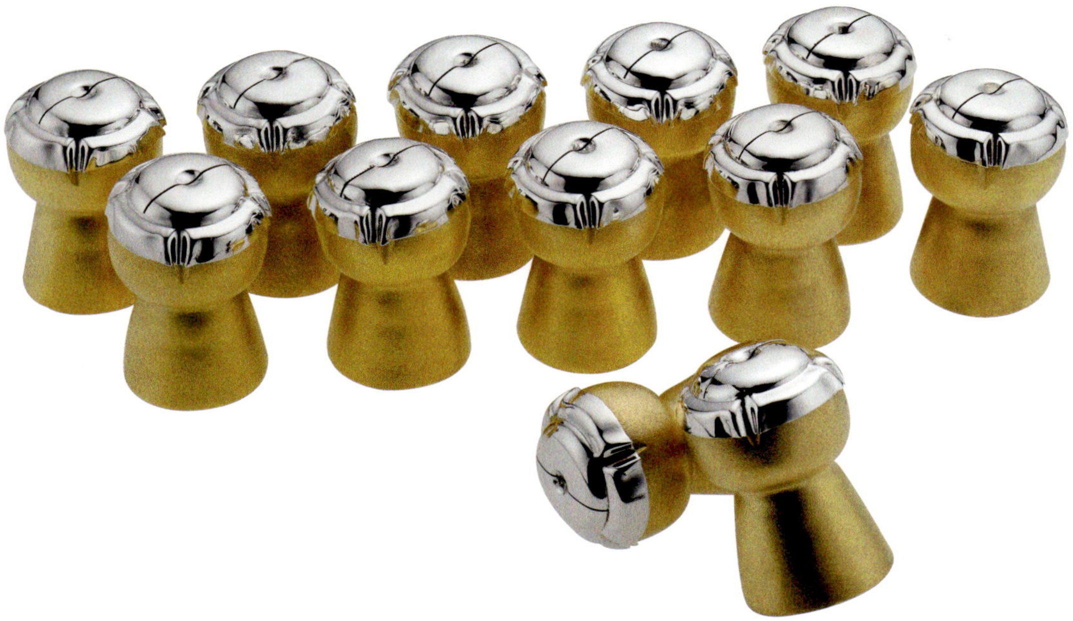

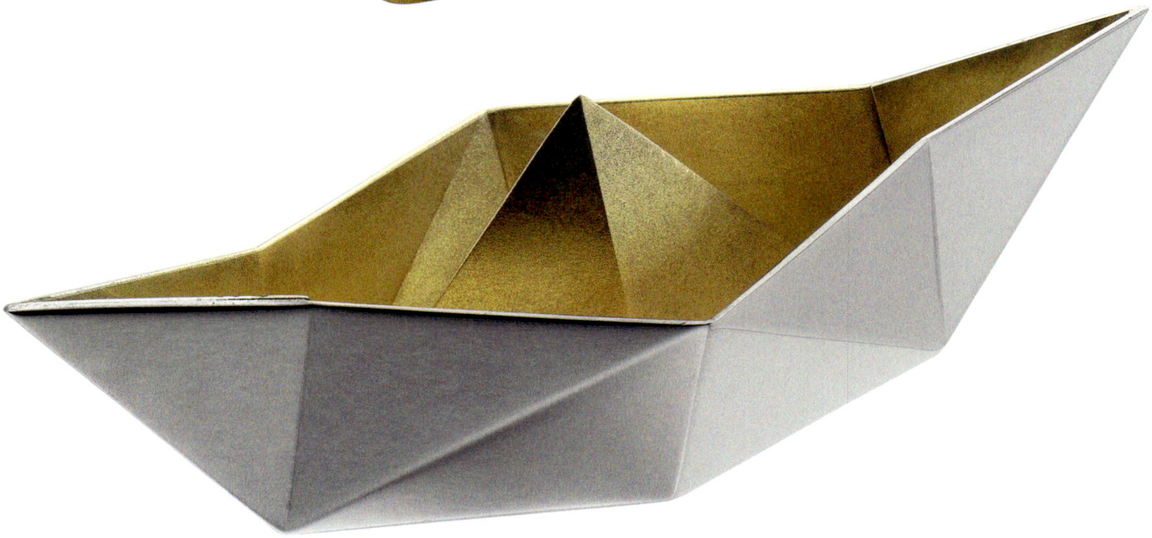

53. Set of champagne cork place-card holders, ca. 1975
Silver and gilded silver

54. Boat paperweight, 1974
Sterling silver and gilded silver

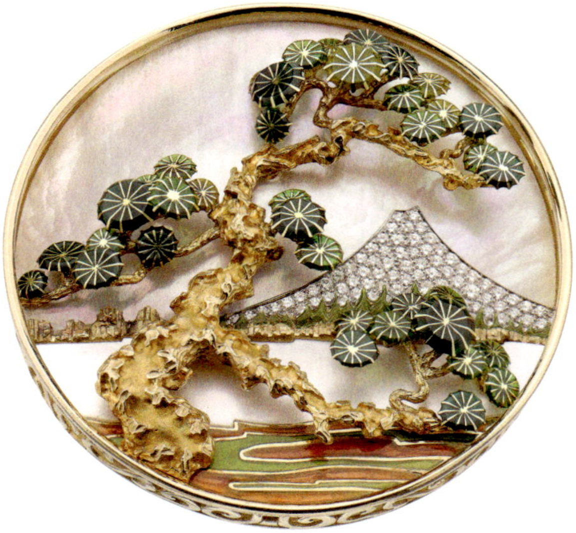

55. Mount Fuji brooch, 1971

Gold and platinum with mother-of-pearl, polychrome enamel, and diamonds

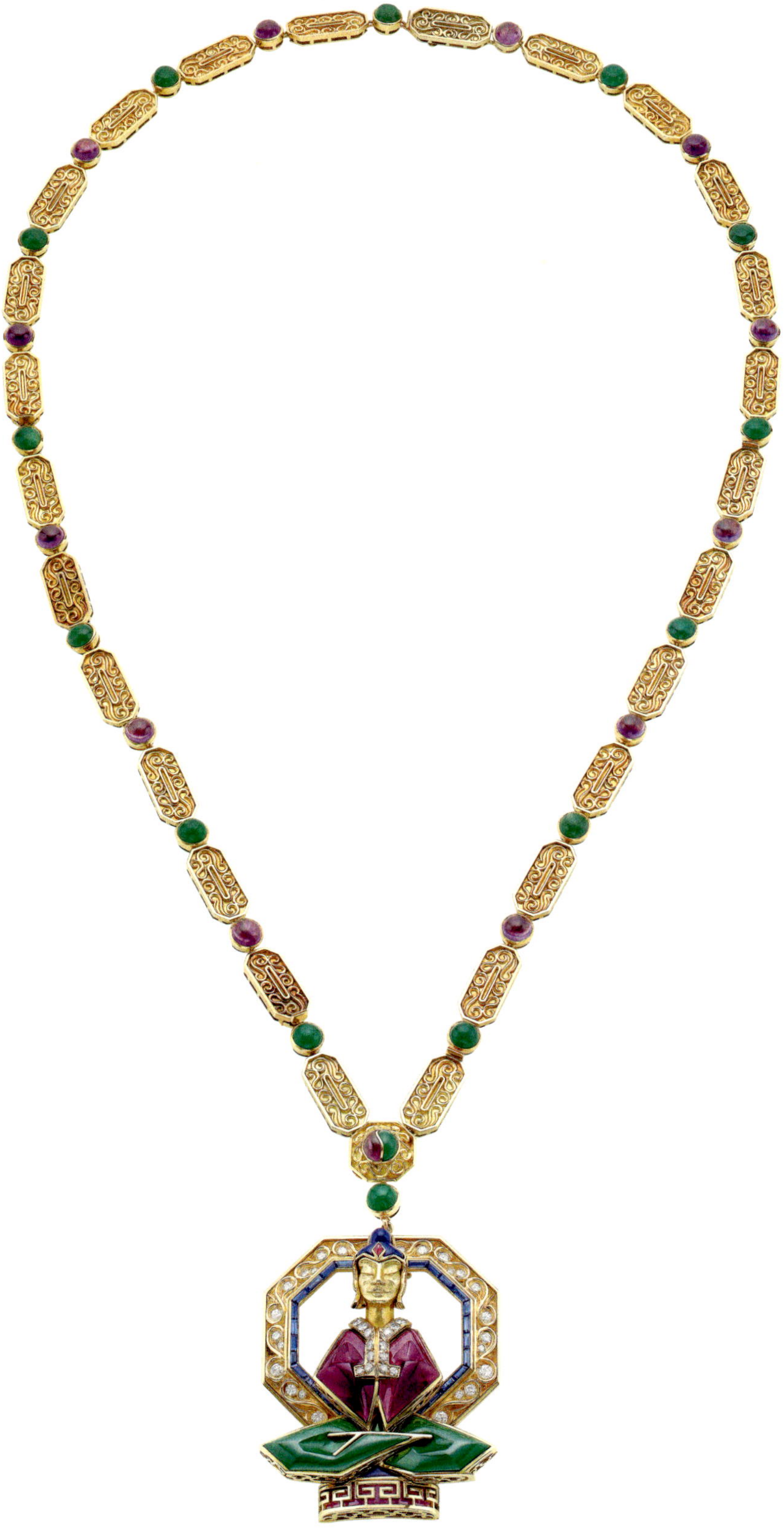

56. Buddha sautoir, 1971

Gold with malachite, amethysts, emeralds, sapphires, lapis lazuli, rubies, and diamonds

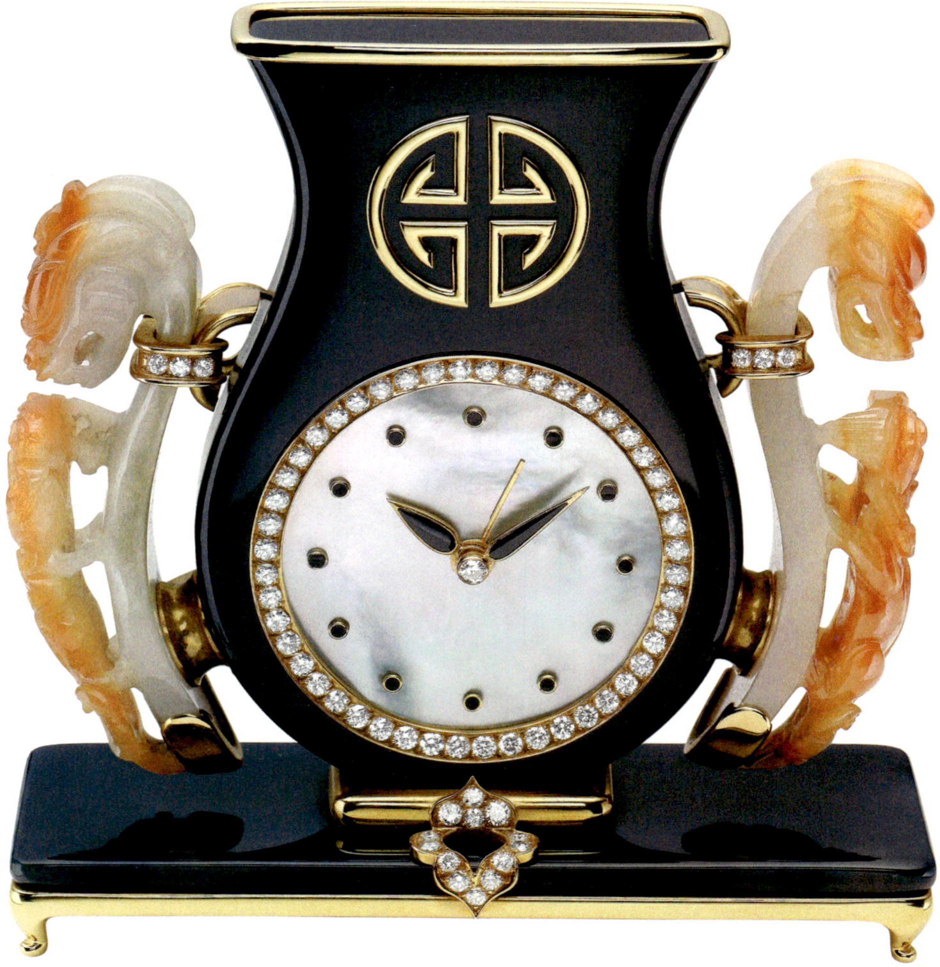

57. Table clock, 1980
Gold with onyx, mother-of-pearl, jade, and diamonds

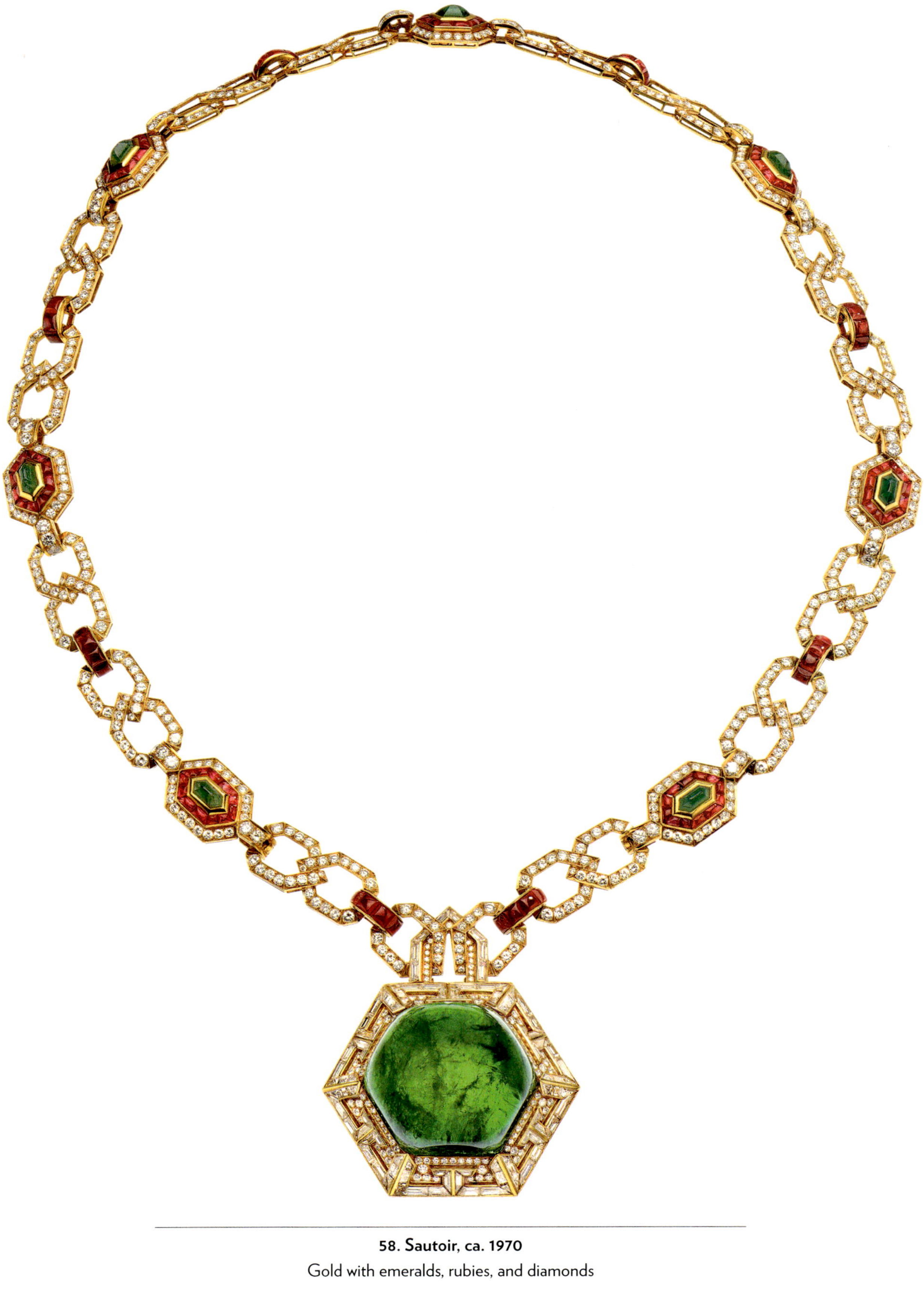

58. Sautoir, ca. 1970
Gold with emeralds, rubies, and diamonds

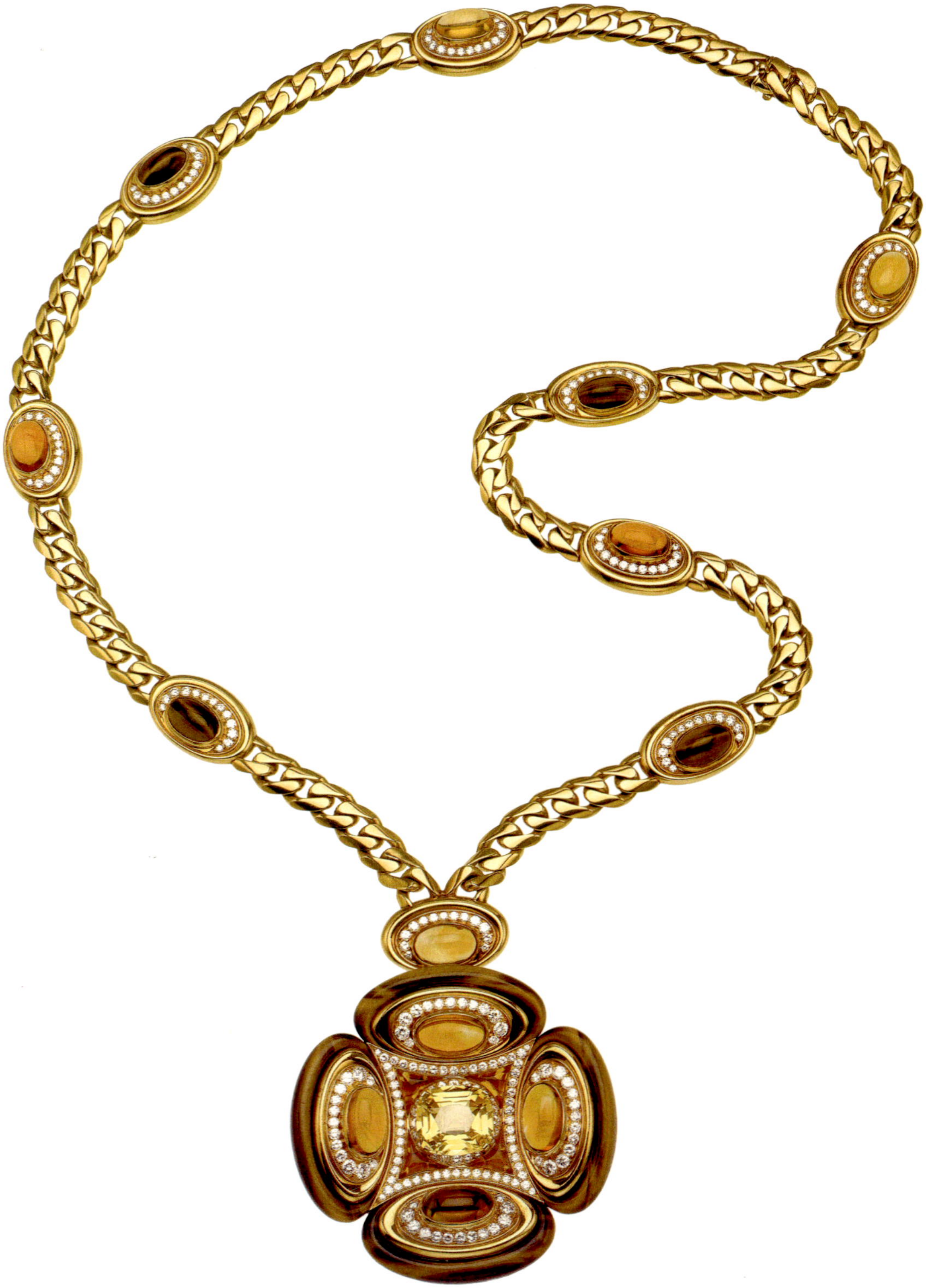

59. Sautoir, ca. 1973

Gold with yellow sapphire, tiger's eye, citrines, and diamonds

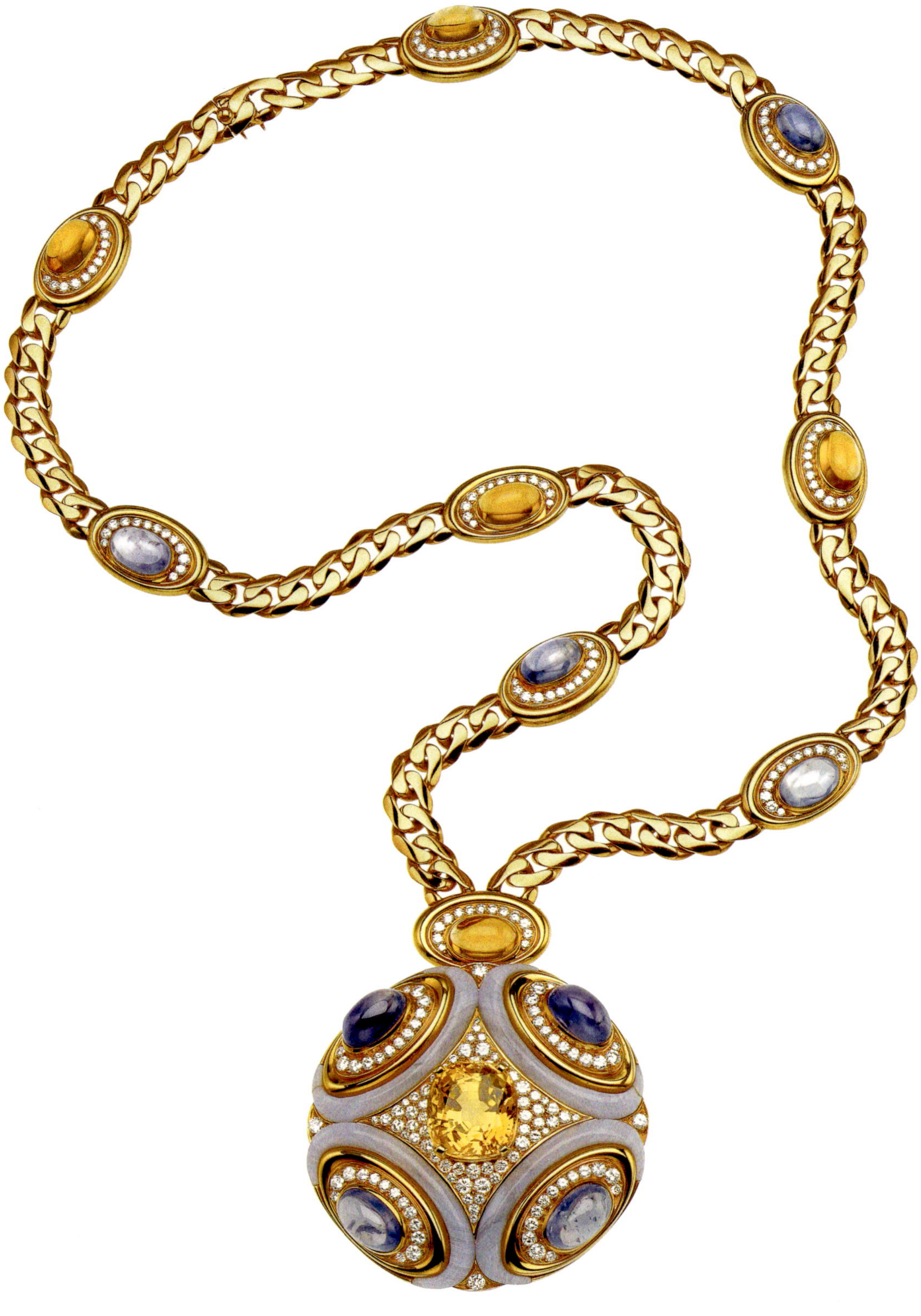

60. Sautoir, ca. 1972

Gold with yellow and blue sapphires, agate, citrines, and diamonds

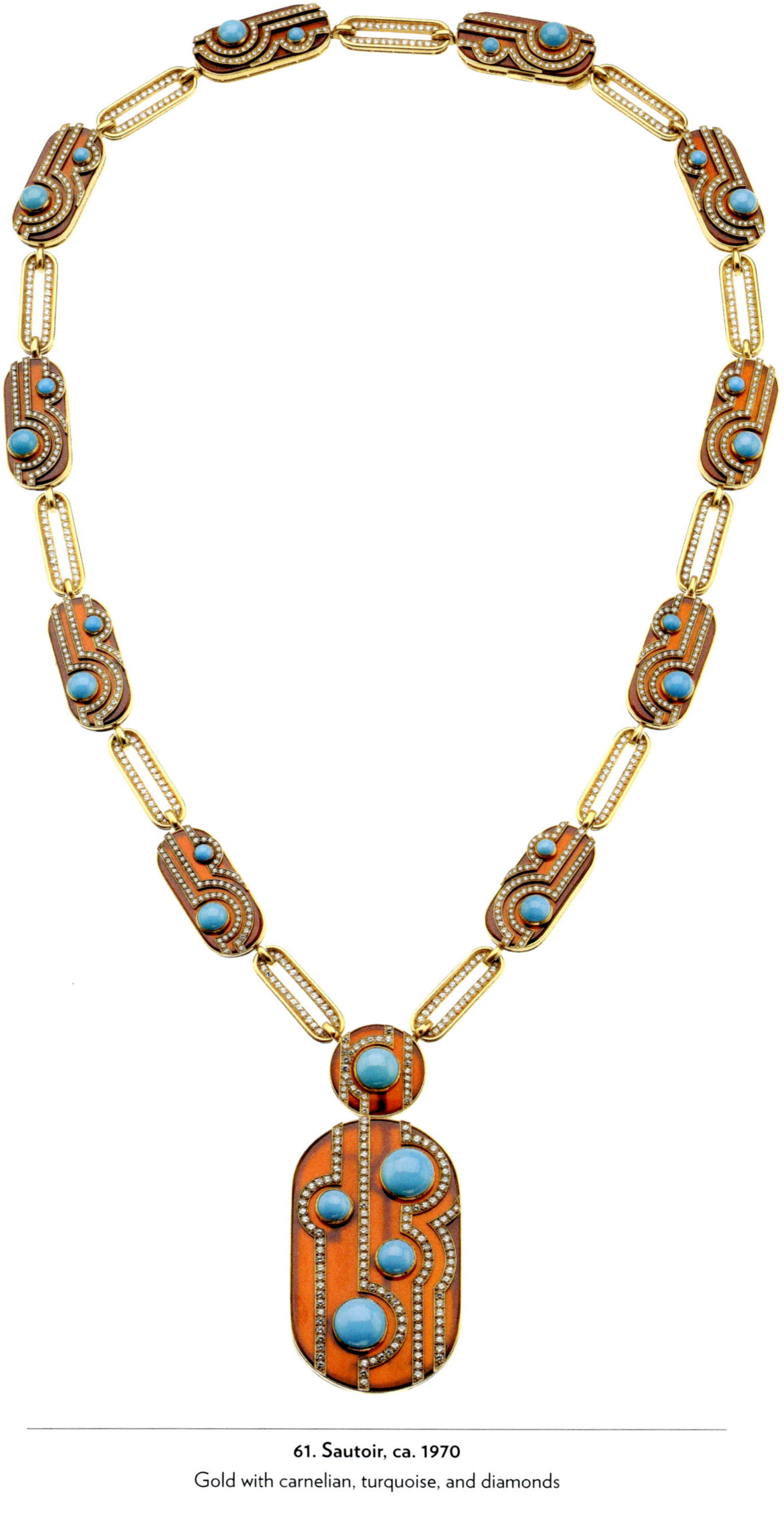

61. Sautoir, ca. 1970

Gold with carnelian, turquoise, and diamonds

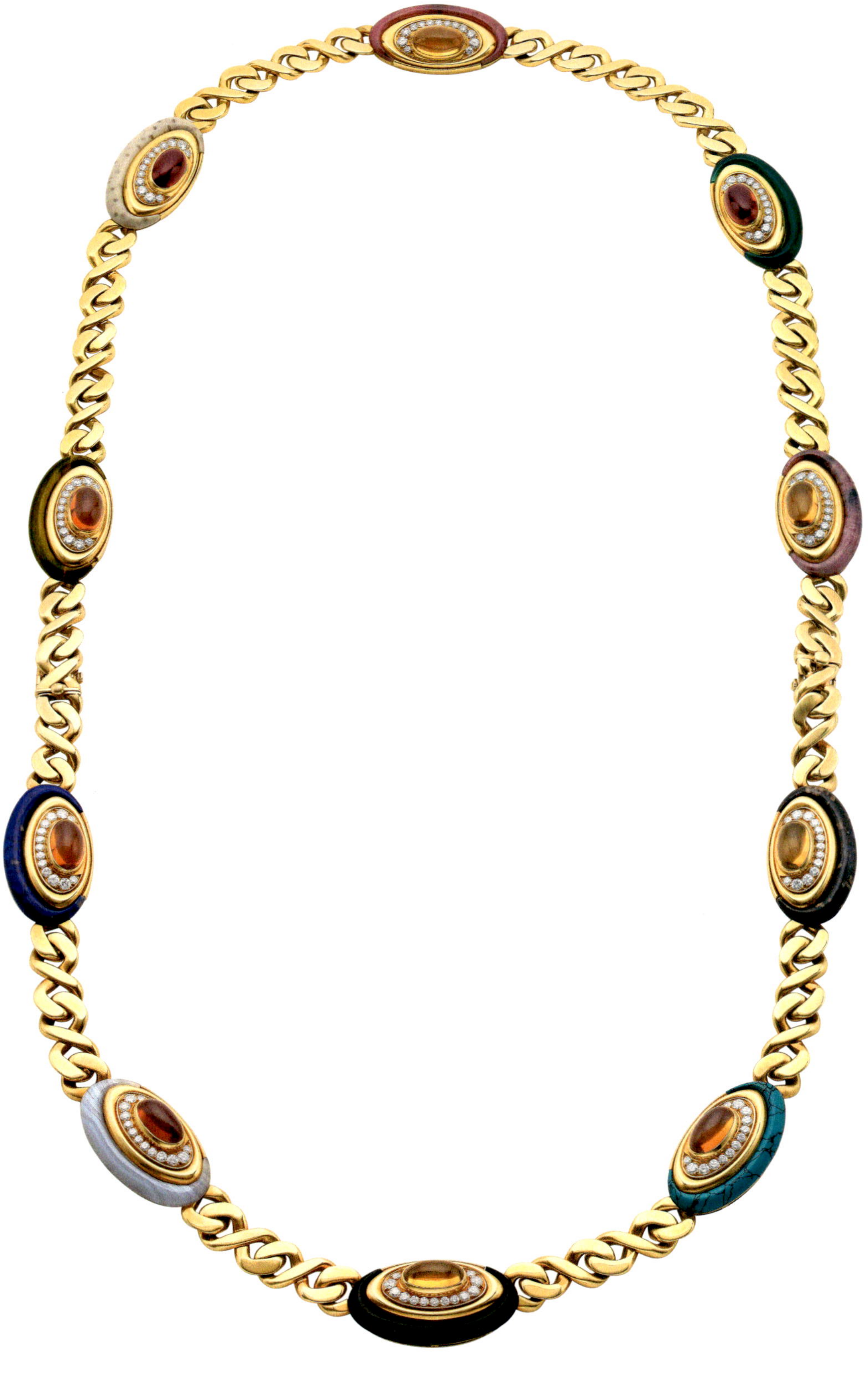

62. Sautoir, ca. 1975
Gold with citrines, colored hardstones, and diamonds

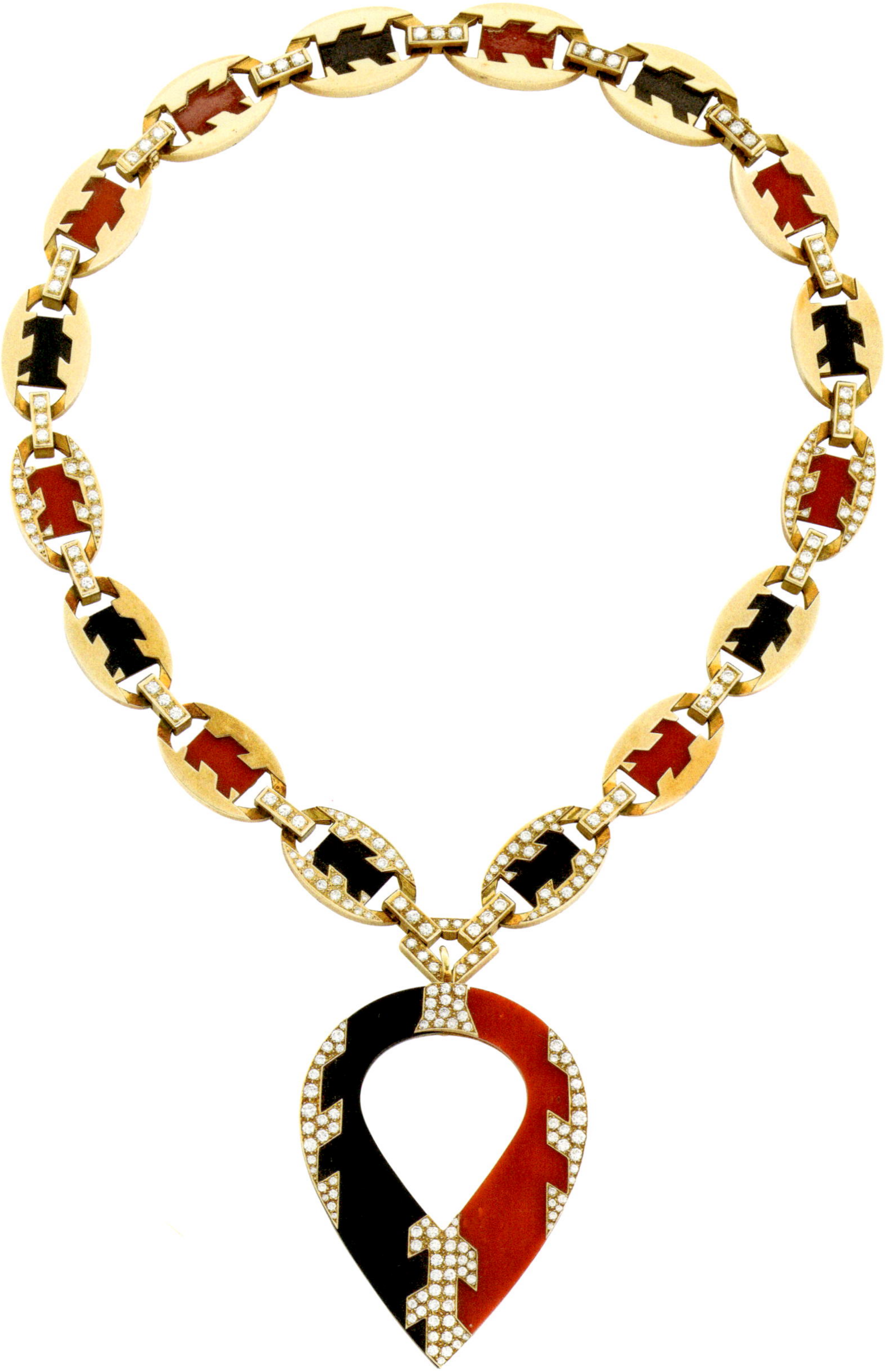

63. Sautoir, 1973
Gold with coral, onyx, and diamonds

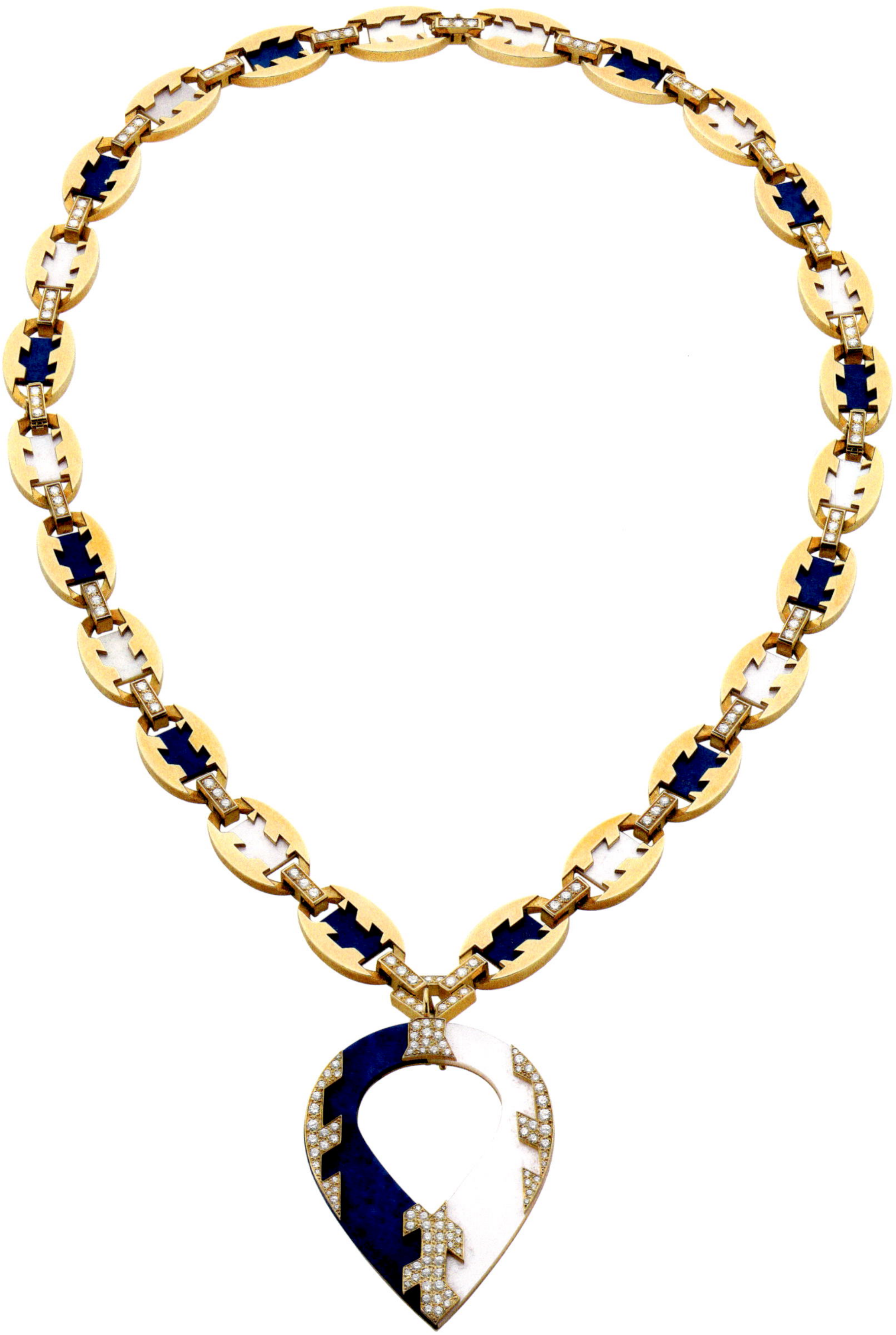

64. Sautoir, 1971

Gold with lapis lazuli, mother-of-pearl, and diamonds

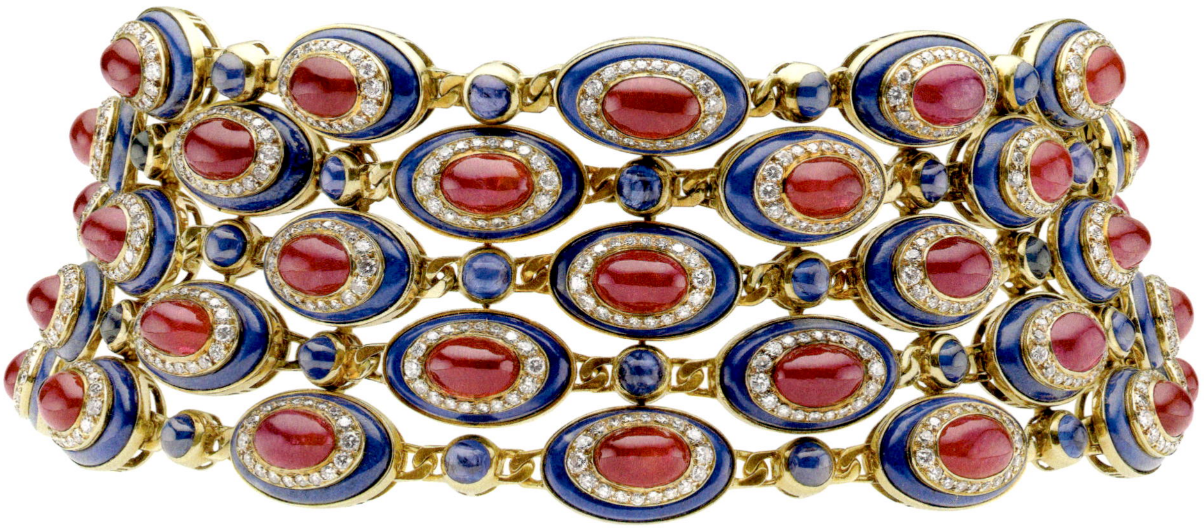

65. Choker, ca. 1979

Gold with rubies, sapphires, lapis lazuli, and diamonds

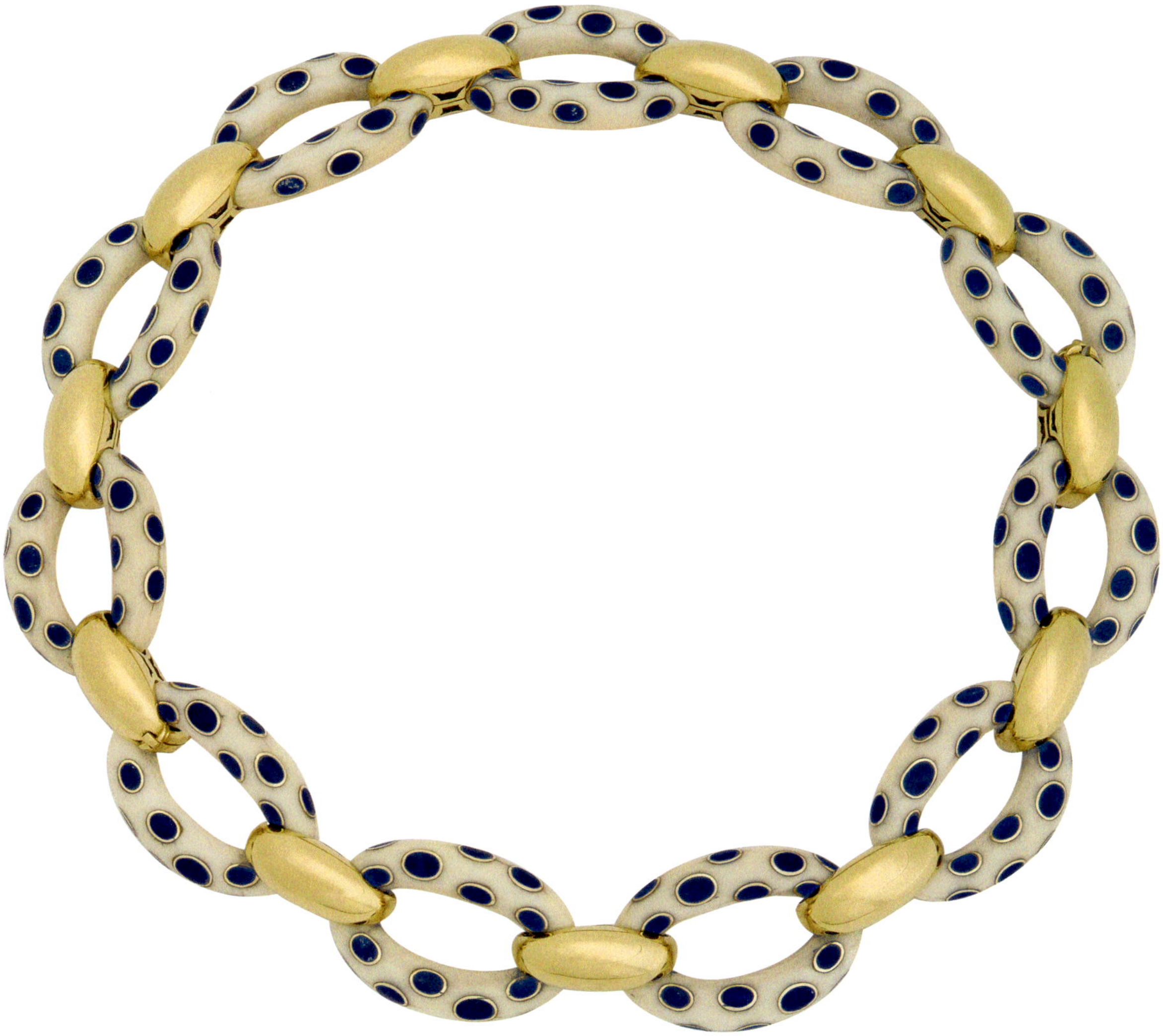

66. Necklace, 1971
Gold with ivory and lapis lazuli

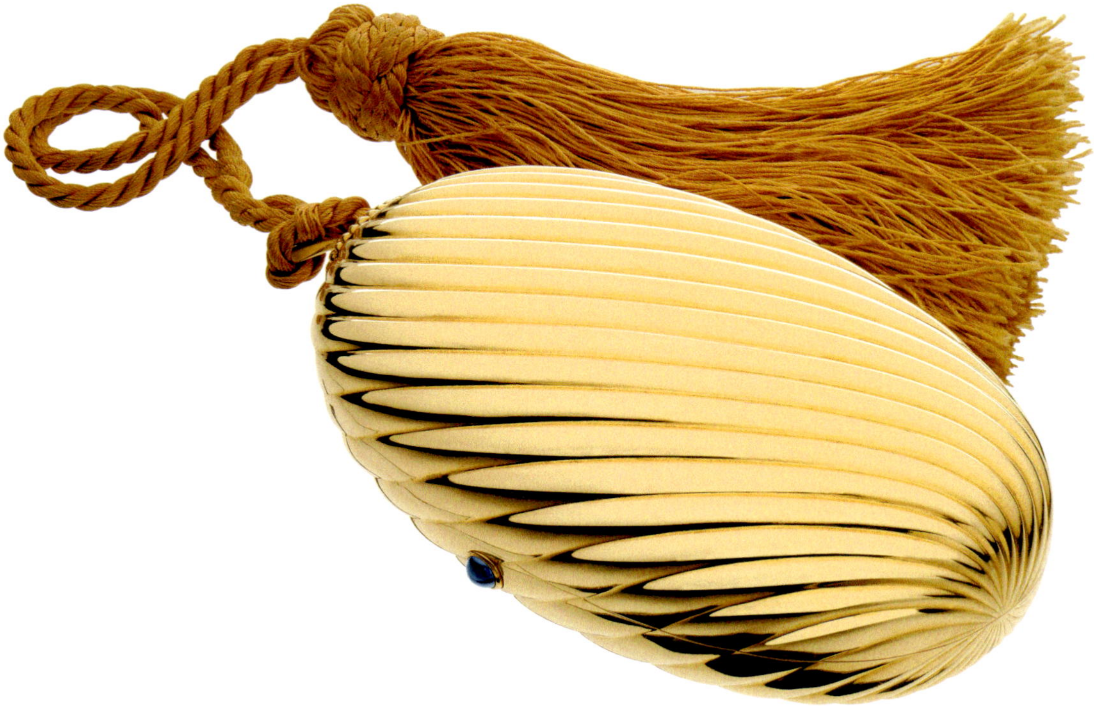

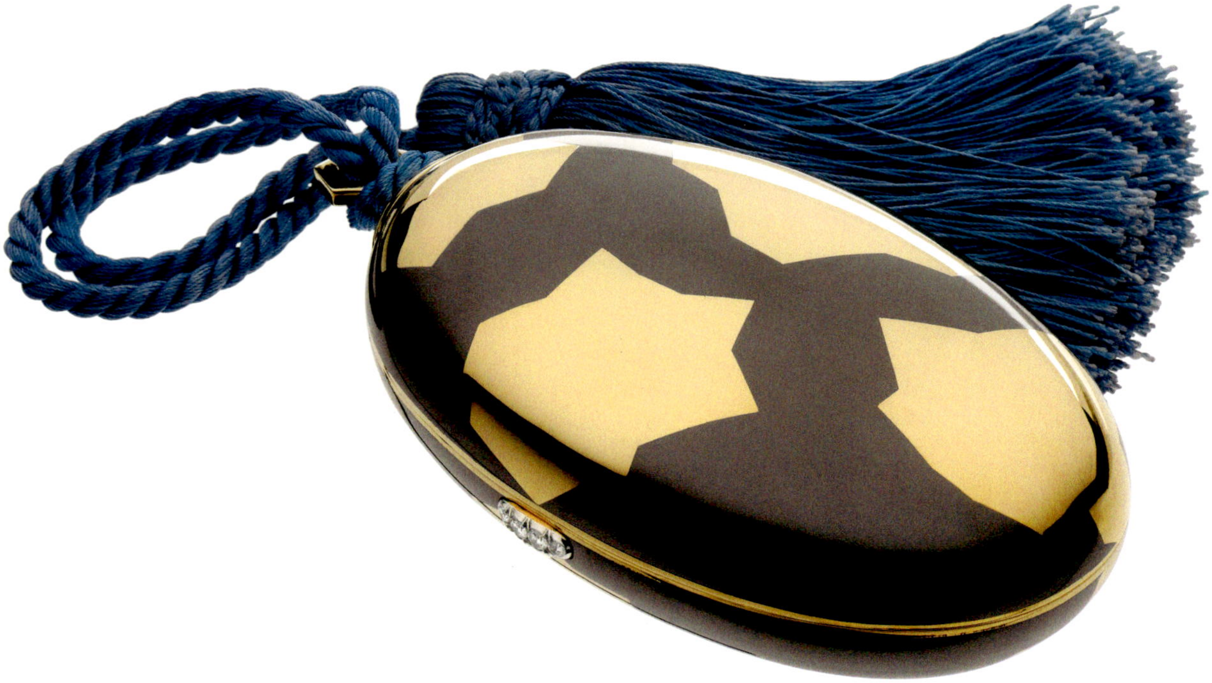

67. Melone evening bag, 1972
Gold with sapphire

68. Melone evening bag, ca. 1972
Gold and burnished steel with diamonds

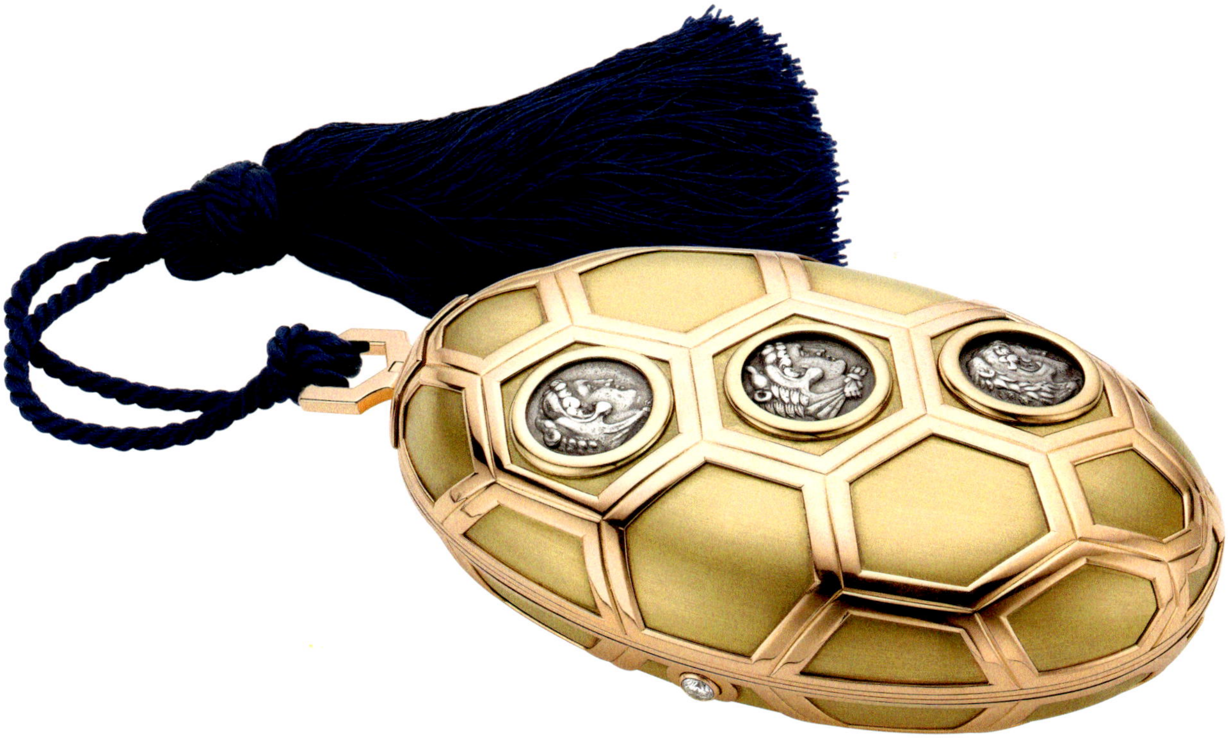

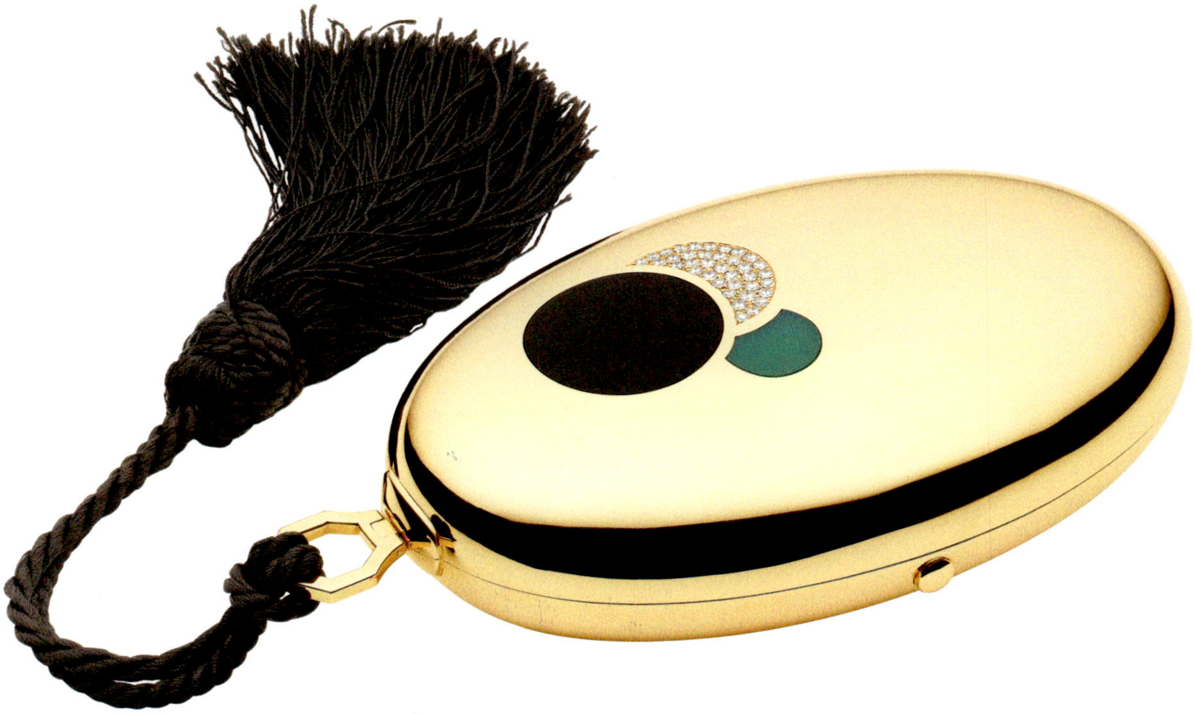

69. Melone evening bag, 1978
Gold with Hellenistic silver coins and diamond

70. Melone evening bag, ca. 1975
Gold with onyx, chrysoprase, and diamonds

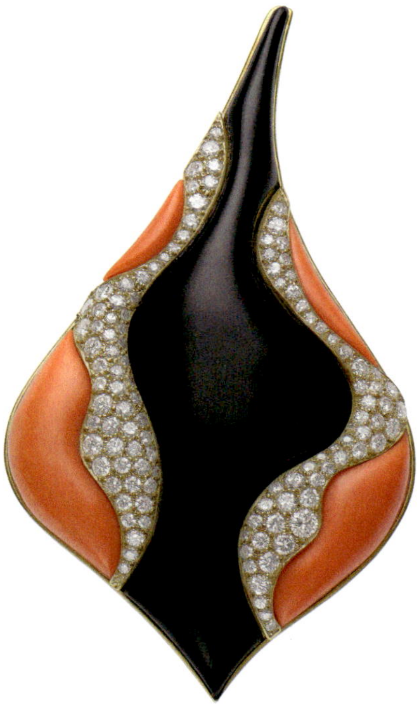

71. Brooch, 1973
Gold with onyx, coral, and diamonds

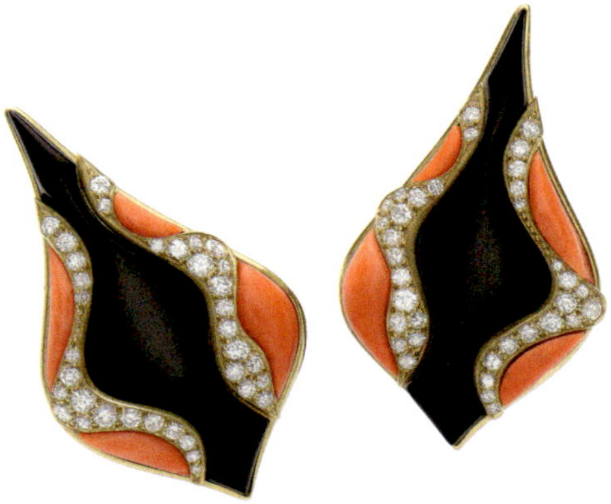

72. Earrings, 1973
Gold with onyx, coral, and diamonds

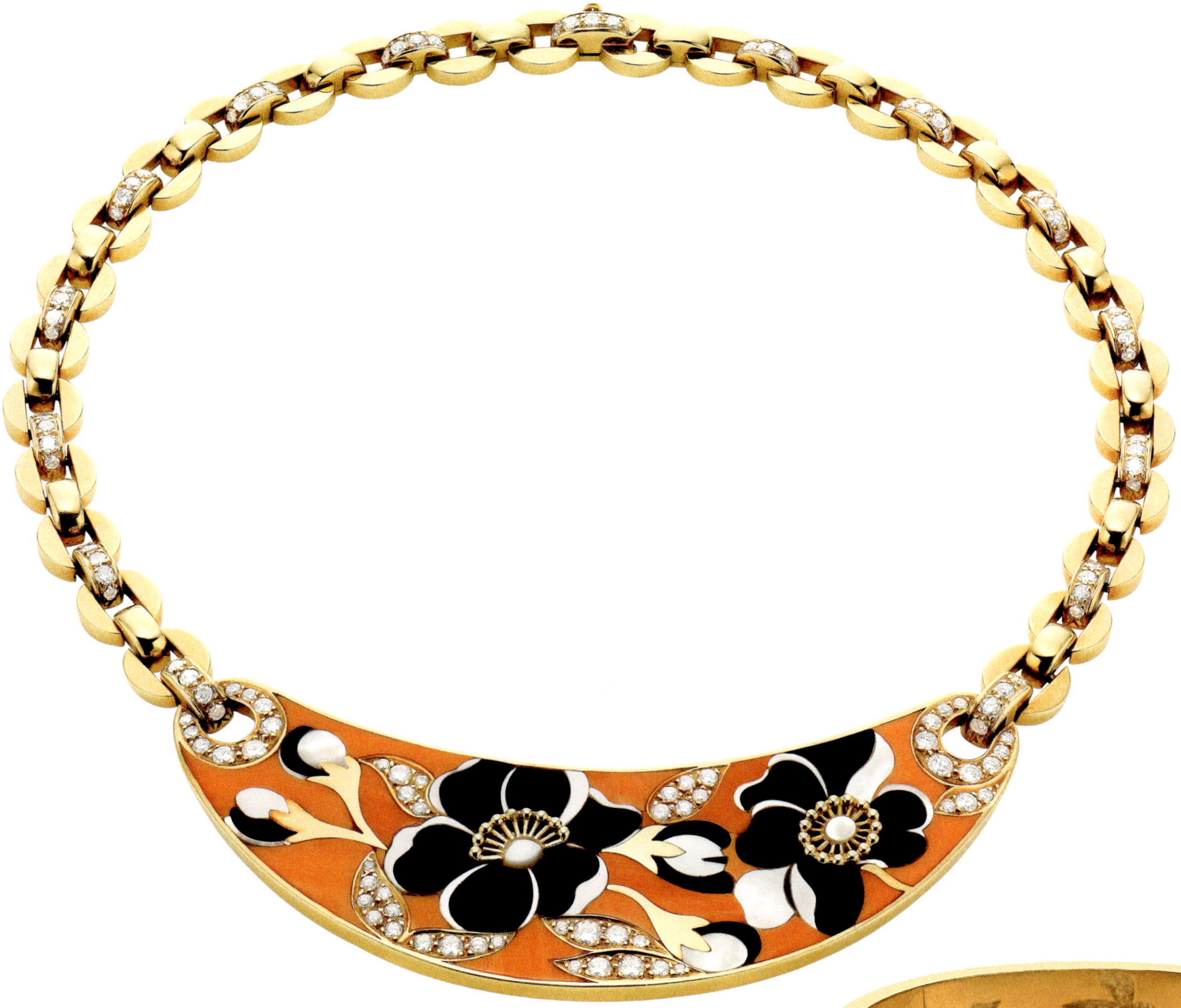

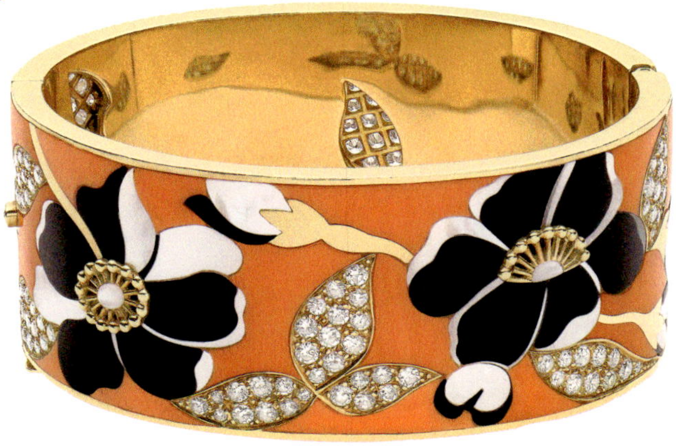

73. Necklace, 1977
Gold with coral, onyx, mother-of-pearl, and diamonds

74. Bangle, 1977
Gold with coral, onyx, mother-of-pearl, and diamonds

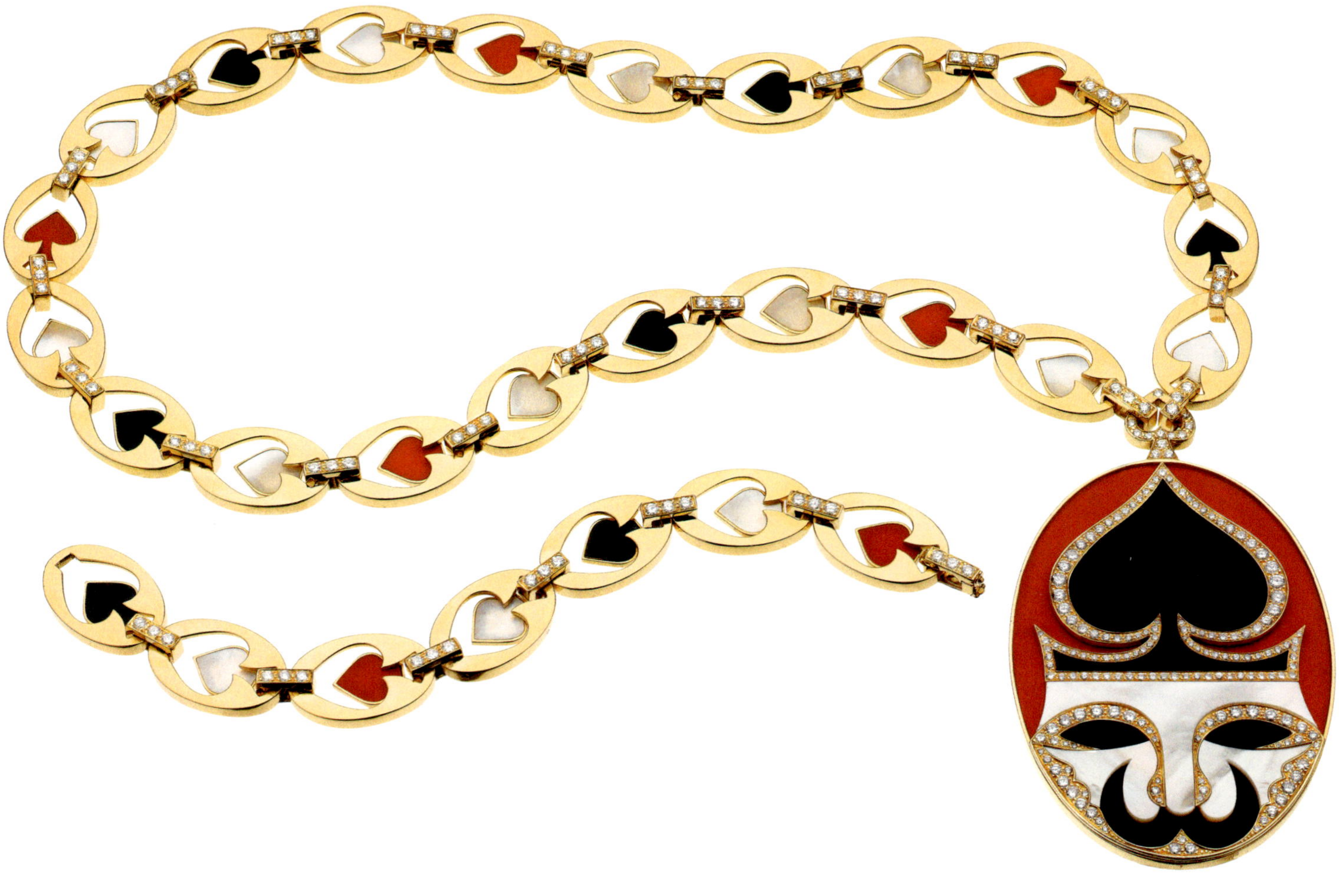

75. Playing card sautoir, 1972
Gold with coral, mother-of-pearl, onyx, and diamonds

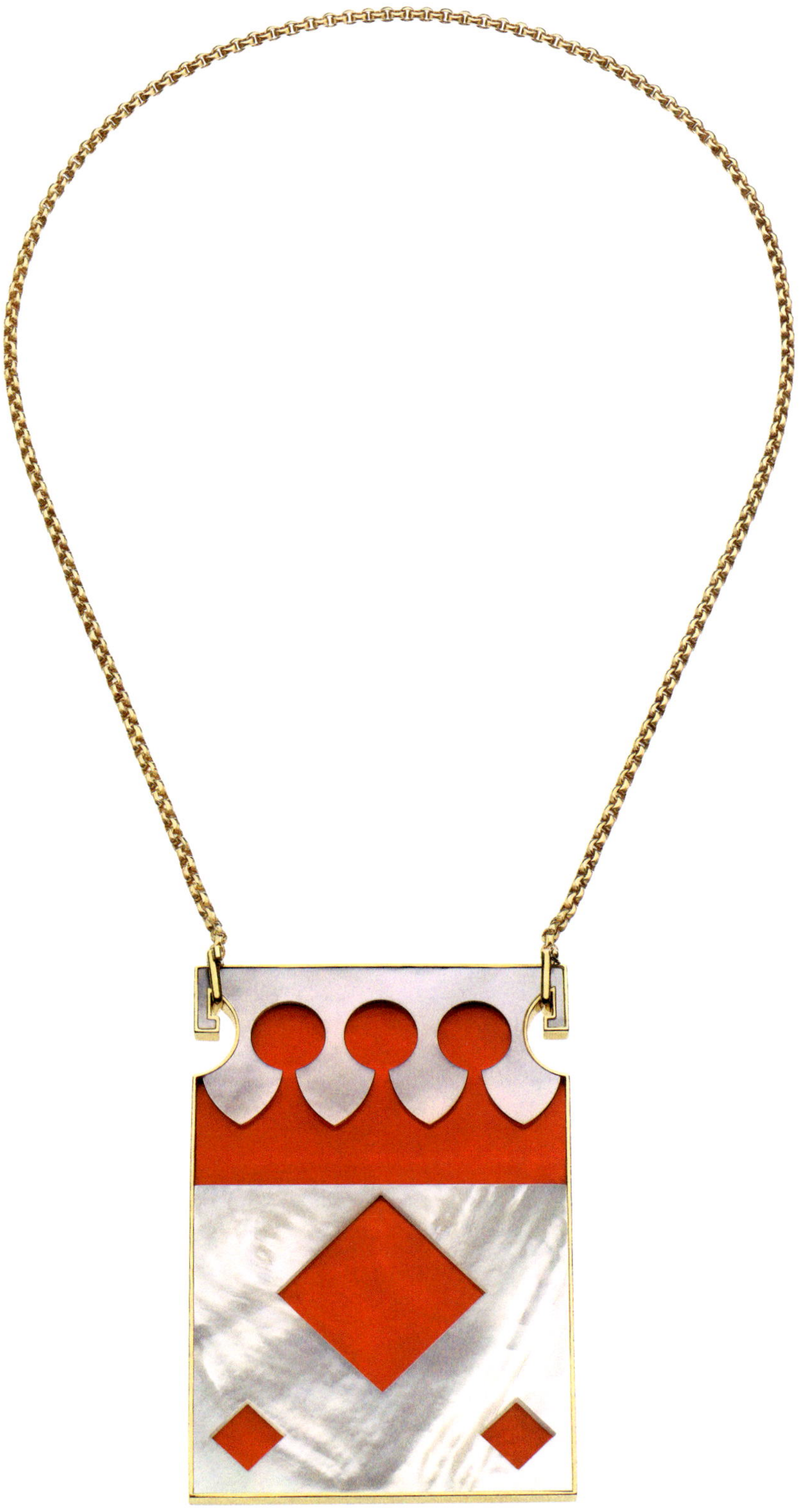

76. Playing card pendant on chain necklet, 1972
Gold with coral and mother-of-pearl

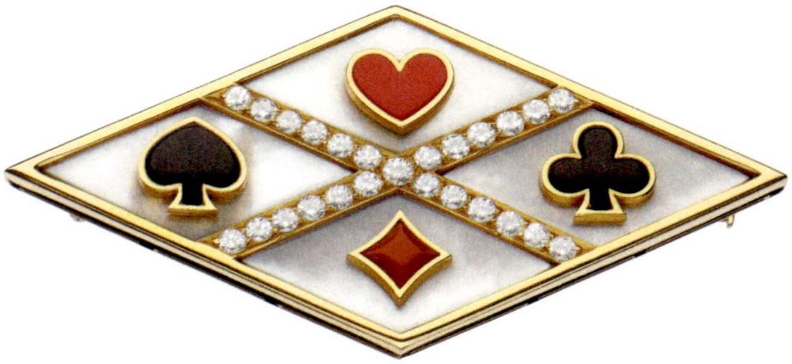

77. Playing card brooch, ca. 1975
Gold with mother-of pearl, coral, onyx, and diamonds

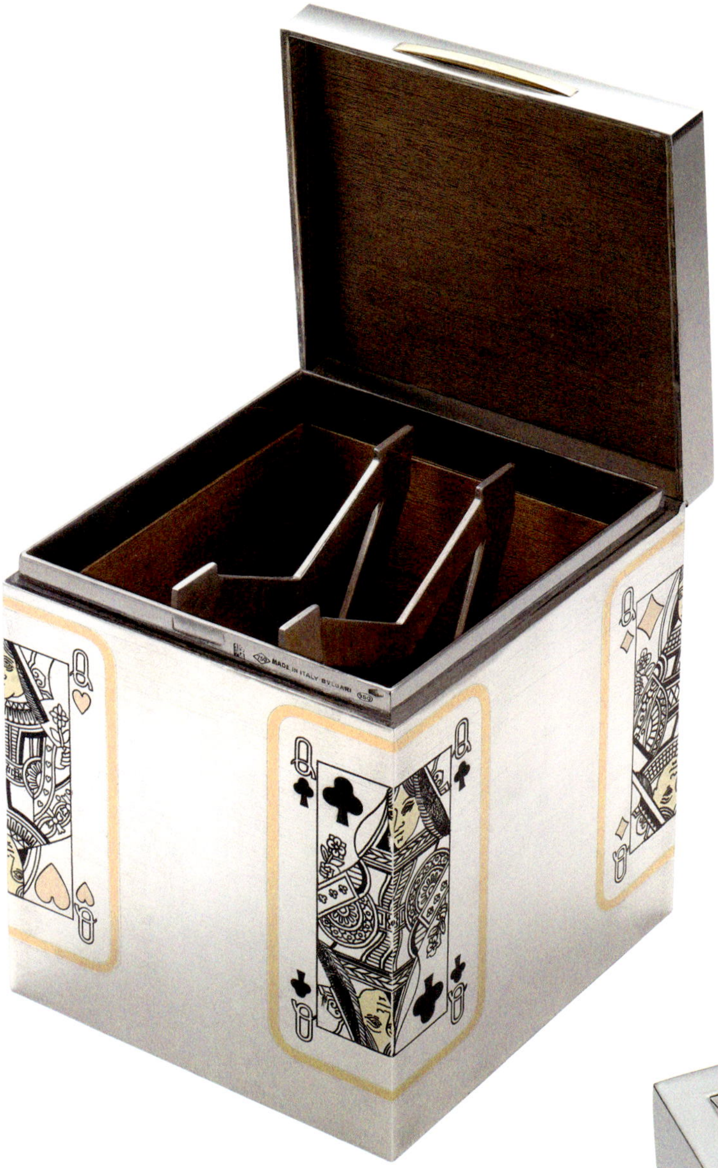

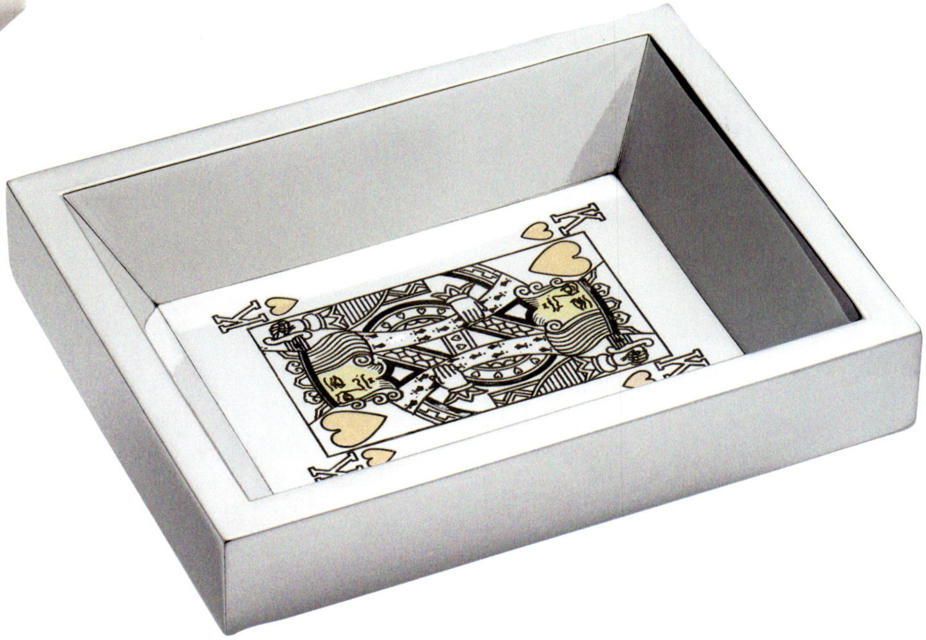

78. Playing card card box, 1974
Silver and two-color gold with black enamel

79. Playing card ashtray, 1974
Silver and two-color gold with enamel

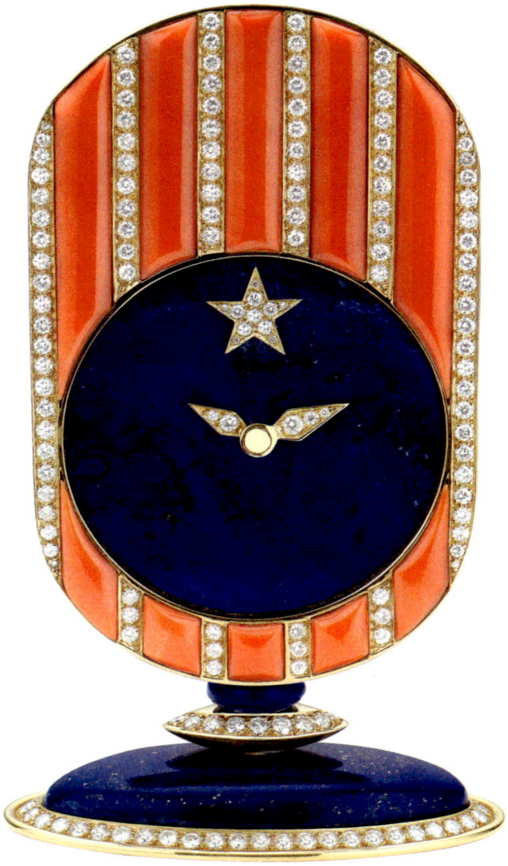

80. Star-Spangled Banner table clock, 1975
Gold with lapis lazuli, coral, and diamonds

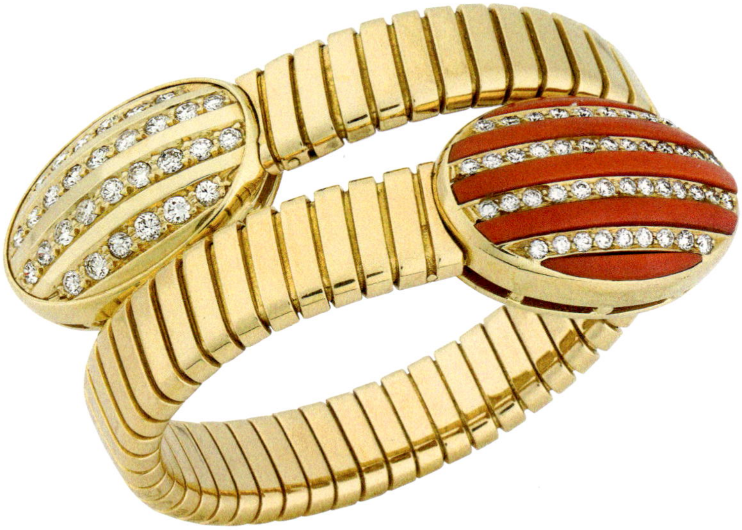

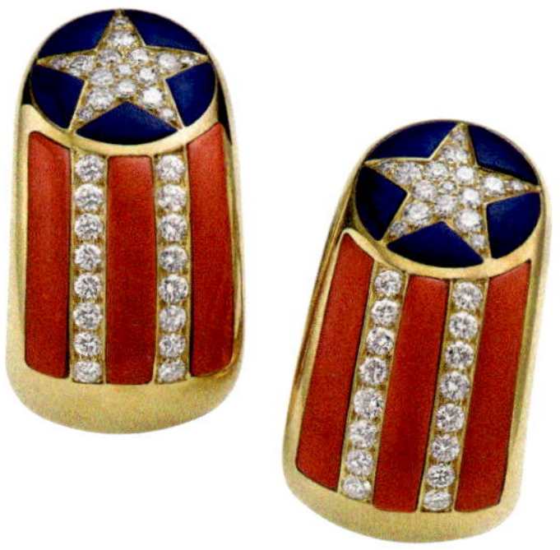

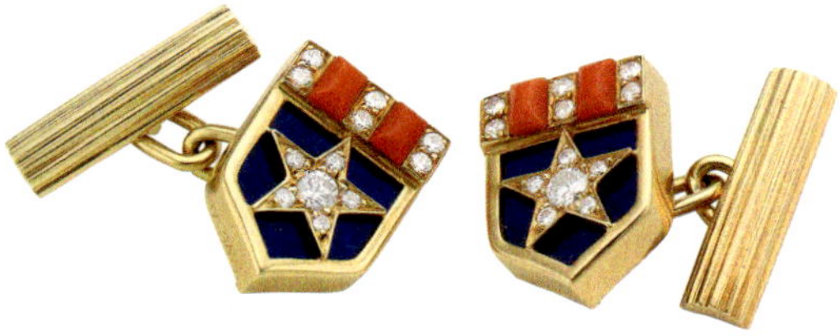

81. Star-Spangled Banner earrings, ca. 1975
Gold with coral, lapis lazuli, and diamonds

82. Star-Spangled Banner bracelet, ca. 1972
Gold with coral and diamonds

83. Star-Spangled Banner cuff links, ca. 1970–1976
Gold with coral, lapis lazuli, and diamonds

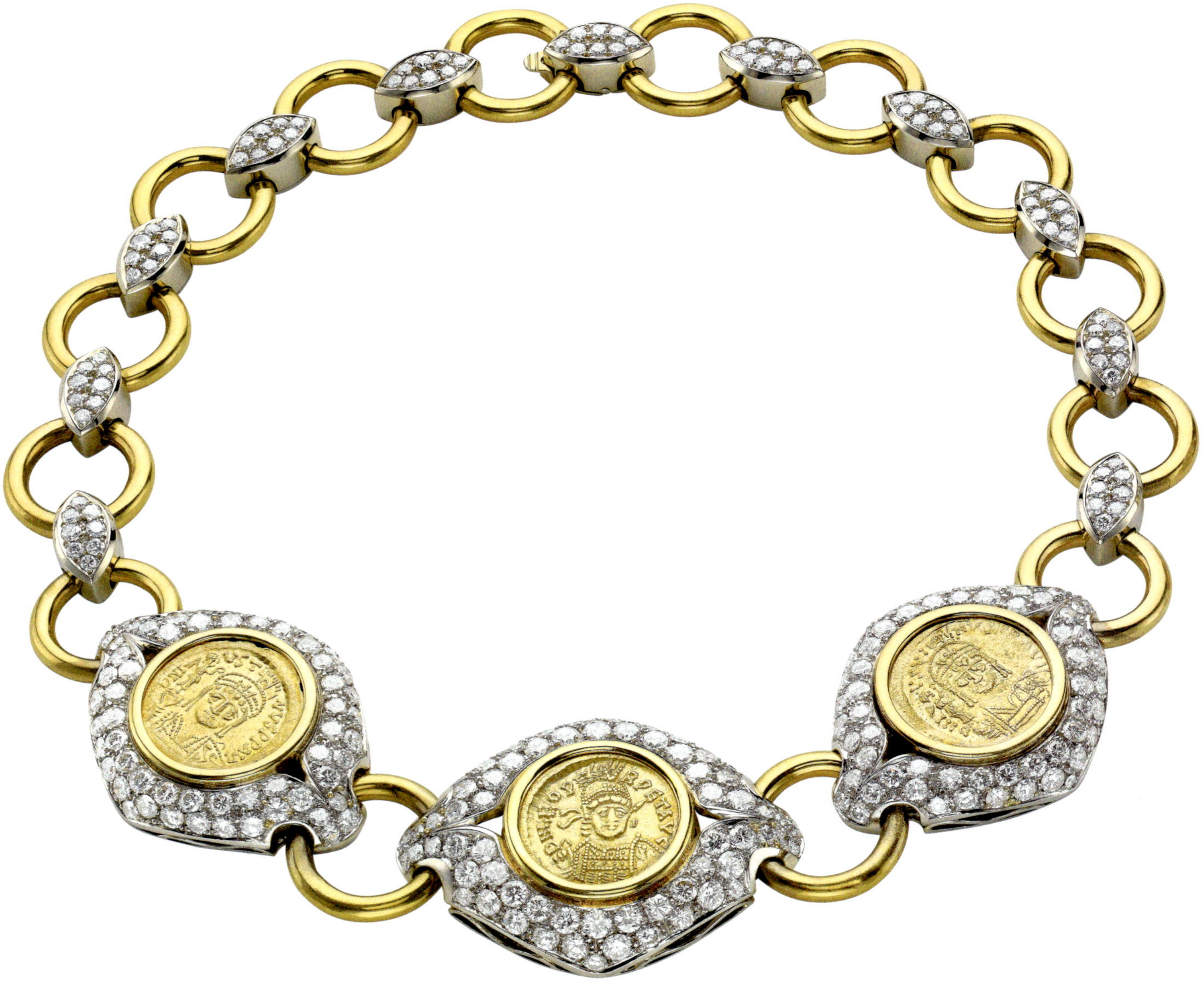

84. Necklace, 1966
Gold and platinum with Byzantine gold coins and diamonds

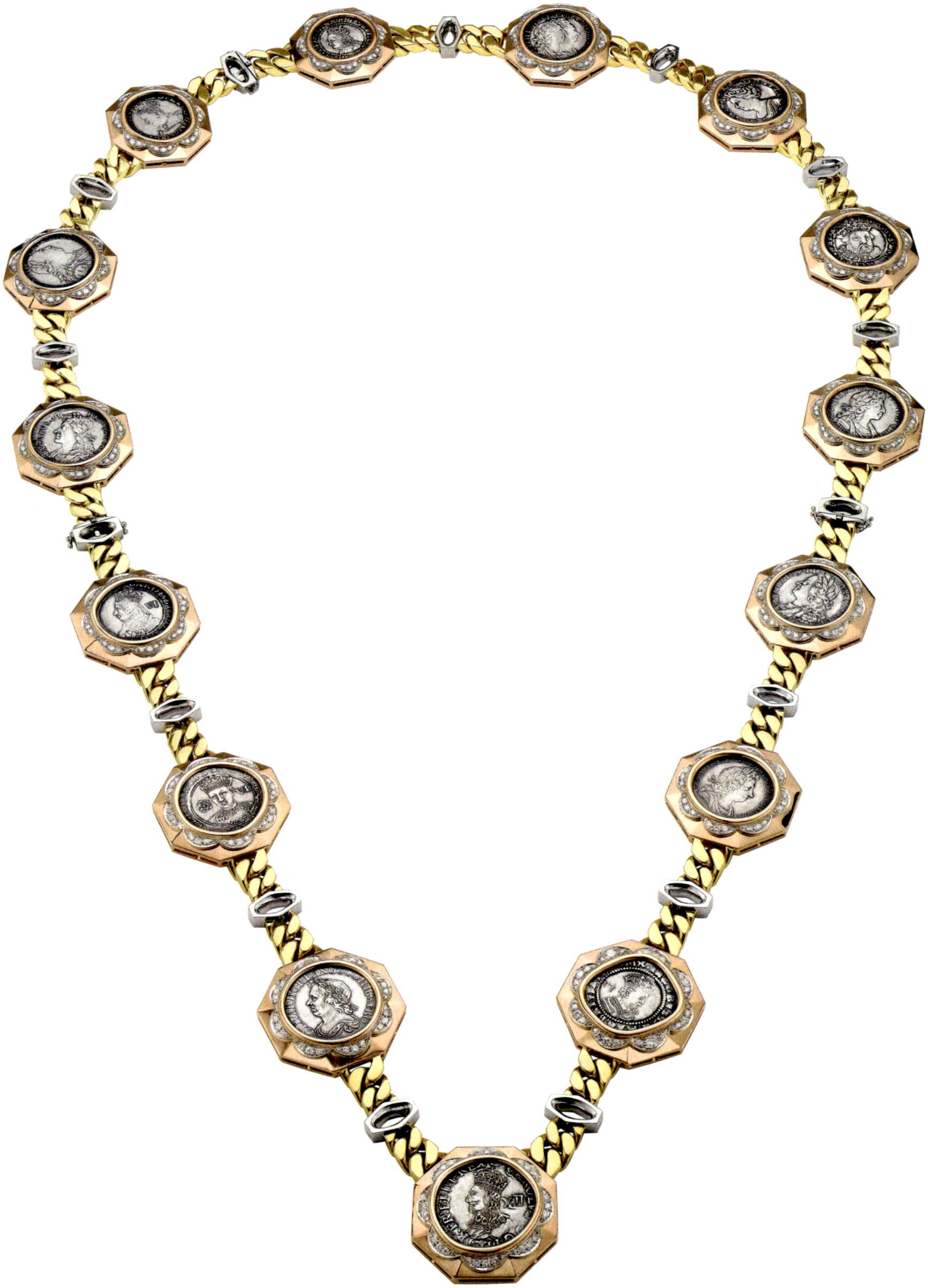

85. Sautoir, ca. 1973

Three-color gold with British silver coins and diamonds

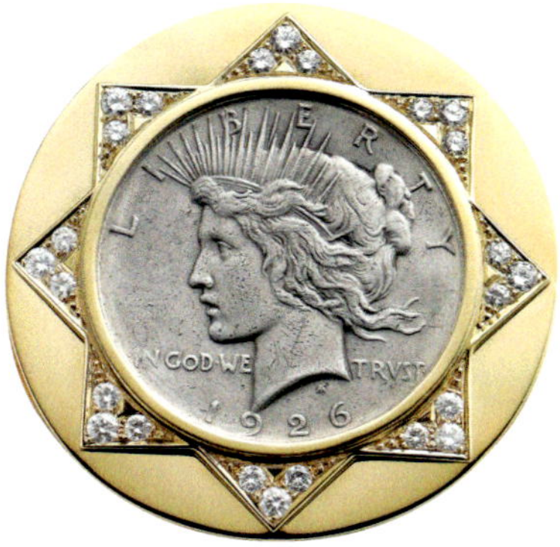

86. Brooch, 1973
Gold with American silver coin and diamonds

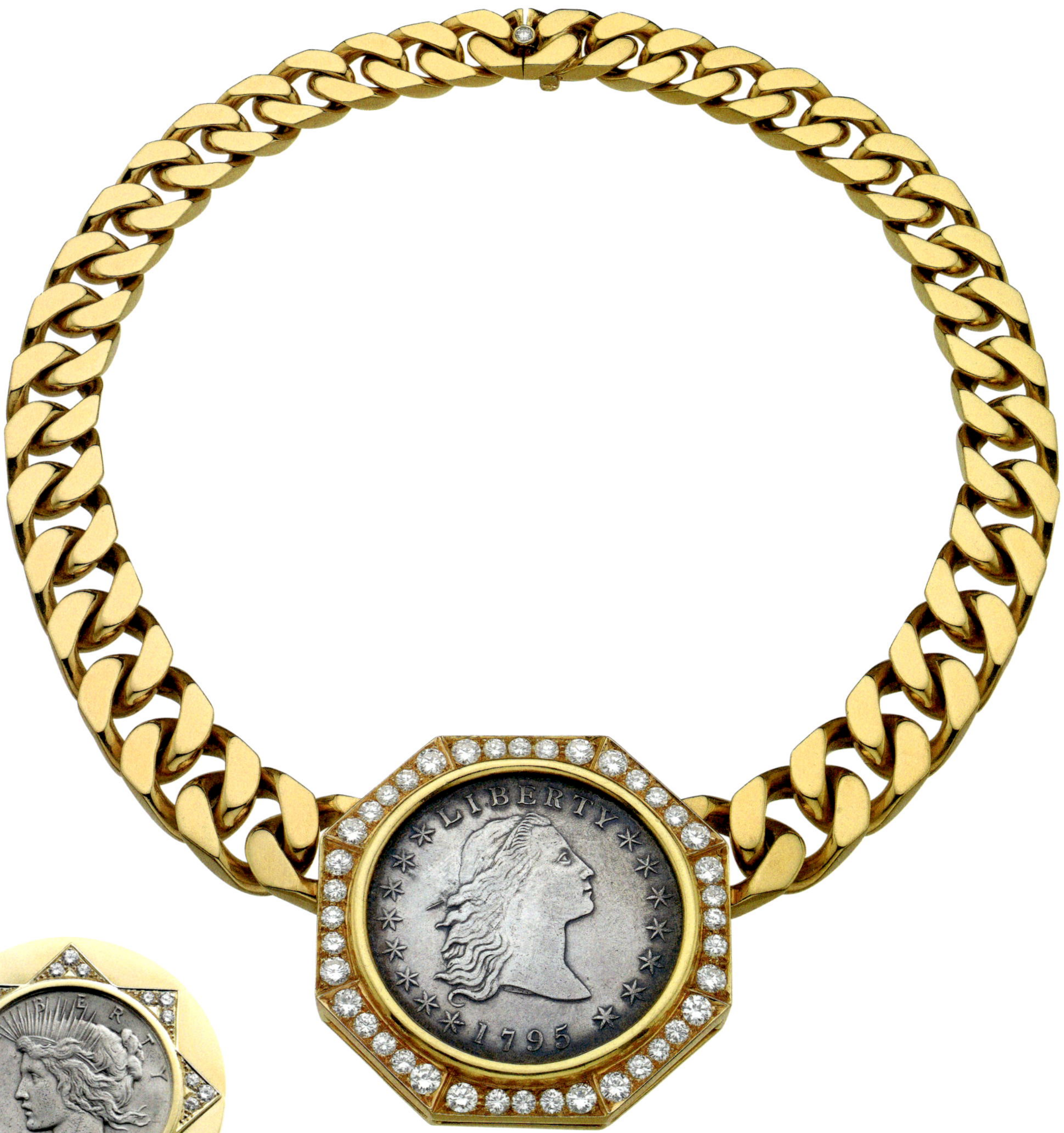

87. Necklace, ca. 1975
Gold with American silver coin and diamonds

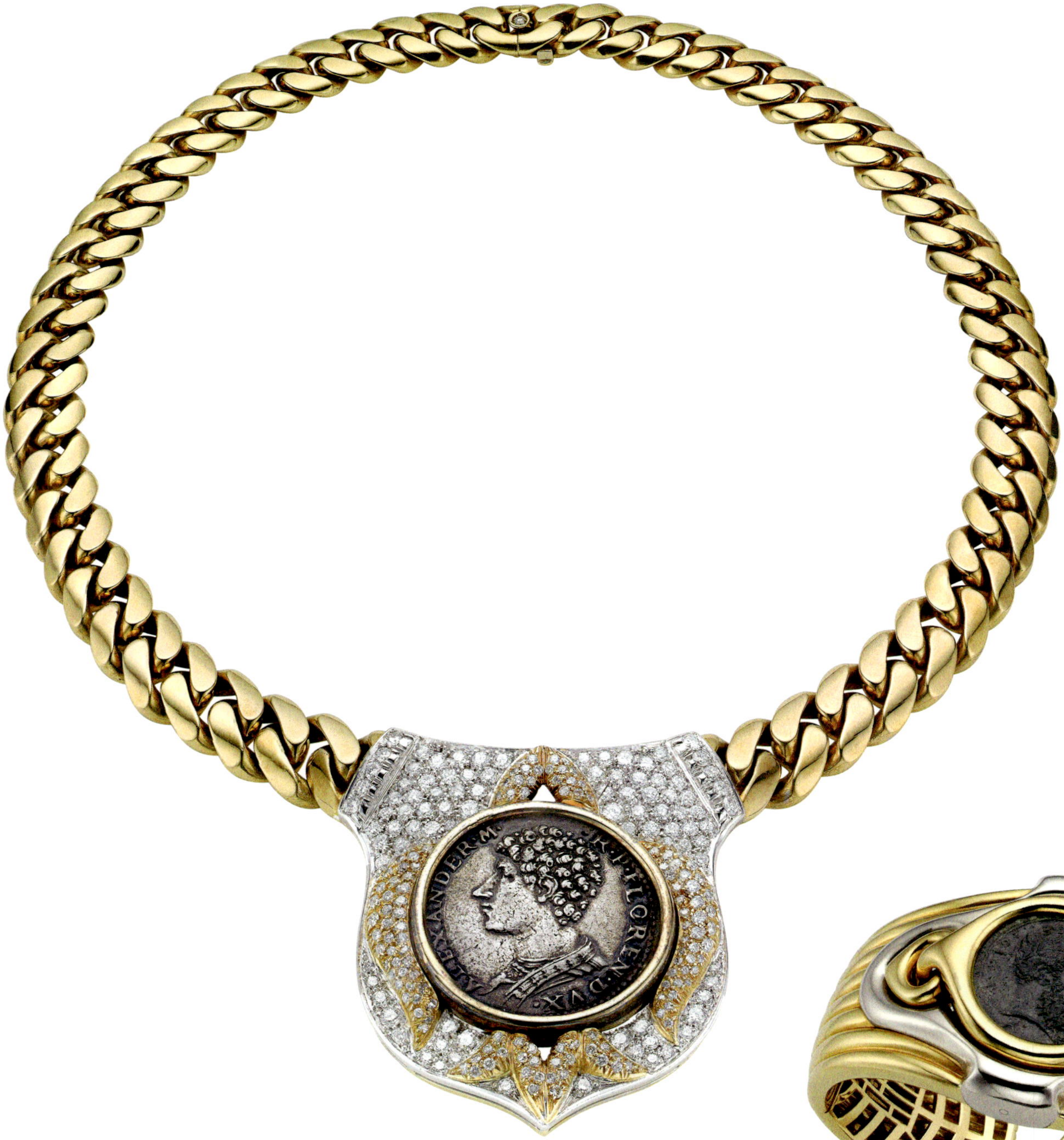

88. Necklace, ca. 1978
Gold with Florentine Renaissance silver coin and diamonds

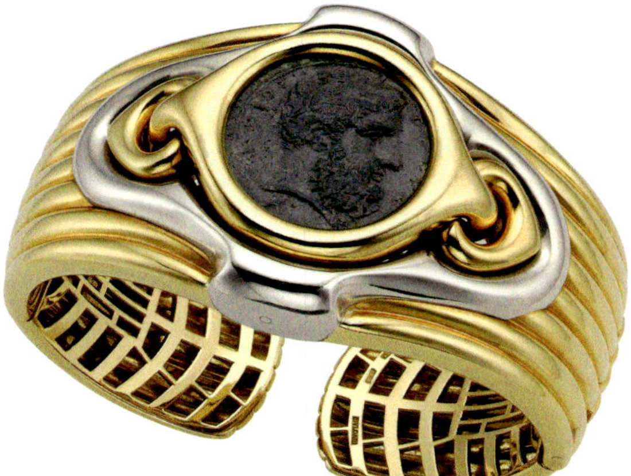

89. Bangle, 1983
Two-color gold with Greek bronze coin

The Elizabeth Taylor Collection

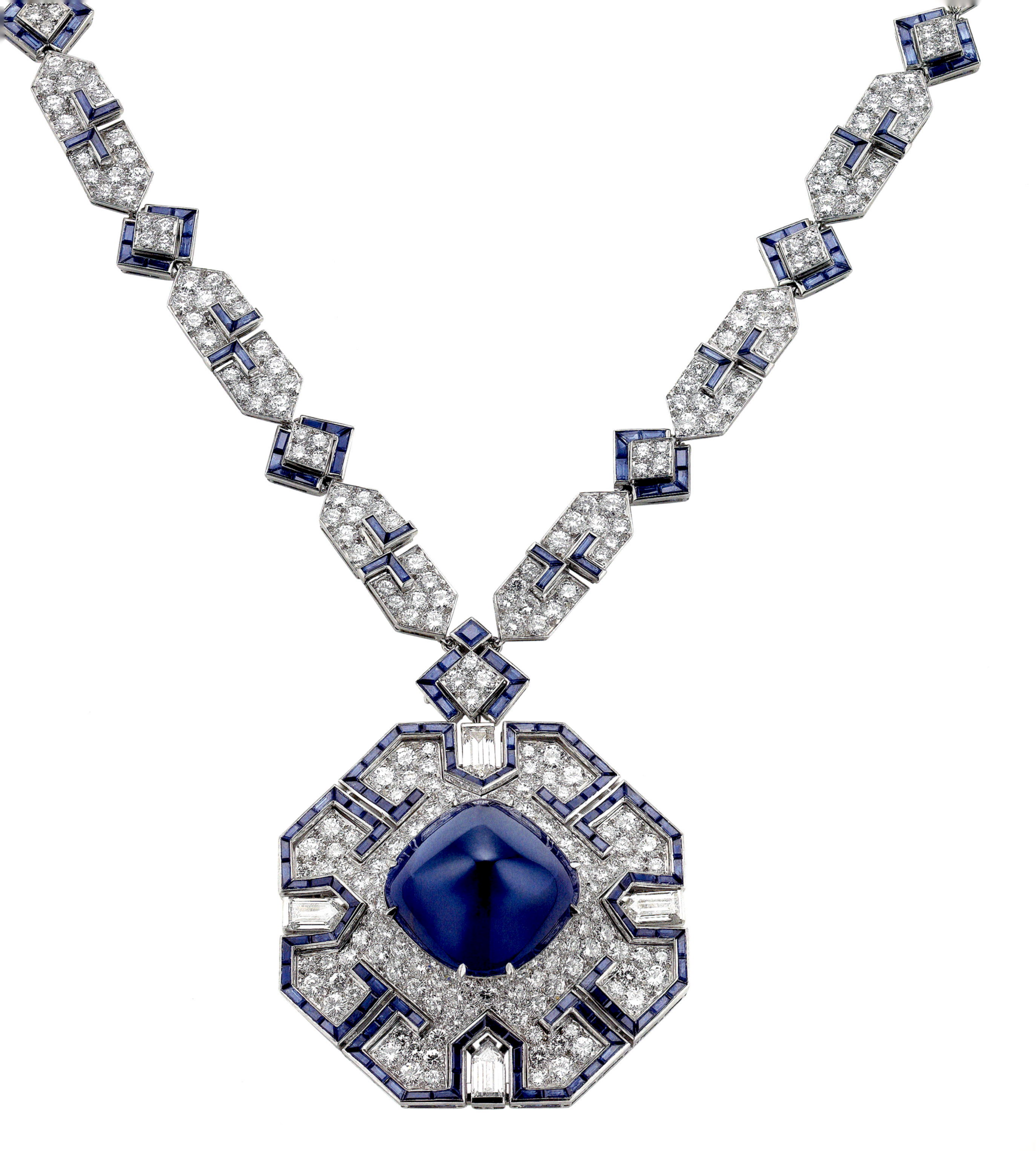

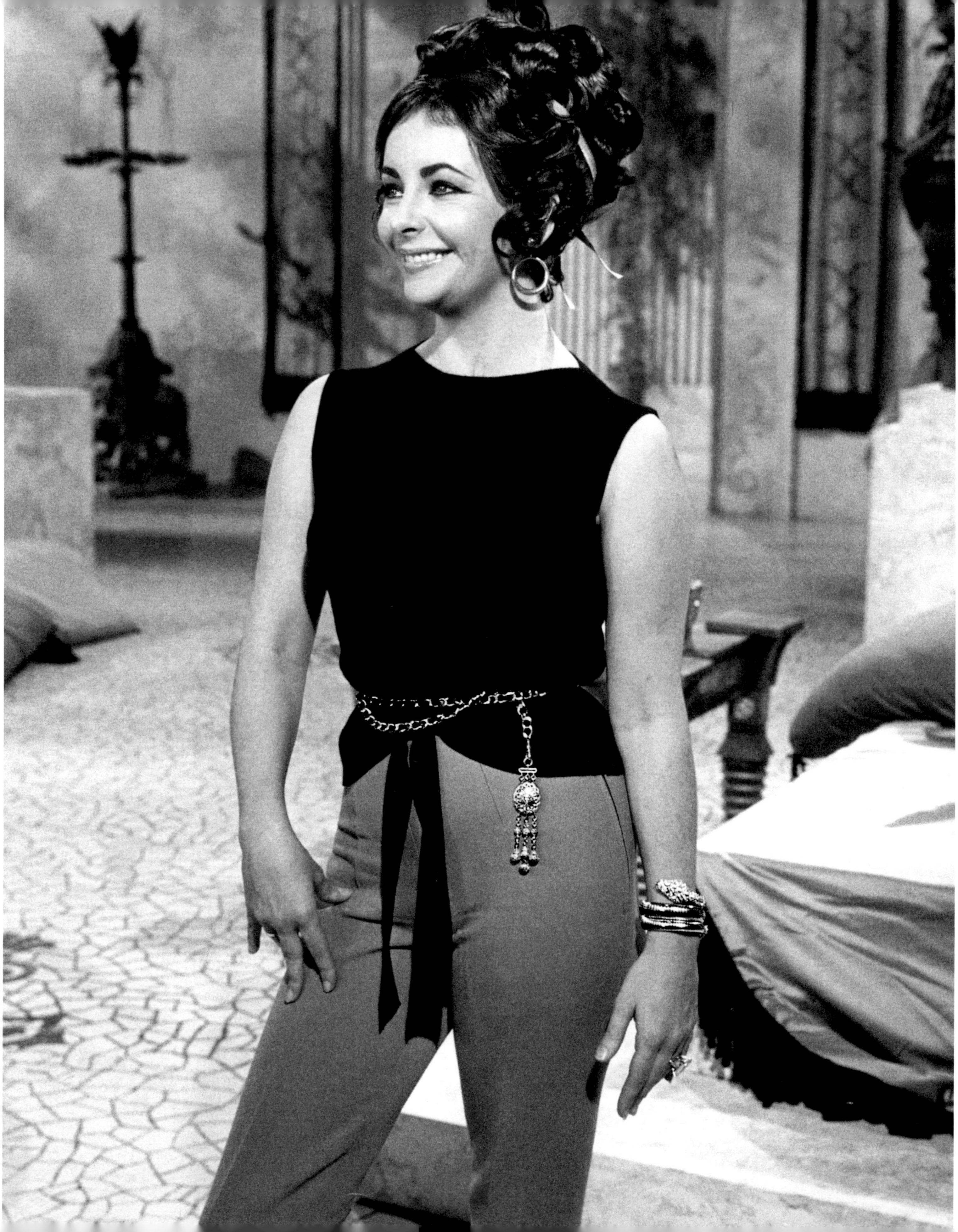

The Elizabeth Taylor Collection

All the jewels in this section, except the ruby and diamond pendant necklace (cat. 98), come from the personal collection of Dame Elizabeth Taylor.[1] They illustrate the tastes of one of the most famous film actresses of the twentieth century, a star whose passion for jewelry has become legendary. In her book *Elizabeth Taylor: My Love Affair with Jewelry* the actress presents her collection, one that comprises important pieces from many of the most prominent twentieth-century jewelers, including Boucheron, Cartier, JAR, Tiffany, Schlumberger, Van Cleef and Arpels, and, of course, Bulgari.[2] The collection features exceptional gemstones: the Krupp diamond and the Taylor-Burton diamond,[3] as well as gems of extraordinary historical interest, such as the natural pearl known as La Peregrina[4] and the engraved Taj Mahal diamond.[5]

Considering herself merely the temporary custodian of such magnificent works, Taylor wished that they be sold after her death. Thus impressive auctions of her jewels, as well as couture clothing, personal belongings, and art, were held in 2011 at Christie's New York. With earnings totaling more than 150 million dollars for the jewelry alone, it is not surprising that this has since been regarded as one of the most important jewelry auctions in recent times.

Drawing from the many photographs and publications about the actress, it can easily be said that Elizabeth Taylor had a particular predilection for Bulgari jewelry.[6] Ever since she discovered the shop on via dei Condotti in Rome, Taylor appeared for countless important occasions wearing Bulgari jewels. In her book she recalls: "Undeniably, one of the biggest advantages to working on *Cleopatra* in Rome was Bulgari's . . . shop. I used to visit Gianni Bulgari in the afternoons and we'd sit . . . and swap stories."[7] In 1966, at the time she received the Academy Award for Best Actress, she was immortalized wearing her magnificent Bulgari emerald necklace (cat. 92; see also fig. 45). She subsequently wore this necklace when she was introduced to Queen Elizabeth II; later in a famous portrait by Helmut Newton (1989), who photographed her in her Beverly Hills swimming pool, with her parrot on her shoulder;[8] and more recently, in 2003, at the Cannes Film Festival for an amfAR (the Foundation for AIDS Research) event. There are countless photos that show Taylor wearing Bulgari jewels on both formal and informal occasions, and she even decided to wear them in three of her films, *The V.I.P.s* (1963, see fig. 1), *Boom!* (1968, see fig. 9), and *Ash Wednesday* (1973, see fig. 46).

The selection of the pieces for her collection is indicative of the attention the actress paid to Bulgari's creations throughout her life. Numerous iconic Bulgari jewels are present: the *tremblant* brooches of the late 1950s to early 1960s; the serpent bracelet-watch (one of the first examples in gold, with a diamond head and tail and emerald eyes; see fig. 44); the sautoir, dating to 1969; and the necklaces with antique coins from the late 1970s to early 1980s (cat. 97; see also figs. 11, 43).

Particularly admirable examples of her *tremblant* brooches include one from 1959 with yellow diamonds in shades ranging from golden yellow to cognac (cat. 90) and an emerald version of 1960

Fig. 44. Elizabeth Taylor on the set of *Cleopatra*, wearing her Bulgari snake bracelet-watch, 1962

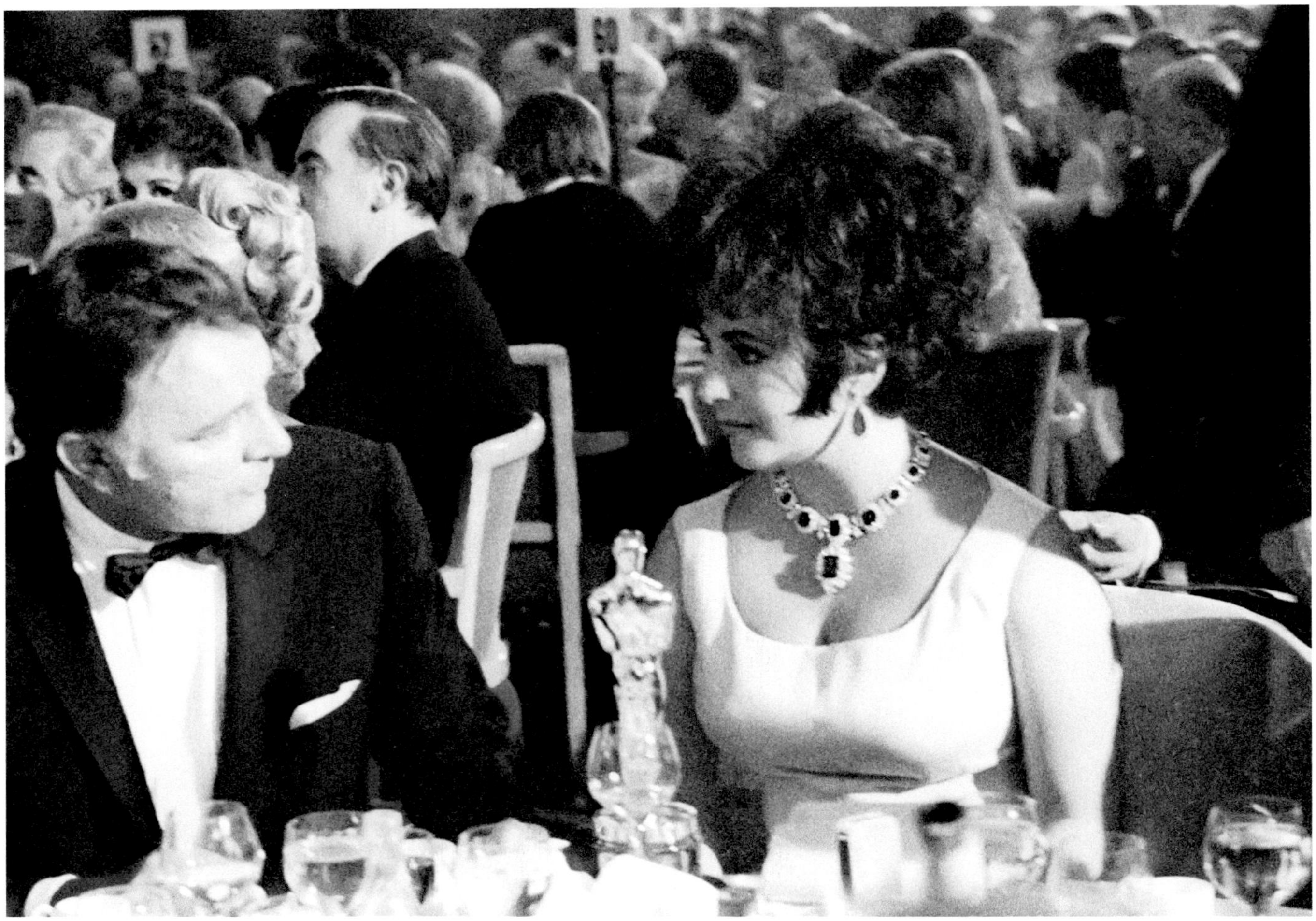

Fig. 45. Taylor, in her Bulgari necklace of platinum, emeralds, and diamonds (cat. 92), with Richard Burton at the British Academy of Film and Television Arts Awards, London, 1967

(cat. 91). A pair of long drop earrings, a ring (cat. 93), and a bracelet, all made from emeralds, completed the "green set" together with the marvelous emerald and diamond brooch and necklace. Such was the beauty of these emeralds that the press often referred to them as "the Grand Duchess Vladimir's Suite," although the principal stones of that famous collection had in fact been set into a tiara owned by Barbara Hutton (see fig. 5).[9]

The elegant diamond sautoir of 1969 (cat. 96; see also fig. 49), with its calibré-cut sapphires and octagonal pendant crowned by a sugarloaf cabochon Burmese sapphire of 52.72 carats, is a particularly valuable and exquisite piece—one that also anticipated Bulgari's iconic sautoirs of the 1970s. Interestingly, it is one of the rare sautoirs, if not the only one of its time, that was mounted in platinum rather than yellow gold.

Any reference to these jewels inevitably entails mention of the scandal that involved this beautiful actress in 1962 when, during filming of the blockbuster *Cleopatra*, Taylor and British actor Richard Burton fell in love and engaged in an adulterous affair. Occupying the headlines worldwide, the story

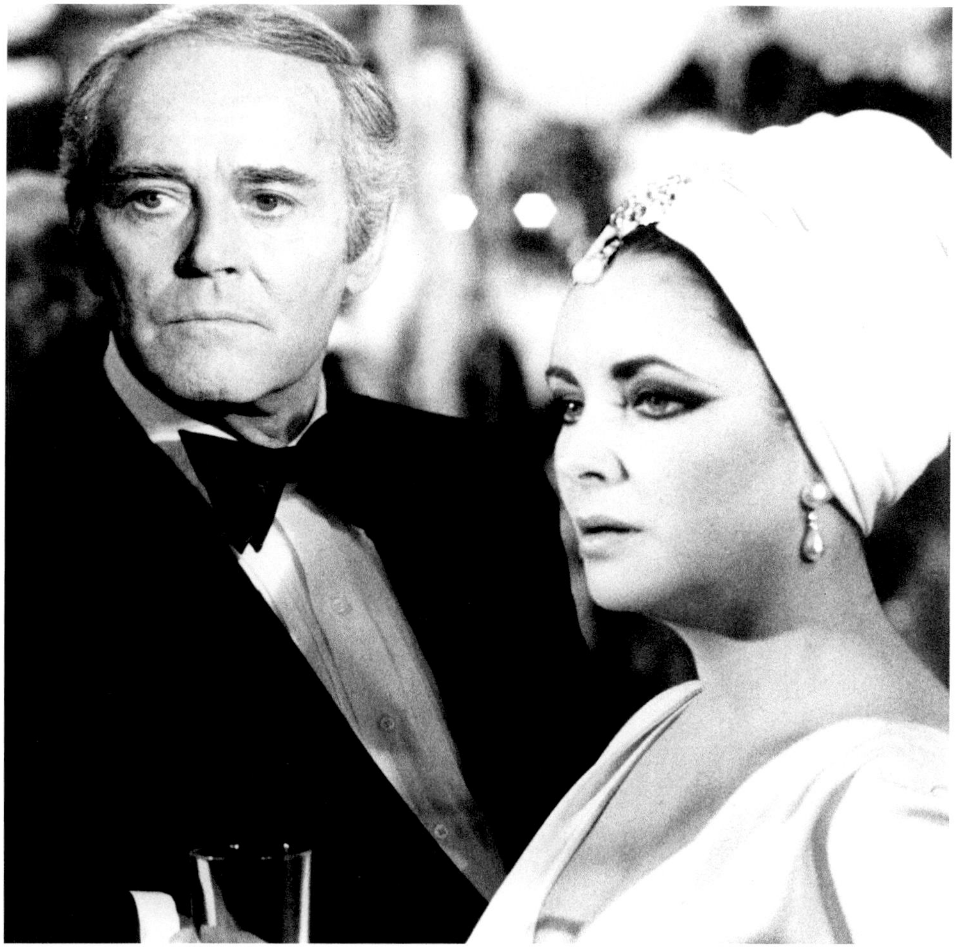

Fig. 46. The actress, wearing her own Bulgari drop earrings of pearls and diamonds, with Henry Fonda in *Ash Wednesday*, 1973

unfolded at Cinecittà and, naturally, at Bulgari. Taylor's fourth husband, Eddie Fisher, understood the powerful effect jewelry had on his wife and was accustomed to buying her pieces from Bulgari. For Burton, however, it was a new experience, and he purportedly quipped, "I introduced Liz to beer, she introduced me to Bulgari."[10] A salesperson from the via dei Condotti shop recalled taking a selection of jewels to the film set, where Burton picked out a diamond and emerald ring. A few days later, a beautiful and elegant lady walked into the Bulgari shop asking if the ring could be resized; the lady turned out to be Burton's wife, Sybil. Fisher also made a desperate attempt to save his marriage by giving Taylor three magnificent Bulgari jewels with yellow and white diamonds for her thirtieth birthday: the *tremblant* brooch (cat. 90) and a ring and pendant earrings set with pear-shaped yellow diamonds of 15.68 and 16.2 carats, respectively. A few months later, however, by which time the couple had already separated, Fisher sent Taylor the bill for the jewels. In her book, she comments, "Did I end up paying the bill? Mmmm, probably."[11]

During an interview years later, the actress recalled Burton's generosity in buying her Bulgari jewels, and how happy it made her to choose them with him.[12] Among the most important pieces Taylor

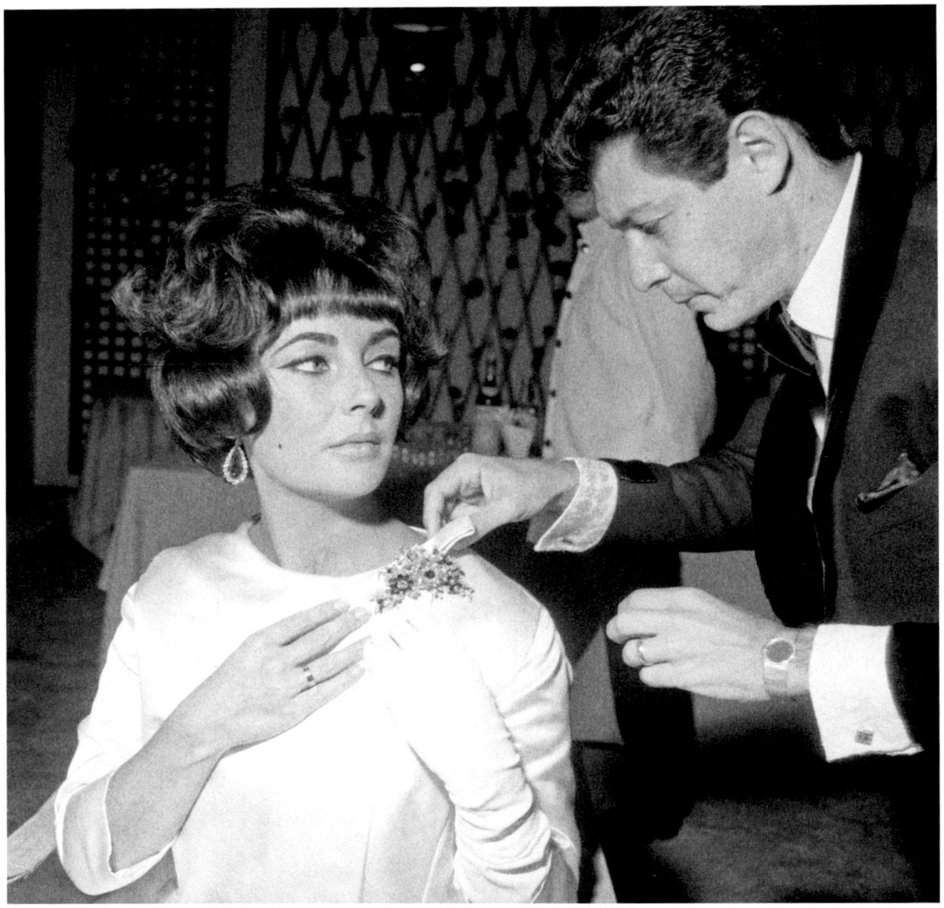

Fig. 47. Eddie Fisher adjusting his wife's Bulgari *tremblant* brooch (cat. 91), Rome, 1961

received from the British actor is the "green set" brooch featuring an exceptional Colombian octagonal, step-cut 23.44-carat emerald surrounded by radiating pear-shaped diamonds, which he gave her in 1962 as an engagement gift (see figs. 1, 48). Two years later, in 1964, he bought her the emerald necklace as a wedding gift. The brooch was subsequently adapted to also be attached as a centerpiece for the necklace. On her fortieth birthday, in 1972, Taylor received the sautoir with its deep velvety blue sugarloaf Burmese cabochon sapphire and a matching ring (cat. 95).

Paolo Bulgari, recalling the couple's visits to the via dei Condotti shop, said: "I remember they were both always very interested in the history behind every piece of jewelry they looked at. . . . When he picked up a piece, he looked to her to see her reaction: there was always an electricity in the air, a kind of telepathy so he always knew what she preferred. I think they had a very special relationship with jewels."[13]

The platinum cluster ring set with an octagonal step-cut emerald of approximately 7.4 carats with a border of pear-shaped diamonds was the first present Burton gave Taylor. The actress chose to sell it in 2002 at a charity auction to raise money for the Elizabeth Taylor AIDS Foundation.[14] Following the sale, in a letter to the new owners, Taylor wrote, "Wear it with love!"[15]

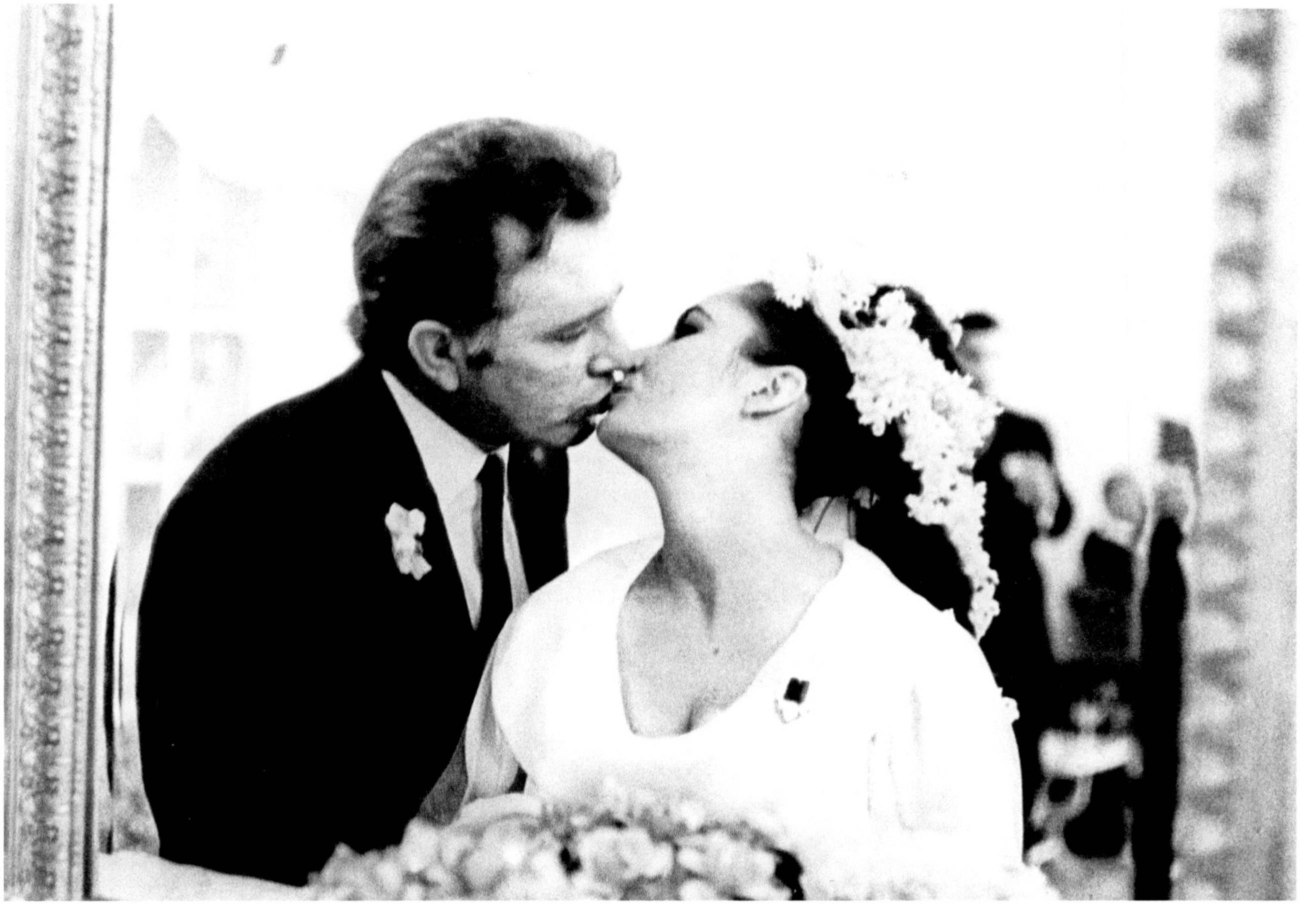

Fig. 48. Taylor, wearing her Bulgari Colombian emerald brooch (shown attached to necklace, cat. 92), with Richard Burton on their wedding day, 1964

For the same 2002 charity auction, Taylor asked each of her favorite jewelers to make and contribute a bespoke item of jewelry. Bulgari presented a ruby and diamond heart-shaped pendant suspended on a gold and ruby-bead chain (cat. 98), now in a distinguished private collection. The use of the red heart, symbol of love, clearly denotes Taylor's passionate involvement in the fight against AIDS. From 1984 until her death in 2011 Elizabeth Taylor spoke out against hypocrisy and discrimination toward people with HIV and AIDS, and she asked for compassion and care amid this major epidemic. She lent her voice, her generosity, and indeed her heart to raising the public's awareness of, and to changing its attitude toward, the disease.

An air of mystery surrounds the gold hand mirror bearing an Egyptian-inspired design of a raptor that is set with calibré-cut turquoise (cat. 94). Although it is inscribed Bulgari, and there is confirmation in the archival records of its creation in 1962 (when *Cleopatra* was being filmed), the donor of the gift to the actress remains anonymous. The present may have come from an admirer, for it was a known fact that Taylor received jewels from her friends and from her husbands. (This helps explain how she amassed her vast and extraordinary collection despite her statement, "I never planned to acquire a lot of jewels."[16]) It is just as likely that the film company, Twentieth Century Fox, commissioned Bulgari to make the mirror with its very obvious Egyptian attributes as a memento for the actress who had played the role of the queen.[17] Yet the existence of this magnificent mirror was little known until it was illustrated, in 2011, in the Christie's auction catalogue *The Collection of Elizabeth Taylor*.

As a result of the sale of Taylor's holdings, seven magnificent pieces of jewelry were bought back by Bulgari for the company's own permanent collection. By doing this, Bulgari fulfilled Taylor's wish that her jewels be shared by many and bring delight to others. Commenting on her wish to sell her collection, she said, "I wanted to share my collection with others so that they could get a glimpse of the joys, the thrills, and the pure happiness that these beautiful creations have given me."[18]

1. During Elizabeth Taylor's lifetime she was given numerous awards for her humanitarian work: she received the French Legion of Honor in 1987, was named a Dame Commander of the Order of the British Empire in 2000, and received a Presidential Citizens Medal in 2001. By the end of her life the fame she achieved for her humanitarian commitments arguably equaled her renown as a legendary star of the stage and screen.

2. Elizabeth Taylor, *Elizabeth Taylor: My Love Affair with Jewelry* (London: Thames & Hudson, 2002).

3. The Krupp diamond is an Asscher-cut 33.19-carat gem mounted as a ring. It was included in the collection of jewels sold at Christie's New York in 2011, as lot 80, and was renamed the "Elizabeth Taylor diamond" for the occasion. The Taylor-Burton diamond is a 69.42-carat pear-shaped gem; it was bought by Richard Burton in 1969 for a record price at that time and given to Taylor as the centerpiece of a necklace. The actress sold this diamond during her lifetime.

4. La Peregrina is the name of a natural drop pearl found in the Gulf of Panama by a slave at the beginning of the sixteenth century. A wedding present from King Philip II of Spain to his English queen, Mary Tudor, it was subsequently returned to the Spanish crown, and was worn by countless queens. Immortalized by Diego Velázquez in his magnificent court portraits, the pearl belonged to the Bonaparte family during the nineteenth century, and was bought by Richard Burton in 1969.

5. It is generally thought that in 1627, upon the order of the Mughal Shah Jahangir, the diamond was engraved with the name of his wife. This jewel was shown in the exhibition *Masterpieces of French Jewelry* at the Legion of Honor, San Francsico, February 10–June 10, 1997.

6. Taylor, *My Love Affair with Jewelry*; see also *The Collection of Elizabeth Taylor: The Legendary Jewels, Evening Sale* (New York: Christie's, 2011).

7. Taylor, *My Love Affair with Jewelry*, 56.

8. Helmut Newton chose this portrait photograph of Elizabeth Taylor for the front cover of the second edition of his book *Portraits* (Munich: Schirmer/Mosel, 1993).

9. Stefano Papi and Alexandra Rhodes, *Famous Jewelry Collectors* (London: Thames and Hudson, 1999), 182–183.

10. Amanda Triossi and Daniela Mascetti, *Bulgari* (Milan: Electa, 2007), 34–35.

11. Taylor, *My Love Affair with Jewelry*, 111.

12. "I used to get so excited, I would jump on top of him and practically make love to him in Bulgari," *New York Times* (Sunday Style), September 29, 2002.

13. *The Collection of Elizabeth Taylor*, 115.

14. From 1984 Elizabeth Taylor became committed to the fight against HIV/AIDS and became the principal spokesperson for amfAR. In 1991 she started her own organization, the Elizabeth Taylor AIDS Foundation, mainly to support the provision of direct services to people living with HIV/AIDS.

15. Amanda Triossi, *Bulgari: 125 Years of Italian Magnificence*, exh. cat. (Milan: Skira, 2010), 378.

16. *The Collection of Elizabeth Taylor*, 32.

17. Incidentally, Taylor's contract with Fox was the first million-dollar contract in the history of moviemaking.

18. *The Collection of Elizabeth Taylor*, 1.

Fig. 49. Taylor, wearing her spectacular Bulgari sautoir of platinum, sapphires, and diamonds (cat. 96), 1988

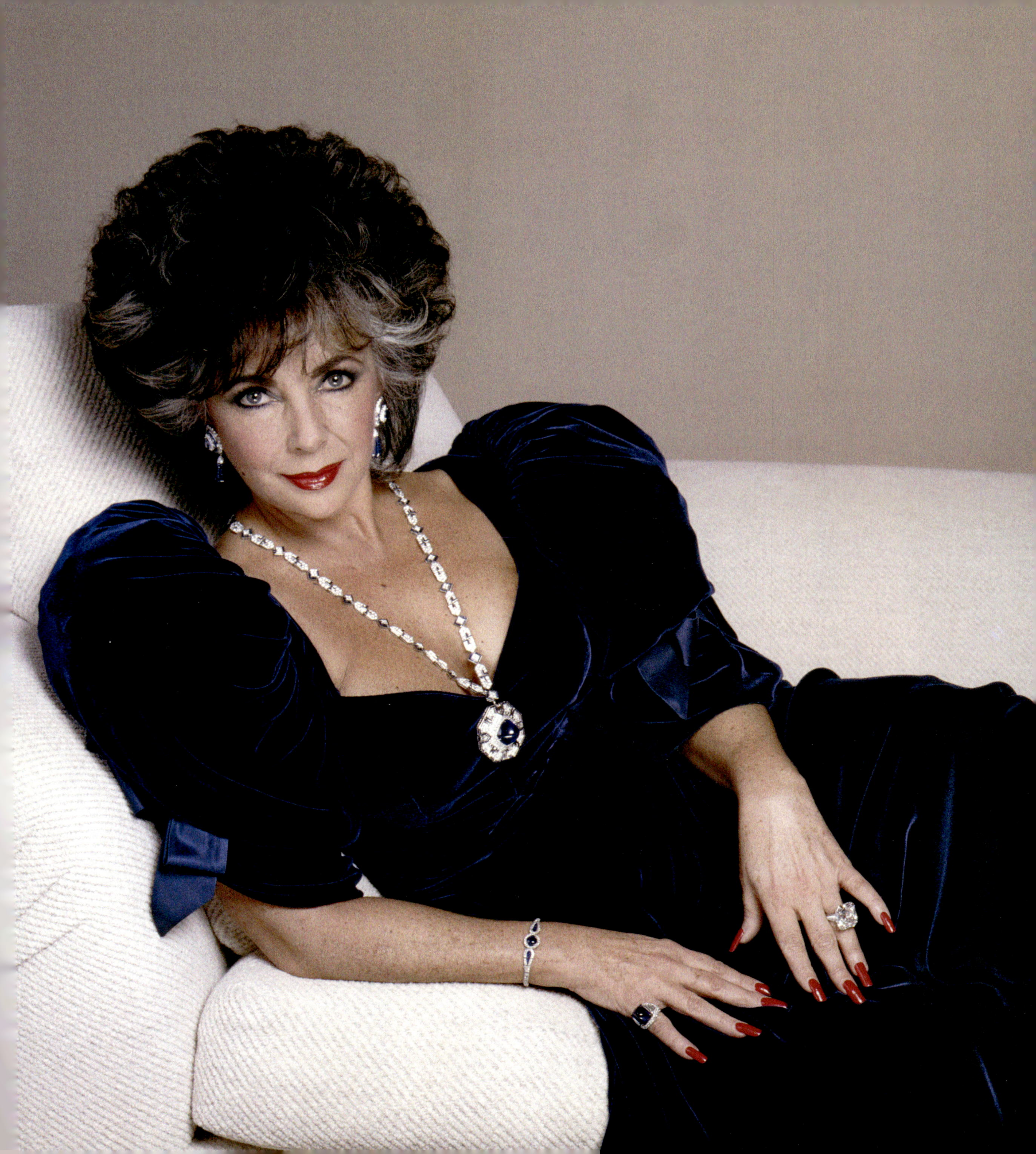

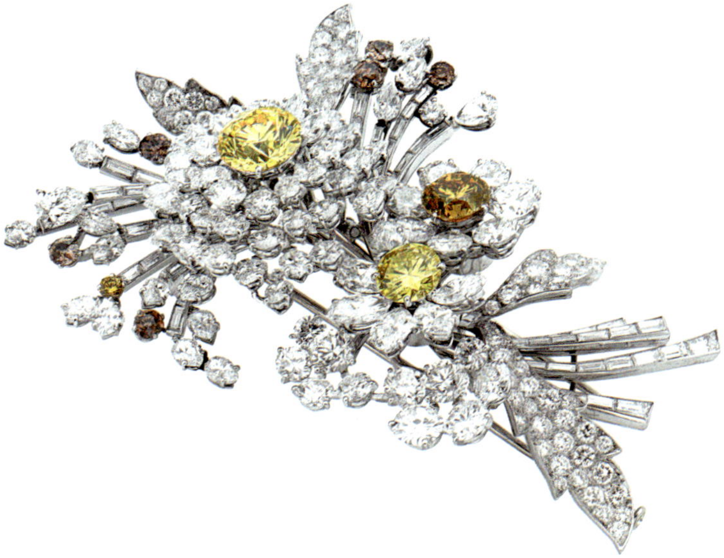

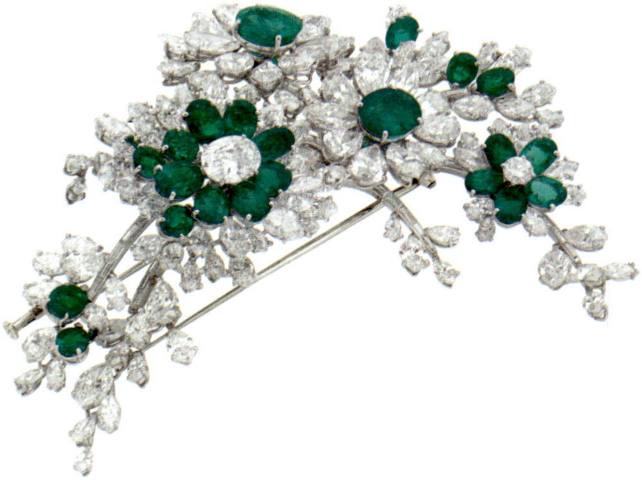

90. *Tremblant* brooch, 1959
Platinum with colored and white diamonds

91. *Tremblant* brooch, 1960
Platinum with emeralds and diamonds

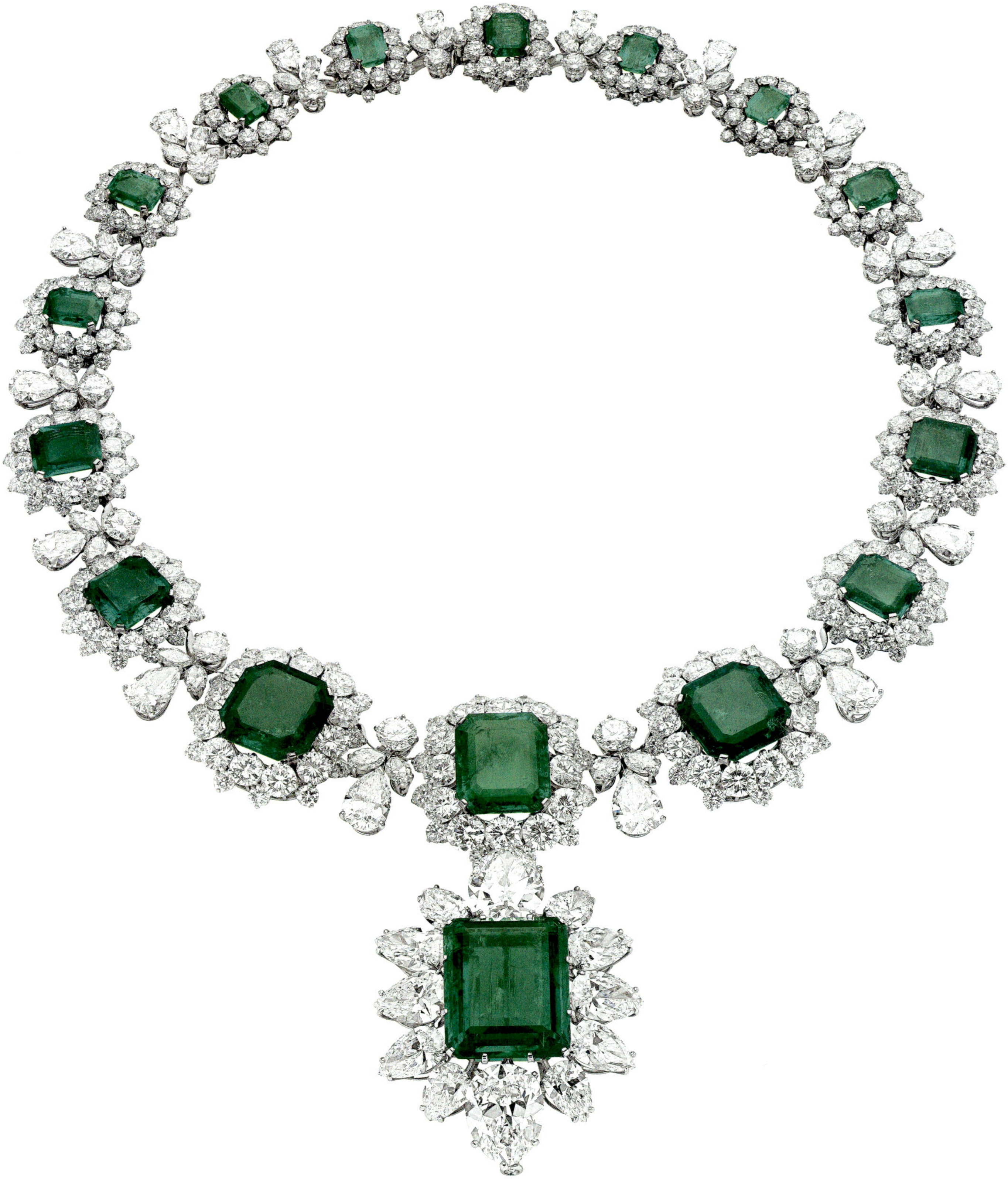

92. Necklace, 1962, with pendant/brooch, 1958
Platinum with emeralds and diamonds

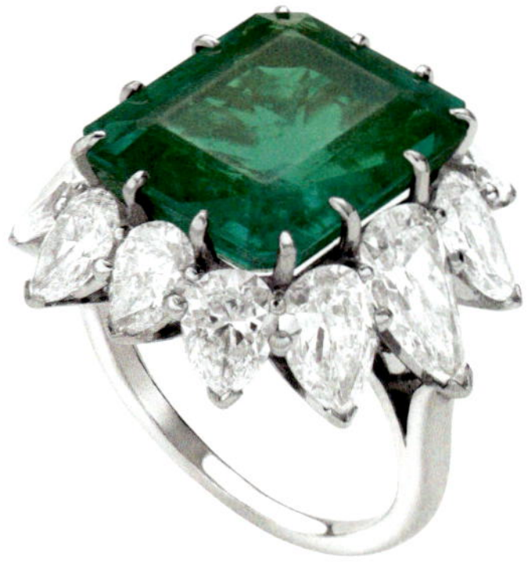

93. Ring, 1961
Platinum with emerald and diamonds

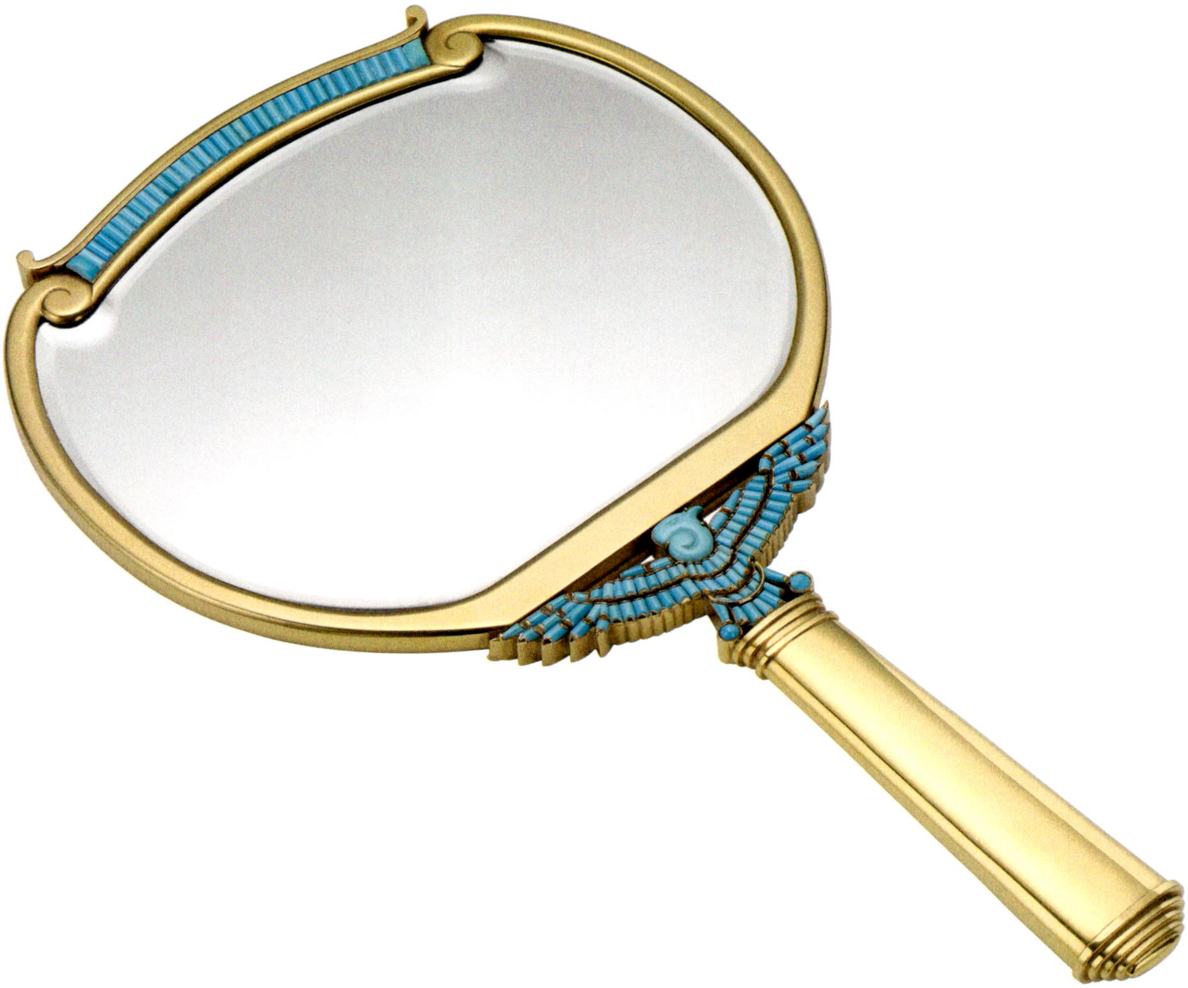

94. Mirror, 1962
Gold with turquoise

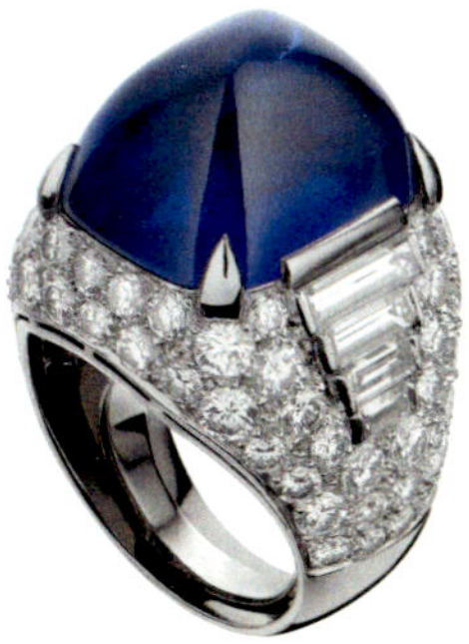

95. *Trombino* ring, 1971

Platinum with sapphire and diamonds

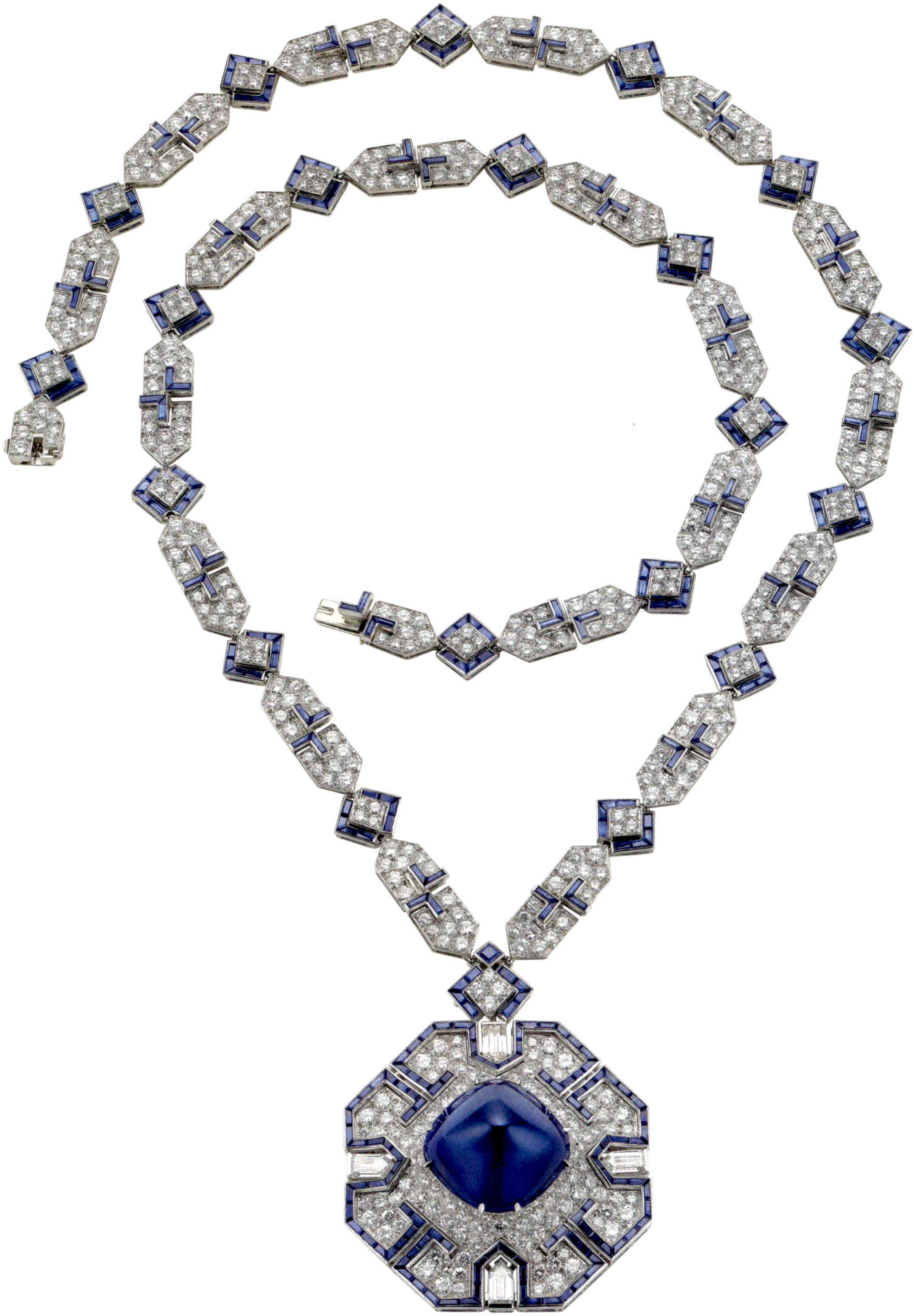

96. Sautoir, 1969

Platinum with sapphires and diamonds

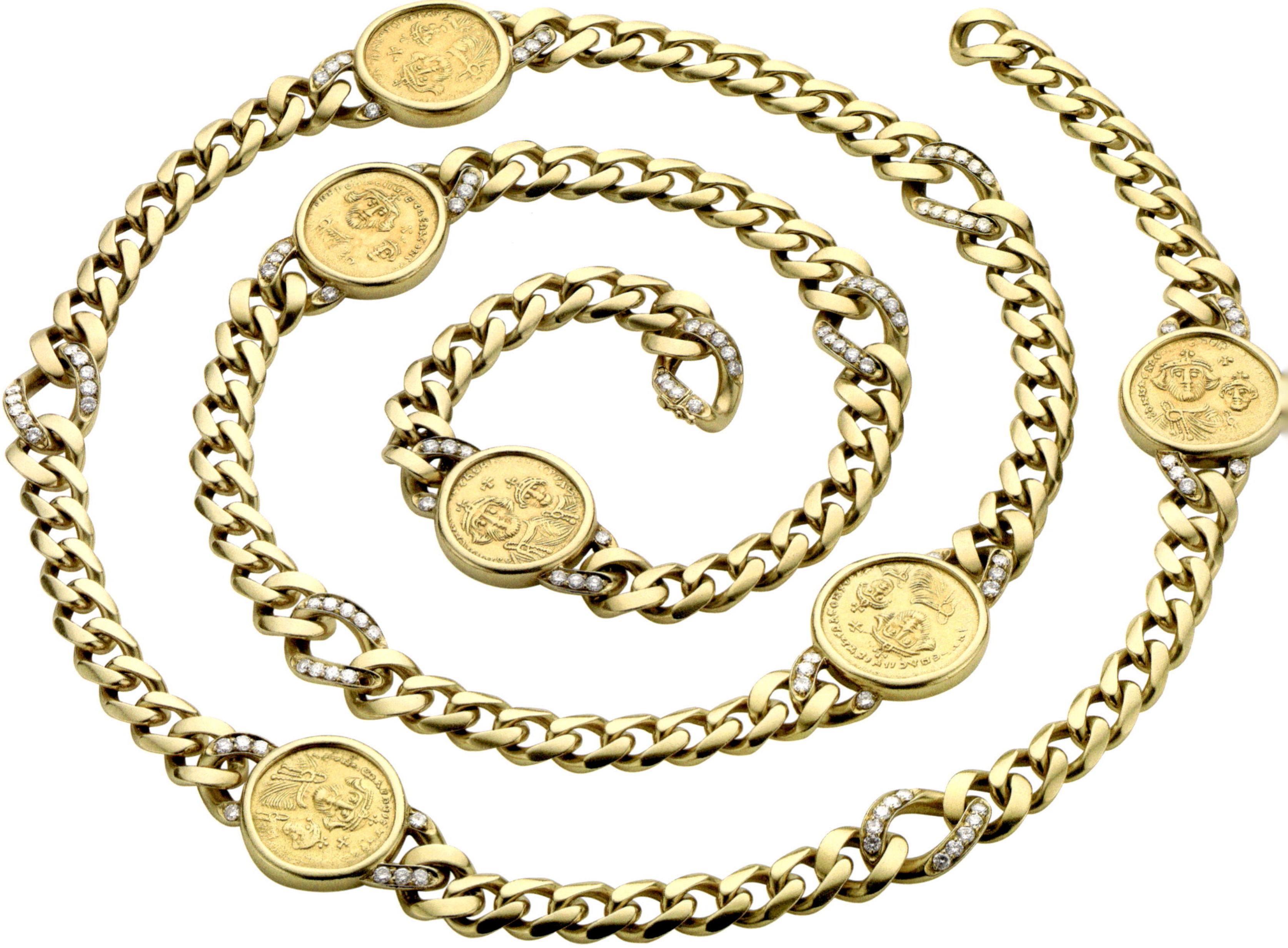

97. Sautoir, 1975

Gold with Byzantine gold coins and diamonds

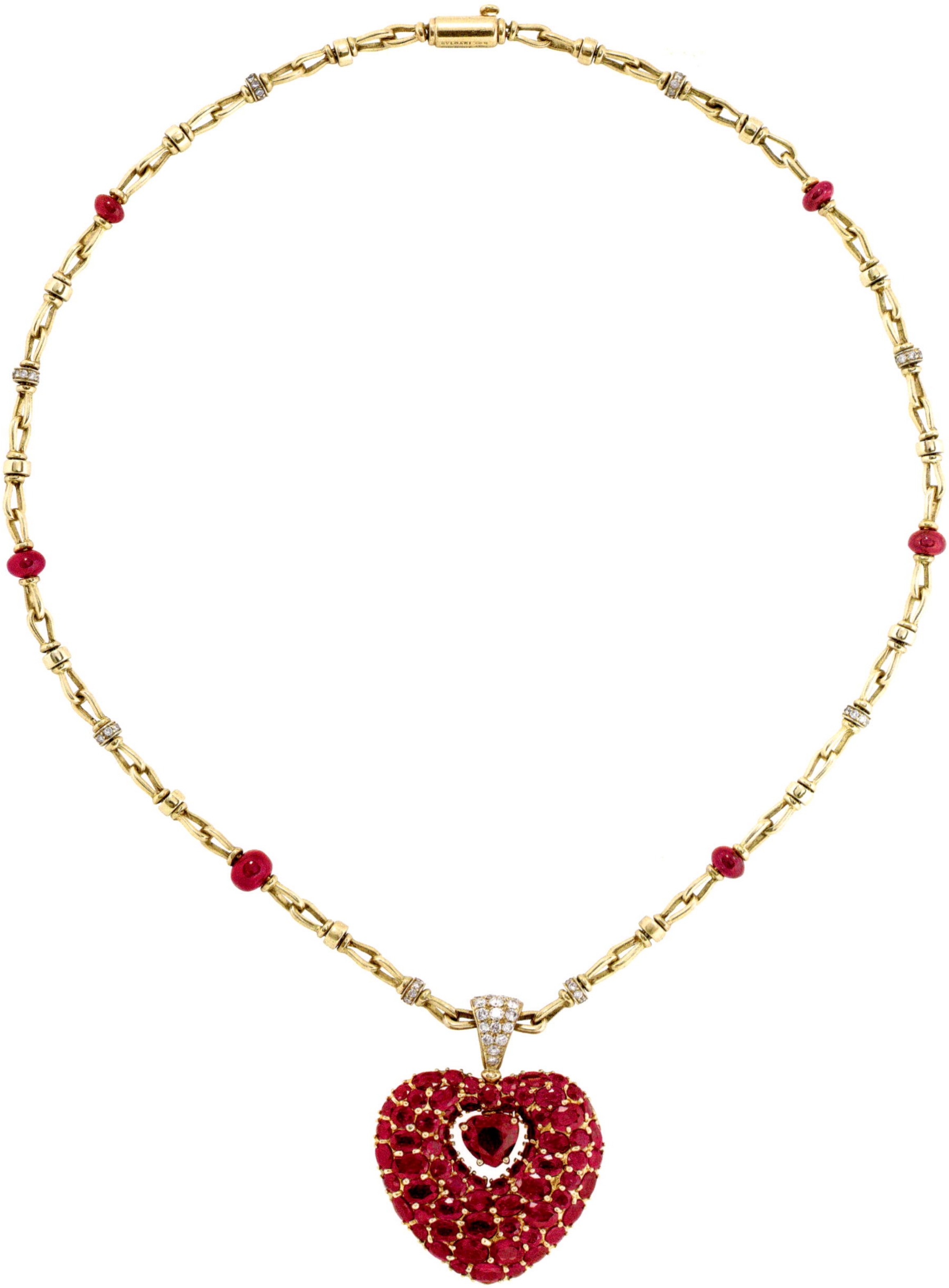

98. Necklace, 2002
Gold with rubies and diamonds

1980s

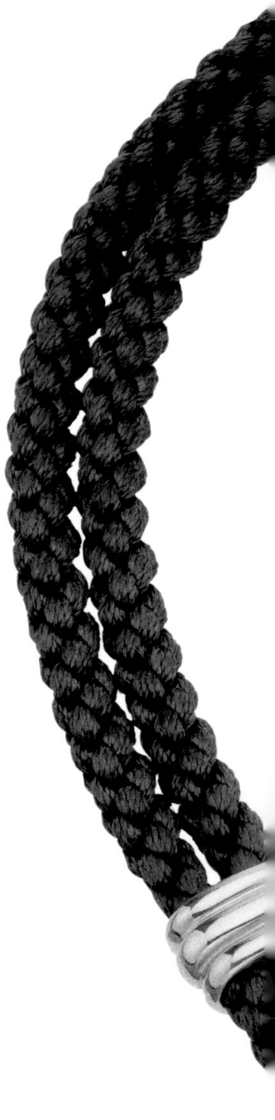

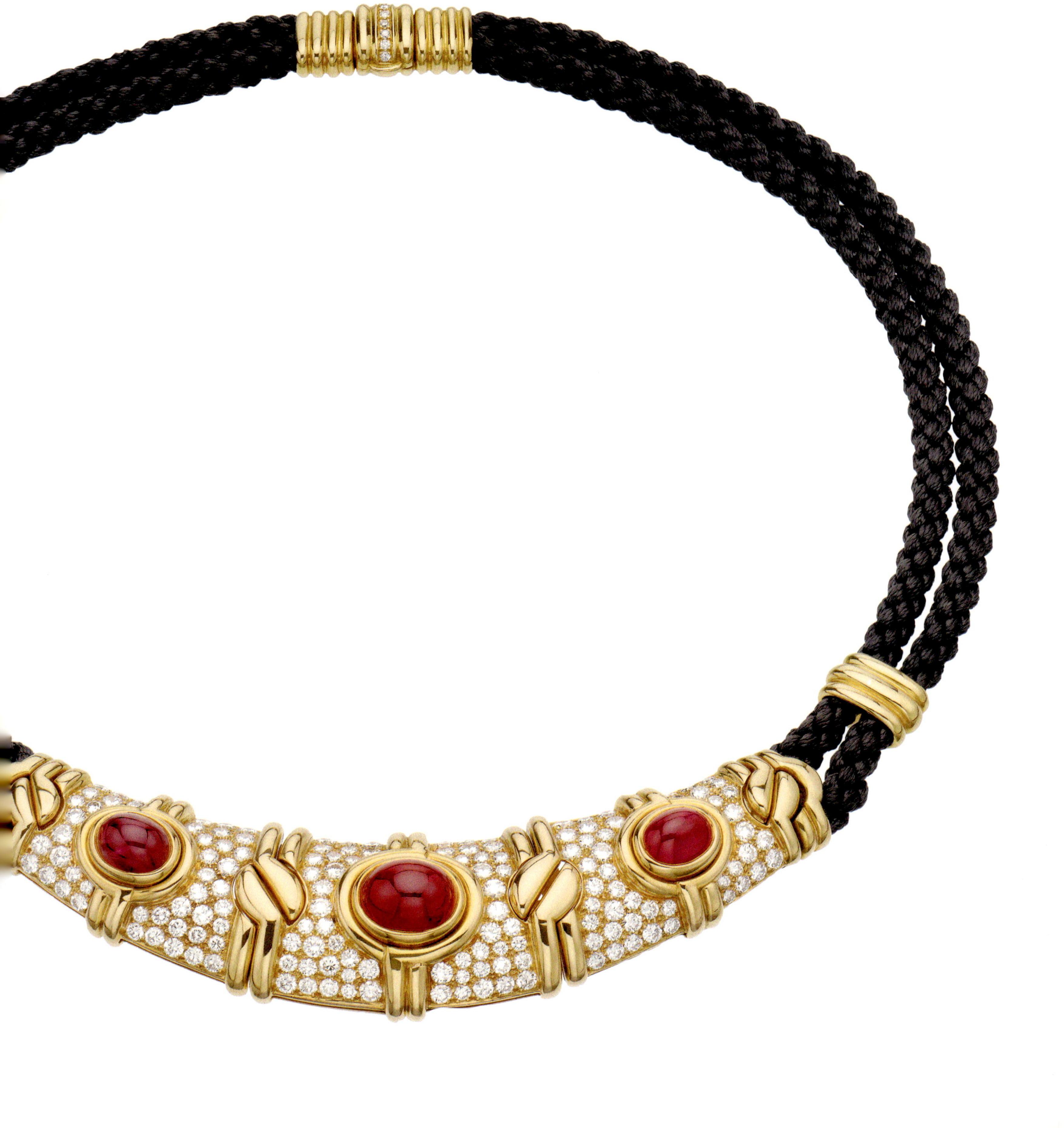

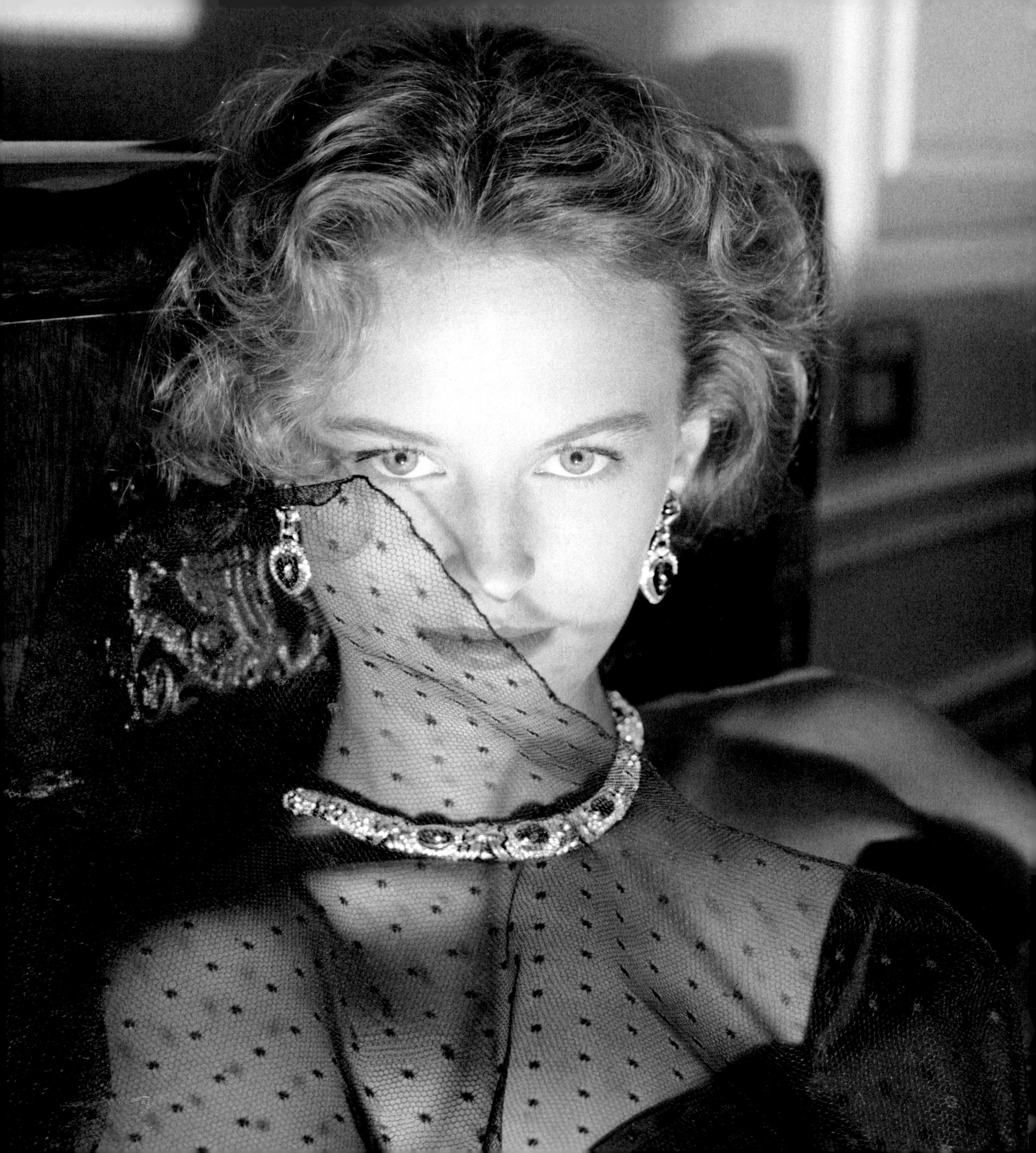

1980s: Unconventional Designs and Modular Lines

Andy Warhol immediately grasped the significance of Bulgari in the 1980s, remarking in an interview with Nicola Bulgari: "Well, I think your jewelry is the 1980s. Everybody's trying to copy this look."[1] As evidence of the artist's statement, in the 1995 film *Casino*, which takes place in the Las Vegas of 1983, director Martin Scorsese (who painstakingly reconstructs the period settings and costumes in all of his films) has Robert De Niro offer his on-screen wife, Sharon Stone, a large, elegant case brimming with Bulgari creations—the consummate symbols of 1980s jewelry (fig. 51). Warhol himself featured Bulgari jewels on the cover of his magazine, *Interview* (see fig. 52).

This was the decade when all the evolving features of Bulgari's design crystallized into signature forms replete with volume, strong colors, clean lines, stylized decorative motifs, and antique themes. Color effects were so important that valuable gems were often mounted with stones of relatively little worth if the result achieved the desired aesthetic. Key characteristics of the decade's creations were unconventionality on one hand and wearability on the other, resulting in such successes as "BVLGARI-BVLGARI" wristwatches and modular jewelry.

A new collection known as BCI (Bulgari Collection Internationale, later Bulgari High Jewelry) was launched in 1980. Consisting of unique pieces mounted with exceptionally valuable gems (in contrast to designs produced in multiples for a broader market), the line was displayed in rotation in all the Bulgari shops. Between 1979 and 1994 the new collection enjoyed the contributions of the designer Omar Torres, who designed striking, colorful, and spirited creations with soft, rounded contours. Regarding his use of curved lines, he said, "I can't picture jewels without seeing the curves of the ears and the cheekbones."[2]

Among the most representative creations of this era were Bulgari's impressive necklaces, which were sometimes accompanied by assortments of large, matching earrings (see cats. 106, 108, 114). The highly structured and tailored fashions of the eighties perfectly displayed these bold and sleek neckpieces. Intriguingly, these new works incorporated decoration into their construction, such as with the modular pieces (see below). In the previous decade, ornamentation had been limited mostly to the pendant; however, by the 1980s, the body of the necklace was both structure and decoration at the same time.

The popularity of yellow gold, which began in the 1970s, continued into this decade; a variety of gold necklaces were set with diamonds, large emeralds, sapphires, or rubies, nearly always in combination with other diversely colored gems. Other examples used dark materials such as black mother-of-pearl, onyx, or hematite with diamonds and colored stones (see cat. 101). As the years progressed, so did the vividness of the color combinations, drawing from rubies, amethysts, sapphires, peridots, and citrines.

Fig. 50. A model wearing Bulgari jewels, in a photograph published in *Vogue*, 1988

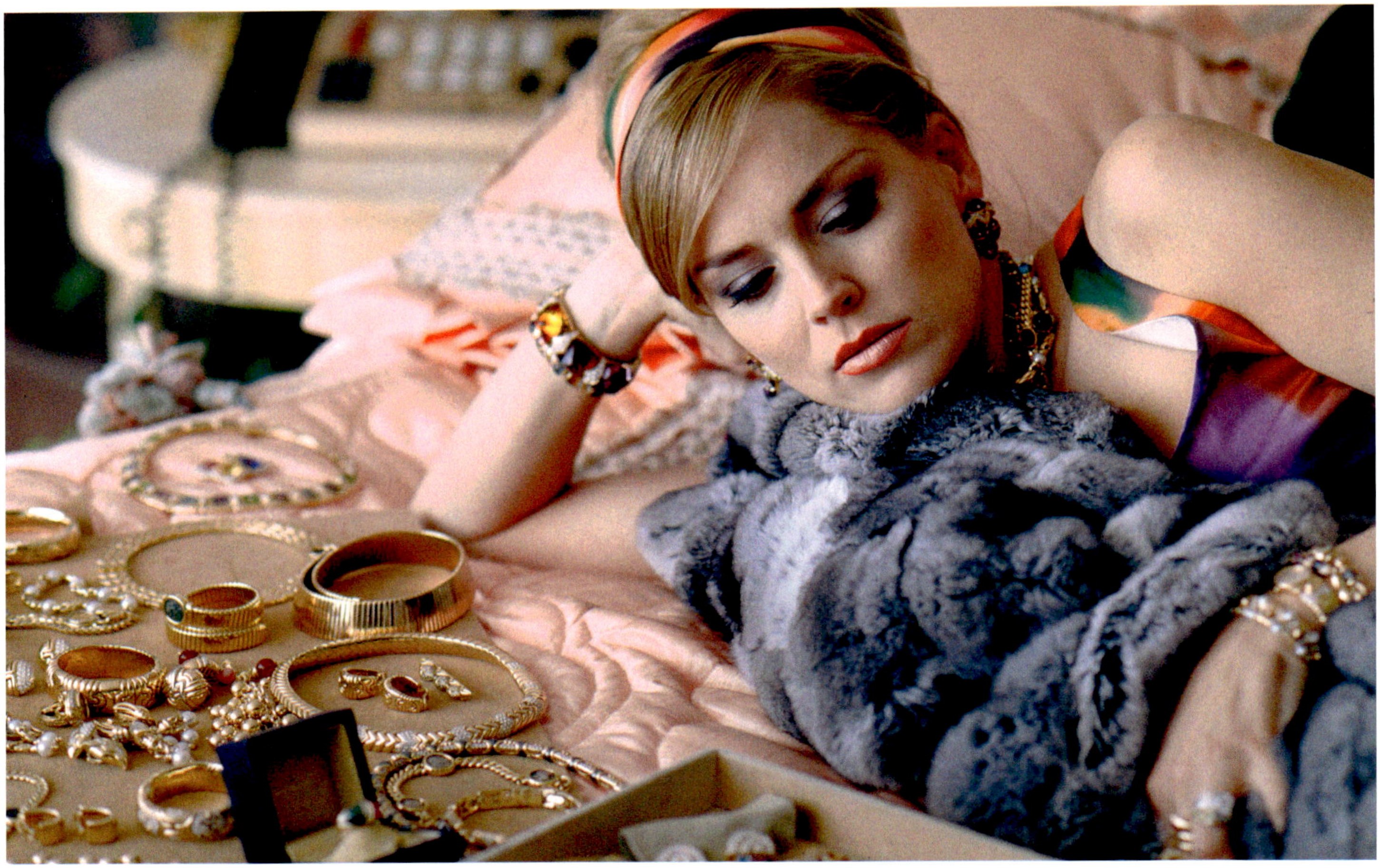

Fig. 51. Sharon Stone surrounded by 1980s Bulgari jewelry in *Casino* (1995)

Torres himself defined these new chromatic blends as the "harmony of colors." Given a color wheel including the complete spectrum, he felt the most subtle harmonies were obtained by combining consecutive hues such as violet, blue, and green. The most striking results, however, were achieved by joining those from opposite ends of the spectrum, such as violet with yellow, or green with red. Perfect examples of these color arrangements are found in two necklaces produced respectively in 1988 and 1989 (cats. 109, 110), where the proportions and combinations exquisitely culminate in startling vibrancy.

This decade also witnessed Bulgari's increasing use of calibré-cut colored gems—stones cut to fit together snugly—a technique that had featured extensively in jewelry of the twenties. Bulgari's revival in the eighties of the calibré cut came with a twist: the small colored gemstones, cut and shaped to perfectly fit the required form of the mount, were presented with polished buff-top tables (in the style of a cabochon) rather than faceted ones. This method was not only sophisticated, requiring great time and skill, but it was also expensive: in the process of recutting each gem to a standard shape and size for a perfect fit, many carats were lost (furthermore, during this process some stones were broken).

The collection of Carré (square) brooches of 1987 (see cats. 104, 105; see also fig. 53b), whose design recalls the geometric patterns seen in gardens or mosaic floors, proved an ideal vehicle for Bulgari

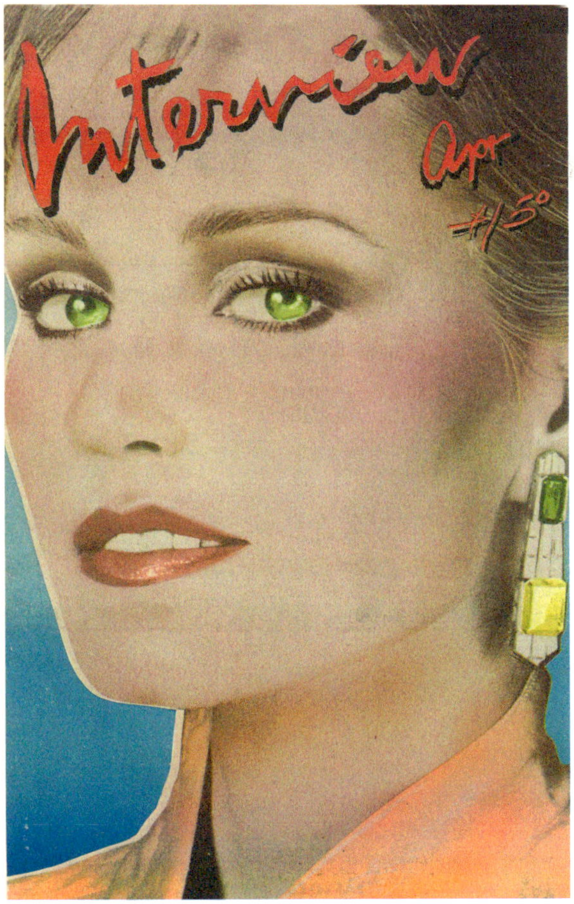

Fig. 52. Jessica Lange, in Bulgari earrings of yellow gold, Colombian emeralds, and yellow diamonds, on the cover of Andy Warhol's *Interview* magazine, April 1979

to experiment with extremely diverse color combinations. The repeating checked motif produced a great variety of visual effects through the use of different juxtapositions of calibré-cut gemstones. The same was true of the "kilim" bracelets of 1988–1989 (see fig. 53a), so called for their resemblances to Oriental carpets. They were constructed as wide, articulated bands and are set with various colored cabochon gemstones, also arranged in geometric patterns. The example here (cat. 103) is set with three sugarloaf cabochon emeralds together weighing 22.23 carats.

As jewelry fashion evolved, so did the firm. In 1984 the young Francesco Trapani (nephew of Gianni, Paolo, and Nicola Bulgari) became its chief executive officer, flanked by his uncles Paolo as president and Nicola as vice president. It was clear to Trapani that if Bulgari was to compete in the future, it needed to present a consistent image for its products and expand its sales worldwide. The end of the eighties saw numerous store openings: Milan (1986), London (1988), and Saint Moritz and Munich (1989) in Europe; and Tokyo (1987) and Osaka, Singapore, and Hong Kong (1988) in Asia. In 1989 a second impressive shop was opened in New York at 730 Fifth Avenue, on the corner of 57th Street, occupying the ground floor and first level of Manhattan's landmark Crown Building.

Earlier in the decade, in 1980, Bulgari Distribuzione was established to plan, design, manufacture, and distribute jewelry and other precious objects to the Bulgari branches worldwide. This new company ensured uniformity in the design and production of each creation, as well as the branding and interior look of Bulgari's network of shops. It also oversaw creative innovations, employing new designers from areas as remote as the automobile industry and architecture to develop sophisticated methods and technologies that could be freshly applied to jewelry.

Complementing the wider presence of Bulgari around the world, a significant new approach to its branding took place. In the late seventies, Bulgari was the first jeweler to elevate its name to the status of a logo, taking inspiration from the capital typeface that had first appeared over the via dei Condotti shop in 1934 (see fig. 20), in imitation of the lapidary inscriptions used in ancient Rome. Such lettering had been periodically revived since the fifteenth century, primarily for use in public inscriptions; in Italy, in the late 1920s and throughout the 1930s, it was exalted in monumental dimensions on municipal buildings. After displaying the lapidary lettering on its shop sign, Bulgari began engraving it on its jewels and printing it inside its jewelry cases.

The first example of the logo as an integral part of a work's design was on the famous "BVLGARI-BVLGARI" watch. This piece's distinguishing features are a case formed by a horizontal cross section of a cylinder, and a black enamel dial framed by a gold bezel inscribed twice with Bulgari's logo. The design itself derived from of an earlier gold, digital model inscribed *BVLGARI ROMA*. This unintentional prototype was produced in 1975, in a limited series of one hundred samples that were intended as gifts for Bulgari's most loyal customers. Its unexpected success led the company to use the same case for some mechanical models and then, in 1977, for the "BVLGARI-BVLGARI" archetype. This watch was immediately successful in all its manifestations (see cat. 42) and became one of Bulgari's major icons.

Another emblematic design originating in the eighties was Bulgari's modular jewelry, which, like the coin jewelry of the previous decade, represented the revival of another ancient tradition. As early as the fourth century BC, Hellenistic craftsmen were the first in the West to perceive the advantages of reproducing a series of similarly designed elements, reducing the time involved both in the creative process and in manufacturing the pieces. They created identical, stamped-out rosettes and amphora motifs that were subsequently applied to necklaces, earrings, and hair ornaments. In the nineteenth century the Castellani family of jewelers was among the first to use the same concept, manufacturing identical rosettes and disk-shaped motifs for numerous and diverse jewels.

An awareness of the enormous changes in the market led to the creation of Bulgari's modular works. The rapidly growing desire for mid-priced jewelry stimulated a radical change in the very notion of production, and the module was advantageous because it could be easily adapted to different pieces of jewelry: a single element in a ring could be repeated many times in a necklace, for example. Once a satisfactory design was made, its module could be repeated in a wide number of shapes and jewels. Reducing the intrinsic value of the piece to accommodate the mass production needed for a wider-ranging clientele was essential, and developing an incisive design that was not only recognizable, but also highly refined from an aesthetic point of view, offered another kind of value.[3]

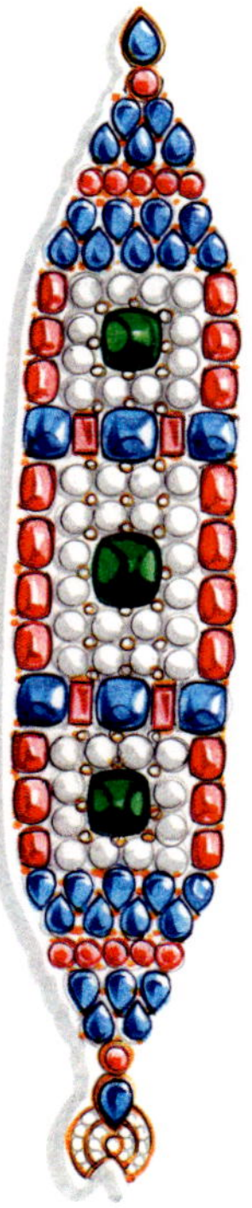

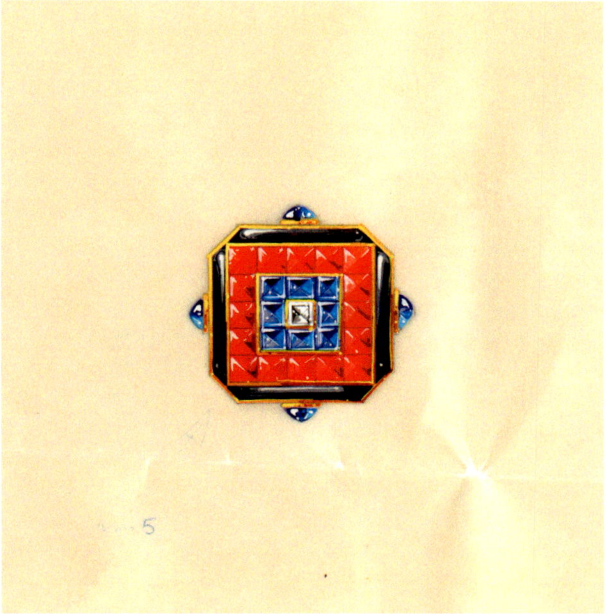

Figs. 53a–b. Original design sketches for kilim bracelet and Carré brooch, ca. 1980s

In 1982 the creation of Parentesi (parenthesis) marked Bulgari's first line of modular jewelry, which was eponymously characterized by a graphic motif reminiscent of a succession of parentheses (see figs. 54a–c, 55). There are various anecdotes about the origin of its inspiration. One story tells of a Bulgari brother (the story does not say which), en route to the via dei Condotti shop one day, noticing how the curbstones were shaped and joined together, inspiring him to reproduce the shape of the join in jewelry. Another anecdote describes how Gianni Bulgari, while doodling a pattern of consecutive algebraic brackets, was suddenly struck by the thought of it repeated on a jewel.[4]

Whatever its exact inception, this line not only became iconic in the 1980s, but, according to statistics, is one of the most copied jewelry designs of all time. With well-defined aesthetics, the Parentesi pieces were not only accessible and easy to wear, but also decorative and suitable for any occasion. Parentesi items, easily recognized as Bulgari, became status symbols and highly sought-after designer accessories. The Parentesi range was just what the 1980s woman was looking for: modern, wearable jewels that departed from the conventional formality of high jewelry.

Objects in the Parentesi line were—and still are—created using modular elements with simple, well-defined shapes and with no additional ornamentation. Because they are reproduced in series and combined to form a variety of homogeneous designs, there is no need to add decoration—the modular design itself creates visual interest. In the production process, each module is cast in a series (this method is known as "microfusion"), and then finished and assembled by hand.

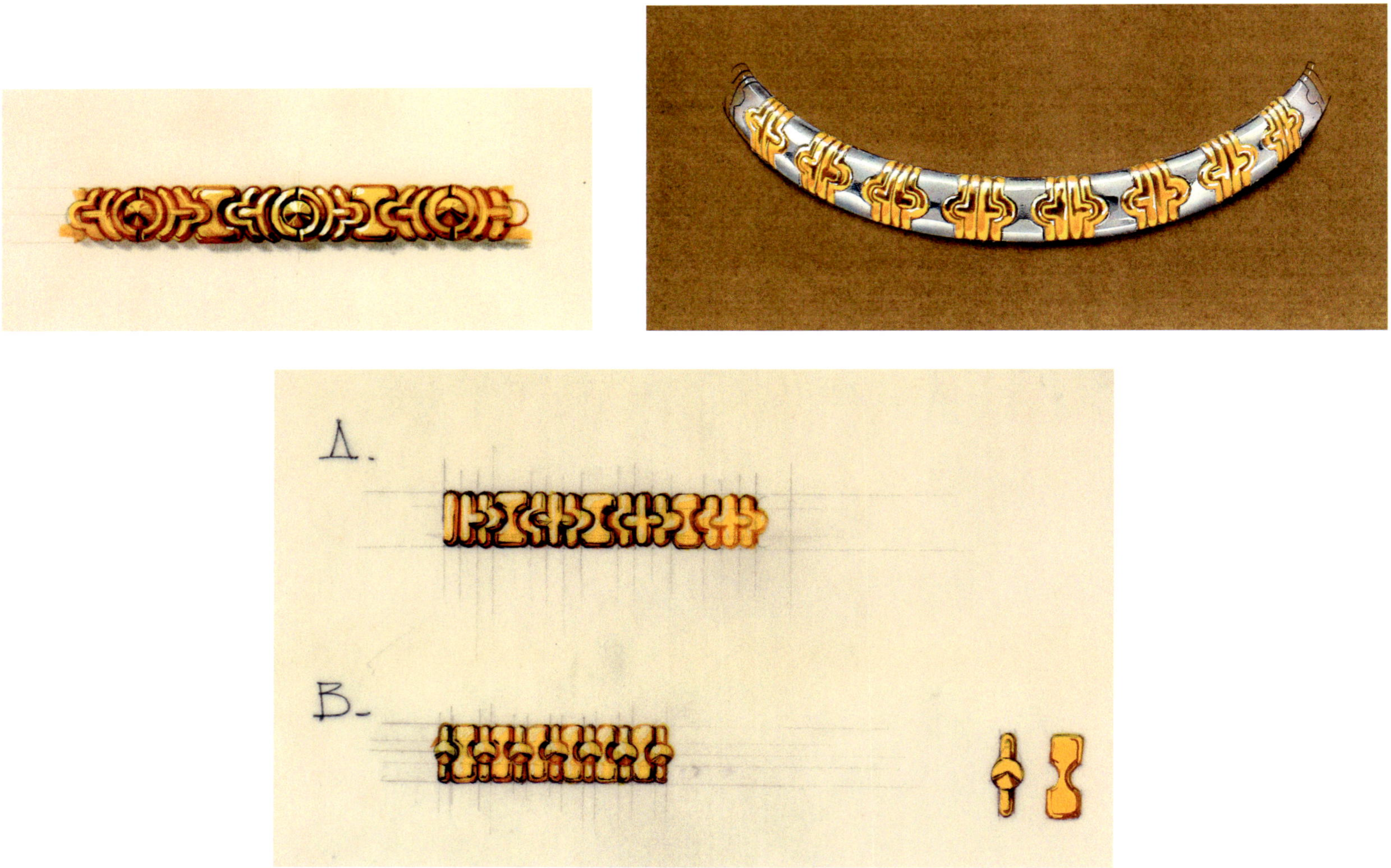

Figs. 54a–c. Original design sketches for the Parentesi collection, ca. 1980s

The basic format consists of gold Parentesi motifs that alternate with gold connecting elements, which can be embellished with diamonds (see cat. 99). However, the item can be less expensive if the connecting elements are made from steel, hematite, coral, mother-of-pearl, or other semiprecious stones. The module is highly adaptable because it can incorporate colored cabochon stones or antique coins and can be modified to slide on silk cords or flattened *tubogas*. Jewels can be extended in length and easily sized to different wrists or necks simply by the addition or removal of one or more elements. After 1982 various other modular lines based on different designs were introduced, and new versions of Parentesi have continued into the twenty-first century.

In addition to its highly successful Parentesi line, Bulgari created another innovation in the early 1980s by mounting important stones on simple silk cords offered in a wide range of colors to easily match any outfit (see cat. 100); thus expensive gemstones were easily transformed into highly wearable ornaments. These more casual jewels were appreciated by Bulgari's clientele not because they were more affordable—they were still expensive—but because they were versatile. For example, a silk-cord necklace

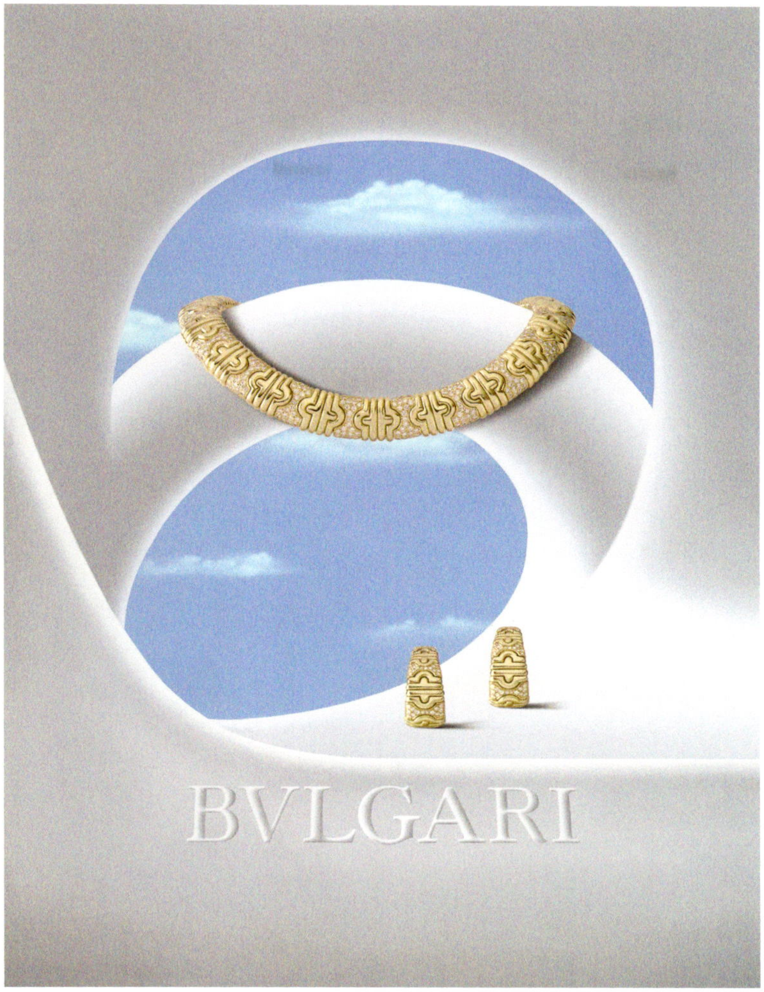

Fig. 55. Bulgari advertisement for the Parentesi collection, ca. 1989–1991

could be worn with jeans as well as an evening gown; Nicola Bulgari purportedly said that Bulgari jewels should be worn to a picnic and to a ball.[5]

As the 1980s drew to a close, Bulgari was not simply synonymous with Italy, jewelry, and elegance, it was also an international presence whose styles were recognized and admired by a wider and more diversified clientele. Its many innovations of the period, including the "BVLGARI-BVLGARI" and Parentesi lines, established the company as one of the most important names in fine jewelry—its flagship store on via dei Condotti still representing the finest Italian artistry.

1. Quoted in Andy Warhol, "Nicola Bulgari: Wearable Wealth," *Interview*, November 1980, 62–63.

2. Quoted in interview with Nicola Bulgari, *Palm Beach Daily News*, May 20, 1981.

3. See interviews with Gianni Bulgari published in the *International Daily News* (London), September 20–21, 1981; and *Gioia* (Milan), April 5, 1982, cited in Amanda Triossi and Daniela Mascetti, *Bulgari* (Milan: Electa, 2007), 112.

4. For a fuller story behind the design, see Triossi and Mascetti, *Bulgari*, 153.

5. Quoted in interview with Nicola Bulgari, *Vogue*, October 1995.

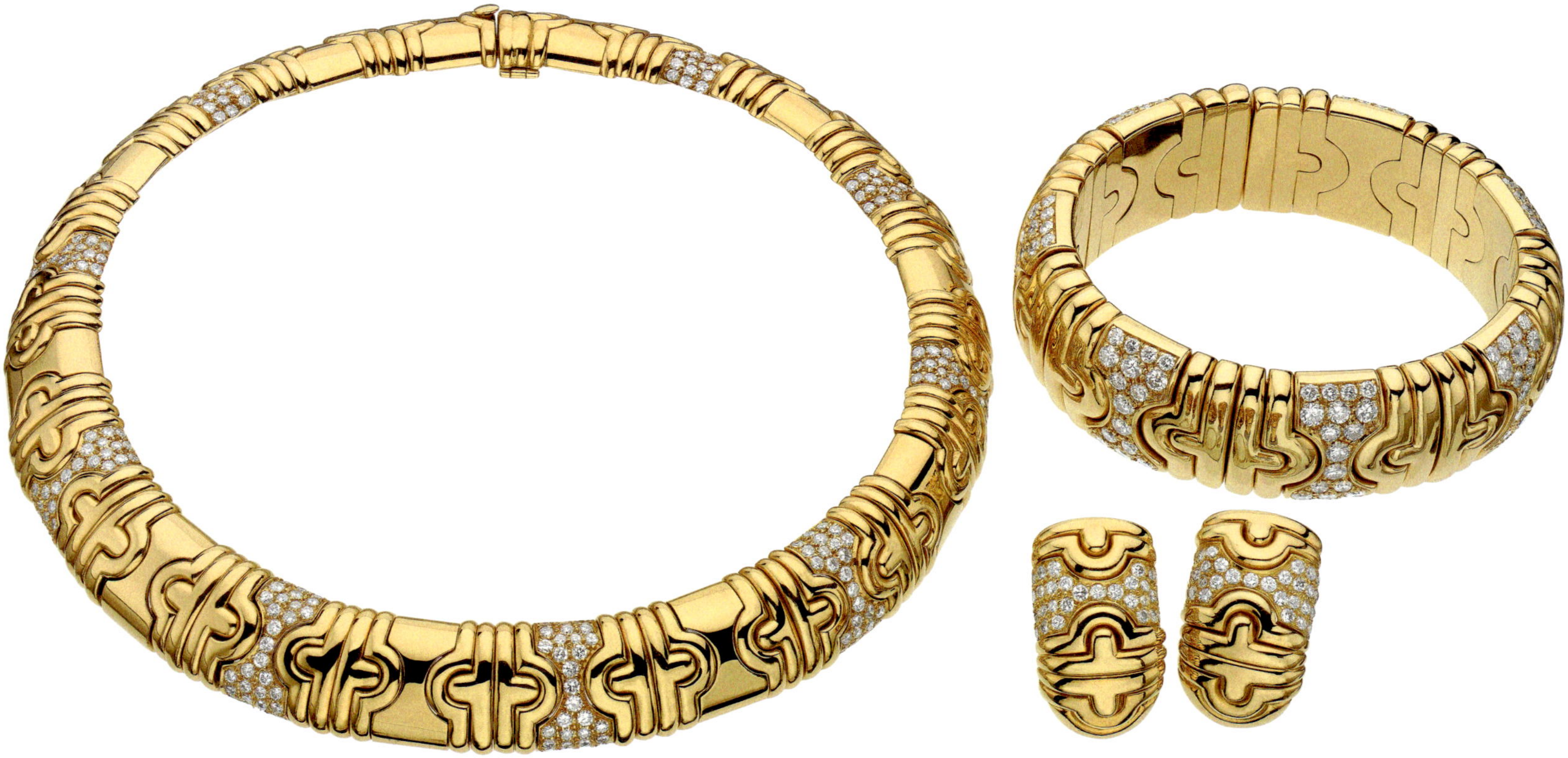

99. Parentesi parure, ca. 1982
Gold with diamonds

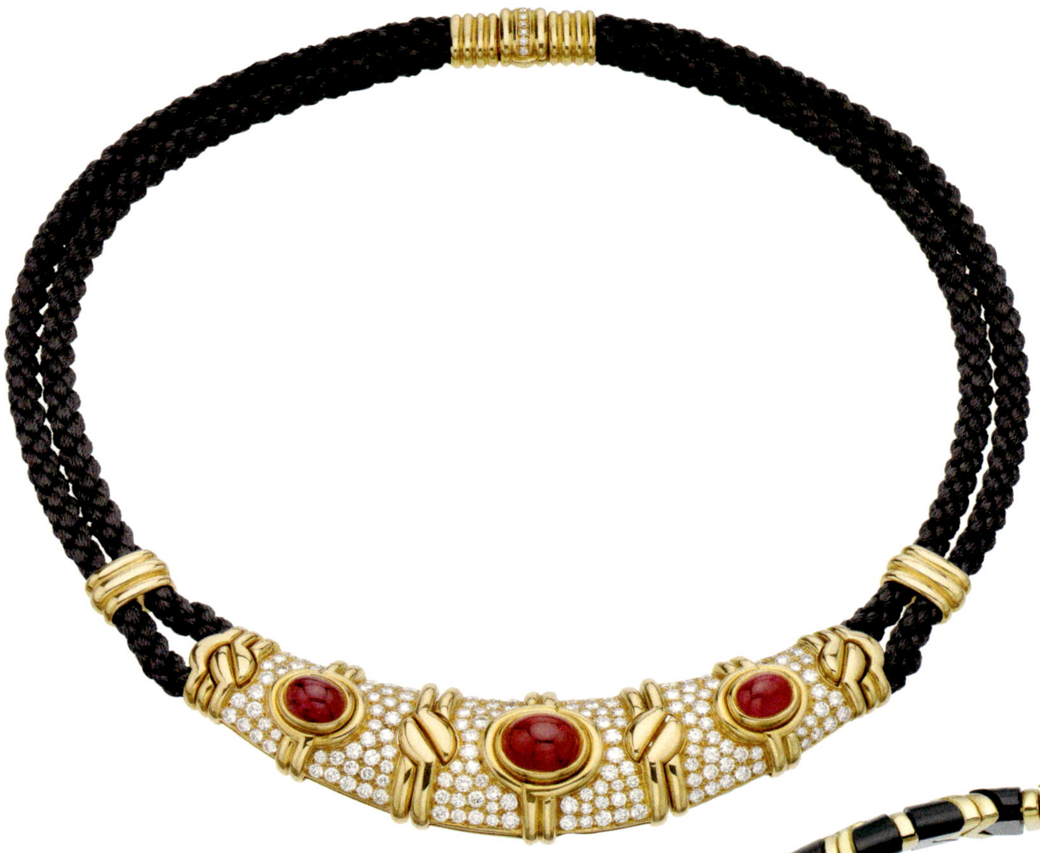

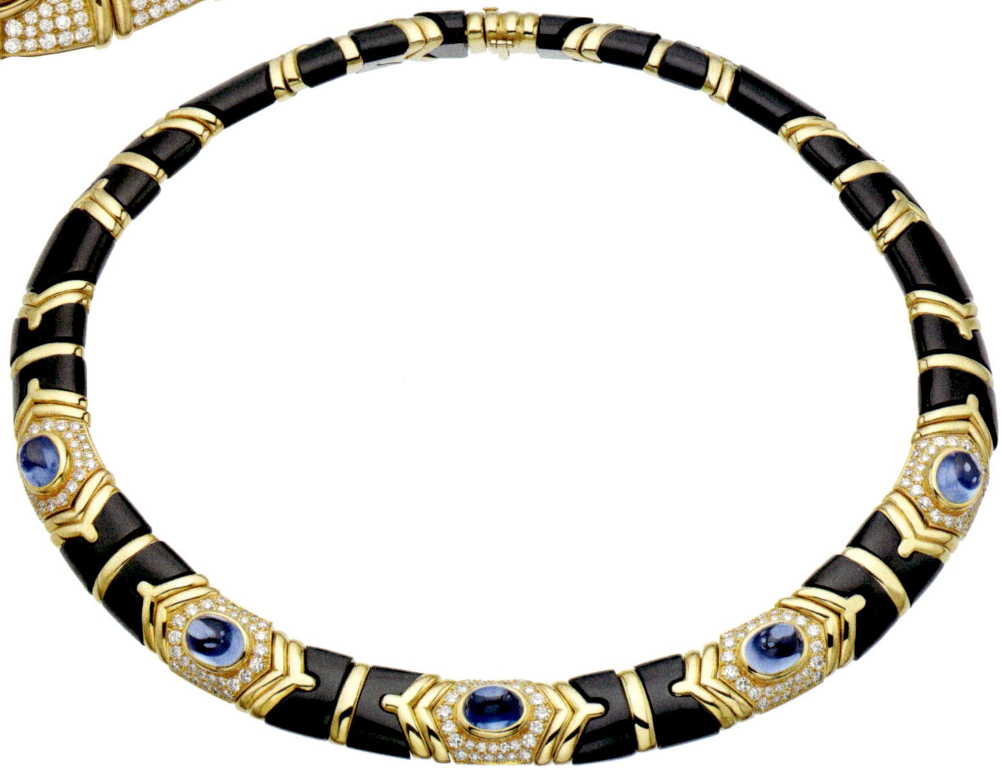

100. Necklace, ca. 1984
Gold with silk cord, rubies, and diamonds

101. Necklace, 1985
Gold with sapphires, onyx, and diamonds

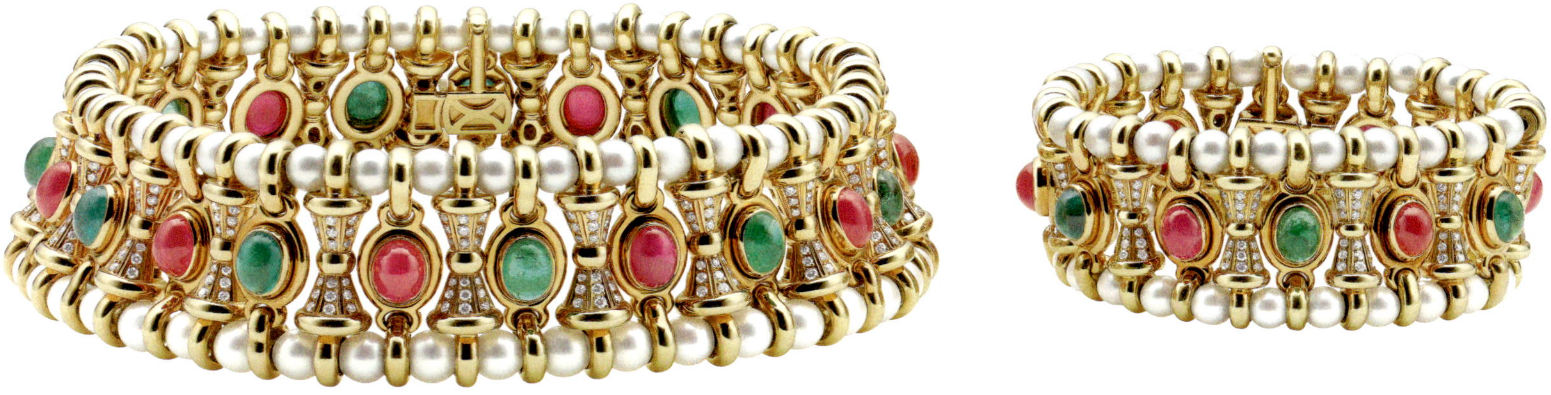

102. Choker and bracelet, 1987
Gold with cultured pearls, emeralds, rubies, and diamonds

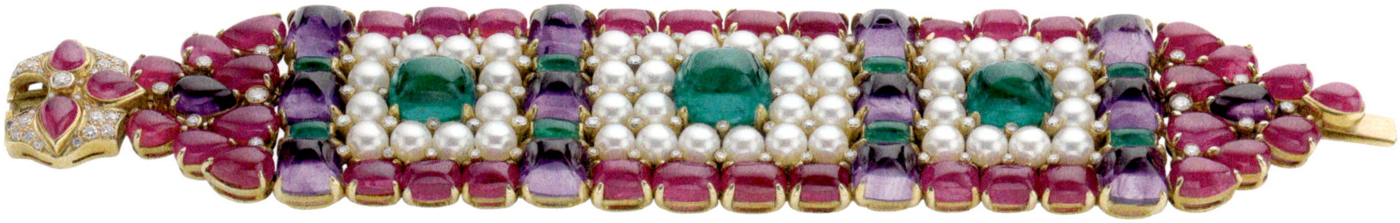

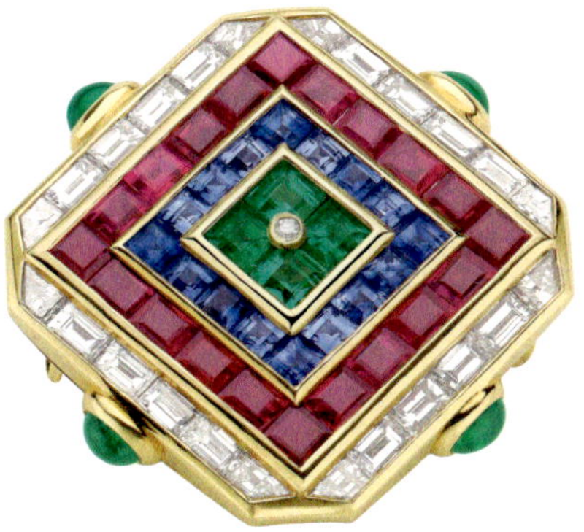

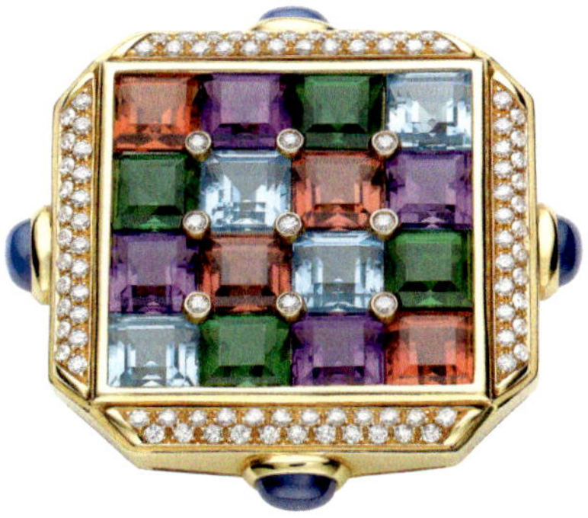

103. Kilim bracelet, 1988
Gold with emeralds, amethysts, rubies, cultured pearls, and diamonds

104. Carré brooch, 1987
Gold with emeralds, rubies, sapphires, and diamonds

105. Carré brooch, 1987
Gold with aquamarines, amethysts, red and green tourmalines, sapphires, and diamonds

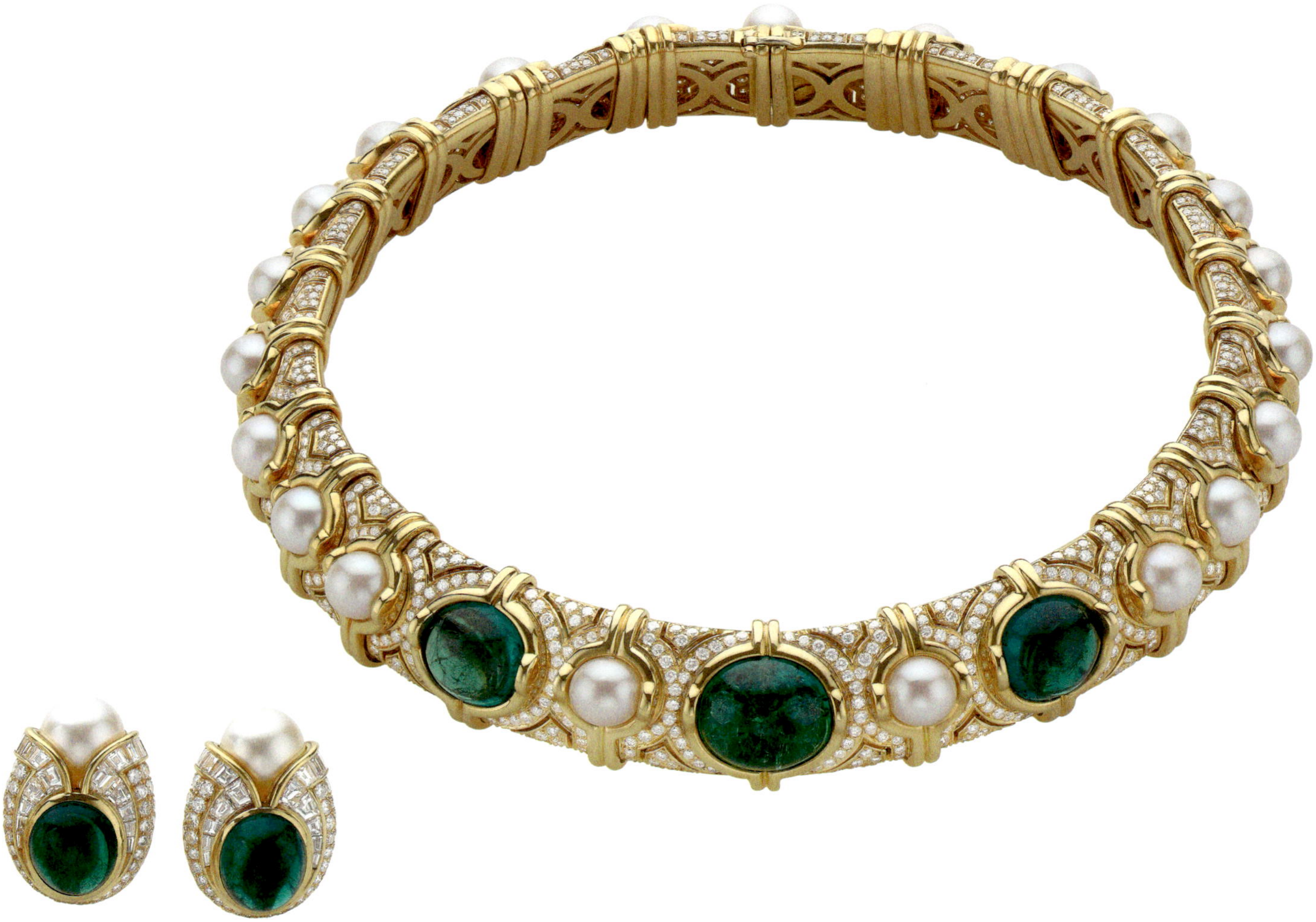

106. Choker and earrings, 1987
Gold with cultured pearls, emeralds, and diamonds

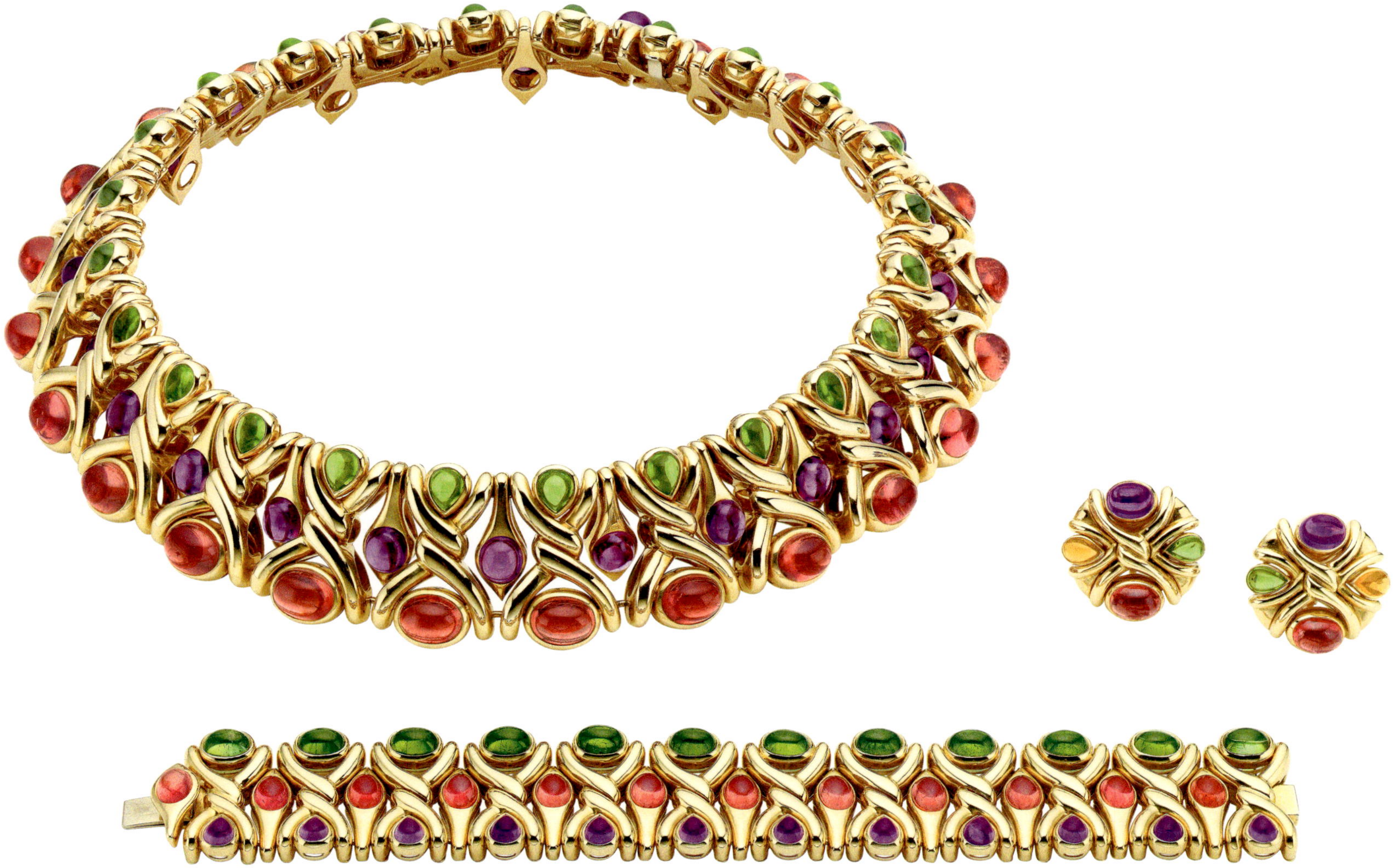

107. Parure, 1988

Gold with pink tourmalines, amethysts, and peridots

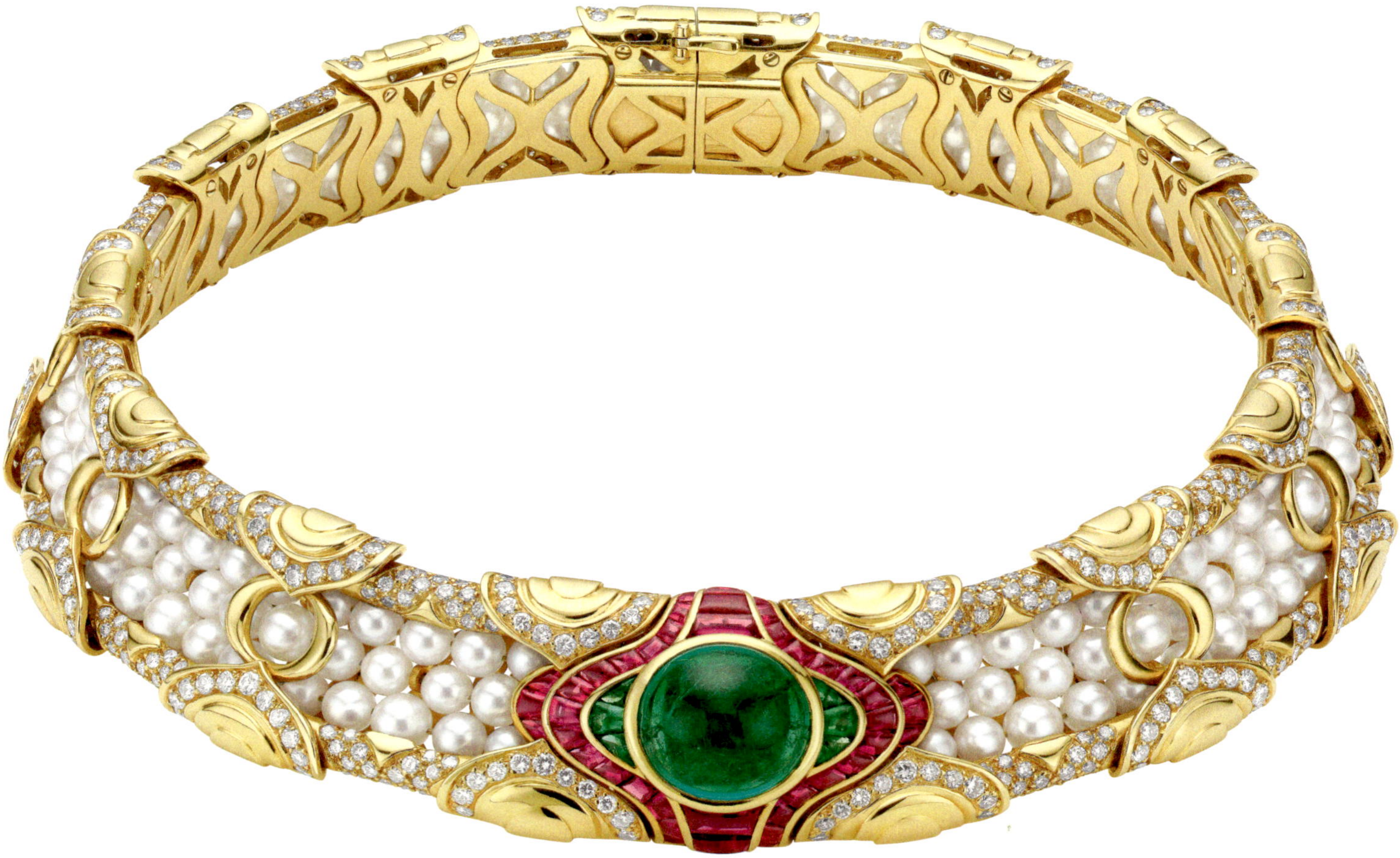

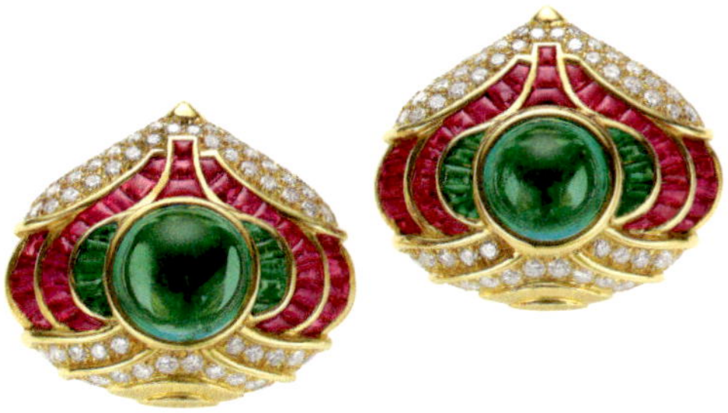

108. Earrings, 1988
Gold with emeralds, rubies, and diamonds

109. Choker, 1988
Gold with cultured pearls, emeralds, rubies, and diamonds

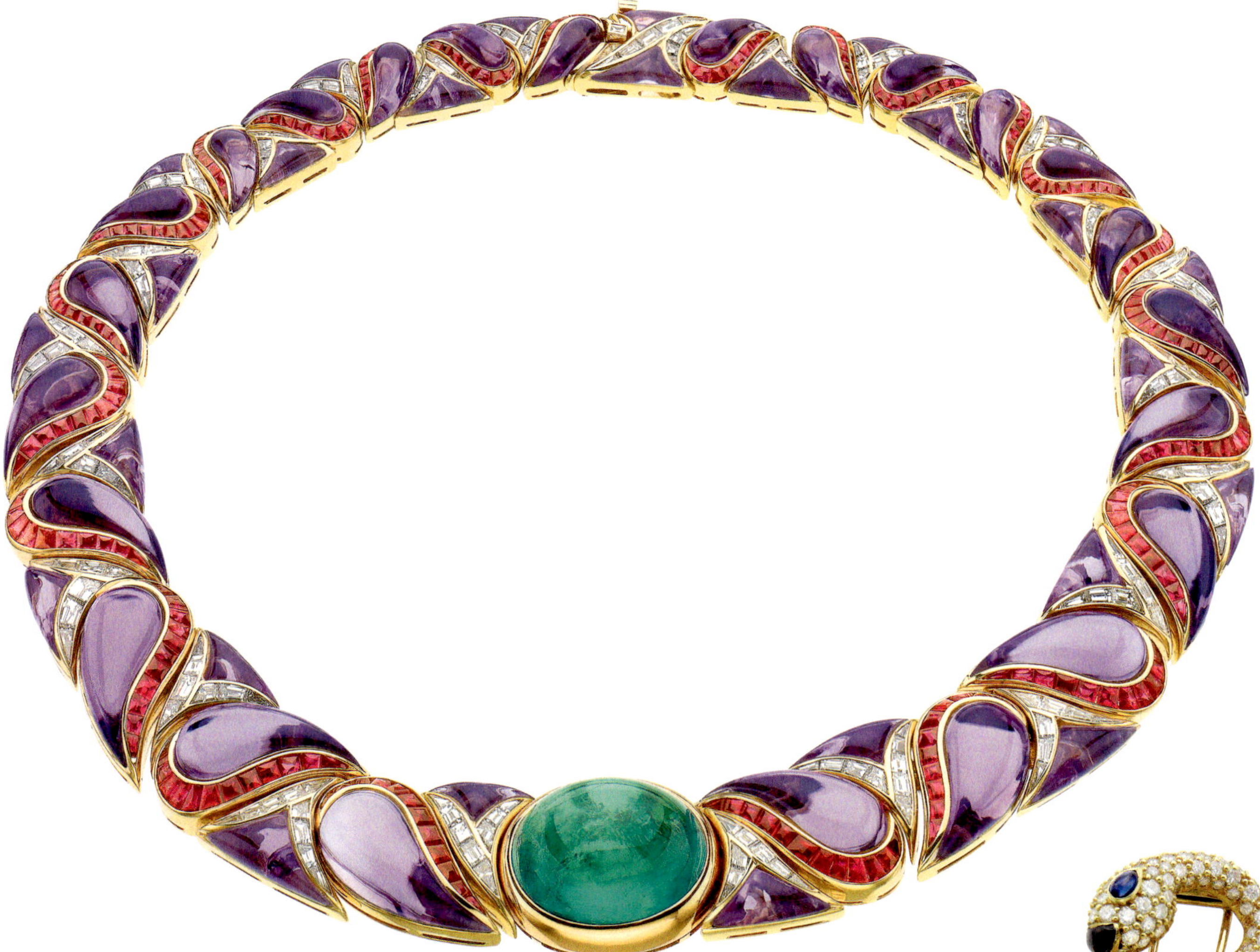

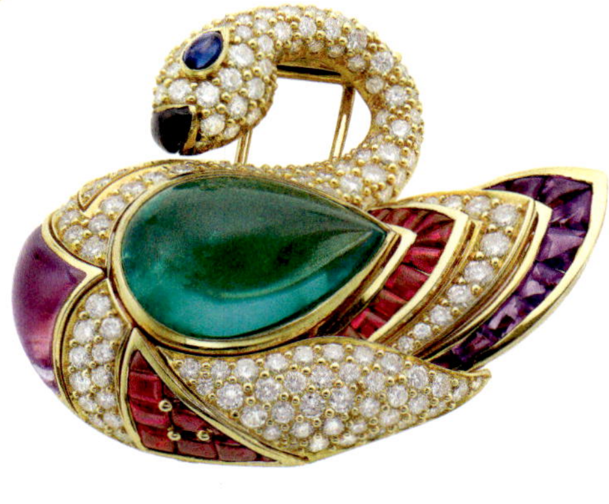

110. Necklace, 1989
Gold with emerald, amethysts, rubies, and diamonds

111. Swan brooch, 1990
Gold with emerald, sapphire, onyx, amethysts, rubies, and diamonds

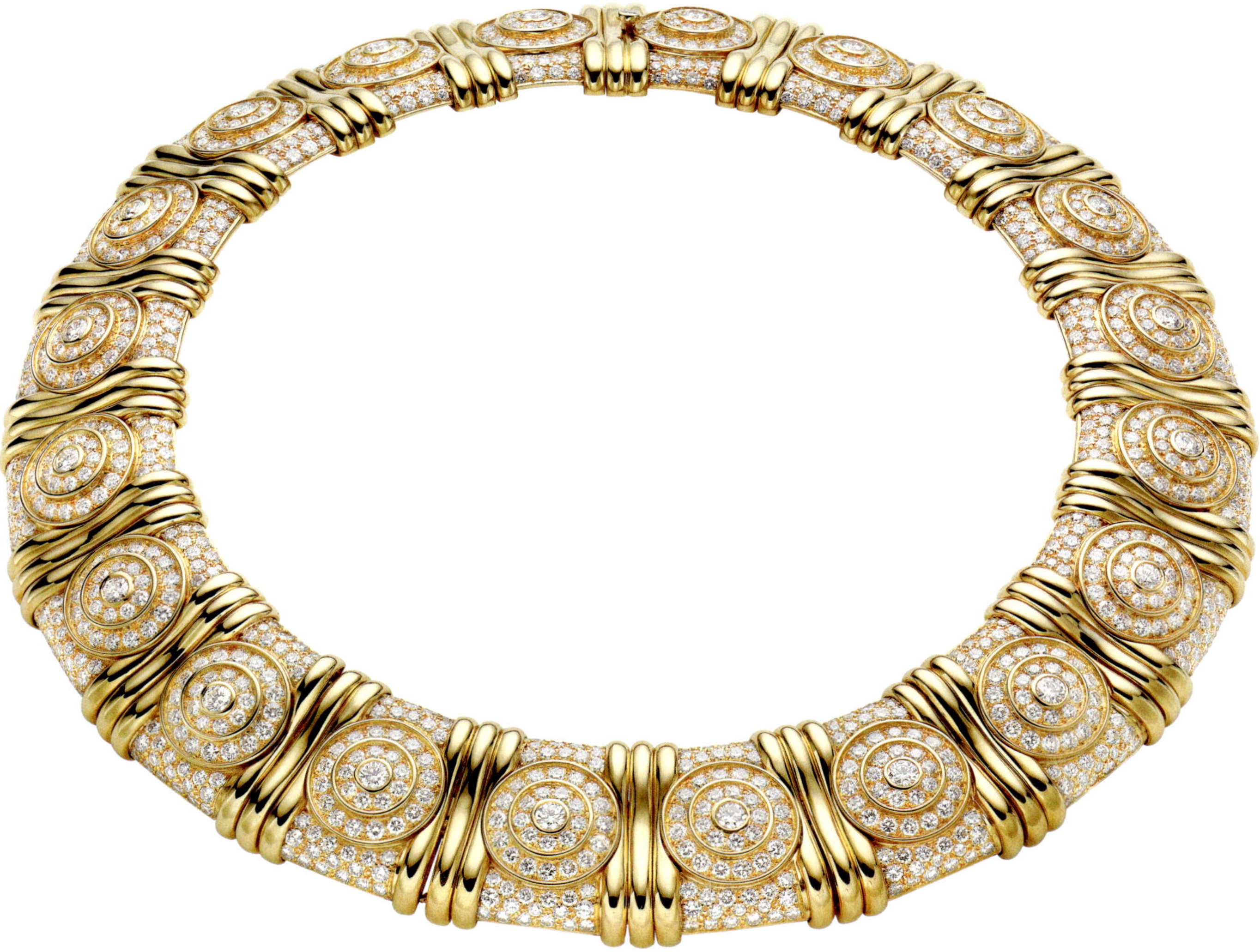

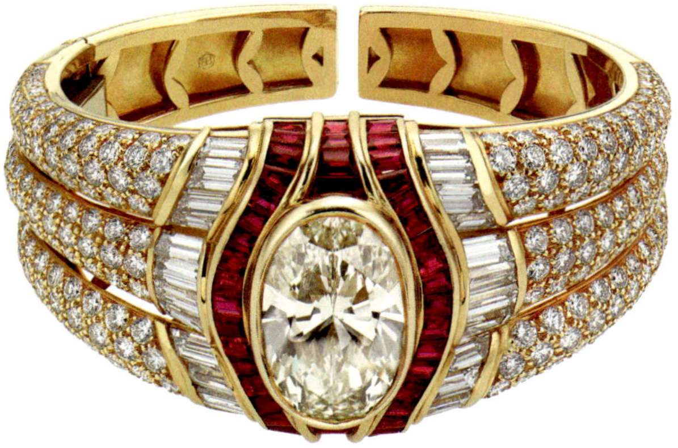

112. Bangle, 1988
Gold with rubies, yellow diamond, and white diamonds

113. Necklace, 1988
Gold with diamonds

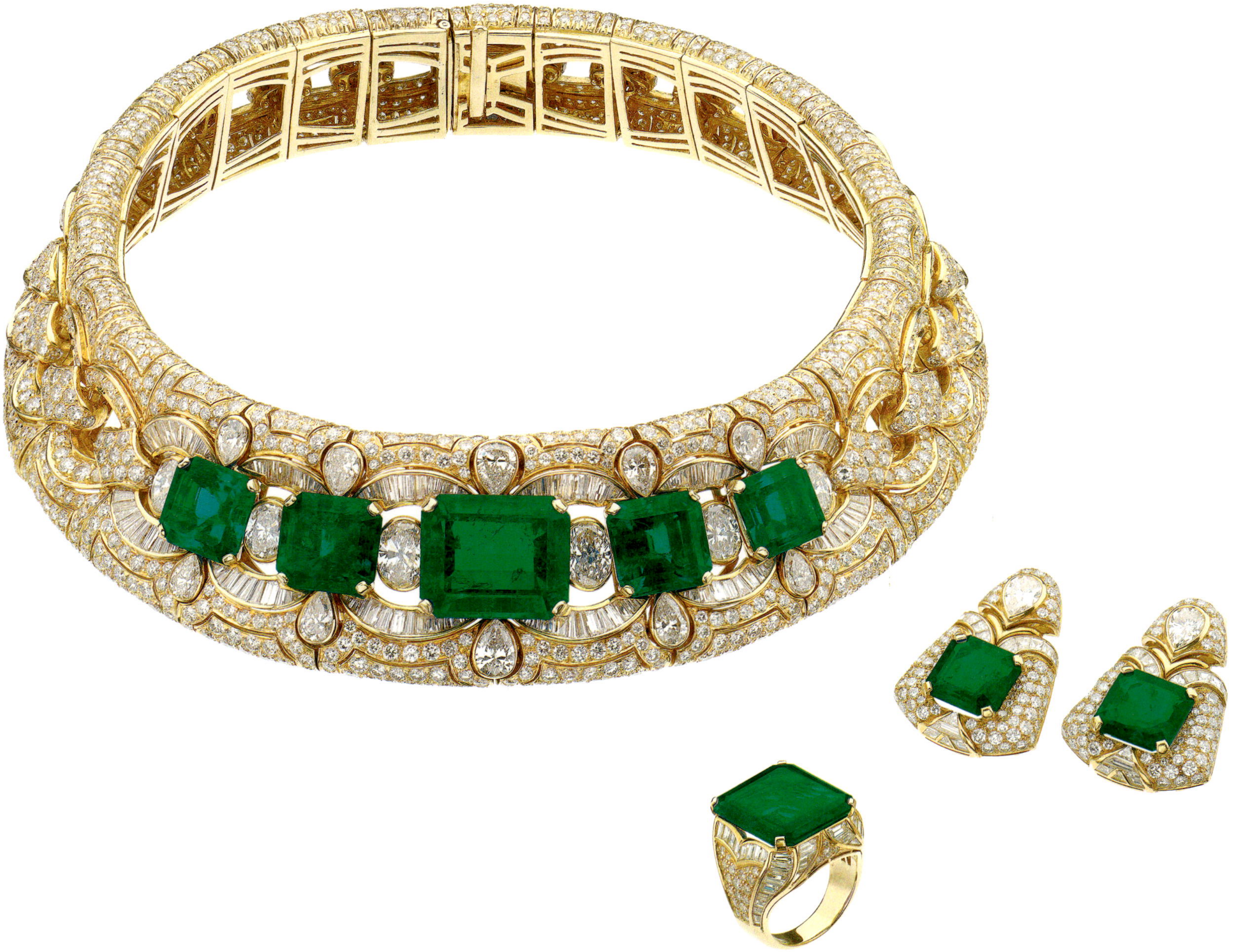

114. Parure, 1989–1992

Gold with emeralds and diamonds

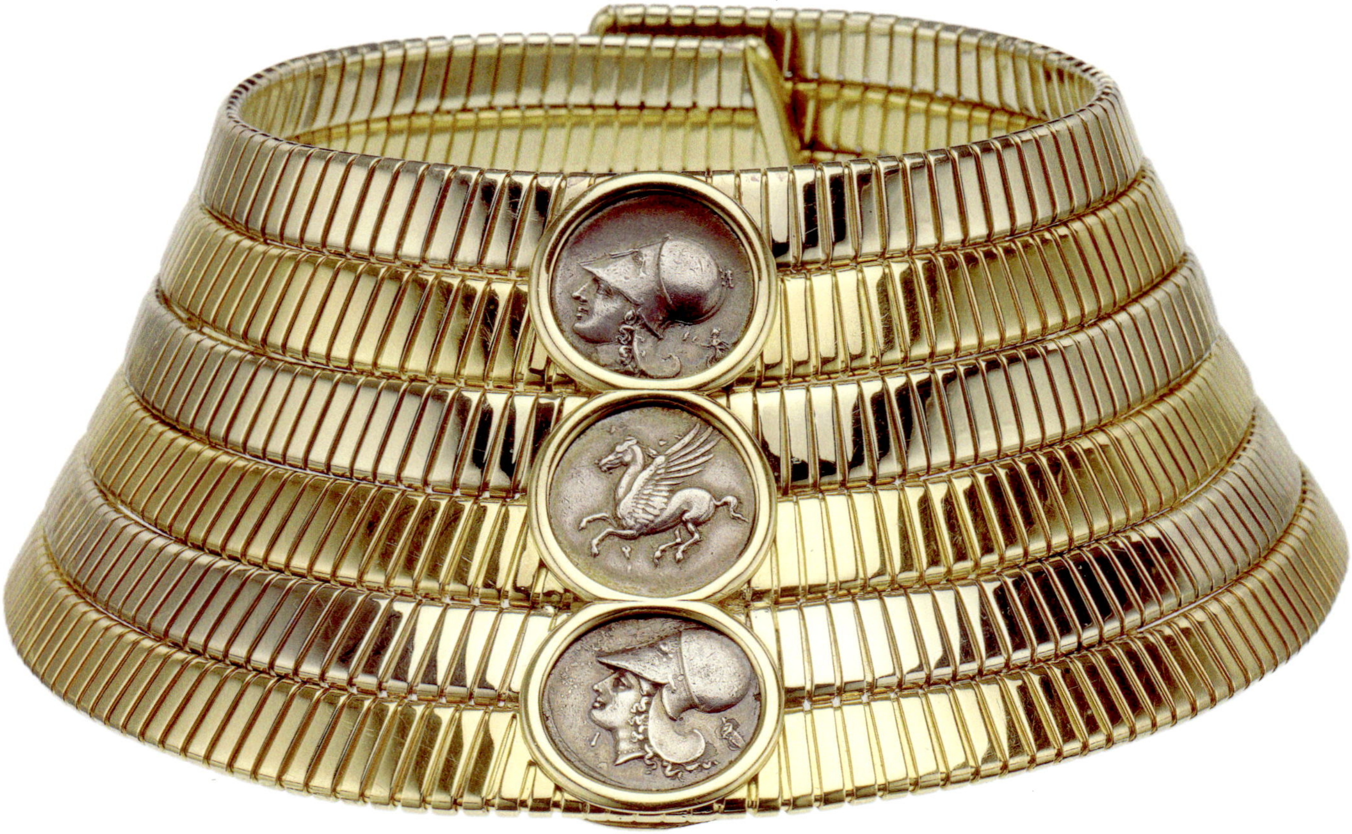

115. *Tubogas* choker, 1974
Two-color gold with Greek silver coins

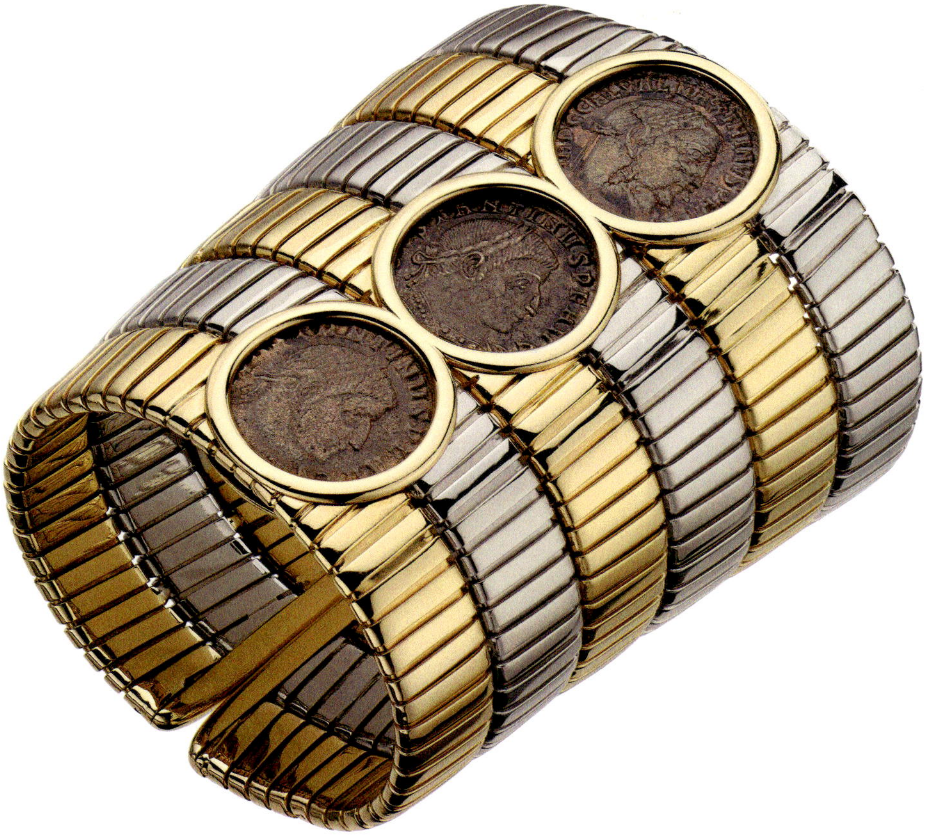

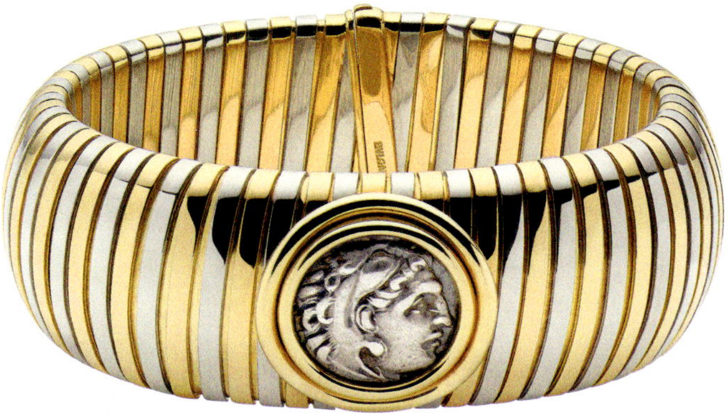

116. *Tubogas* bracelet, ca. 1982
Two-color gold with Hellenistic silver coin

117. *Tubogas* bracelet, ca. 1975
Two-color gold with Imperial Roman bronze coins

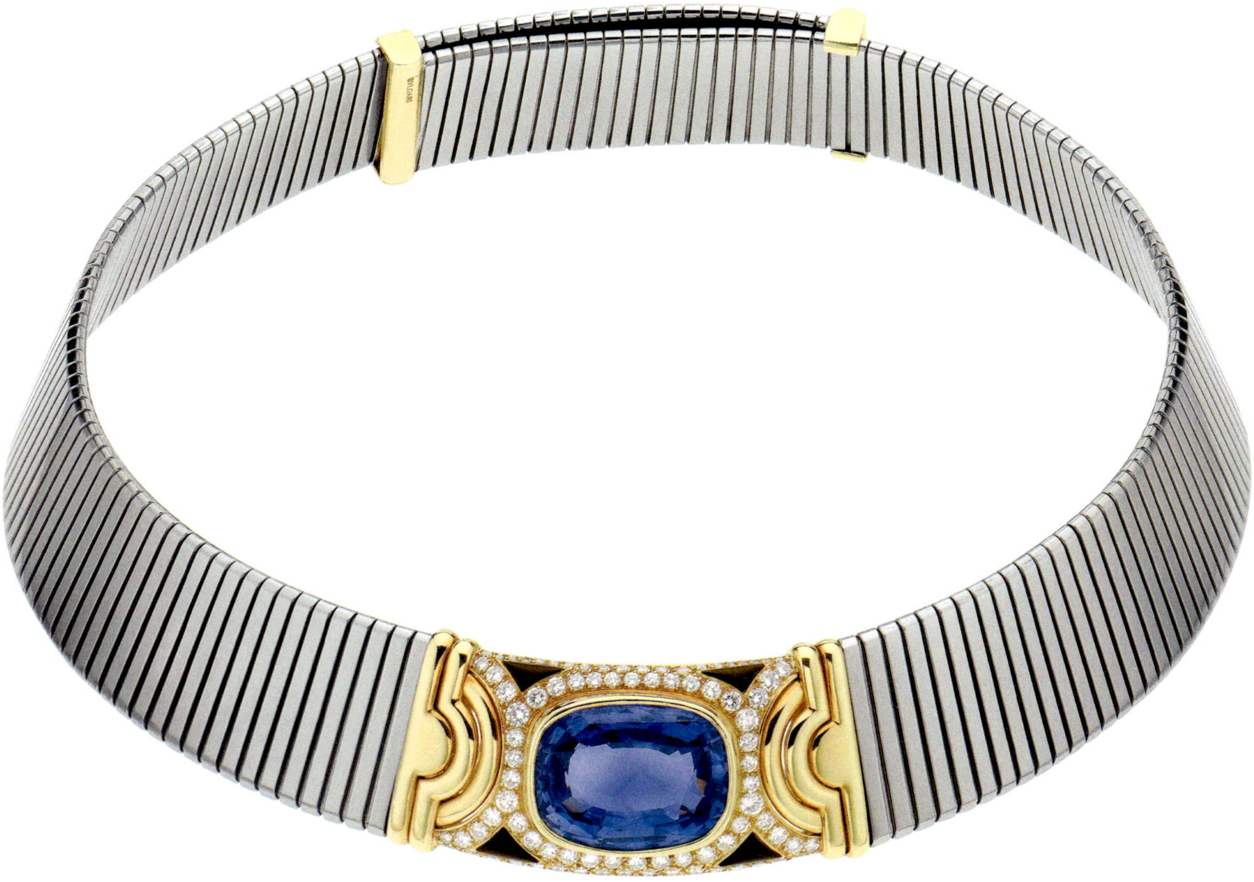

118. *Tubogas* choker, ca. 1983
Steel and gold with sapphire, onyx, and diamonds

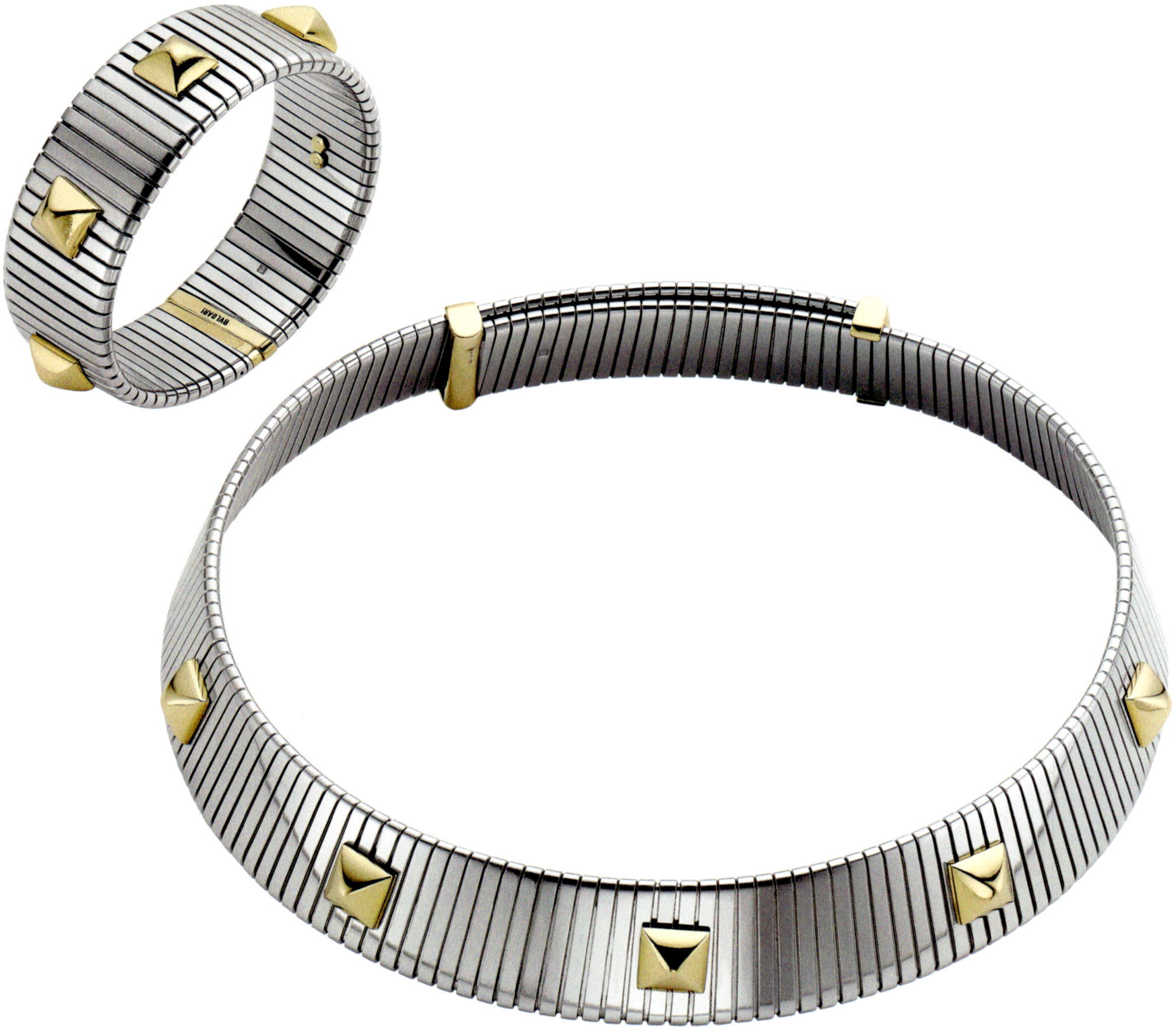

119. *Tubogas* choker and bracelet, 1982–1984
Steel and gold

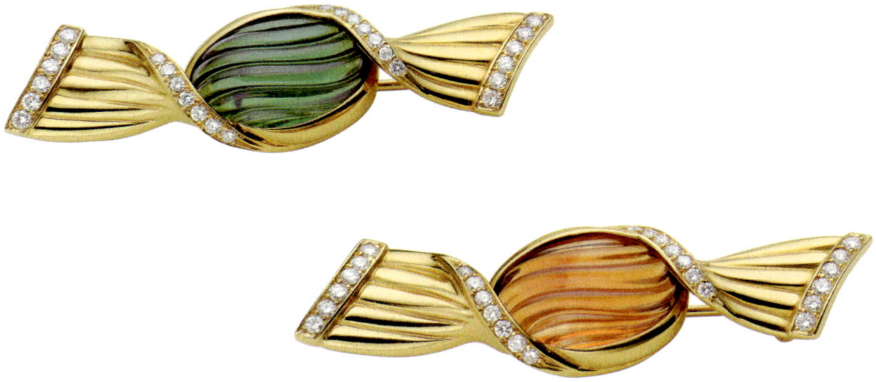

120. Caramella brooch, ca. 1983
Gold with green tourmaline and diamonds

121. Caramella brooch, ca. 1983
Gold with citrine and diamonds

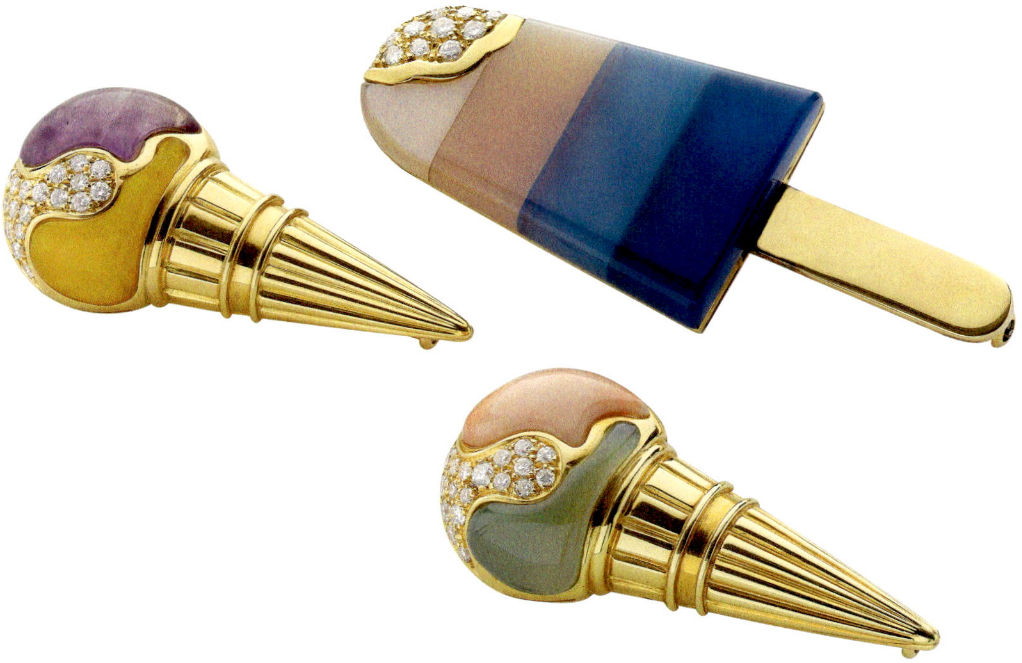

122. Ice cream cone brooch, ca. 1986
Gold with amethyst, yellow chalcedony, and diamonds

123. Ice pop brooch, ca. 1986
Gold with polychrome chalcedony and diamonds

124. Ice cream cone brooch, ca. 1986
Gold with coral, green chalcedony, and diamonds

Catalogue of the Exhibition

Unless otherwise noted, dimensions indicate height x width, or height x width x depth. Figures for necklaces and bracelets indicate length (measured end to end with the piece open) x width. Measurements for rings are taken at the bezel.
This list reflects the most complete information available at the time of publication.

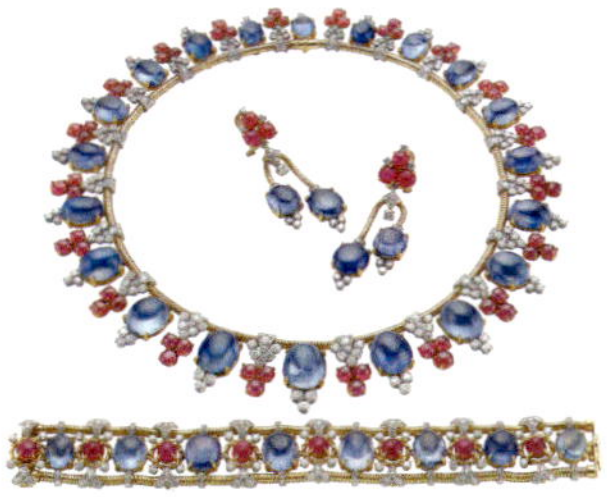

1. Parure, 1955–1956
Gold and platinum with sapphires, rubies, and diamonds
Necklace: 42 x 4 cm
Earrings: 6 x 2 cm
Bracelet: 18 x 3 cm
Private collection

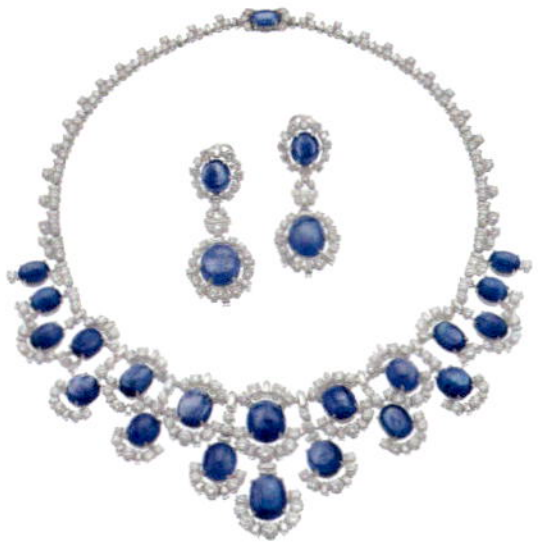

2. Necklace and pendant earrings, 1955
Platinum with sapphires and diamonds
Necklace: 41 x 4.9 cm
Earrings: 5.6 x 2 cm
Bulgari Heritage Collection, inv. 5076 N1589, 5074 E1830

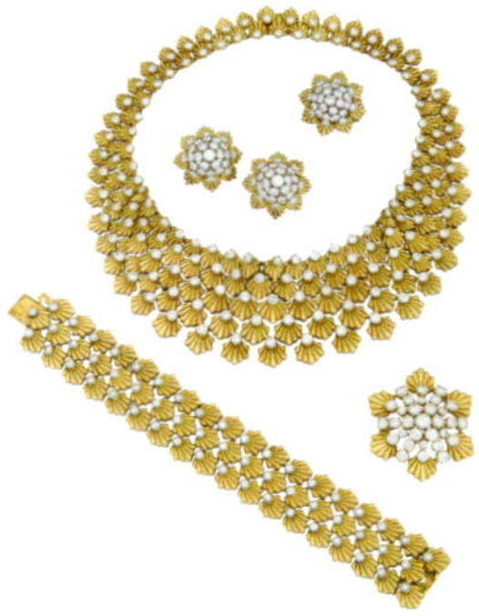

3. Parure, 1954–1958
Gold and platinum with diamonds
Necklace: 31 x 5 cm.
Earrings: 3 x 3 cm. Brooch: 5 x 5 cm. Ring: 4 x 4 cm.
Bracelet: 19 x 2.9 cm.
Private collection

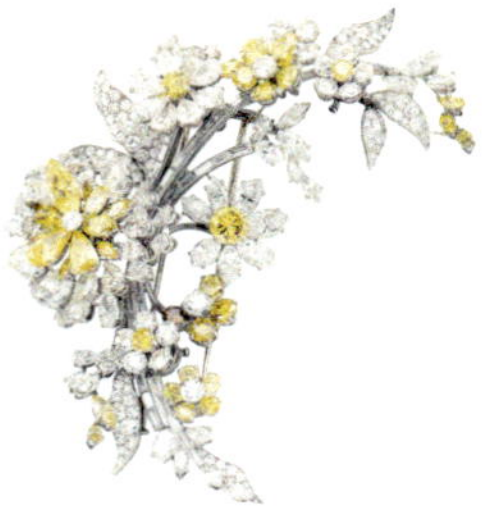

4. *Tremblant* brooch, 1960
Platinum with yellow and white diamonds
8.5 x 4 cm
Bulgari Heritage Collection, inv. 407 P29

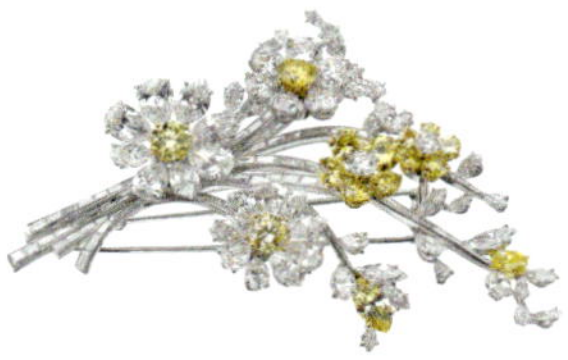

5. *Tremblant* brooch, 1962
Platinum with yellow and white diamonds
9.5 x 5 cm
Bulgari Heritage Collection, inv. 4998 P154

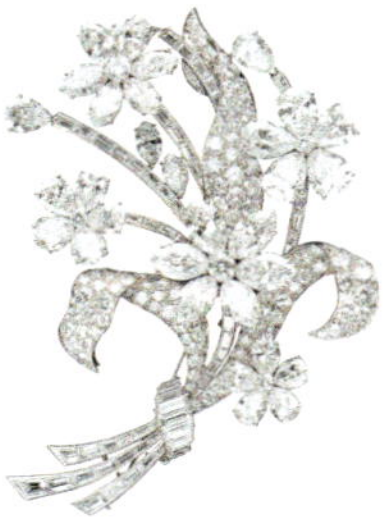

6. *Tremblant* brooch, 1958
Platinum with diamonds
8.5 x 5.2 cm
Bulgari Heritage Collection, inv. 408 P35

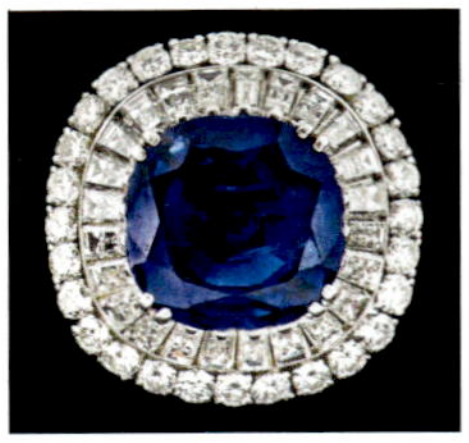

7. Ring, ca. 1960
Platinum with sapphires and diamonds
3 x 3 cm
Private collection

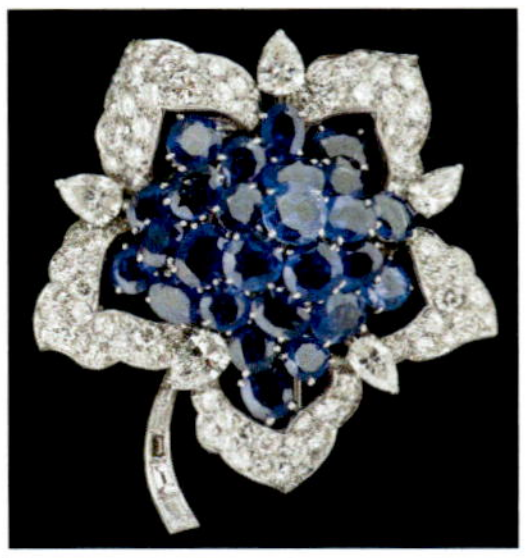

8. Brooch, 1961
Platinum with sapphires and diamonds
6.5 x 2 cm
Private collection

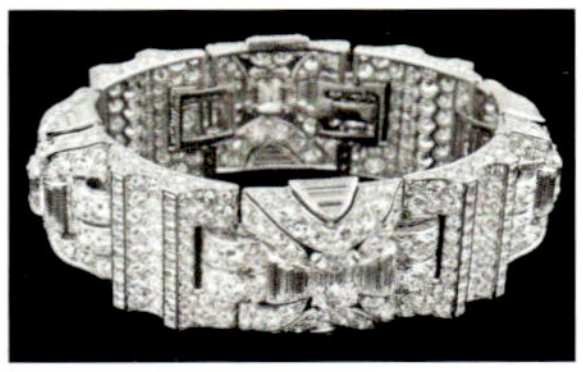

9. Bracelet, ca. 1950
Platinum with diamonds
18.4 x 2.4 cm
Private collection

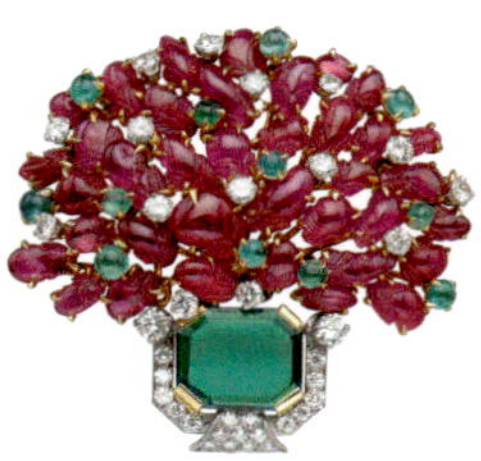

10. *Giardinetto* brooch, ca. 1959
Gold and platinum with emeralds, rubies, and diamonds
5 x 5 cm
Bulgari Heritage Collection, inv. 5000 P206

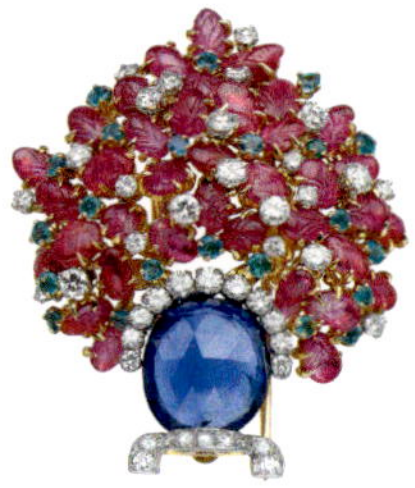

11. *Giardinetto* brooch, 1964
Gold and platinum with sapphire, rubies, emeralds, and diamonds
4.8 x 4 cm
Bulgari Heritage Collection, inv. 5111 P149

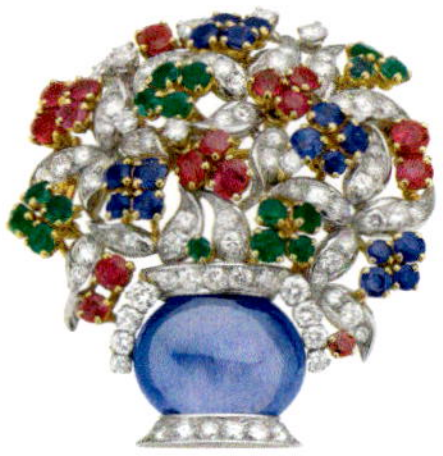

12. *Giardinetto* brooch, 1960
Gold and platinum with sapphires, emeralds, rubies, and diamonds
4 x 4.5 cm
Bulgari Heritage Collection, inv. 7068 P359

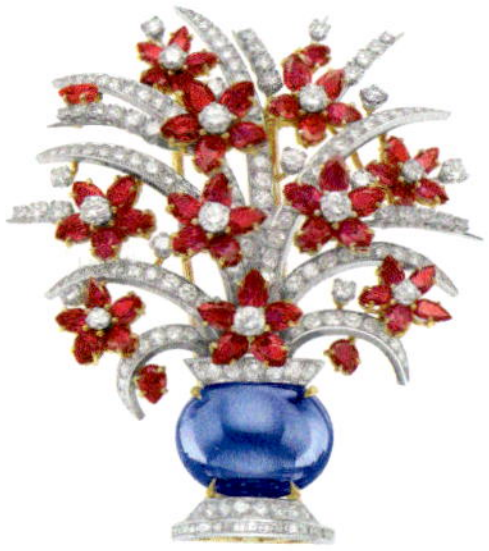

13. *Giardinetto* brooch, 1966
Gold and platinum with sapphire, rubies, and diamonds
7 x 6 cm
Bulgari Heritage Collection, inv. 348159 P403

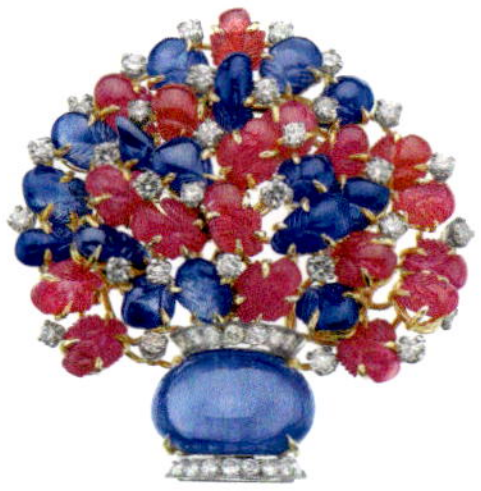

14. *Giardinetto* brooch, 1968
Gold with sapphires, rubies, and diamonds
4.5 x 4 cm
Bulgari Heritage Collection, inv. 5115 P313

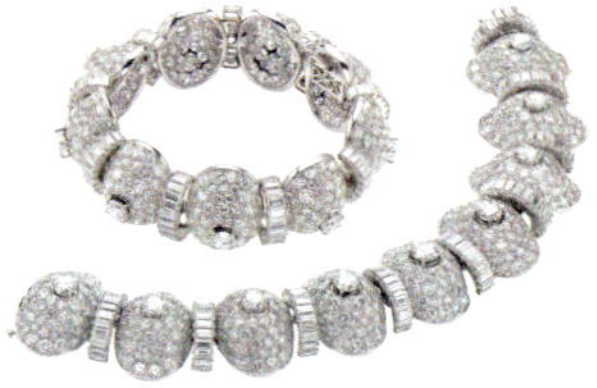

15. Bracelets, 1955 and 1959
Platinum with diamonds
Each 19.8 x 2.2 cm
Formerly in the collection of Ellen Barkin
Bulgari Heritage Collection, inv. 4924 B527, 4925 B528

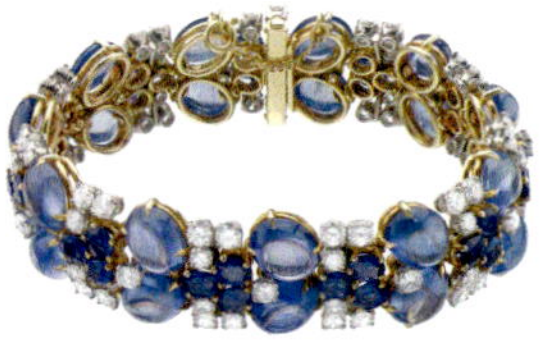

16. Bracelet, 1960
Gold with sapphires and diamonds
19.5 x 2 cm
Bulgari Heritage Collection, inv. 4956 B501

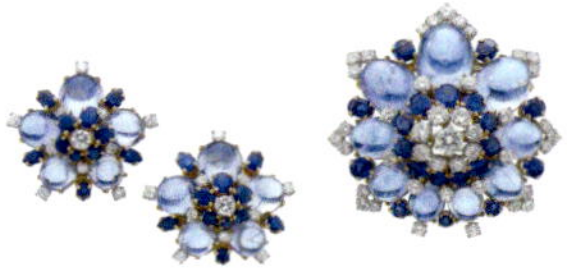

17. Brooch and earrings, 1960
Gold with sapphires and diamonds
Brooch: 4.5 x 4.2 cm
Earrings: 3 x 2.8 cm
Bulgari Heritage Collection, inv. 4955 P259, 4960 E1719

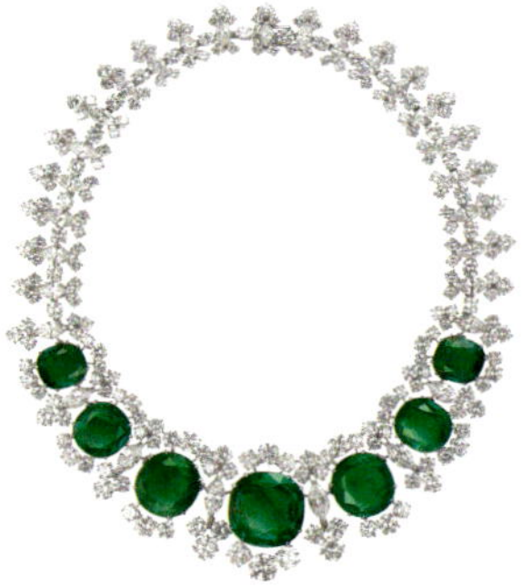

18. Necklace, 1961
Platinum with emeralds and diamonds
39.7 x 4 cm
Bulgari Heritage Collection, inv. 405 N622

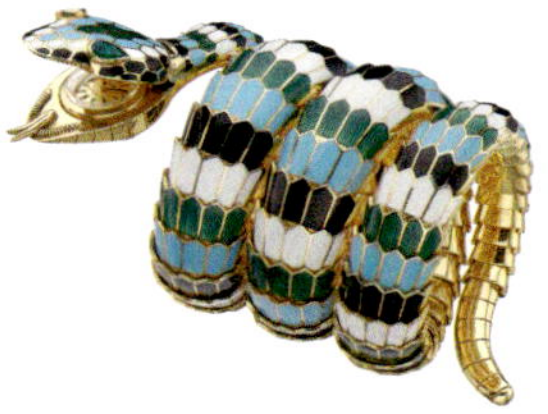

19. Snake bracelet-watch, 1967
Gold with polychrome enamel and emeralds
44 x 2 cm
Bulgari Heritage Collection, inv. 5035 W43

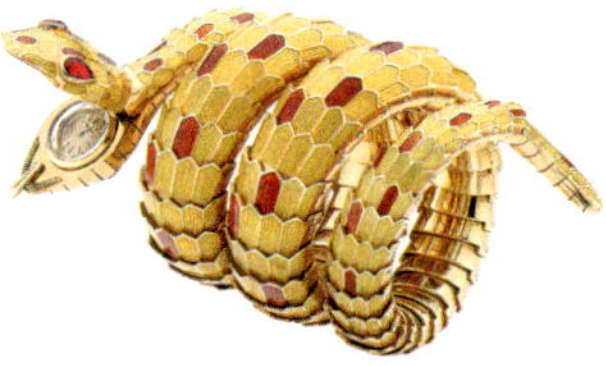

20. Snake bracelet-watch, ca. 1967
Gold with yellow and red enamel and rubies
43 x 2 cm
Bulgari Heritage Collection, inv. 5814 W47

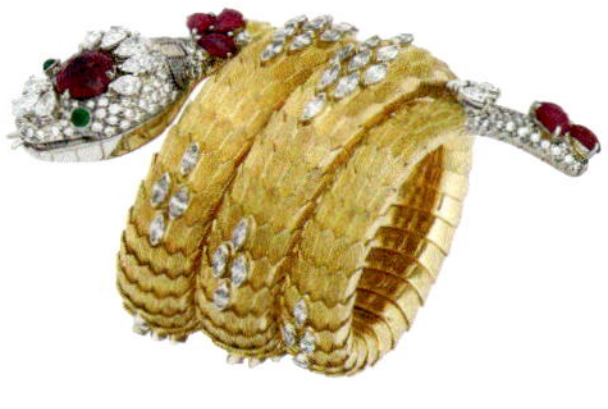

21. Snake bracelet-watch, ca. 1962
Gold with rubies, emeralds, and diamonds
57.5 x 1.5 cm
Private collection

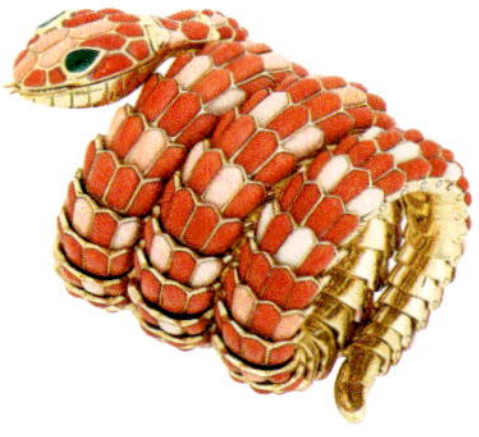

22. Snake bracelet-watch, ca. 1965
Gold with coral, emeralds, and diamonds
59 x 1.5 cm
Private collection

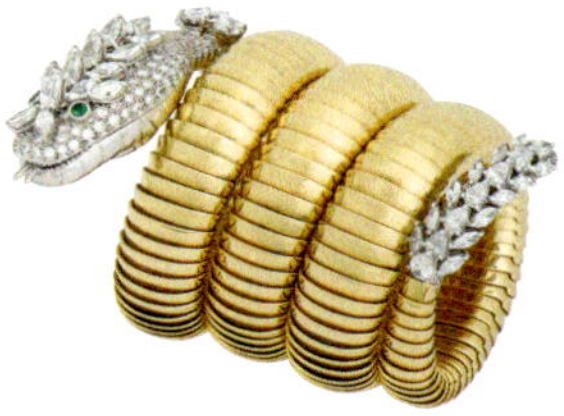

23. Snake bracelet-watch, ca. 1962
Gold and platinum with emeralds and diamonds
72 x 1.5 cm
Private collection

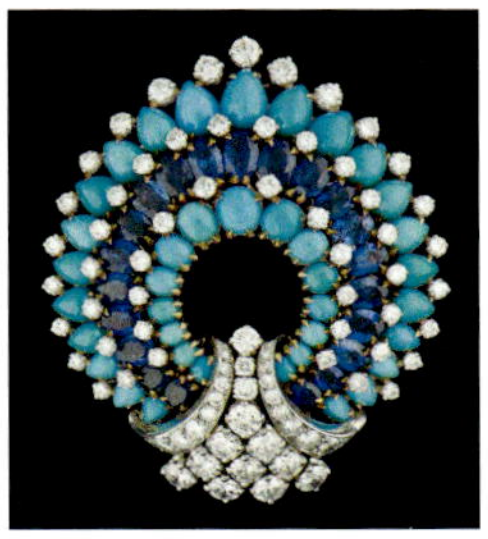

24. Brooch, 1959
Platinum with turquoise, sapphires, and diamonds
5.5 x 4.6 cm
Private collection

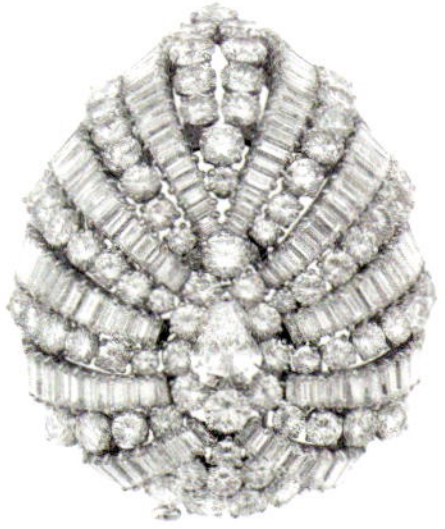

25. Shield brooch, 1967
Platinum with diamonds
6 x 4 cm
Bulgari Heritage Collection, inv. 8044 P390

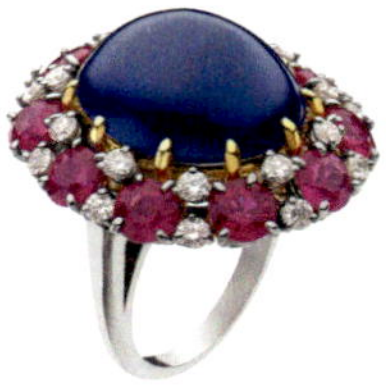

26. Ring, ca. 1960
Platinum and gold with sapphire, rubies, and diamonds
3 x 2 cm
Bulgari Heritage Collection, inv. 4935 RS295

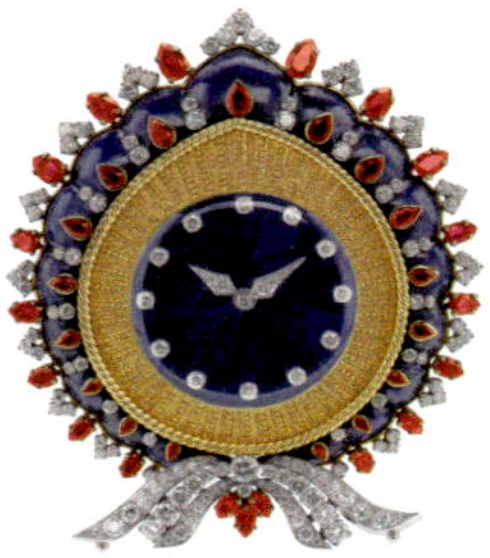

27. Table clock, 1968
Gold and platinum with lapis lazuli, rubies, and diamonds
9 x 7.5 cm
Bulgari Heritage Collection, inv. 432 V10

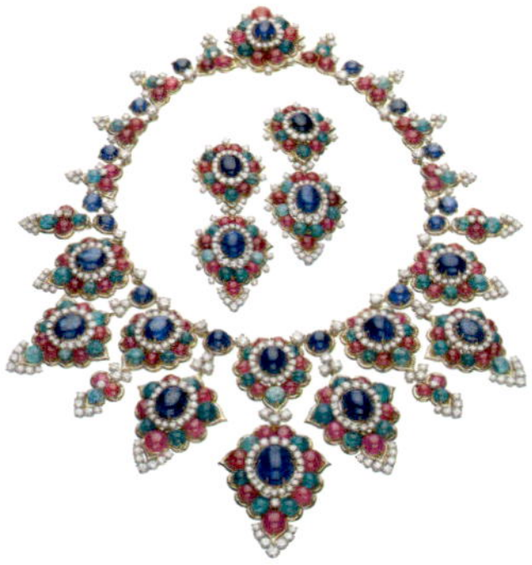

28. Necklace and pendant earrings, 1967
Gold with sapphires, emeralds, rubies, and diamonds
Necklace: 32.5 x 7.3 cm
Earrings: 7.3 x 2.8 cm
Formerly in the collection of Mayrink Veiga
Bulgari Heritage Collection, inv. 5125 N1397, 5140 E1562

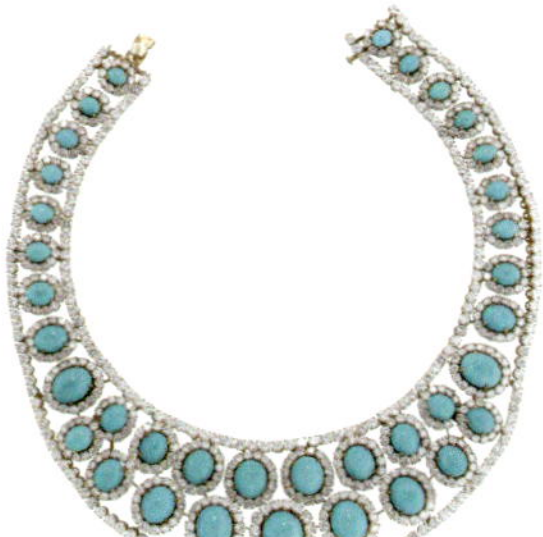

29. Necklace, 1972
Platinum with turquoise and diamonds
39.1 x 17.8 cm (with 5.1 cm extension, not shown)
Collection of Jennifer Tilly

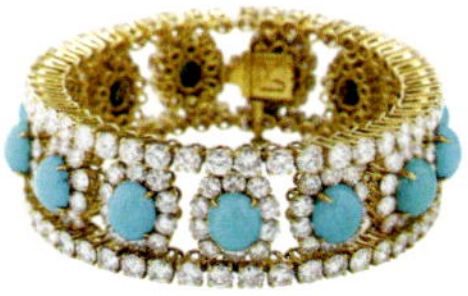

30. Bracelet, 1972
Platinum with turquoise and diamonds
17.8 x 1.9 cm
Collection of Jennifer Tilly

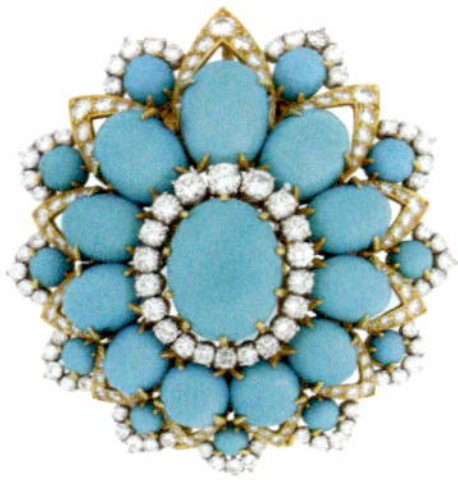

31. Brooch, ca. 1969
Platinum with turquoise and diamonds
6.3 x 5 cm
Collection of Jennifer Tilly

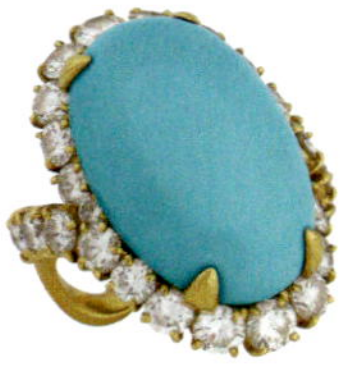

32. Ring, ca. 1969
Platinum with turquoise and diamonds
2.5 x 1.3 cm
Collection of Jennifer Tilly

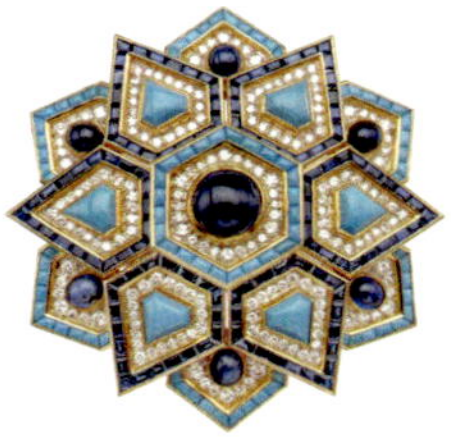

33. Brooch, 1969
Gold and platinum with turquoise, sapphires, and diamonds
5 x 5 cm
Bulgari Heritage Collection, inv. 4992 P111

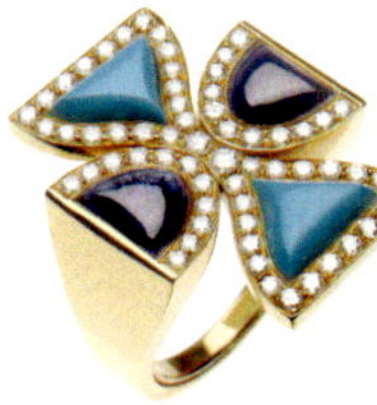

34. Ring, ca. 1975
Gold with sapphires, turquoise, and diamonds
3 x 2.8 cm
Bulgari Heritage Collection, inv. 4934 RS186

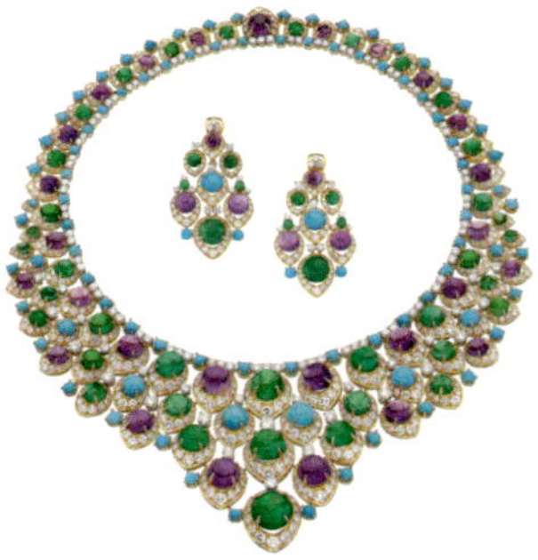

35. Bib necklace and pendant earrings, 1965
Gold with emeralds, amethysts, turquoise, and diamonds
Necklace: 39 x 6 cm
Earrings: 6 x 3.5 cm
Formerly in the collection of Lyn Revson
Bulgari Heritage Collection, inv. 401 N565, 762 E527

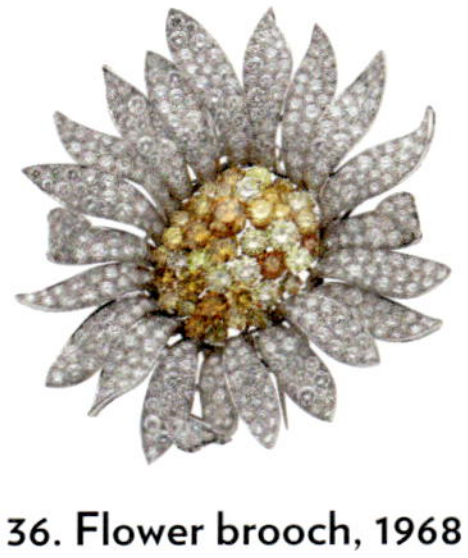

36. Flower brooch, 1968
Platinum and gold with yellow and white diamonds
8.5 x 8 cm
Bulgari Heritage Collection, inv. 7338 P367

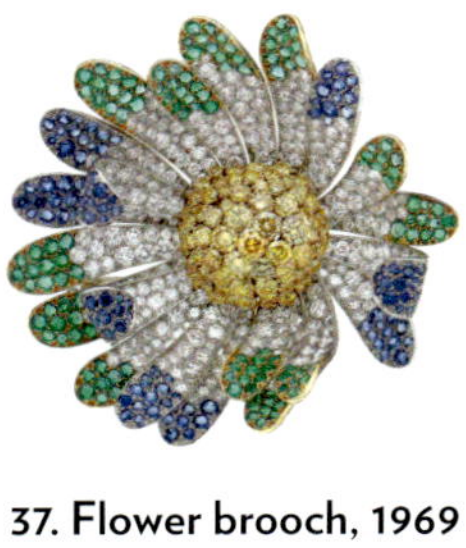

37. Flower brooch, 1969
Platinum with emeralds, sapphires, and yellow and white diamonds
7 x 7 cm
Bulgari Heritage Collection, inv. 6174 P346

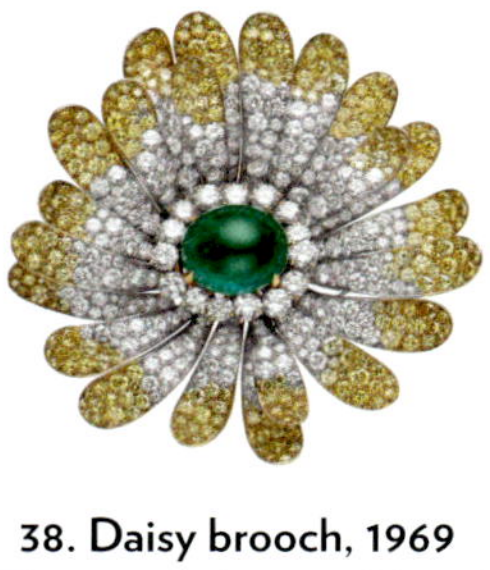

38. Daisy brooch, 1969
Platinum with emerald and yellow and white diamonds
7 x 7.5 cm
Bulgari Heritage Collection, inv. 348607 P410

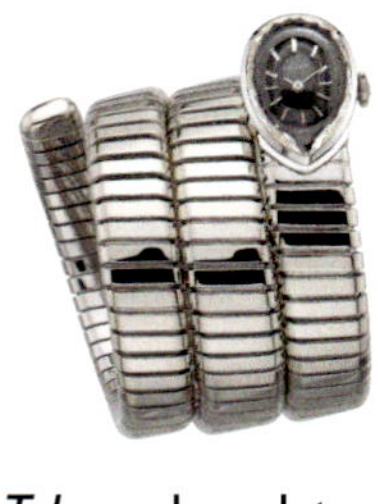

39. *Tubogas* bracelet-watch, ca. 1960
White gold
36 x 1.5 cm
Bulgari Heritage Collection, inv. 5032 W40

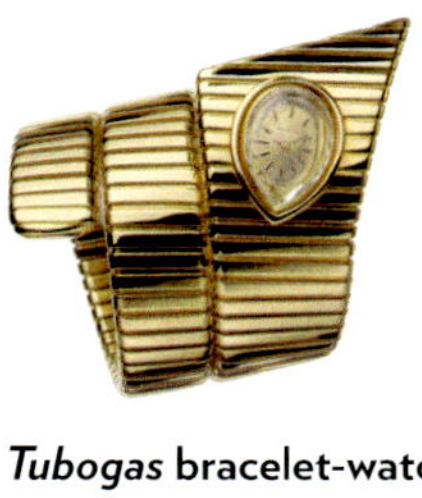

40. *Tubogas* bracelet-watch, ca. 1972
Gold
26 x 3.5 cm
Bulgari Heritage Collection, inv. 439 W26

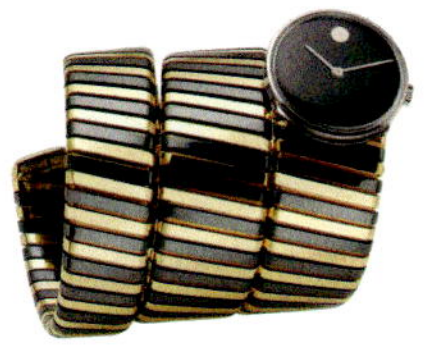

41. *Tubogas* bracelet-watch, ca. 1972
Gold and burnished steel
36 x 2 cm
Bulgari Heritage Collection, inv. 5952 08

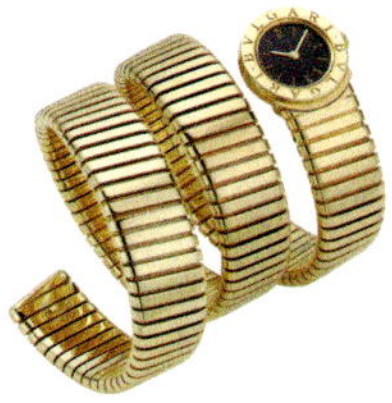

42. *Tubogas* "BVLGARI-BVLGARI" bracelet-watch, 1980
Gold
40 x 1.8 cm
Bulgari Heritage Collection, inv. 5955 13

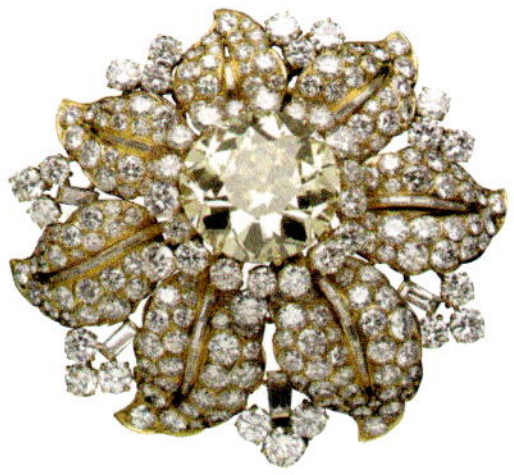

43. Brooch, ca. 1968
Gold with diamonds
5.8 x 5.8 cm
Private collection

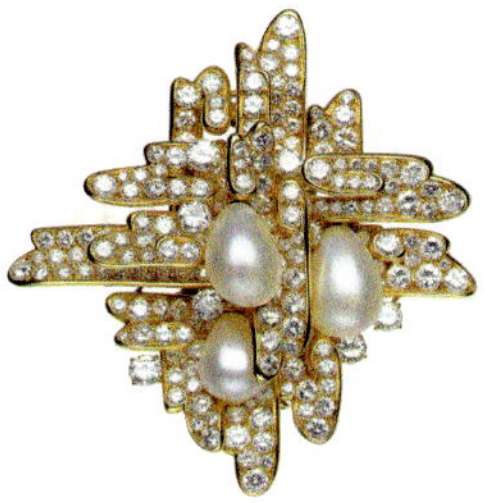

44. Brooch, 1970
Gold with natural pearls and diamonds
8 x 7.2 cm
Bulgari Heritage Collection, inv. 4952 P112

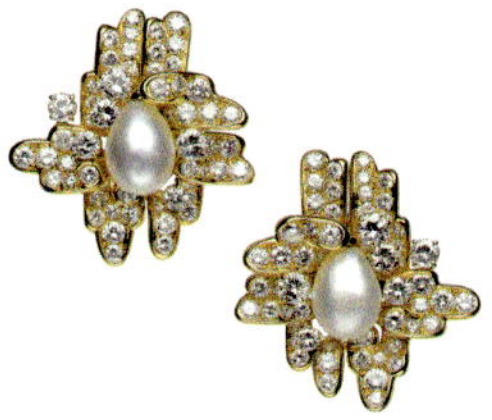

45. Earrings, 1970
Gold with natural pearls and diamonds
3.9 x 3.9 cm
Bulgari Heritage Collection, inv. 4957 E792

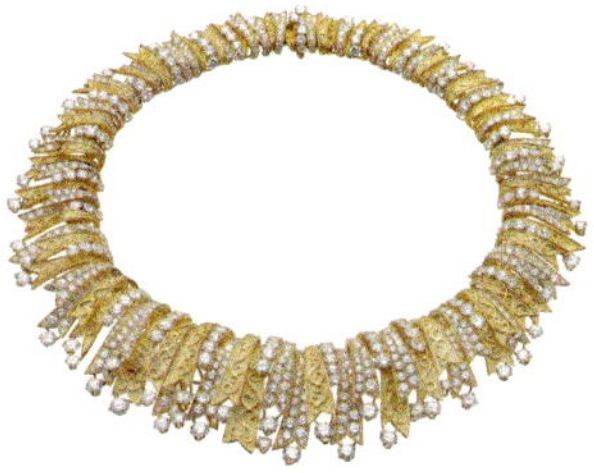

46. Fireworks necklace, 1969
Gold with diamonds
39 x 4.2 cm
Bulgari Heritage Collection, inv. 4880 N734

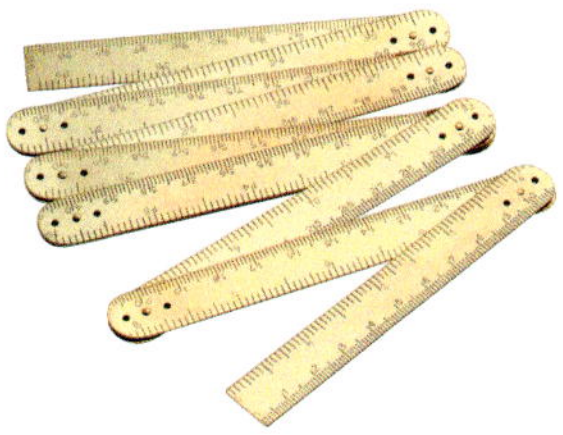

47. Measuring stick, ca. 1970
Gold
100 x 1.4 cm
Bulgari Heritage Collection, inv. 5122 V97

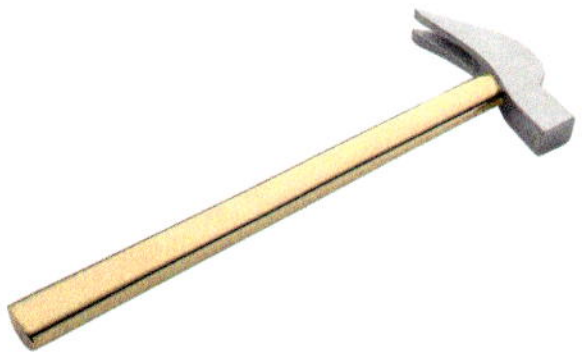

48. Hammer, 1972
Two-color gold
27 x 9 x 1.9 cm
Bulgari Heritage Collection, inv. 6089 V120

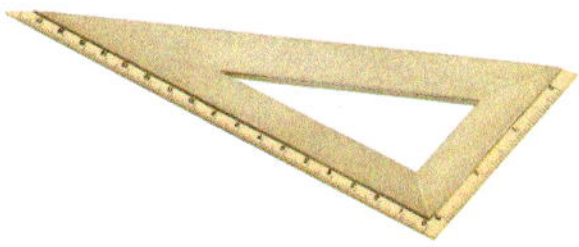

49. Square, ca. 1970
Gilded silver and gold
19 x 9.5 cm
Bulgari Heritage Collection, inv. 6080 V122

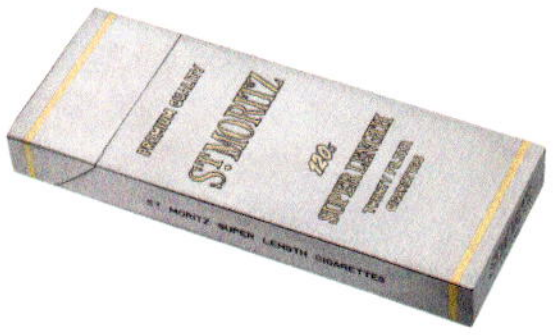

50. "St. Moritz" cigarette case, 1977
Silver and gold
12.3 x 4.7 x 1.6 cm
Bulgari Heritage Collection, inv. 4936 D100

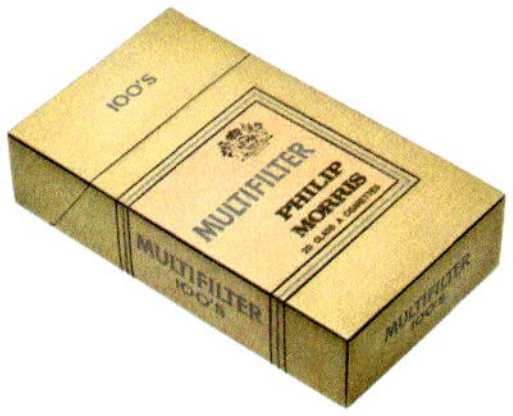

51. "Multifilter Philip Morris" cigarette case, 1977
Two-color gold with white and black enamel
10 x 5.5 x 2.4 cm
Bulgari Heritage Collection, inv. 6888 V136

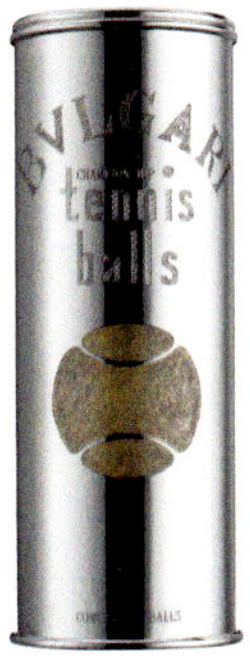

52. Tennis-ball canister, 1980
Silver and gold
21.5 x 7.5 x 7.5 cm
Bulgari Heritage Collection, inv. 7366 V147

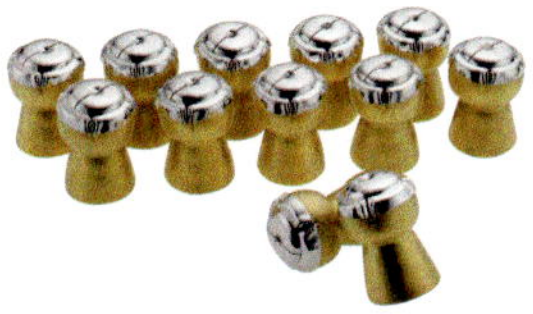

53. Set of champagne cork place-card holders, ca. 1975
Silver and gilded silver
Each 4.4 x 2.5 cm
Bulgari Heritage Collection, inv. 4940 V47

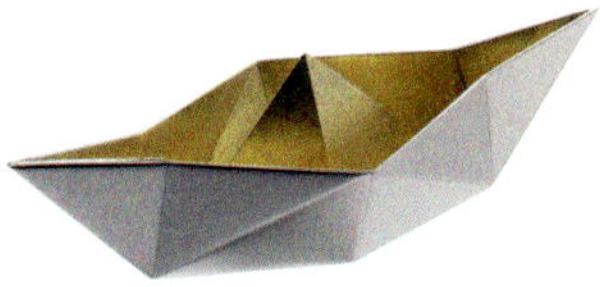

54. Boat paperweight, 1974
Sterling silver and gilded silver
14 x 6 x 3 cm
Bulgari Heritage Collection, inv. 5773 V103

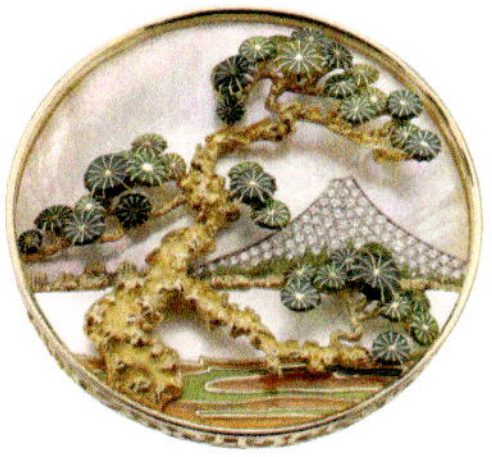

55. Mount Fuji brooch, 1971
Gold and platinum with mother-of-pearl, polychrome enamel, and diamonds
6.5 x 6.5 cm
Bulgari Heritage Collection, inv. 5003 P245

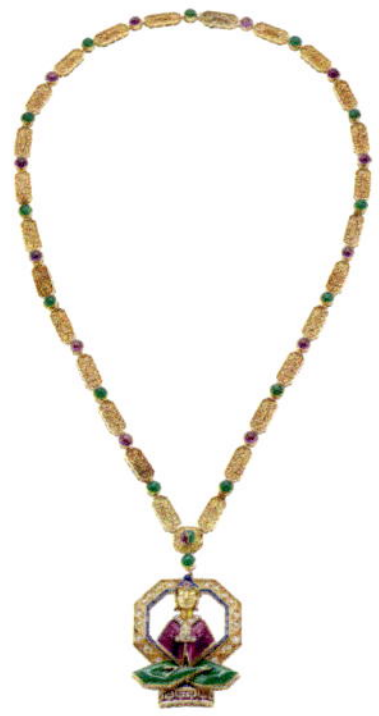

56. Buddha sautoir, 1971
Gold with malachite, amethysts, emeralds, sapphires, lapis lazuli, rubies, and diamonds
Chain: 81.8 x 1 cm
Pendant: 6.5 x 5.1 cm
Bulgari Heritage Collection, inv. 348162 N2230

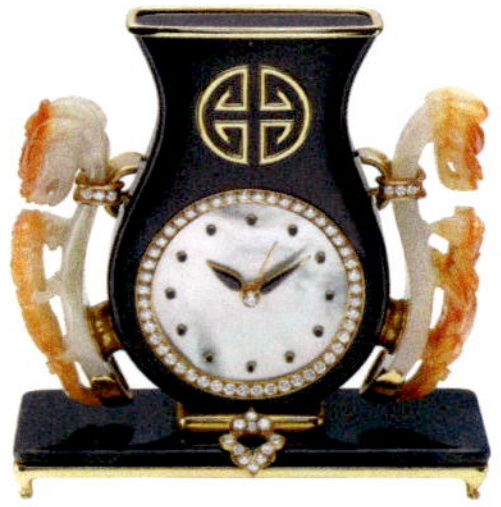

57. Table clock, 1980
Gold with onyx, mother-of-pearl, jade, and diamonds
10.1 x 9.8 x 4.1 cm
Bulgari Heritage Collection, inv. 7103 W66

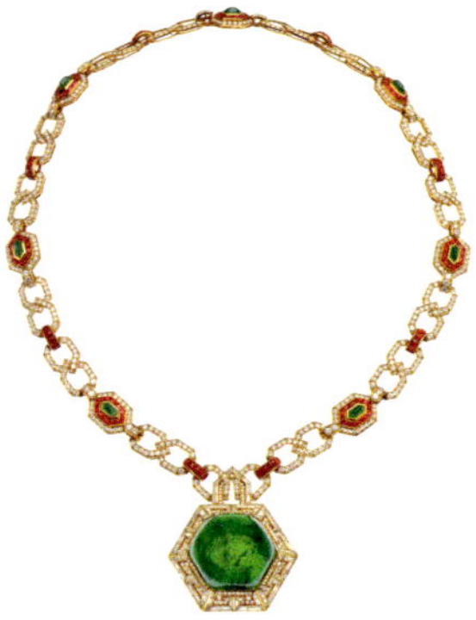

58. Sautoir, ca. 1970
Gold with emeralds, rubies, and diamonds
Chain: 75 x 2 cm
Pendant: 5.5 x 4.6 cm
Bulgari Heritage Collection, inv. 4883 N755

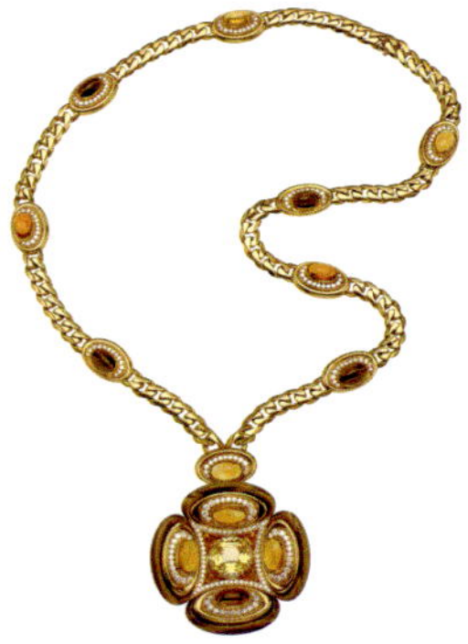

59. Sautoir, ca. 1973
Gold with yellow sapphire, tiger's eye, citrines, and diamonds
Chain: 73 x 2 cm. Pendant/brooch: 6.5 x 6.5 cm
Bulgari Heritage Collection, inv. 5120 N753

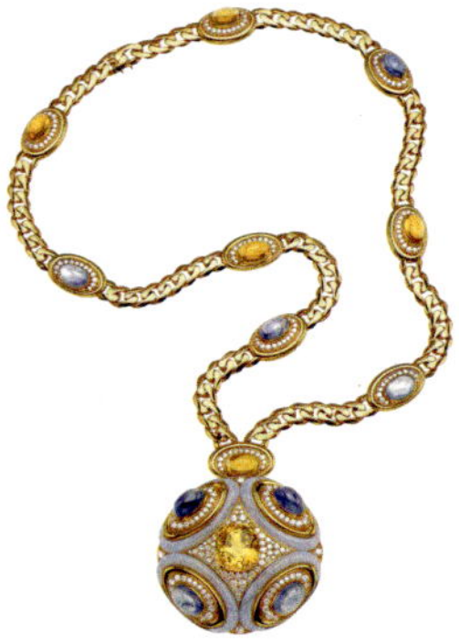

60. Sautoir, ca. 1972
Gold with yellow and blue sapphires, agate, citrines, and diamonds
Chain: 72 x 2 cm
Pendant/brooch: 6 x 6 cm
Bulgari Heritage Collection, inv. 5065 N754

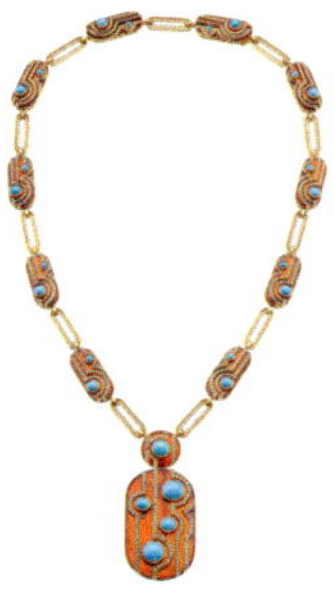

61. Sautoir, ca. 1970
Gold with carnelian, turquoise, and diamonds
Chain: 73 x 2 cm
Pendant/brooch: 6.5 x 4 cm
Bulgari Heritage Collection, inv. 5118 N752

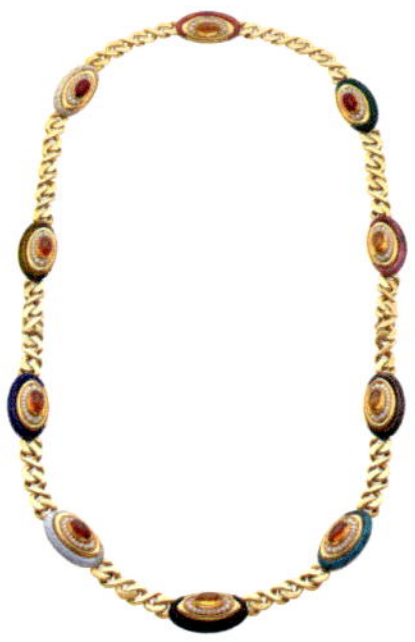

62. Sautoir, ca. 1975
Gold with citrines, colored hardstones, and diamonds
94.5 x 1.8 cm
Bulgari Heritage Collection, inv. 348161 N2231

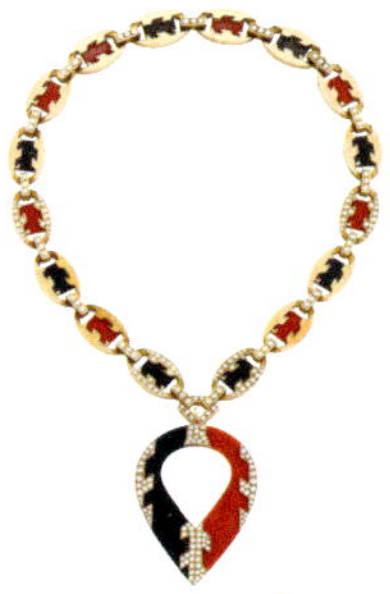

63. Sautoir, 1973
Gold with coral, onyx, and diamonds
Chain: 80 x 1.8 cm (including extension/bracelet, not shown)
Pendant/brooch: 7.3 x 5.3 cm
Collection of Linda S. Chaiken

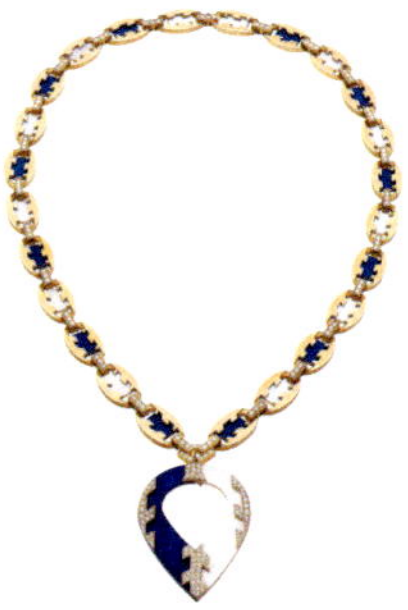

64. Sautoir, 1971
Gold with lapis lazuli, mother-of-pearl, and diamonds
Chain: 80 x 1.8 cm (including extension/bracelet, not shown)
Pendant/brooch: 7.3 x 5.3 cm
Bulgari Heritage Collection, inv. 6835 N1880

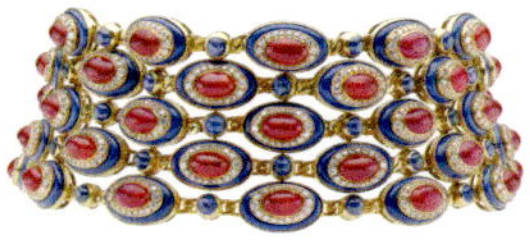

65. Choker, ca. 1979
Gold with rubies, sapphires, lapis lazuli, and diamonds
36 x 5 cm
Bulgari Heritage Collection, inv. 7309 N1990

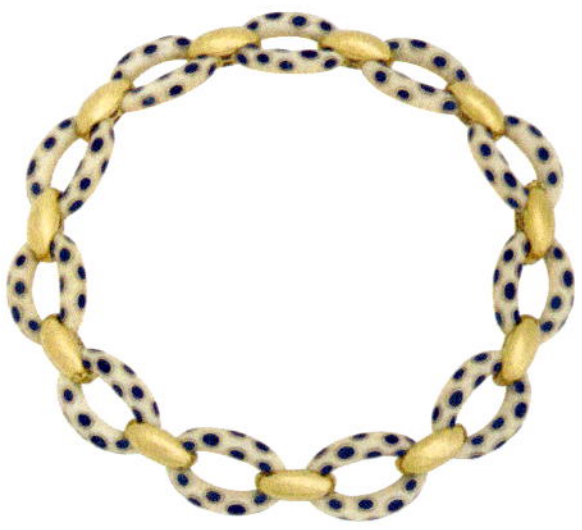

66. Necklace, 1971
Gold with ivory and lapis lazuli
43.5 x 2.5 cm
Private collection

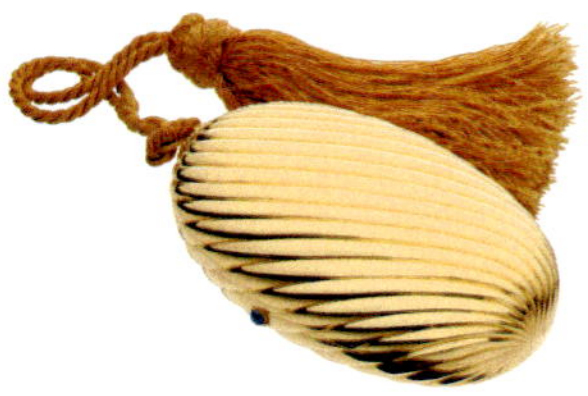

67. Melone evening bag, 1972
Gold with sapphire
14 x 9 x 2.5 cm
Bulgari Heritage Collection, inv. 5045 V35

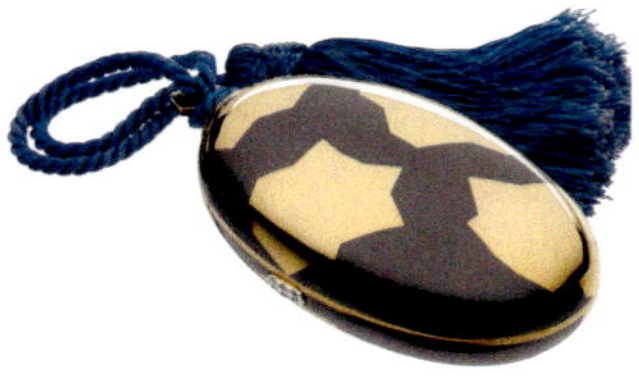

68. Melone evening bag, ca. 1972
Gold and burnished steel with diamonds
14 x 9 x 3 cm
Formerly in the collection of Lyn Revson
Bulgari Heritage Collection, inv. 5046 V36

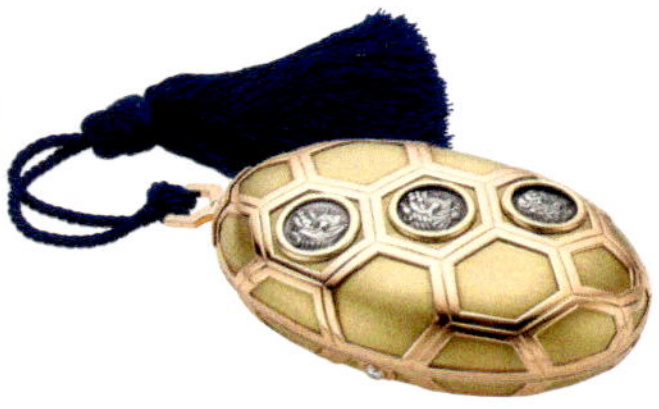

69. Melone evening bag, 1978
Gold with Hellenistic silver coins and diamond
16 x 10 x 3 cm
Bulgari Heritage Collection, inv. 5058 V92

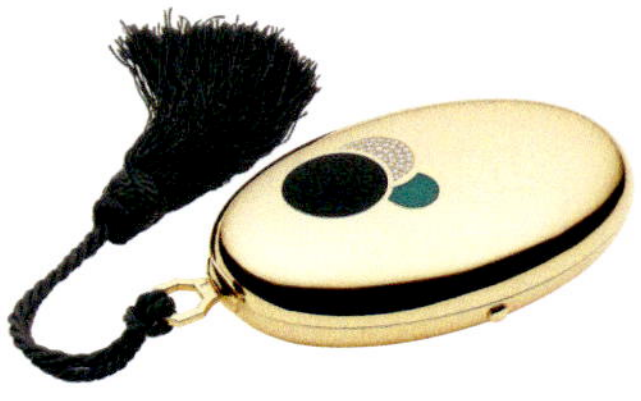

70. Melone evening bag, ca. 1975
Gold with onyx, chrysoprase, and diamonds
19 x 10 x 5.5 cm
Bulgari Heritage Collection, inv. 7181 V138

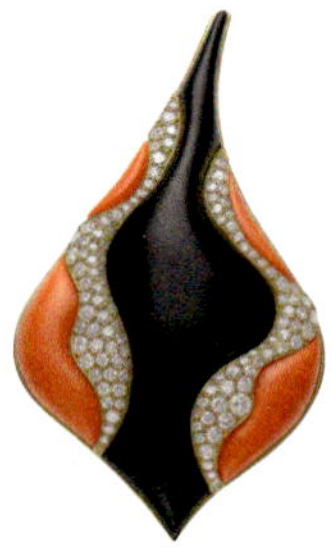

71. Brooch, 1973
Gold with onyx, coral, and diamonds
7.5 x 4 cm
Bulgari Heritage Collection, inv. 348147 P404

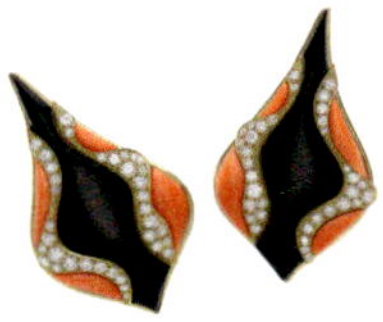

72. Earrings, 1973
Gold with onyx, coral, and diamonds
3.8 x 2.2 cm
Bulgari Heritage Collection, inv. 348148 E2556

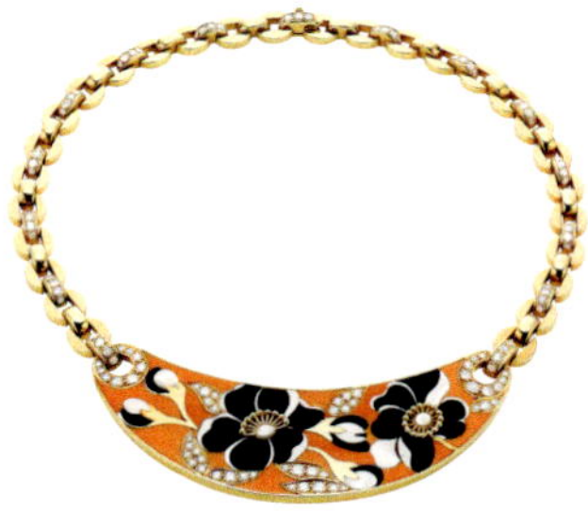

73. Necklace, 1977
Gold with coral, onyx, mother-of-pearl, and diamonds
40 x 2.8 cm
Bulgari Heritage Collection, inv. 7145 N1959

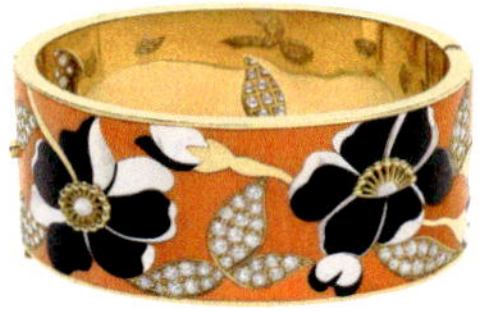

74. Bangle, 1977
Gold with coral, onyx, mother-of-pearl, and diamonds
19.5 x 3 cm
Bulgari Heritage Collection, inv. 7146 B667

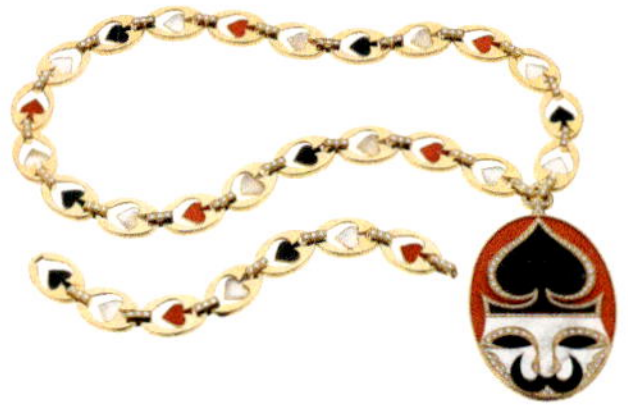

75. Playing card sautoir, 1972
Gold with coral, mother-of-pearl, onyx, and diamonds
Chain: 58 x 1.8 cm, with extension/bracelet of 19.5 cm
Pendant: 9.9 x 5.8 cm
Bulgari Heritage Collection, inv. 5066 N1324

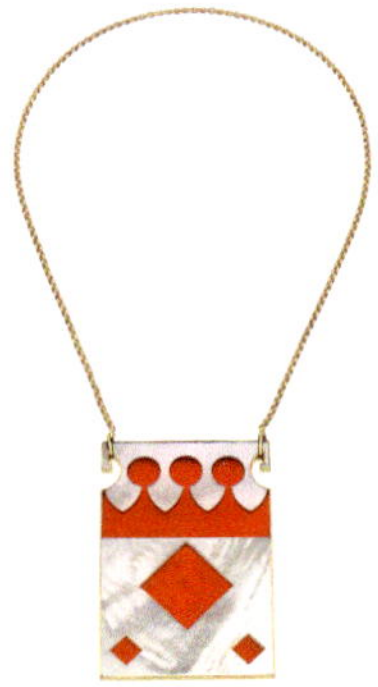

76. Playing card pendant on chain necklet, 1972
Gold with coral and mother-of-pearl
Chain necklet: 45 x 0.2 cm
Pendant: 8 x 5.4 cm
Bulgari Heritage Collection, inv. 5743 N1626

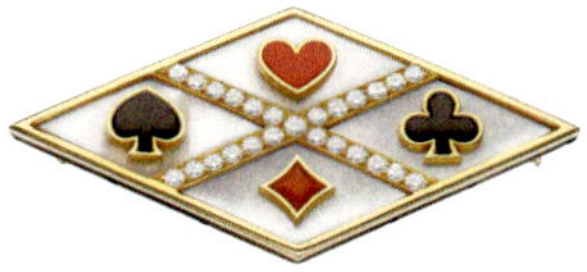

77. Playing card brooch, ca. 1975
Gold with mother-of pearl, coral, onyx, and diamonds
6.5 x 3.2 cm
Bulgari Heritage Collection, inv. 5070 P113

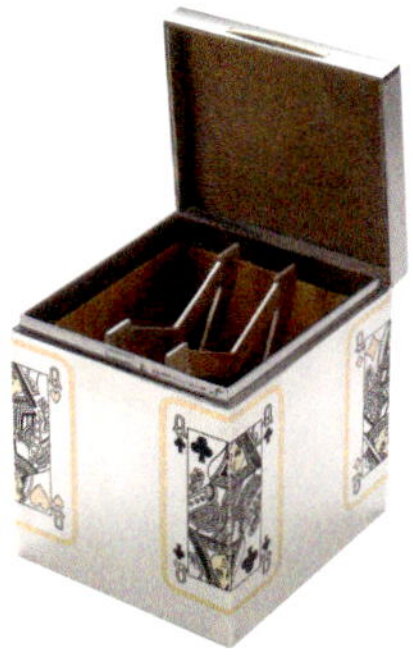

78. Playing card card box, 1974
Silver and two-color gold with black enamel
10 x 8.5 x 8.5 cm
Bulgari Heritage Collection, inv. 348662 D126

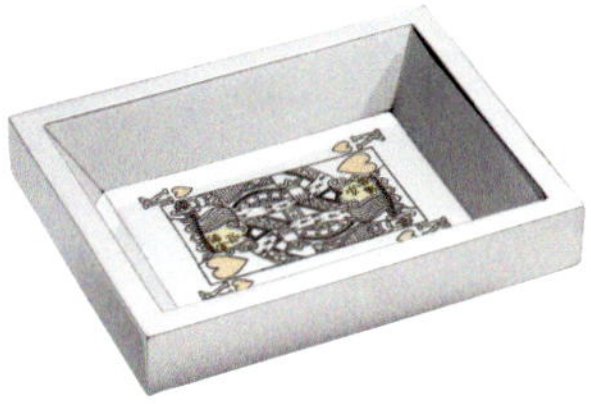

79. Playing card ashtray, 1974
Silver and two-color gold with enamel
11 x 8.8 x 2 cm
Bulgari Heritage Collection, inv. 5768 V104

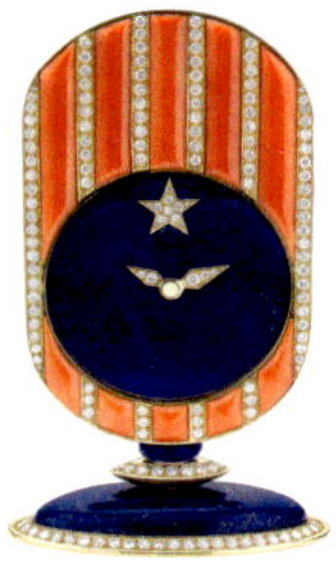

80. Star-Spangled Banner table clock, 1975
Gold with lapis lazuli, coral, and diamonds
9 x 5 x 1.2 cm
Bulgari Heritage Collection, inv. 348703 W74

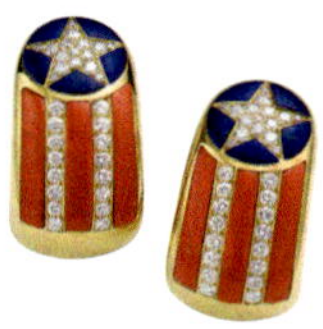

81. Star-Spangled Banner earrings, ca. 1975
Gold with coral, lapis lazuli, and diamonds
3 x 2.3 cm
Bulgari Heritage Collection, inv. 4943 E1063

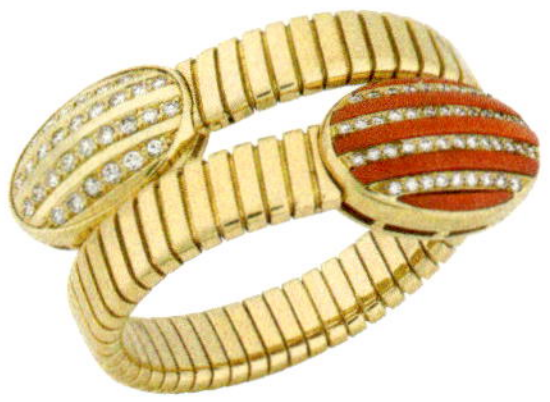

82. Star-Spangled Banner bracelet, ca. 1972
Gold with coral and diamonds
13.7 x 5.5 cm
Collection of Claire M. A. Beaulieu

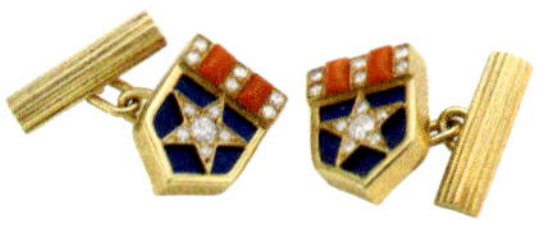

83. Star-Spangled Banner cuff links, ca. 1970–1976
Gold with coral, lapis lazuli, and diamonds
1.5 x 1 cm
Collection of Camilla Dietz Bergeron Ltd.

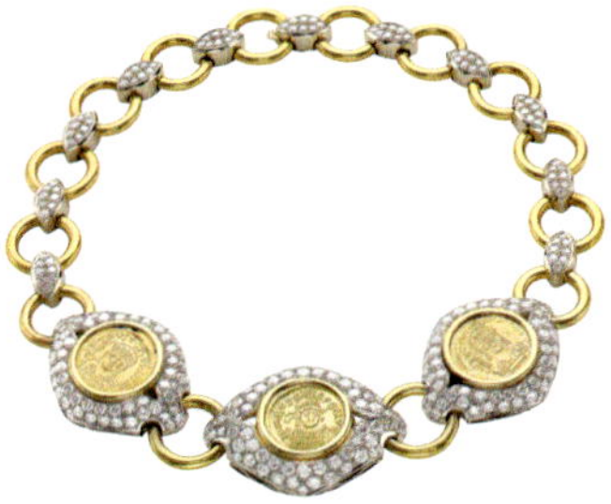

84. Necklace, 1966
Gold and platinum with Byzantine gold coins and diamonds
40 x 3 cm
Bulgari Heritage Collection, inv. 6151 N1801

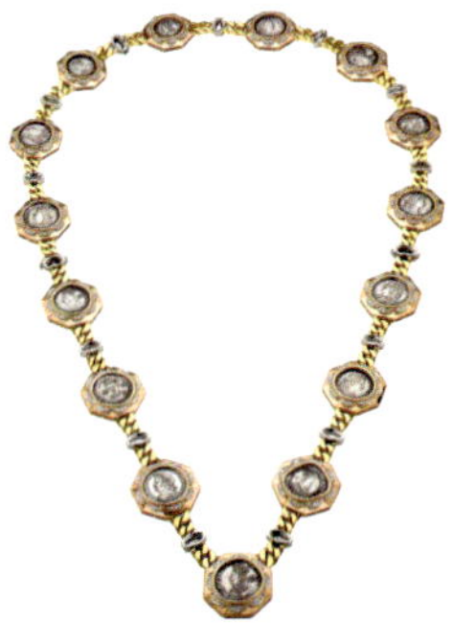

85. Sautoir, ca. 1973
Three-color gold with British silver coins and diamonds
115 x 4 cm
Formerly in the di Portanova Collection
Bulgari Heritage Collection, inv. 7733 N2043

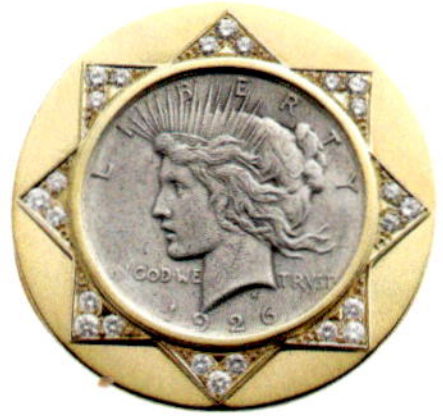

86. Brooch, 1973
Gold with American silver coin and diamonds
6 x 6 cm
Bulgari Heritage Collection, inv. 5944 P345

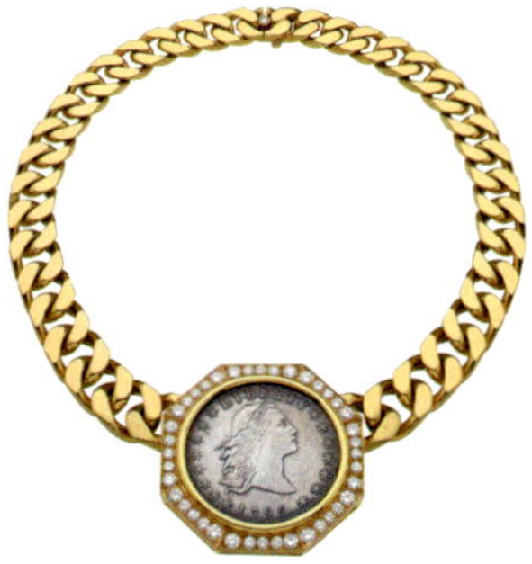

87. Necklace, ca. 1975
Gold with American silver coin and diamonds
39.5 x 5 cm
Bulgari Heritage Collection, inv. 4912 N1514

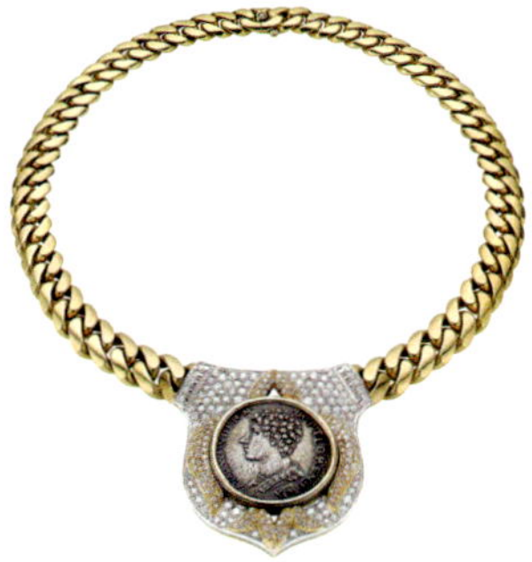

88. Necklace, ca. 1978
Gold with Florentine Renaissance silver coin and diamonds
40 x 4.5 cm
Bulgari Heritage Collection, inv. 347898 N2175

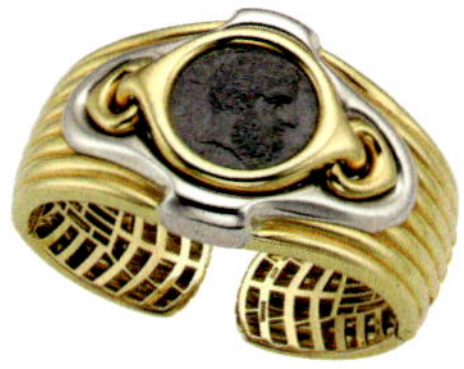

89. Bangle, 1983
Two-color gold with Greek bronze coin
14 x 3.9 cm
Bulgari Heritage Collection, inv. 6178 B607

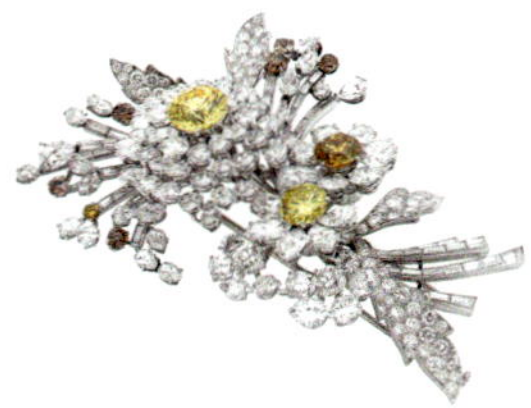

90. *Tremblant* brooch, 1959
Platinum with colored and white diamonds
8 x 5.6 cm
Formerly in the collection of Elizabeth Taylor
Collection of Jennifer Tilly

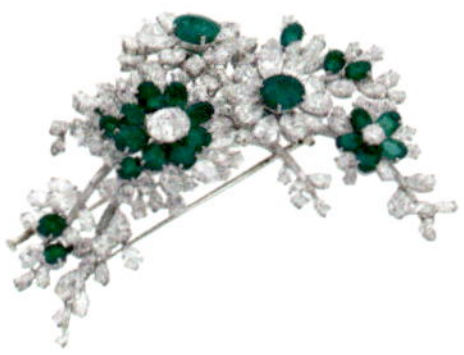

91. *Tremblant* brooch, 1960
Platinum with emeralds and diamonds
8 x 6 cm
Formerly in the collection of Elizabeth Taylor
Bulgari Heritage Collection, inv. 6683 P392

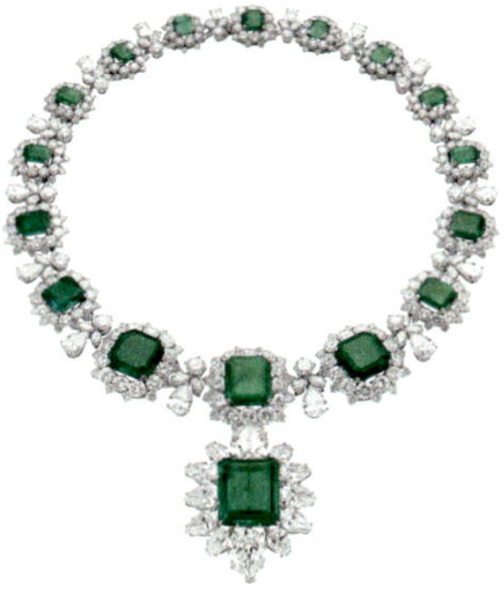

92. Necklace, 1962, with pendant/brooch, 1958
Platinum with emeralds and diamonds
Necklace: 37 x 2.7 cm
Pendant/brooch: 4.9 x 3.4 cm
Formerly in the collection of Elizabeth Taylor
Bulgari Heritage Collection, inv. 6676 N2169, 347870 P393

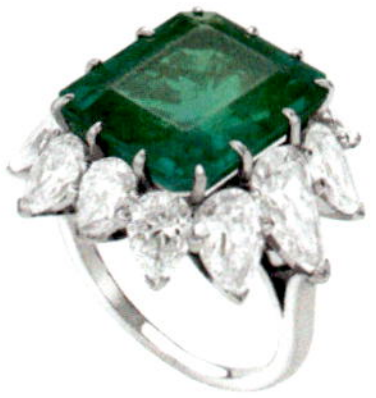

93. Ring, 1961
Platinum with emerald and diamonds
2 x 1.5 cm
Formerly in the collection of Elizabeth Taylor
Bulgari Heritage Collection, inv. 6679 RE226

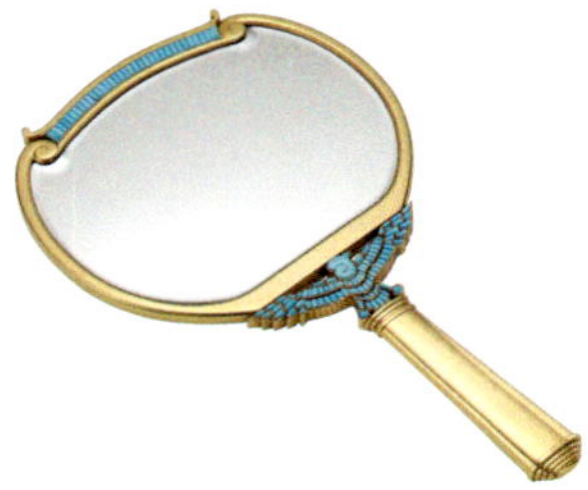

94. Mirror, 1962
Gold with turquoise
28.5 x 15.5 cm
Formerly in the collection of Elizabeth Taylor
Bulgari Heritage Collection, inv. 347871 V171

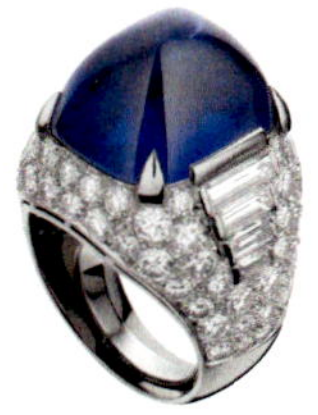

95. *Trombino* ring, 1971
Platinum with sapphire and diamonds
3.4 x 1.8 cm
Formerly in the collection of Elizabeth Taylor
Bulgari Heritage Collection, inv. 6677 RS437

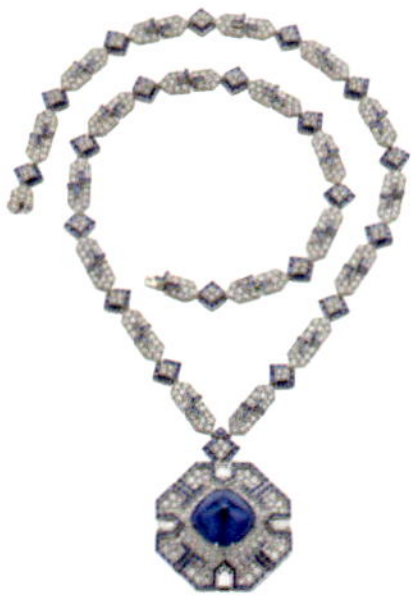

96. Sautoir, 1969
Platinum with sapphires and diamonds
Chain: 74 x 1 cm
Pendant/brooch: 4.9 x 4.9 cm
Formerly in the collection of Elizabeth Taylor
Bulgari Heritage Collection, inv. 6675 N2170

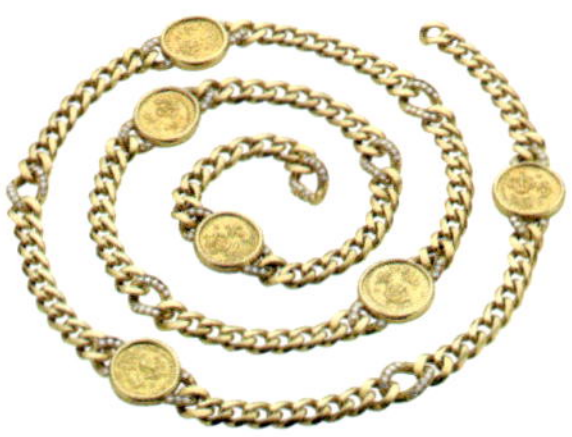

97. Sautoir, 1975
Gold with Byzantine gold coins and diamonds
98 x 2.2 cm
Formerly in the collection of Elizabeth Taylor
Bulgari Heritage Collection, inv. 6672 N2171

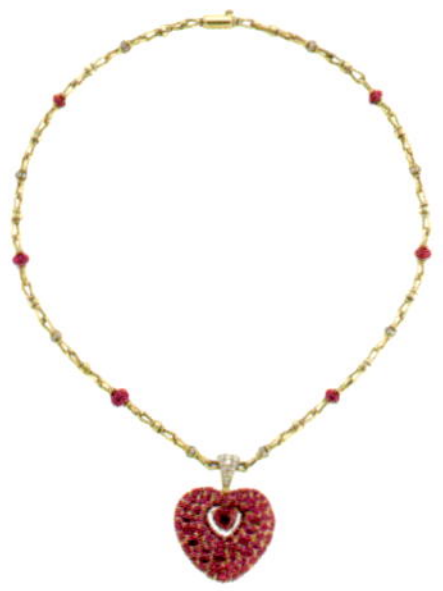

98. Necklace, 2002
Gold with rubies and diamonds
Chain: 43.1 cm (length)
Pendant: 3.8 x 2.5 cm
Commissioned by Elizabeth Taylor for auction to benefit the Elizabeth Taylor AIDS Foundation at Christie's New York, 2002
Collection of Jennifer Tilly

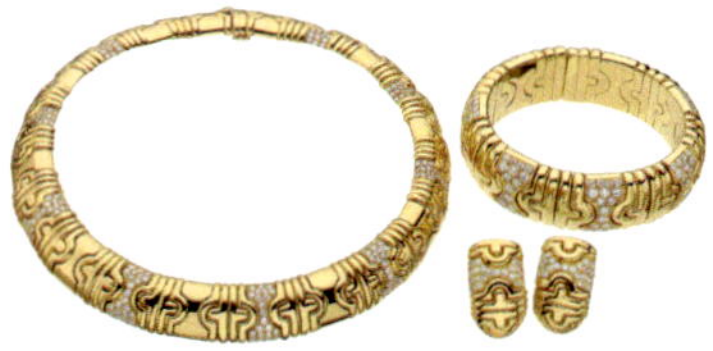

99. Parentesi parure, ca. 1982
Gold with diamonds
Necklace: 33 x 1.2 cm
Earrings: 2.2 x 1.1 cm
Bangle: 15.5 x 1.5 cm
Bulgari Heritage Collection, inv. 5068 N1500, 5063 E1735, 5072 B508

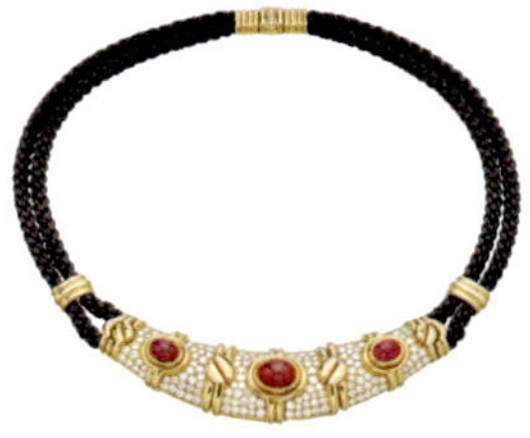

100. Necklace, ca. 1984
Gold with silk cord, rubies, and diamonds
39.5 x 2 cm
Bulgari Heritage Collection, inv. 4969 N794

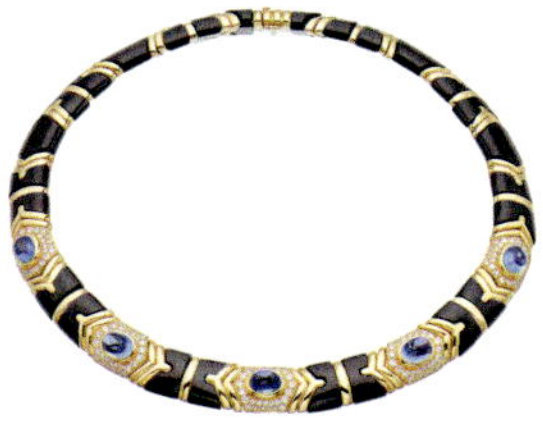

101. Necklace, 1985
Gold with sapphires, onyx, and diamonds
40 x 1 cm
Bulgari Heritage Collection, inv. 4895 N1352

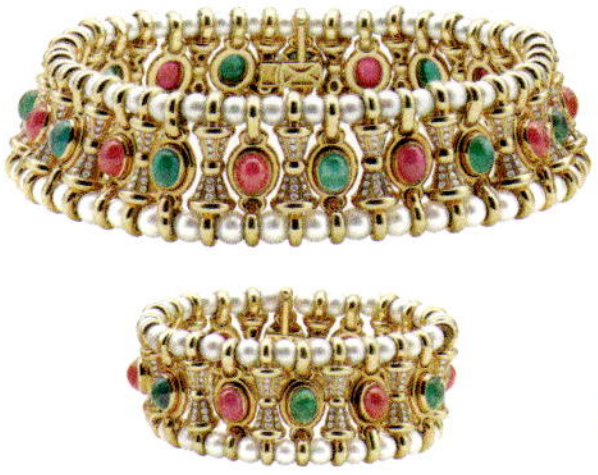

102. Choker and bracelet, 1987
Gold with cultured pearls, emeralds, rubies, and diamonds
Choker: 35 x 3 cm
Bracelet: 19 x 2.8 cm
Bulgari Heritage Collection, inv. 7208 N1968, 7209 B672

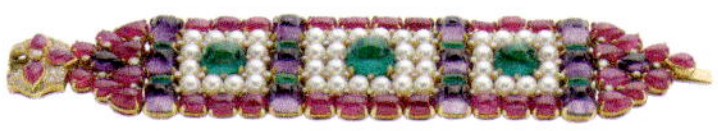

103. Kilim bracelet, 1988
Gold with emeralds, amethysts, rubies, cultured pearls, and diamonds
17 x 3 cm
Bulgari Heritage Collection, inv. 7260 B681

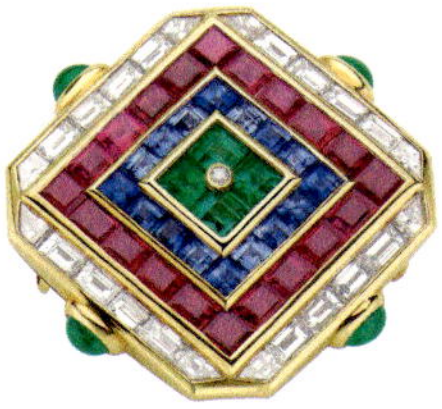

104. Carré brooch, 1987
Gold with emeralds, rubies, sapphires, and diamonds
3.5 x 3.5 cm
Bulgari Heritage Collection, inv. 7740 P381

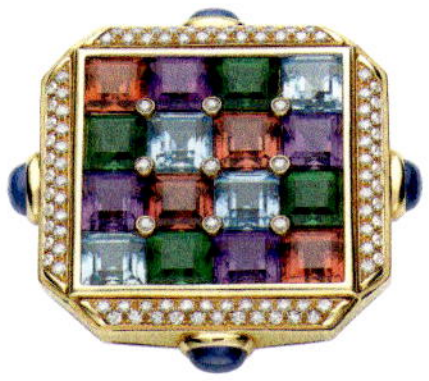

105. Carré brooch, 1987
Gold with aquamarines, amethysts, red and green tourmalines, sapphires, and diamonds
4.5 x 4.5 cm
Bulgari Heritage Collection, inv. 6716 P355

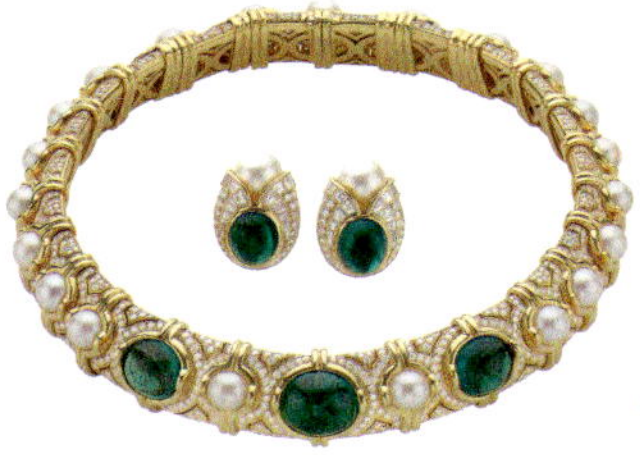

106. Choker and earrings, 1987
Gold with cultured pearls, emeralds, and diamonds
Choker: 38 x 2 cm
Earrings: 3 x 2 cm
Bulgari Heritage Collection, inv. 5975 N1720, 5977 E1993

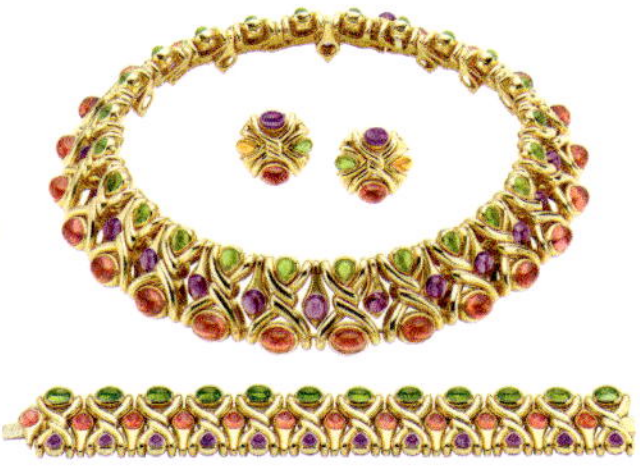

107. Parure, 1988
Gold with pink tourmalines, amethysts, peridots, and citrines
Necklace: 40 x 2.5 cm
Earrings: 2.2 x 2.2 cm
Bracelet: 20 x 2.5 cm
Bulgari Heritage Collection, inv. 7090 N1939, 7091 E2203, 7092 B661

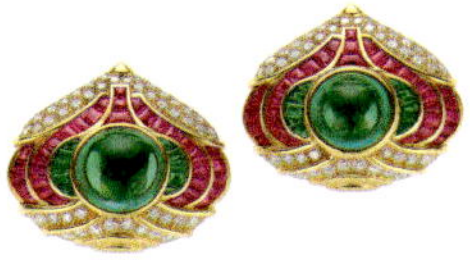

108. Earrings, 1988
Gold with emeralds, rubies, and diamonds
2.7 x 2.5 cm
Bulgari Heritage Collection, inv. 348164 E247

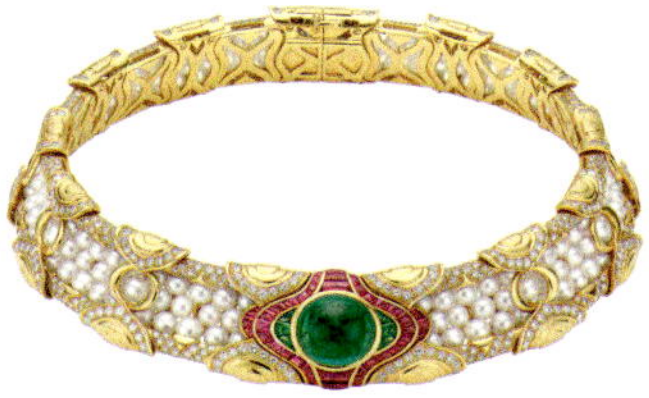

109. Choker, 1988
Gold with cultured pearls, emeralds, rubies, and diamonds
38 x 2 cm
Bulgari Heritage Collection, inv. 348163 N405

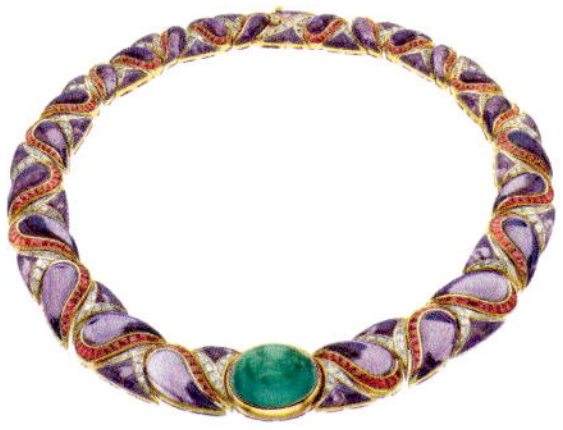

110. Necklace, 1989
Gold with emerald, amethysts, rubies, and diamonds
37 x 3 cm
Bulgari Heritage Collection, inv. 4873 N442

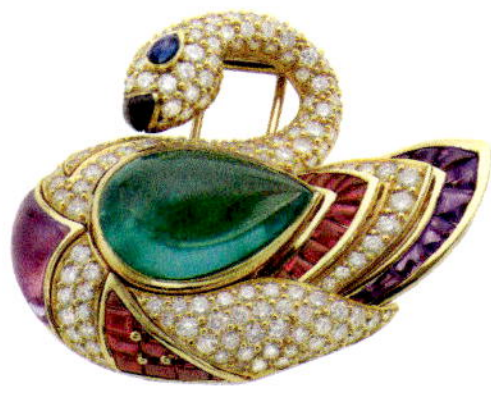

111. Swan brooch, 1990
Gold with emerald, sapphire, onyx, amethysts, rubies, and diamonds
5 x 4 cm
Bulgari Heritage Collection, inv. 7934 P388

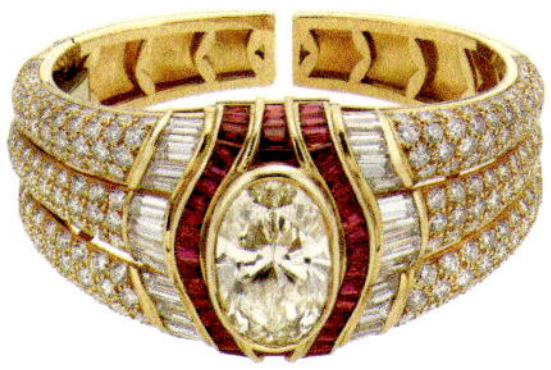

112. Bangle, 1988
Gold with rubies, yellow diamond, and white diamonds
14 x 3.5 cm
Bulgari Heritage Collection, inv. 6180 B87

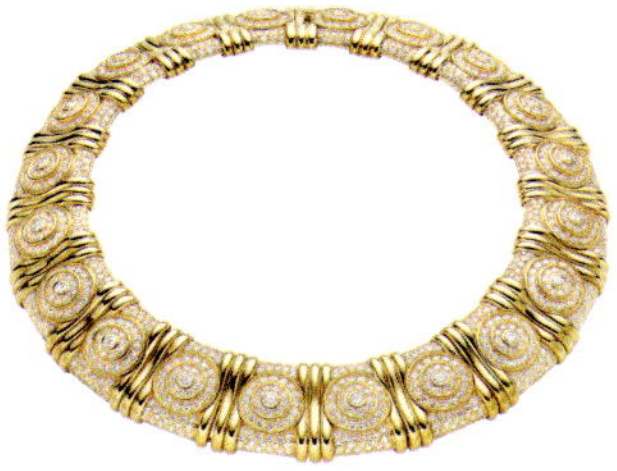

113. Necklace, 1988
Gold with diamonds
45 x 3.8 cm
Bulgari Heritage Collection, inv. 6184 CL888801 N1770

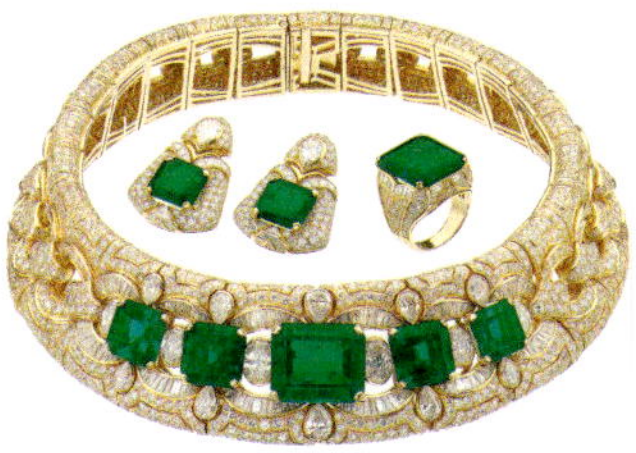

114. Parure, 1989–1992
Gold with emeralds and diamonds
Necklace: 36 x 3 cm
Earrings: 3.5 x 2.5 cm
Ring: 2.9 x 1.7 cm
Bulgari Heritage Collection, inv. 5128 N417, 5143 E356, 5139 RE75

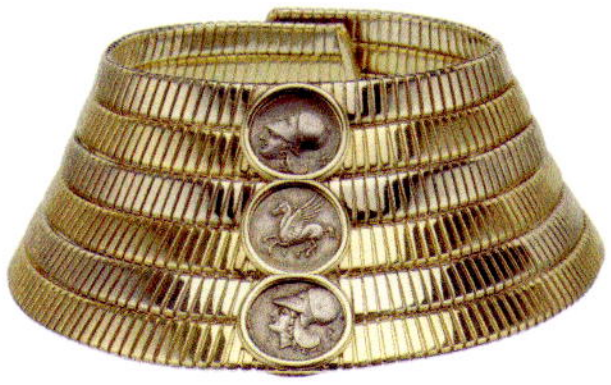

115. *Tubogas* choker, 1974
Two-color gold with Greek silver coins
27 cm (top) and 41 cm (base) x 7 cm
Bulgari Heritage Collection, inv. 404 N607

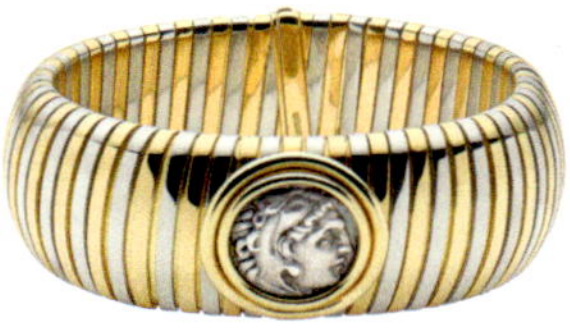

116. *Tubogas* bracelet, ca. 1982
Two-color gold with Hellenistic silver coin
19.5 x 2.3 cm
Bulgari Heritage Collection, inv. 7147 B666

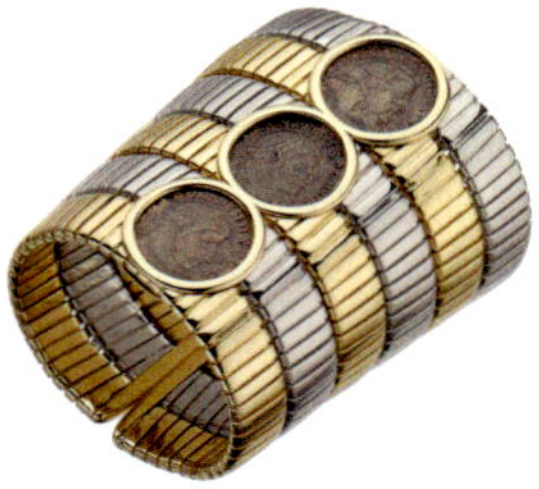

117. *Tubogas* bracelet, ca. 1975
Two-color gold with Imperial Roman bronze coins
16.5 x 6.3 cm
Bulgari Heritage Collection, inv. 4922 B499

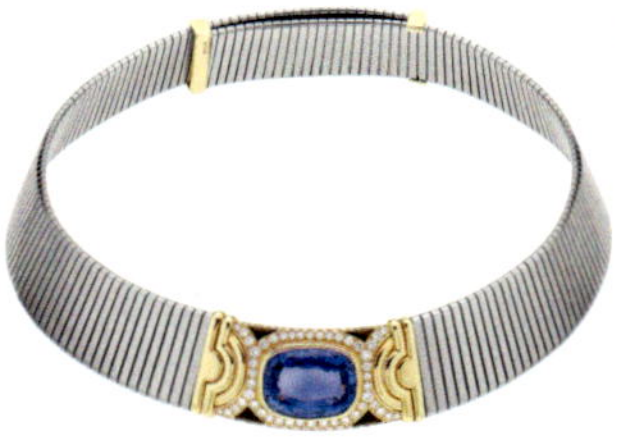

118. *Tubogas* choker, ca. 1983
Steel and gold with sapphire, onyx, and diamonds
50 x 2 cm
Bulgari Heritage Collection, inv. 4913 N1546

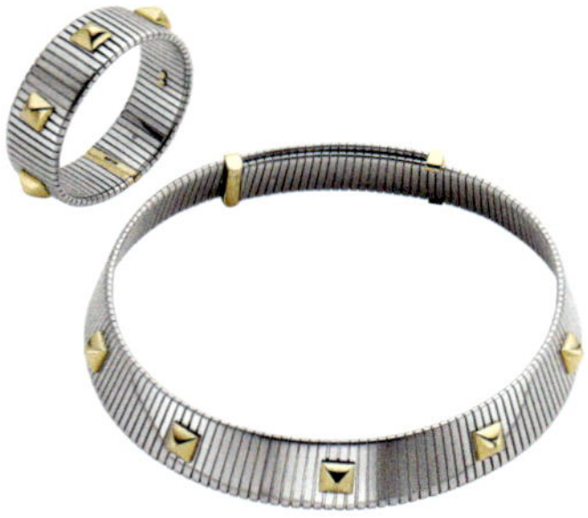

119. *Tubogas* choker and bracelet, 1982–1984
Steel and gold
Choker: 48 x 2 cm
Bracelet: 16 x 2 cm
Bulgari Heritage Collection, inv. 6335 N1822, 6334 B629

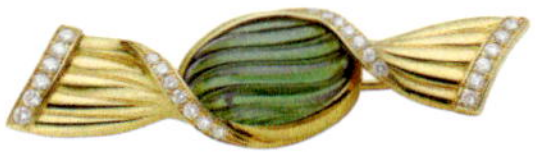

120. Caramella brooch, ca. 1983
Gold with green tourmaline and diamonds
4.5 x 1.2 cm
Bulgari Heritage Collection, inv. 347885 P394

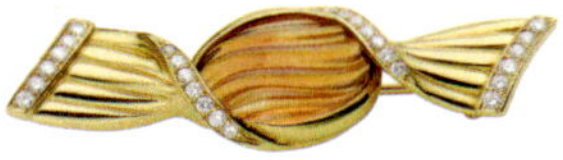

121. Caramella brooch, ca. 1983
Gold with citrine and diamonds
5 x 1 cm
Bulgari Heritage Collection, inv. 347886 P395

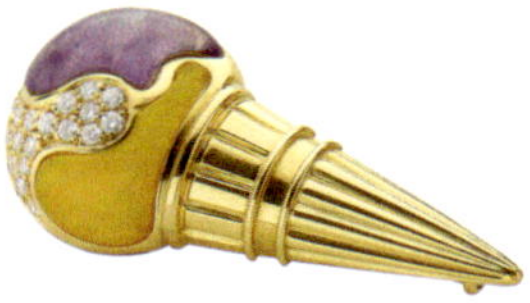

122. Ice cream cone brooch, ca. 1986
Gold with amethyst, yellow chalcedony, and diamonds
4.4 x 2 cm
Bulgari Heritage Collection, inv. 6140 P342

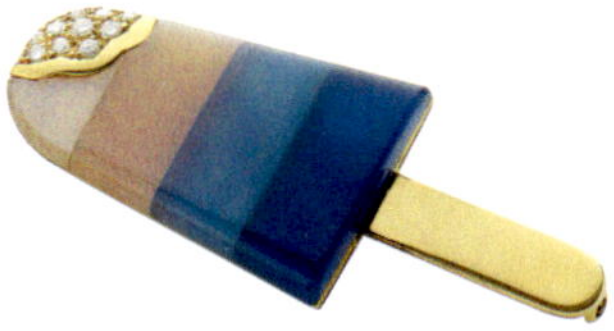

123. Ice pop brooch, ca. 1986
Gold with polychrome chalcedony and diamonds
6.2 x 2.5 cm
Bulgari Heritage Collection, inv. 6139 P343

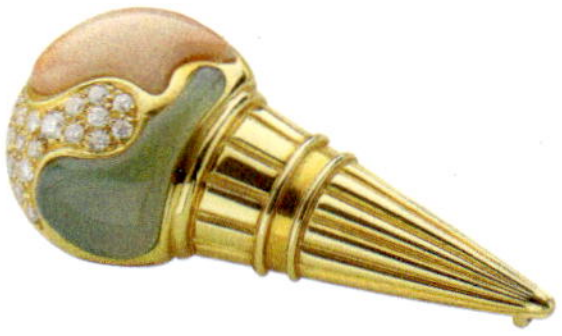

124. Ice cream cone brooch, ca. 1986
Gold with coral, green chalcedony, and diamonds
4 x 1.7 cm
Bulgari Heritage Collection, inv. 6225 P352

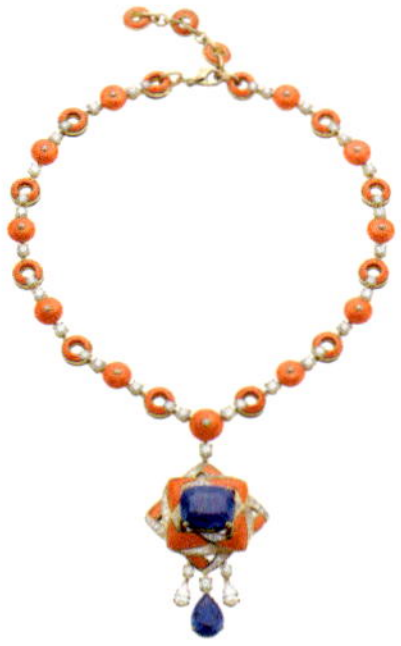

125. Necklace, 2009
Gold with sapphires, coral, and diamonds
Chain: 44 x 1 cm
Pendant: 6.5 x 4 cm
Collection of Jill and Allen Chozen

Acknowledgments

The Fine Arts Museums of San Francisco wish to thank our president, Diane B. Wilsey, and the Board of Trustees, who supported the presentation of this exhibition alongside Colin B. Bailey, director of Museums; Richard Benefield, deputy director; Michele Gutierrez-Canepa, chief administrative officer and chief financial officer; and Julian Cox, chief administrative curator and founding curator of photography for the Fine Arts Museums. Special thanks are given to Martin Chapman, curator in charge of European decorative arts and sculpture, who organized the exhibition for the Museums and contributed a lively introductory essay to this catalogue, and associate curator Maria Santangelo, who so ably provided her expertise with the checklist and images.

Our sincerest gratitude is offered to the esteemed staff of the Bulgari Corporation of America and the Bulgari Heritage and Exhibition Department, Rome, for their cooperation in lending such rare and beautiful objects to this exhibition, and for their collaboration in its presentation and in the production of this catalogue. Thanks are also due to author Amanda Triossi for her delightful essay and section introductions, Rhoda Poetzel Billingsley for her translations of these texts, and Ottavio Sbragia for his invaluable support to the author concerning the historical aspects of her essay.

This volume could not have been produced without the leadership and guidance of Leslie Dutcher, director of publications; the skilled project management of Danica Michels Hodge, editor; and the expert assistance of Lucy Medrich, associate editor. The team at DelMonico • Prestel deserves special acknowledgment for their collaboration, especially Mary DelMonico, publisher; Karen Farquhar, production manager; and Katy Homans, who produced such a beautiful design.

For the coordination and installation of the exhibition at the de Young Museum, thanks are due to Krista Brugnara, director of exhibitions; Sarah Hammond, senior exhibitions coordinator; Therese Chen, director of collections management; and Craig Harris, manager of installation and preparation. For institutional support of the exhibition we thank Renay Conlin, director of development, and her team; Maureen Keefe, director of marketing and communications, and her entire department; and Lisa Podos, director of strategic projects. Further thanks go to the members of the Museums' extended staff, including the entire installation, conservation, and education teams.

We are indebted not only to Bulgari for the many objects on loan to this exhibition, but also to the private lenders who made their precious jewelry available for others to enjoy, including Claire M. A. Beaulieu, Camilla Dietz Bergeron Ltd., Linda S. Chaiken, Jill and Allen Chozen, Denise Hale, Jennifer Tilly, and Diane B. Wilsey. Finally, we would like to acknowledge the generosity of those whose financial support made this presentation possible, including early patrons Carl and Yurie Pascarella, Denise Fitch, Dr. Alan R. Malouf, and Wells Fargo.

Published by the Fine Arts Museums of San Francisco and DelMonico Books, an imprint of Prestel Publishing, on the occasion of the exhibition *The Art of Bulgari: La Dolce Vita and Beyond, 1950–1990* at the de Young Museum, San Francisco, September 21, 2013–February 17, 2014.

This exhibition is organized by the Fine Arts Museums of San Francisco in collaboration with Bulgari.

Sponsorship support is provided by the following:

Curator's Circle
Mr. and Mrs. Carl F. Pascarella

Benefactor's Circle
Mrs. George Hopper Fitch
Dr. Alan R. Malouf
Wells Fargo

Library of Congress Cataloging-in-Publication Data
Chapman, Martin.
The art of Bulgari : la dolce vita and beyond, 1950-1990 / Martin Chapman and Amanda Triossi.
pages cm
ISBN 978-3-7913-5323-4 (hardback)
1. Bulgari (Firm : Italy)—Exhibitions. 2. Jewelry—Italy—History—20th century—Exhibitions. I. Triossi, Amanda. II. M.H. de Young Memorial Museum. III. Title.
NK7398.B79A4 2013
739.270945—dc23

2013020332

Fine Arts Museums of San Francisco
Golden Gate Park
50 Hagiwara Tea Garden Drive
San Francisco, CA 94118-4502
www.famsf.org

Leslie Dutcher, Director of Publications
Danica Michels Hodge, Editor
Lucy Medrich, Associate Editor

Project management by Danica Michels Hodge
Translations by Rhoda Poetzel Billingsley
Proofreading by Susan Richmond
Production management by Karen Farquhar
Design and typesetting by Katy Homans
Separations by GHP, West Haven, Connecticut
Printed and bound in China

DelMonico Books is an imprint of Prestel, a member of Verlagsgruppe Random House GmbH

Prestel Verlag
Neumarkter Strasse 28
81673 Munich
TEL: 49 89 4136 0
FAX: 49 89 4136 2335
www.prestel.de

Prestel Publishing Ltd.
14–17 Wells Street
London W1T 3PD
TEL: 44 20 7323 5004
FAX: 44 20 7323 0271

Prestel Publishing
900 Broadway, Suite 603
New York, NY 10003
TEL: 212 995 2720
FAX: 212 995 2733
E-MAIL: sales@prestel-usa.com
www.prestel.com

Photography Credits

Unless otherwise indicated below, all jewelry photographs are by Antonio Barrella, Studio Orizzonte Roma, and archival photographs and jewelry design sketches are courtesy Bulgari Historical Archive, Rome.

Front cover: composite photograph courtesy Bulgari, Rome. Page 1: daisy brooch, 1969 (cat. 38). Pages 2–3: photograph by Guy Bourdin, originally published in French *Vogue*, reproduced by permission of Art + Commerce. Page 4: necklace, 1961 (detail, cat. 18). Pages 34–35: snake bracelet-watch, ca. 1962 (detail, cat. 21). Pages 36–37: necklace, 1954–1958 (detail, cat. 3). Pages 52–53: necklace, 1967 (detail, cat. 28). Pages 78–79: Buddha sautoir, 1971 (detail, cat. 56). Pages 122–123: sautoir, 1969 (detail, cat. 96). Pages 140–141: necklace, ca. 1984 (detail, cat. 100).

Figure illustrations: 1, 43, 46: Photofest. 3: Margaret Norton / Time & Life Pictures / Getty Images. 5: courtesy of the Cecil Beaton Studio Archive at Sotheby's. 7, 47: © Bettmann/CORBIS. 8: courtesy of Denise Hale. 9: © 1968 Universal Pictures. 10: © Jack Nisberg / Roger-Viollet. 12: Ron Galella/ Ron Galella Collection / Getty Images. 13: © The Richard Avedon Foundation, originally published in *Vogue*. 14: Alfredo Agomeri. 21: © Ivan Crosceno / AP / AP / Corbis. 22: Archivio Crescenzi, Rome. 24: AP Photo / Jim Pringle. 25: Darlene Hammond / Archive Photos / Getty Images. 26: © Bettman / Corbis / AP Images. 27: Archivi Farabola. 30: Licio D'Alosio / Reporters Associati. 31: Rex USA. 33, 38, 50: © Gian Paolo Barbieri. 34: © Gaio Bacci, Rome. 35: Jeffrey Mayer / WireImage / Getty Images. 36: © Karen Radkai. 37: Archivio Storico Illario. 39: Alice Ghergo, © Archivio Ghergo. 41: © The Richard Avedon Foundation, originally published in French *Vogue*. 44: AP Images / La Presse / Umberto Salvemini. 45: Bentley Archive / Popperfoto / Hulton Archive / Getty Images. 48: William Lovelace / Hulton Archive / Getty Images. 49: Terry O'Neill / Getty Images. 51: ©1995 Universal City Studios, Inc. and Syalis Droits Audiovisuels. 52: Courtesy BMP Media Holdings, LLC. 55: Raffaello Benedetto Brà.

Plates and catalogue: 3, 21-23, 29-32, 66, 82, 98: Zale Richard Rubins. 7-9, 24: Randy Dodson. 45: Jorge Bachmann.

Back cover: Gamma-Keystone via Getty Images